CHARLES MORGAN

and the Development of
Southern Transportation

CHARLES MORGAN

AND THE
DEVELOPMENT OF
SOUTHERN
TRANSPORTATION

JAMES P. BAUGHMAN

VANDERBILT
UNIVERSITY PRESS
NASHVILLE, 1968

FOR SUSAN, JACK, AND PETER

AND FOR MIMI

NOTE ON SOURCES
AND ACKNOWLEDGMENTS

BECAUSE of gaps in the business and personal papers of Charles Morgan, this study has relied heavily on other sources of information. Several of these have been especially rewarding and bear notice.

Among manuscript materials, the notarial, conveyance, and mortgage records of Orleans Parish, Louisiana, were of greatest value. Because of that state's unique French heritage, many business charters, contracts, and agreements could be executed before a notary and were thus preserved in his records. These archives, filed under the name of each notary, are available in the Orleans Parish Courthouse, New Orleans, and are a great source for social and economic history—although little used. For business history, it is necessary to determine which notaries were most frequently used by the firms in question and then to read through the chronological records of those individuals. As the footnotes for this study indicate, the task yields many riches.

Second in value among manuscript sources consulted were the records of predecessor companies held by Southern Pacific Company (Texas and Louisiana Lines), Houston, Texas. In the custody of the Secretary and the Auditor are the fragmentary records of the Morgan Line and the minute books, stock ledgers, contract files, and financial records of such important railroad companies as Houston and Texas Central; Galveston, Harrisburg, and San Antonio; Texas and New Orleans; New Orleans, Opelousas, and Great Western; Louisiana Western; Gulf, Western Texas, and Pacific; Houston Direct Navigation; and, of course, Morgan's Louisiana and Texas. Reference to these archives is indispensable for any study of southwestern economic history.

Among federal archival records, those of the Customs Service, the Post Office Department, the Quartermaster General, the Bureau of Ships, and the Costa Rican Claims Commission were most useful. The published documents and reports of both houses of Congress were invaluable.

A particularly valuable source only recently opened to scholars was the Dun & Bradstreet Collection held by Baker Library, Harvard Graduate School of Business Administration. Here may be found extensive credit and financial reports on hundreds of thousands of nineteenth-century individuals and firms which supplement the printed and equally useful Corporate Records Collection also found at Baker. The latter is especially rich in annual reports, prospectuses, brokers' circulars, and receivership papers.

The most extensive use possible has been made of legal documents, travelers' accounts, and newspapers. These sources have added factual and interpretive elements in hundreds of ways. The perceptive and argumentative press of nineteenth-century New Orleans, where more than half a dozen dailies flourished, provided information and discussion unavailable elsewhere.

Finally, and in addition to those authors cited in this text, there are several individuals without whose knowledge and counsel this book would have been impossible: Professor Edward H. Phillips of Austin College; Professors Gerald M. Capers, William R. Hogan and Thomas L. Karnes of Tulane University; Professor Philip F. Detweiler of Trinity University, San Antonio; Professor Ralph W. Hidy of Harvard University and Mrs. Hidy; Messrs. Robert G. Ottman, H. D. Gray, J. V. Watson, and Joseph L. Bart, Jr., all now or formerly of the Southern Pacific Company; Mr. Morgan Whitney of New Orleans; the late Mr. Harry J. Heaney of Houston, Texas; Mrs. Charles Bailey of New York; Miss Barbara Kovitz of Cambridge; and my father, Mr. J. L. Baughman of Corpus Christi. Each knows his contribution and to each is due the author's special gratitude.

CONTENTS

INTRODUCTION

CHARLES MORGAN
was Connecticut born and New York reared. Manhattan was his home, Brooklyn his final resting place. Yet for most of his adult life he poured his energy, abilities, and resources into the development of steamship, railroad, and port facilities in the states and republics bordering the Gulf of Mexico. His efforts made his name a synonym for transportation in the Gulf Southwest.

Although a "Yankee" by southern standards, Morgan was in no sense a "carpetbagger." Connecticut and New York provided his cultural background and set the conditions that led to his choice of business as a career. And, as his early business training and experience accumulated, his native environment encouraged him to specialize as a businessman concerned with transportation. Environment also channeled his investments and skills specifically into shipowning and agency, sail and steam liner service, and the coasting trades.

It was along the Atlantic and Gulf coasts of the southern United States and northern Latin America that Morgan chose to apply his functional and technological specialities. He made this crucial locational decision in the 1830s, thus binding his own destiny with the volatile history of the regions that he served. Despite his birth, his goals and actions (in their own ways) became as intensely "southern" as those of the defenders of slavery. He is a classic case of an easterner with capital and purpose who found profitable employment for his resources in the less-developed areas of the South. He began opportunistically, but he soon became an important factor in regional economic growth.

In this historical appraisal of Morgan's career, I have purposely selected the biographical form because his personal goals, resources, and actions were so often the binding agents of economic change. I have sought the man in the context of his times; or, to put it more precisely, the interaction of a businessman and the environment that shaped, and was shaped by, his decisions. The focus is as much on the process of *mutual* accommodation as upon the products of change.

Such personalization of economic affairs is certainly germane to the writing of American economic history. For if the "American system" is definable at all, one of its major components has surely been decentralized, private, often unco-ordinated, economic decision-making. The pragmatic pursuit of individual goals, in an environment of freedom and plenty, has been an untidy but persistent force in the economic and political development of the American Republic.

It is also necessary, however, to offset the uniqueness and specificity inherent in biography by casting Morgan within the patterns which have emerged from the historical study of business. Not only must we come to know Morgan as Morgan, we must also appreciate him as a businessman and as a factor in the economic development of the areas in which he operated. This dual approach is in sympathy with those ideals of "business history," recently summarized by Harold F. Williamson; that is, to

identify and analyse the critical or strategic decisions of the management, suggest the extent to which the company's operations were typical or atypical of other firms, indicate whether it played an active or passive role in the industry, and evaluate any contributions it may have made to general economic growth and development.[1]

As an introduction to Morgan the man, it is helpful to know the business and economic roles he played.

MORGAN THE BUSINESSMAN

It is difficult in some respects, to identify what "business" Morgan pursued. New York city directories, for example, give a misleading picture. From 1819 through 1833, he was listed as a "grocer" while from 1834 through 1841 his occupation was not listed. In 1842 he appeared as a "merchant" but the following year was redesignated a "founder," which he remained through 1853. In 1854 he was identified as a "president" and retained this distinction until 1856 when his classification became "bankers and steamships." This was revised to merely "steam-

1. "The Uses of Business History: A Comment," *Business History*, VII (January 1965), 57.

ships" in 1858 and back to "merchant" in 1863. The latter was then irregularly interchanged with "steamships" until Morgan's death in 1878.

New Orleans directories are a poorer source, and even the respected and confidential credit reports of Dun & Bradstreet are sketchy. No New Orleans city directory between 1837 and 1878 would even yield Morgan's name although that city was the center of his enterprise. The reader does find the names of his agents and lines but never is their principal and owner identified. The credit reports associate him primarily with the Morgan Iron Works of New York and carry no appraisal of his shipping activities until 1865.[2]

These examples underscore a lack of awareness of the extent of Morgan's activities among his contemporaries and the necessity of finding a more precise classification for his business career.

One is tempted to appropriate N. S. B. Gras's conceptions of "mercantile," "industrial," and "financial" capitalism and assign Morgan to the first of those eras. Perhaps "mercantile" holds for his career before 1832 when he could be called a "shipping and commission merchant," but this definition is of diminishing utility thereafter. An alternative formulation might be the "owner-manager" to "general entrepreneur" progression developed by Thomas C. Cochran. Yet here there are difficulties, too, as Morgan demonstrates less ubiquity of investment and more intimate control over his various enterprises than do Cochran's ideal types.

Equity and decision-making were united in all of Morgan's business activities, and the power of the purse remained in his hands. In Heinz Hartmann's terms, he was thus "the source of all formal authority" in his enterprises and exercised or delegated his power accordingly. He fits Philip Selznick's organizational description of the "entrepreneur" quite well: he clearly set the "mission and role" of his enterprises and saw to it that organization and policy "sensitized" his managers to think and act within the letter and spirit of his plans and instructions; and he was certainly and primarily responsible for "the defense of institutional integrity" and "the ordering of internal conflict."[3]

2. Dun & Bradstreet Credit Ledgers (Baker Library, Harvard University, hereafter cited as "D. & B."), N. Y. vol. 316, pp. 48, 83, 1G, 1W; vol. 341, pp. 162, 200a/54; vol. 348, p. 857; La., vol. 9, p. 164; vol. 10, p. 544; vol. 11, p. 1C; vol. 12, p. 324; vol. 5, p. 14; vol. 6, p. 51; Tex., vol. 15b, pp. 182, 287, 353.

3. For the various works of Gras, Cochran, Hartmann, and Selznick, see bibliography.

A more workable description of Morgan's business function, however, is that of "transportation specialist." In this context all his investments fall into place as complementary to his basic business goal—the ownership and profitable operation of common carriers. Morgan's consistent perception and pursuit of this goal, the resulting functional, technological, and geographical specializations that it entailed, and the breadth of his accomplishments are what make him important in the history of American transportation. His career is especially illustrative of the process by which businessmen moved the United States from an era of closely held, regional, short-haul transportation monopolies to one of integrated and national transport systems.

An early commitment to functional specialization as a common carrier was Morgan's most "critical" decision and shaped his entire career. A preoccupation with maritime enterprises was not unusual among Americans of Morgan's generation. But few of them made such definite and early commitments to the specialized mixture of common carriage, steamships, liner service, and coasting trades that he represented—only Cornelius Vanderbilt is comparable. Similarly, while regional transportation monopolies were not uncommon in the nineteenth-century United States, Morgan's systematic development and domination of the Gulf of Mexico was uniquely his own. Other decisions crucial to the course and viability of his enterprises may be categorized as locational, technological, and operational.

Morgan's three key locational decisions were keeping his headquarters in New York City, restricting his business to the coasting trades, and his preoccupation with the Gulf of Mexico and its hinterland. The first of these decisions made him a part of America's leading maritime community and, over time, broadened his personal and financial contacts and influence in many positive ways. New York was always his center of capital, information, and top-level decision-making.

The second of these locational decisions afforded Morgan the opportunities of the most cherished and protected American trade routes. Safe from foreign competition, generally outside of the tariff controversy, the coasting trades were a New York specialty, and Morgan became a specialist's specialist. Unlike the foreign trades, however, concentration in coastal shipping made him vulnerable to the effects of steadily improving land transportation. And, in time, the challenge of the railroad came to consume his entire business attention.

Morgan's preference for the Gulf trades plunged him into two whirl-pools of nineteenth-century American conflict—sectionalism and west-ward expansion. The Texas Revolution, the Mexican War, the Gold Rush, the Civil War, and Reconstruction were intimately entwined with his business life.

Technologically, Morgan's crucial decision was his early and consistent employment of steamships. He was truly a pioneer in commercial steam navigation in the United States, and his success validates his early confi-dence in this transportation innovation. Conversely, he lagged behind many of his contemporaries in appreciating the utilities of the railroad, but he became exceptionally adept at expanding his strength at sea into an integrated water-rail system.

Operationally, Morgan's preference for proprietary or closely held corporate enterprises and his penchant for liner service as opposed to tramp shipping were basic. He relied upon family members to fill key managerial positions and invested them with authority and responsibility by procurations granting "full power of authority for him in his name and behalf, and to use, to conduct, manage, and transact his affairs" in specific geographical areas or for specific segments of his business. These documents were typically without limit of time, but were revocable at Morgan's pleasure.[4]

The informal ways in which Morgan exercised or influenced decision-making within his enterprises were of greater significance, how-ever. Time and again he shaped ultimate policy by assuming control on the spot or by correspondence. He traveled regularly between New York, Louisiana, and Texas and kept "desks" in all of his agencies. He fre-quently financed both sizable and routine projects on the spot, almost out of pocket, and repeatedly projected his personality into his business.

In his preference for owner-management and closely held companies, Morgan was typical of the shipping fraternity of nineteenth-century America—raised as they were on the ancient ship-share, venture tradition of equity-holding. He was atypical, however, in the degree to which he carried this tradition over into related enterprises, and especially into

4. See, e.g., Procuration, Morgan to Cornelius B. Payne, June 3, 1858; Abroga-tion of Power, Morgan to Payne, April 24, 1860; Procuration, Morgan to Israel C. Harris, April 24, 1860; Procurations, Morgan to Charles A. Whitney and Alex-ander C. Hutchinson, April 29, May 28, 1867, September 16, 1869. Acts before Selim Magner, Notarial Archives (Orleans Parish, La.), hereafter cited as "N. A. (Orleans)."

railroads. Most, if not all, of the shipping merchants who made similar moves into railroading felt much more comfortable with corporations than he did—witness Cornelius Vanderbilt, the Forbeses, Moses Taylor, and others.

But Morgan's conservatism in spreading the equity in his enterprises was an effective control device for most of his career. He was convinced that it reduced his risk and increased his flexibility of decision—he had few partners, boards, or stockholders to worry about. Theoretically, his policy also had the advantage of reducing fixed costs in his business, as he had fewer stock or bond obligations to cover. He ultimately came to see advantages in corporations in terms of capital mobilization, the spreading of risk, the integration of diverse activities, and perpetual life, but he lagged behind the business community as a whole in utilizing the corporate form. Interestingly enough, however, lack of incorporation in no way impeded his actions for the major portion of his career.

What sort of business and economic world did Morgan inhabit because of his other "crucial" operational decision: to specialize in the operation of water carriers in coastal liner service? We must appreciate the parameters and norms of this world before judgments as to Morgan's performance or innovations can be made.

"A liner is usually defined as a ship plying a fixed route, sailing according to a pre-determined timetable, and offering cargo space at fixed rates to all those who wish to engage such space."[5] The demand for such service is crucial to its appearance and sustenance because it is a derived demand. From the shipper's point of view, the "purchase of cargo space is merely a detail in a larger transaction" concerning the acquisition or disposition of goods. If the buying or selling prices of his goods are sensitive *above all else* to transport costs, he will demand the tramp carrier who offers the lowest price. As the shipper's transport needs tend toward precise mixtures of consignment size, speed, frequency of voyage, and care in handling, however, he is willing to pay a premium price to the line carrier who can respond in kind.[6]

Demand for liner service thus derives what elasticity it has more from the nature of the goods to be carried than from changes in the price of

5. S. G. Sturmey, "Some Aspects of Ocean Liner Economics," *Paper before the Manchester Statistical Society*, pp. 1–2.

6. The analysis in this and the next fifteen paragraphs draws upon the brilliant work of Thomas Thorburn and S. G. Sturmey as cited in the bibliography.

transport. Its price elasticity is low, except in relation to goods with seasonal price fluctuations or to those that can use a tramp or nonwater alternative. To the extent that there are no such substitutes, commodity-by-commodity, for the mixture of price and convenience offered by the liner, the demand for its service remains inelastic.

In offering and pricing their service, then, line operators such as Morgan consider their costs, the supply and quality of cargo space and harbor services in the markets they serve, and the demand for water transport in general and liner service in particular. How do each of these factors condition the ship operators' decisions?

The prime elements of the line operator's costs are those related to the size, speed, equipment, and manning of his vessels and to the capacities of the ports and the needs of the trades he serves. As S. G. Sturmey defines them, these costs may be categorized as "organizational over-heads," including "interest on capital or normal profit, depreciation, office expenses, and insurance;" "voyage overheads," including crew costs, ship's stores, maintenance, repairs, and port charges; and "voyage variables," including cargo-handling charges and unforeseen events.

In the American coasting trade in which Morgan specialized, all opera-tors were *theoretically* subject to the same factor prices and hence to the same cost curve. For by federal legislation of 1817, the coasting trades were restricted to American-flag vessels. To qualify as such, a ship had to be 100 per cent of American construction, 100 per cent of her officers had to be American citizens; and 75 per cent of her crew likewise.

Morgan thus could not hope to achieve comparative advantages in costs by reason of his having access to factor markets appreciably cheaper than those available to his competitors. They were all restricted to the same domestic supply which clustered along the upper Atlantic seaboard. Within that market, however, Morgan could and did secure comparative cost advantages through economies of scale in purchasing, through backward integration, through exploitation of cyclical and spa-tial price differentials, and through his power to demand rebates from shippers and suppliers. His factor advantages were also the result of a continued striving for technological improvement of his capital equip-ment and more efficient management of human, financial, and material resources.

Prudent decisions and timing were crucial in determining what cargo capacity to offer, and where, when, and how to blend it with the supply of harbor services and the demand for liner transport. Like all water carriers, Morgan had four major means of varying the cargo capacity he offered: he could increase the cargo or decrease the time per trip made by his ships; he could lay-up vessels or reactivate them and deploy them in various spatial and temporal patterns; he could build new ships or break up old ones; or he could try to improve his managerial skill and his technology so as to increase the productivity of his resources. The first of these alternatives was available within narrow limits (certainly not more than ± 5 per cent); the third required a lead time of six to eight months; and the last came only after long periods of development. The second and the first thus provided day-to-day managerial flexibility and required day-to-day managerial decision.

The supply and quality of harbor services available to Morgan had cost, technological, and geographical determinants. In the short run, the costs of such harbor services as pilotage, lighterage, stevedoring, wharfage, and storage were relatively fixed, being reviewed and reset by the proprietors or regulators of waterfront facilities only periodically. Over the long run, however, the level of harbor costs and the quality of harbor services could be influenced from the demand side by high-volume and frequent line carriers such as Morgan—by negotiating either preferential rates and services or rebates.

When ports competed among themselves for shippers and carriers, they often varied their charges and services to induce liners to call and shippers to use their gateway instead of patronizing alternative ports. While inducements to shippers usually affected only those located in a narrow zone where port hinterlands overlapped, inducements to line carriers were usually quite effective in securing their patronage. For, as Morgan well knew, the line carrier able to command or enjoy such benefits improved his comparative cost advantage. Similar communities of interest existed between line operators and land transport facilities perpendicular to the coastline.

As for the demand for liner service, its price elasticity was low and the flow of traffic uneven. Incoming cargoes and outgoing cargoes rarely were equal, forcing the liners either to seek supplementary goods in direct price competition with tramps, to operate undercapacity, or to sail in ballast. These circumstances only increased the import of the employment and deployment decisions that Morgan and his managers had to make daily.

One tendency working in the carrier's favor, however, was the characteristic inertia of shippers as best observed by Thomas Thorburn:

Many decisions regarding the water transport of goods are made without consideration being paid to alternative means of transport. The freight rate offered by the shipowner is then accepted without further inquiry. Most likely an investigation of possible alternative transports is made now and then . . . [but] The outcome of such an investigation usually decides the means of transport for some time onward.[7]

Under such conditions, what was the nature of Morgan's competitive world? First, because of the price inelasticity of demand for liners, there was rarely a market freight rate to which he had to adhere. This is quite the opposite of the tramp market in which price is the basis of competition. Like most line operators, Morgan could usually pursue an independent rate-making policy which sought to construct a tariff which, *in the aggregate,* would cover his long-term total costs.

Within his aggregate tariff, however, Morgan was again typical of line operators in that he tuned individual freight rates more to estimates of what the traffic would bear than to calculations of incremental costs. Because his costs were relatively impervious to adjustment in the short run, Morgan behaved in the short run as do most line owners: they "consider profits in terms of rates, not of costs, and . . . seek to maintain profits by rate increases rather than by cost reduction."[8] The availability of alternative water or land transport set the upper limits of what the traffic bore.

Morgan had little challenge from tramps as alternative water competition, for his specialized mixtures of price and convenience were always carefully tuned to demand. Also, his line carried consignments too small to attract the tramp even if the Morgan price was not right. More frequently, Morgan had to cope with competition from other line operators. His very success bred them, for as his rates approximated what the traffic would bear, marginal competitors were bound to appear.

With respect to interline rivalry, however, price (rate) competition was less likely in the long run than was co-operation in rate-making. The lifeblood of a line is the goodwill and faithfulness of its customers, and it will usually slash its rates to the bone rather than lay-up its vessels or abandon service. It is because there is thus almost no lower limit to price

7. *Supply and Demand of Water Transport,* p. 157.
8. Sturmey, "Some Aspects of Ocean Liner Economics," p. 3.

competition that line operators on the same route usually act in concert to stabilize rates. Their goals, in this case, are rates which cover their costs and which earn them an acceptable profit, but which are not high enough to attract new line competitors or to drive shippers away to tramp or land-transport alternatives.

The appearance of competing land transport, of course, deranges the market. And, as Morgan learned, it was much easier to stabilize all-water markets than those in which all-water, all-rail, and rail-water alternatives existed side by side.

As for "risk," Morgan defined it simply as the chance of financial loss connected with business activity. He was optimistic and pragmatic and was primarily motivated by the possibilities of profit inherent in the American system. And, at one time or another, he exhibited all of Arthur S. Dewing's classic motives for entrepreneurial growth: ambition, creative impulse, profits, and the euphoria of speculation.[9] Each shipping line and railroad was considered a venture to be undertaken primarily on its own merits and only later, when sustenance might be in question, was its place in the total profit picture systematically evaluated.

This was pure mercantile tradition and characterized Morgan's investments until the Civil War. Thereafter, there was more concern with integration of operations and balancing of profits and losses, but Morgan would surely have echoed J. H. Goodwin's opinion that "a Trial Balance is a sufficient 'Balance Sheet' to satisfy any business man."[10]

With his ships, where relative capital intensity was less and possible trade routes greater, Morgan was inclined to take more speculative chances—with the "out" of redeployment of his vessels as a backstop. With railroads, however, he recognized their inherent indivisibilities and "sunk" costs with a less "opportunistic" and a more "developmental" view of return on investment.[11] Only when he began to link his steamships with railroads after the Civil War did he tend toward developmental investment for his steamships in the sense of improved port facilities.

Morgan's attitude toward government was typical of his pragmatism and that of his generation. On the whole, he refrained from national and

9. *The Financial Policy of Corporations*, II, 853–858.

10. *Goodwin's Improved Book-Keeping and Business Manual*, pp. 107 and 61.

11. The terms are those used by Arthur M. Johnson and Barry E. Supple, in *Boston Capitalists and Western Railroads: A Study in the Nineteenth-Century Railroad Investment Process*.

state politics except where his direct interests were involved. He took no part in the public testimonials and patronage squabbles so characteristic of many of his New York business brethren.[12] He did lobby and intrigue for charters, contracts, diplomatic protection, and public financial aid, but always on the pragmatic level of self-interest, never in any abstract way. He used government assistance where and when he could; he fought government regulation when he thought it unfair to him; and he carried out his projects without government assistance or regulation when these were either inappropriate or unavailable. In short, Morgan was realistic and optimistic on the question of government economic activity and saw it as a malleable possibility rather than as a restriction on his activities.

The prime benefit which he received from the federal government was its restriction of the coasting trades to American-flag vessels. Morgan had nothing to do with the origins of this policy in 1817, but he enjoyed its results. As John G. B. Hutchins has shown, a consistent cabotage policy protected what became the most successful segment of the American merchant marine, and Morgan was one of the leading exploiters of this *mare clausum*.[13]

He also sought and received more direct assistance in the form of ocean mail-subsidies. Staggered payment made these funds of little use in large purchases, but the possession of mail contracts was unquestionably an advantage in credit-seeking. Curiously, mail contracts in Morgan's case were more compensatory than stimulatory. Not once did he receive a domestic mail contract *before* he opened service on the route in question. The contracts did strengthen his competitive position; that is, it was hard enough to beat Morgan, but to beat him when he held a mail contract was nigh impossible. On foreign routes, such as to Nicaragua and Mexico, however, mail subsidies did play a stimulatory role in evoking Morgan steamship service.

Equal in importance to the mail contracts was Morgan's sale of services to the United States in the form of war and peacetime charters, marine-

12. The only public petition known to have been signed by Morgan was one of 1853 requesting reorganization of the New York City Common Council and Mayor's Office. His name was seventh of more than 10,000. New York *Tribune*, March 3, 7, 1853. By contrast, many other New York merchants were active political partisans. See, e.g., the works of Foner, Rawley, Neu, and Lowitt as cited in the bibliography.

13. John G. B. Hutchins, *The American Maritime Industries and Public Policy, 1789–1914*, pp. 542–579.

engine and ironclad construction, and troop and store transportation. The revenue from this work, particularly during the Mexican and Civil wars, was important at crucial junctures in his career. In the first case, it increased his profits and expanded his service just as the Gulf economy was hitting its stride. In the second case, it tided him over the loss of his ships and their income caused by southern secession.

Federal regulation in no way impaired Morgan's seaborne activities. He was liable to federal safety inspection of his vessels—disasters to his vessels helped provoke this regulation—but the quality of his ships after 1840 far exceeded federal standards. He was often a litigant before the federal bench, however, and played a major role in defining federal-state jurisdiction concerning the taxation and safety regulation of interstate corporations. Indeed, he controlled his personal domicile to increase, where possible, his access to the federal courts.

Morgan was much more involved with state and local governments than with federal authorities; this involvement increased as he moved into railroad and port development. Before the Civil War he had a few run-ins with state and local authorities over their taxation of his interstate enterprises; then and later he stimulated a number of landmark cases in this area. Real estate and tax difficulties with such municipalities as New Orleans and Galveston also came to be major factors in his business decisions. The problems of railroad construction—involving as they did right-of-way and the possibilities of state and local aid—further enmeshed him in regional politics. The uncertainties of Reconstruction also complicated the picture.

Since Morgan specialized in an industry which carried a high "social overhead," and because of the quasi-monopolies inherent in line carriage, it was inevitable that his actions would be liable to public criticism. There were "Morgan-haters" and anti-Morgan newspapers like the Carrollton *Louisiana State Register* and (for a while) the New Orleans *Republican*. It is also easy to appreciate the feelings of shippers in remote ports served by no alternative transport to external markets when they complained about Morgan's high rates and "monopoly" position. These are the traditional charges borne by any common carrier. And Morgan's susceptibility was increased by his success and his relative lack of responsibility to partners, shareholders, or the government. Since his was a proprietary and personal business, he was easy to single out for comment.

Yet, on the whole, his actions fell within nineteenth-century social maxims—in contrast, say, to Oakes Ames, Cornelius K. Garrison, Jay Gould, or Cornelius Vanderbilt among his partners and rivals. He had a few spectacular moral lapses—such as his conduct in Nicaragua during the 1850s, his ownership of slaves, and his trading with both sides during the Civil War. The first of these brought him the social criticism he deserved; the second passed unknown to anyone who might have made anything of it; and the third was known but, curiously, ignored.

More typically, however, one finds acceptance and commendation of his business and personal conduct by contemporaries:

Mr. Morgan's name is a tower of strength in any enterprise he chooses to take hold of.[14]

When Charles Morgan takes hold of a great enterprise complete success is sure to be the result.[15]

There is no danger of being deceived or disappointed by him, for it is well known that all contract obligations are held sacred by him, and that while he will not undertake what he is unable to accomplish, he can be depended upon to do what he agrees to do.[16]

Mr. Morgan is one of those citizens of whom a republic should be sincerely proud—a gentleman without assumption, and a champion in the cause of progress, combining three elements of success—faith, enthusiasm, and the greatest spirit of enterprise. . . . We welcome him to New Orleans, the city of his love and adoption.[17]

My only object when building this boat, and when naming her, was to give her the name of some one who was identified in the prosperity of the South . . . I knew of no name more appropriate than that of Charles Morgan—a man who had more enterprise to carry out the successful commerce of the entire South, and this city in particular, than any other. His energy, enterprise and capital formed and built our first trade into the Lone Star State— Texas—from which her trade flowed into our markets by millions; and when opposition through different channels of commerce was about to rob the river of a portion of that commerce, his foresight conceived at a glance the necessity of more expedition, when, as by magic, he extended with dispatch the

14. New Orleans *Daily Picayune*, December 13, 1871.
15. *Ibid.*, March 13, 1872.
16. *Ibid.*, May 14, 1875.
17. *Ibid.*, March 4, 1874.

railroads from this city into the interior . . . Such acts of enterprise from Mr. Morgan were the cause of my naming this boat in honor of him.[18]

Had the *Strong Man's* gigantic vigor been preserved to him even for a semi-decade more, he would have lived to see the accomplishment of what he manifestly intended . . . We refrain from pausing here to pay any tribute to the far-seeking sagacity, the indomitable energy, and the unflagging perseverance of this successful millionaire—a merchant prince, whose wide possessions and enormous wealth, were the spoils of a battle in life which he had fought with a courage, determination, skill, and endurance . . . One cannot help but admire these characteristics which made his acquisitions far more honorable to him, than the greater millions of an Astor obtained by inheritance and the rise in real estate caused by enterprise and labors of such men as Charles Morgan.[19]

His career has been a notable one in the business annals of New York. . . . in all his . . . residence there of nearly seventy years duration he lived a quiet, unostentatious life, following his business with energy and diligence, and consequent success. His ample fortune was the result of qualities which some may think are now more rare than when he started his career. His word was never broken. Prompt and fair in business, quiet and courteous in demeanor, liberal and kind to the very large number of men constantly in his employment, not a few of whom have passed from youth to gray hairs in his service, he has left an enviable record in the mercantile history of New York.[20]

Quiet manners, courteous and kindly, considerate of his subordinates, happy and cheerful always in his life and speech, quick, full of nerve, sagacity, and intuition in his judgement of men and things. . . . His conceptions were unusually clear, his methods prompt and decisive, his self-confidence unfailing . . . strong and alert . . . full of reserve power, in splendid health and spirits, he went about like the embodiment of force and thought combined; his will vitalized all his acts and his genial temper softening his way among men to an extent that is rarely to be met.[21]

These judgments by Morgan's peers stand up under historical investigation, and his public image was often an asset to his business. He was secretive about his financial affairs—as were all his contemporaries—but he regularly informed the public of his plans and actions when he thought

18. *Ibid.*, December 22, 1874.
19. New Orleans *Price Current*, May 11, 1878.
20. New York *Herald*, May 9, 1878.
21. *Semi-Centennial Memoir of the Harlan & Hollingsworth Company, Wilmington, Delaware, U.S.A., 1836–1886*, p. 257.

this was in their mutual interest—an open letter "To the Public" was a favorite technique. Measured against the policies of his major opponents, his disclosure of information to the public is commendable.

As for any *broad* social philosophy or consciousness, Morgan was no Andrew Carnegie. Rather, he demonstrated compassion through philanthropy in *specific* instances close to his heart. He was a soft, if thrifty, touch for church building or relief work in the southern towns he served, particularly following the Civil War. He frequently paid funeral and monument expenses for deceased employees.[22] In his hometown of Clinton, Connecticut, he expended $110,000 on the construction and endowment of a twelve-grade school which bears his name.[23] He could not, however, be compared in his philanthropies with such men as Carnegie, John D. Rockefeller, or Collis P. Huntington.

Thus Morgan was, in comparison with other nineteenth-century businessmen of equal means, less responsible to equity-holders and the government and equally responsible to "society." His contemporaries considered his actions commendable. In the absence of major social or legal constraints, he was capable of excess but more often exhibited responsible behavior.

What, then, of Morgan the businessman? He was a functional, technological, and geographical specialist who pursued his basic goals with tenacity and success. His actions contributed to the functional evolution of the common carrier in the United States, he was intimately involved in the commercialization of steam transportation, and he was a leading business figure in the history of the Gulf South.

He operated within the most protected segment of his industry but still faced serious natural, technological, competitive, and political dislocations. For him, unlike some nineteenth-century businessmen, organization, capital and labor supply, and government were problems of lesser importance. In the abstract, he was scarcely an innovator in business policy or administration, as the development of most shipping techniques

22. *Daily Picayune*, December 27, 1871. Two representative monuments are those at Cuero, Texas, honoring Captains James Mainland and Henry Sheppard.

23. The bulk of Morgan's fortune went into Mrs. Mary Jane Morgan's art collection which was auctioned at $1,207,299.30 after her death in 1885. This was the largest public art auction in the United States to its time. New York *Times*, July 4, 5, 6, 1885, March 12, 1886; New York *Sun*, November 28, 1885, February 8, 11, 14, March 1–16, 1886; *Appleton's Annual Cyclopaedia*, XXVI (1886), 347.

far antedated his career. But he was an active, efficient, and competitive force in his industry—a doer and a leader, not a follower.

His greatest assets were his vision, his energy, and the ability to adapt to changing environmental conditions. He began opportunistically but in time came to think much more in developmental terms and of water-rail systems, accepting the higher capital requirements and great social and political involvement that these entailed. His behavior was generally acceptable to society, and while he was not as "big" as some of his contemporaries in wealth or power, he must be counted as successful and influential in his own ways.

While Charles Morgan is thus of notable stature in the *history of business* in the United States, his greater importance lies within the conception of *business in history*.[24] The effects of his activities on the specific areas that he served reveal his greater historical significance.

MORGAN THE ECONOMIC MAN

Economic growth reflects a crazy-quilt pattern of policy and chance. Its course may be charted, its rate can be measured, but its process involves a less quantifiable mixture of economic, political, and social variables related to time and place. These variables and their precedence and interdependence are continually debated by both economic historians and economic planners.

There is agreement, however, that one of the elements shaping United States history has been the existence of a large and relatively independent business community which pursues private goals of profit but, in the process, makes decisions affecting the allocation of economic resources. This circumstance was especially characteristic of nineteenth-century America, when individual and often unco-ordinated "business" policies many times substituted in the growth process for absent national or state "economic" planning.[25]

In studying this economic system, some historians have emphasized its

24. These concepts have been developed by Fritz Redlich, "Approaches to Business History," *Business History Review*, XXXVI (Spring 1962), 61–70; and Arthur H. Cole, "What is Business History?," *ibid.*, 98–106.

25. "Entrepreneurship in Periods of Rapid Growth: The United States in the 19th Century," *Papers Presented at a Conference Sponsored Jointly by the Committee on Economic Growth of the Social Science Research Council and the Harvard University Research Center in Entrepreneurial History, Cambridge, Massachusetts, November 12 and 13, 1954* (mimeo. copy in Baker Library).

inefficiency and point to its exploitative, wasteful, duplicative, and selfish elements. One need turn only to the "robber baron" literature for evidence. Other historians, however, have found strength in the very disorder of the 1800s—in their energetic and optimistic expansionism. As John E. Sawyer suggests, perhaps progress might even be born of error under such "euphoric" economic conditions.[26]

It is not my purpose here to debate the merits of individual or centralized economic decision-making, but rather to portray a man's influence in the context of his times. Given the nineteenth-century system, businessmen like Charles Morgan were of considerable importance: individually and collectively they affected the direction of economic development and implicitly its rate. Most important, what they did became a legacy for later generations of businessmen and planners to accept, reject, or modify. In this sense, what may be satisfactory growth theory today may or may not blend with what Morgan and his contemporaries thought to be desirable activities. Modern growth theory, however, provides a framework useful in suggesting Morgan's historical importance.

One of the classic roles ascribed to the businessman in economic growth theory is that of "innovator." This term may have technological, organizational, or functional connotations, but the general idea suggests one who changes the patterns of resource allocation so as to increase productivity. Recent studies discount the probabilities of one-man innovations and, rather, suggest a complex process in which many individuals and groups interact.[27] In this less glamorous but more likely model of innovation, a businessman like Charles Morgan rests more comfortably. He made no great technical, managerial, or humanitarian breakthroughs, but he was part of several innovative streams in his environment: functionally, he pioneered in common carriage; technologically, he contributed to improving steam transportation; geographically, he was a leader in the economic life of the Gulf South.

Among his contemporaries, Morgan was frequently cited for "innova-

26. John E. Sawyer, "Entrepreneurial Error and Economic Growth," *Explorations in Entrepreneurial History*, First Series, IV (May 1952), 199–204.

27. Most important in the equation of "entrepreneur" and "innovator," of course, are the works of Joseph A. Schumpeter and Arthur H. Cole, especially Schumpeter, "The Creative Response in Economic History," *Journal of Economic History*, VII (November 1947), 149–159; Cole, "An Approach to the Study of Entrepreneurship: A Tribute to Edwin F. Gay," *ibid.*, VI (Supplement, 1946), 1–15; and Cole, *Business Enterprise in Its Social Setting*.

tive" contributions in the technical fields of ship management and ship-building. Modern authorities confirm the judgment of his peers as to the quality of his ships and engines and to his efficiency as a shipping-line manager. Most often, his name is mentioned as a pioneer in the development (in America) of coal-burning sidewheel and screw engines, of iron steamers, of watertight integrity designs, and of dredging equipment. Much of this credit he must share with his sons-in-law, Israel C. Harris, George W. Quintard, and Charles A. Whitney; with Miers Corryell of the Morgan Iron Works of New York; with his highest-ranking, nonrelative executive A. C. Hutchinson; with his marine superintendent James Lawless; and with engineers of the Harlan and Hollingsworth Company of Wilmington, Delaware. Individually and collectively they made such ships as *Columbia, New Orleans, General Rusk, Brashear,* and *Chalmette* notable in American marine engineering history.[28]

In retrospect, however, Morgan's greater economic role lies in his influence upon patterns of investment. Initially, he converted profits earned in trade into a fleet of common-carrier steamships and a marine-engine works. As time passed, he profitably phased out his industrial enterprise to become a transport specialist. Most significantly, as part of this process, he used the exceptional profits of his ships to underwrite railroads and port improvement projects in a region of capital scarcity. Morgan was, thus, intimately involved in those movements of American capital which flowed from North to South, from commerce and industry to transport, and from older to newer transport technologies (sail to steam; ship to rail).

To use current terminology, Morgan's investments relate more to the realm of "social overhead capital" than to "directly productive activities." This is to say that they fall within that area of investment which provides essential services such as transportation and power for the development of industry and agriculture.[29] Most theorists agree that some social-overhead investment is required before directly productive invest-

28. See, e.g., *Semi-Centennial Memoir of the Harlan & Hollingsworth Company,* pp. 250–257; J. Leander Bishop, *A History of American Manufactures* (3rd ed.), III, 130–132; Henry Hall, *Report on the Ship-Building Industry of the United States (Tenth Census of the United States)* VIII, 209–213; William M. Lytle, "Iron Construction in the United States," pp. 219–221; Fred E. Dayton, *Steamboat Days,* pp. 412–418; William A. Fairburn, *Merchant Sail,* II, 1399–1400, 1480–1482.

29. Albert O. Hirschman, *The Strategy of Economic Development,* pp. 83–97.

ment can grow in a given region; but the extent to which these lead or follow or are necessary to each other is hotly contested. The relative shares to be borne by public and private capital are also always in question.

In Morgan's simpler world, however, the predominant view held transportation to be essential to economic development and a prerequisite to the expansion of directly productive investment. In Kenneth Boulding's terms, it was the "image" that was important and not logic or theory.

Given this emphasis on transportation, however, there was a variety of responses. At the opportunistic end of the investment spectrum were those motivated by what R. Harrod has called "visible demand;" and at the other, more developmental, extreme were those induced to invest in transport by their conviction that certain areas must and would grow. In nineteenth-century America, the private sector was more likely to support the opportunistic end of the spectrum and public investment the developmental, but there was definite and productive mixing of interests in between.[30]

Morgan ranged this spectrum throughout his career. Prior to the Civil War, for example, he reacted primarily to visible demand. He opened only those lines for which demand already existed, he charged what the traffic bore, and he varied the frequency of his services and the continuance of his routes according to seasonal and productive realities. He took these actions for competitive business reasons but was *unconsciously* keeping his coastal shipping lines within that initial increment of social-overhead required by the regions he served. He fulfilled an economic as well as a business role, but one was conscious while the other was unconscious.

Similarly, while Morgan's activities were primarily correlated to visible demand in his early years, the quality of his services and the absence of alternative transport induced directly productive investments by others. There is abundant contemporary evidence that the Morgan steamship and railroads had this effect. Granted, causes and effects are difficult to determine in the process of economic growth. The point here, however, is that all evidence consulted in this study indicates that Morgan himself

30. See the illuminating discussion of R. Harrod and his ideas as interpreted and expanded by D. H. Robertson and A. J. Youngson, in Youngson, *Possibilities of Economic Progress*, pp. 82–87; Robert A. Lively, "The American System: A Review Article," *Business History Review*, XXIX (March 1955), 81–95.

and his contemporary observers considered his transportation investments as stimulatory to investment in trade, agriculture, and industry by others. This was the "image" of reality upon which he and they acted. Again, Morgan's profit-motivated investment had broader economic relevance.

After the Civil War, Morgan's enterprises moved farther up the developmental spectrum. Such projects as waterfront improvements, ship channels, and railroads, and his support of public credit during Reconstruction involved broader and longer-term economic perspective. From Morgan's standpoint, his motivation to undertake water-rail systems of higher cost and greater indivisibility was not the result of any transformation into an economic planner, but was the product of changing competitive conditions. His decisions, however, increasingly identified him with those in his society—both public and private—who saw transportation improvements as the magic inducer of economic development. Morgan inevitably became more involved with governments and more convinced of the necessity of better transportation. Both he and the governments directed their attentions far beyond visible demand toward the future growth of areas as a whole.

To say Morgan or any businessman affects economic growth in this way is not to invest him with infallibility. As W. W. Rostow and many others have shown, the criteria relevant to private profit-seeking are not necessarily those policies which may optimize growth.[31] Furthermore, the likelihood of wasteful mistakes is especially high in social-overhead investment.[32] And when private profit-seeking is as large a part of social-overhead investment as it was in Morgan's day, the probability of error (in terms of optimizing growth) increases.

For example, Morgan did make what he considered correct business decisions which may have diverted economic resources to projects of questionable growth-potential. It appears in retrospect that his estimates of the prospects of Morgan City, Louisiana, and Indianola, Texas, were too optimistic; yet he channeled large private and public investments into

31. W. W. Rostow, *The Process of Economic Growth*, pp. 270–271, 297; George W. Wilson, *Essays on Some Unsettled Questions in the Economics of Transportation*, pp. 6–9.

32. Social overhead investment is difficult to appraise: capital-output computation are not easy to construct for this sector, and social or economic sanctions against failure are not always immediate. Hirschman, *Strategy*, pp. 84–85.

those areas. His Nicaraguan ventures were even less productive, in growth terms, for either Central America or the United States. On the other hand, he did initiate or carry through projects which proved to be of positive value to the development of New Orleans, Galveston, and Houston.

The true importance of Morgan, however, is that for competitive *and* altruistic reasons, he became a champion and symbol of growth through transportation. He lived in an optimistic age, he had proven his business ability, and he had access to capital, technology, and labor. To himself and to many contemporaries he became a "can-do" image in an environment of political and economic immaturity and uncertainty.

As a result, he assumed and was delegated responsibilities for mobilization and application of economic resources. He gave continuity and direction to diverse urges to invest and channeled these funds in certain ways. His choices emphasized certain routes, certain ports, certain technologies, and certain market structures. The pattern of his choices became part of the process of economic development in the Gulf South. This interaction of man and environment left neither unchanged.

PART I

"He had talents equal to business,
and aspired no higher."

Tacitus, *Annals.*

1

CONNECTICUT AND NEW YORK,
1795–1837

As a businessman, Charles Morgan belonged to the South. For five decades of the mid-nineteenth century, steamships and railroads of the Morgan Line served and stimulated the cities bordering the Gulf of Mexico. As much as any of his contemporaries, Morgan shaped the patterns of transportation and port development in Louisiana, Texas, and their spheres of influence. Yet this man so attuned to the rhythm of the Gulf was a New Englander by birth and a New Yorker by choice. His story properly begins in the lifetime of Washington and far from the shores of the Mexican Sea.

Americans born in the 1790s were truly children of independence. Their heroes were the champions of the Revolution and the founding fathers. Hamiltonian and Jeffersonian schemes of government; the purchase of Louisiana; the disaster of the Embargo—these were their youthful fare. For most, their majorities coincided with the Peace of Ghent—that psychological milestone along the nation's road to autonomy.

It is not surprising that this vigorous generation of national birth absorbed the optimism and pragmatism of its time. Such men as James Buchanan, Francis Preston Blair, Stephen F. Austin, John M. Clayton, John Slidell, John Bell, Matthew Calbraith Perry, and Rufus Choate found political and martial outlets for their talent and ambition. Others chose clerical or medical callings, yet the curiosity and creativity of the generation were equally reflected in the achievements of Samuel F. B. Morse, George Catlin, and William Cullen Bryant.

But a significant number of these men of the 1790s responded to the

3

challenges and opportunities of their environment as businessmen. Into the time-honored service of trade and banking went such men as James Gore King, Abbott Lawrence, William B. Astor, Erastus Corning, Chauncey Brooks, Johns Hopkins, George Peabody, John Carter Brown, and W. W. Corcoran. America's expanding maritime industry drew the likes of Jacob Bell, Charles H. Marshall, Paul Spofford, Thomas Tileston, Walter R. Jones, Cornelius Vanderbilt, Charles Mallory, and ultimately Daniel Drew. While the ancient business of publishing attracted such men as James Harper, Henry C. Carey, and Thurlow Weed, the nation's infant manufacturing trades owed much to the enterprise of Peter Cooper, Matthias W. Baldwin, Zachariah Allen, Jonas Chickering, Chauncey Jerome, Charles Danforth, Isaac Babbitt, and their fellows.

Charles Morgan was one of this generation of the 1790s whose life encompassed the birth and solidification of the Union and spanned its transition from a commercial to an industrial economy—from waterpower and sail to steampower and rail. Like so many of his American business contemporaries, his roots lay deep in the heritage and values of New England.

The Morgans, whose Welsh surname identifies them as "of the sea," were early colonizers.[1] James Morgan and his younger brothers John and Miles arrived at Boston from Bristol in April 1636. John soon found the Anglican colony of Virginia more to his liking, while Miles settled at Springfield, Massachusetts, there becoming the forebear of such notable Morgans as Junius Spencer, John Pierpont, and the engineer, Charles Hill Morgan. James migrated first to Roxbury, thence to New London in 1650, and soon settled in nearby Pequot (now Groton). From James Morgan were descended the merchant-politicians Edwin Barber and Edwin Denison, the ethnologist Lewis Henry, and the shipowner Charles.

James's grandson Theophilus brought the Morgan name to Killingworth (now Clinton), Connecticut, sometime between 1730 and 1748.

1. Details of the Morgans are gleaned from: Killingworth Land Records, V–XVI; Saybrook Land Records, V, XI; Nathaniel H. Morgan, *Morgan Genealogy: A History of James Morgan of New London, Conn. and His Descendants from 1607 to 1867*; "Morgan," *Dictionary of American Biography*, XIII, 163–189; Oscar Zeichner, *Connecticut's Years of Controversy, 1750–1776*, pp. 168–169; *The Public Records of the State of Connecticut*, VIII, 150, 500–501; IX, 102, *et passim*; Ship Registers and Enrollments, Middletown and Hartford District; and inscriptions in the Morgan cemetery plots, Clinton, Conn., and Green-Wood, Brooklyn, N.Y.

Killingworth was a small but active port, established in 1663 on the north shore of Long Island Sound equidistant along the Boston Post Road from New London and New Haven.[2] Its fine sand beach and protected harbor encouraged maritime occupations, and locally built schooners and sloops had participated in the coasting and West Indies trades from the early 1700s. Corn, other grains, and hay from arable lands edging the shore sustained a sizable farm population, while taking clams, oysters, and shad from the waters of the Sound and of the Indian and nearby Hammonasset rivers was seasonal but lucrative work. Spiritual ministry by such men as the studious Abraham Pierson and Jared Eliot and representation in the Assembly by the likes of Eliot's vitriolic son-in-law Benjamin Gale, had given the town a reputation for Old-Light Congregationalism and reactionary politics. Yet international recognition of the educational and scientific achievements of Pierson, Eliot, and Gale, and of such local craftsmen as Abel Buell, attests to the urbanity of Killingworth's conservatism.

The Morgan men rang true with their environment. Theophilus served as a justice of the peace until his death in 1778. Charles's grandfather, Theophilus, Jr., was a large landholder, a farmer and occasional "West India trader," and an influential Moderate in Connecticut's Revolutionary struggle. Theophilus, Jr.'s twelve children (by two wives) were equally prominent in the transition to statehood. John, the eldest, graduated from Yale in 1774 and soon became the leading shipping merchant of Hartford. The third son, George, born in 1768, remained in Killingworth as manager of his father's properties and on March 25, 1788, with his marriage to Miss Elizabeth Redfield, united two of the town's best families.

George and "Betsey" Morgan were soon established as responsible citizens. From the profits of his planting fields and hay meadows, George erected a $2,500 home on Killingworth's Main Street. His twenty-acre homestead was in the best of neighborhoods, east of town center, adjacent to the property of the wealthy Kelsey family, and a block from Adam

2. For the Morgans' Connecticut environment, see: Daybrooks Nos. 1–2, Adam Stanton General Store Records; David D. Field, *A Statistical Account of the County of Middlesex in Connecticut*, pp. 106–113; Margaret E. Martin, *Merchants and Trade of the Connecticut River Valley, 1750–1820; Clinton: Its Old Houses and Legends;* and Henry Pierce, *Colonial Killingworth: A History of Clinton and Killingworth.*

Stanton's elegant home and store where Betsey often shopped. George's livelihood came from farming, seasonal fishing, and the management of property for himself, for his older and younger brothers John and Charles of Hartford, and for the Redfields. His stature in the community was reflected in public service as sewer commissioner and as captain (1794), then major (1797), of the Seventh Regiment of Connecticut militia.

At variance with the "rags-to-riches" myth surrounding the origins of so many nineteenth-century American businessmen,[3] Charles Morgan was thus born into a comfortable family, in a region undergoing a period of unprecedented prosperity. He was the third of George and Betsey Morgan's children—Elias, born September 26, 1790; John, born December 3, 1791; Charles, born April 21, 1795, and Wealthy Ann, born September 6, 1798—and suffered only the presumable fortunes of a boy with older brothers and a baby sister. Later portraits reflect a strong figure of almost six feet, a firm, if dimpled, chin, and widely spaced eyes framed by thick, sandy hair and eyebrows. Beardless in an age of beards, Morgan's was a genial face, strengthened by a nose of massive proportions. He was remembered by his contemporaries as a quiet, pleasant youth but quick and full of nerve and self-confidence. His schoolmaster always recalled Charles more for his swimming and sailing abilities than for his attendance at Killingworth's one-room "academy."[4]

But Charles's schooldays drew quickly to a close. The Connecticut economy was changing and the young man from Killingworth was directly affected. Each year the rocky soil of the coastal farms seemed more grudging in its yield. And Mr. Jefferson's Embargo dealt Connecticut commerce a crippling blow. The prosperity of 1795 became depression by 1808. In increasing numbers, by necessity or design, Connecticut men sought new opportunities in the commercial centers of the Atlantic seaboard.

3. For further contradiction of the myth, see the works of Miller, Mills, Taussig, and Wyllie, as cited in the bibliography.

4. The "official" (since all were financed by the family) accounts of Morgan's youth are found in: Morgan, *Genealogy*; Lewis E. Stanton, *An Account of the Dedication of Morgan School Building, Clinton, Conn., Thursday, December 7th, 1871*; and *In Memoriam: Charles Morgan*. In true "rags-to-riches" fashion, these accounts portray Morgan as of humble origins, and they have been accepted by later writers. The evidence found in the town records cited above disproves this picture.

New York City, in particular, drew and absorbed this migration. Unlike Boston, whose mercantile circles were closed to most outsiders, or Hartford, whose business community was hardest hit by the bad times, prospering Manhattan seemed a more likely environment for one's betterment. Some came as practicing merchants seeking a more cosmopolitan atmosphere for their enterprise; others came as agents of established firms; some were sea captains picturing fleets where single ships had sailed before. In equal numbers were younger men anxious to advance where fortune led: the Griswolds of Old Lyme had come by 1796, the Howlands of Norwich followed by 1800, and later, the Grinnells, Anson Phelps, William E. Dodge, and others followed. In 1809 fourteen-year-old Charles Morgan joined this New England exodus to New York.[5]

J. A. Scoville, who made the transition himself, recalled the process:

His . . . schooling generally ends when the boy is fourteen years old. He can by that time (if he is smart) parse pretty well, and has reached the "double rule of three" in Daboll. He needs no more towards his future success than a trunk, "Sunday-go-to-meeting clothes," and a Bible. This the family provide, and with a few dollars and a mother's prayer, the young hero goes forth to seek his fortune in the great mart of commerce. . . . He gets a place somewhere in a "store" . . . He hardly comprehends the difference between the business of the great South street house, that sends ships over the world, and the Bowery dry goods shop . . . But wherever this boy strikes, he fastens . . . From the word "go" he begins to learn, to compare, and . . . he will not rest until he knows all about it, its details,—in fact, as much as the principals.[6]

Young Charles was more fortunate than most—his elder brothers had preceded him to the city, and his parents were able to send him cash to supplement his income. He had not the prestigious connections of a William B. Astor, a John Carter Brown, or a W. W. Corcoran, whose families, education, and means were the best in their respective environments of New York, Providence, and Washington. Neither had he experienced the hard knocks of a Cornelius Vanderbilt, a Peter Cooper, or a Daniel Drew. Among his contemporaries, he seems most like Abbott

5. Smith, *Merchants*, pp. 65–71; Albert L. Olson, *Agricultural Economy and the Population in Eighteenth-Century Connecticut*, pp. 1, 5–7, 22–23; Robert G. Albion, *The Rise of New York Port* [*1815–1860*], pp. 242–250.

6. "Walter Barrett" [J. A. Scoville], *The Old Merchants of New York City*, (new ed.), I, 57.

Lawrence of Massachusetts—a rural boy of good breeding and moderate means, drawn by hard times (as Lawrence was to Boston) to his logical regional metropolis.

Like George Peabody, Johns Hopkins, and Erastus Corning, Morgan found his first "place" in the grocery and hardware trades—as a retail clerk in Greenwich Street—but lacked their advantage of beginning in the familiar surroundings of a relative's store. Little is known of Morgan's years of apprenticeship, but, like Scoville's industrious lad, he learned his business lessons well. By 1815, before he was twenty, he had opened his own ships' grocery at 31 Peck Slip.

Morgan married Miss Emily Reeves on July 5, 1817, and was blessed with five children: Emily Ann (1818), Frances Eliza (1823), Charles W. (1825), Henry R. (1827), and Maria Louise (1832). The family elders remained always in Killingworth, and their properties passed on to Charles upon the deaths of his father (1830) and mother (1832). Sentimentally and for his spinster sister Wealthy Ann (who died in 1868), Morgan maintained the Morgan and Redfield properties for years, often vacationing in Killingworth but never residing there permanently. In New York he lived successively at: 38 Oak (1819); 29 Peck Slip (1820); 319 Pearl (1821–1823); 53 Beekman (1824); 58 Beekman (1825–1831); 30 Henry (1832); 22 Henry (1833–1853); and 7 Madison Square (1853–1878).

But there was more to the story than young Morgan himself, for his majority coincided with the boom years of New York Port. Though first in exports and imports since 1797, New York insured its primacy among American ports in the years 1815–1825. "Those years gave the chance of a fresh start to the various ports in their rivalry for trade. . . . New York alone struck while the iron was hot, to make the streams of commerce flow to its wharves." By mid-March 1815, trade had resumed with the West Indies, Europe, and the Orient. Ocean lines sailing on schedule to Europe were in operation by 1818, and a sophisticated auction system had been established to handle a flow of goods swelled by postwar British "dumping" of manufactures. Regular steamboat service to New Haven and other Long Island Sound ports was established in 1815, and in 1817 the Erie Canal bill became law. Meanwhile, other New Yorkers were expanding trade with the cotton ports. When the Erie Canal opened on November 4, 1825, "all that New York had been quietly accomplishing" had become obvious to other American ports—geographical advantage, timing, and business skill had bound Europe, the southern ports, and the West with sinews of New York commerce—"and by that time it was too late for them to catch up."[7]

The young man from Connecticut grew with this "Rise of New York Port." Like so many New Englanders in the Empire City, Morgan centered his business attention on the shipping industry, and he was among the best of his contemporaries in his perception of opportunity and his flexibility in adapting to change.

Although nominally a "grocer," Morgan's major capital commitment was to the sailing packets, which were New York City's great innovation and specialty. Between 1819 and his withdrawal from sailing investments in 1846, he held equity in eighteen packets which served in ten different lines—from New York to Charleston, Savannah, New Orleans, Kingston, and Liverpool. He also held shares in at least fifteen tramp vessels trading to the Atlantic coasts of the United States, the West Indies, and Europe (see Table 1.1).

In these ventures Morgan fulfilled a variety of owning and operating functions which reflect the ancient and intricate pattern that interwove trade and maritime transportation. Variously described as a "grocer," "chandler," or "shipping merchant," he simultaneously acted as importer, exporter, wholesaler, and retailer and often combined in his person all of the marketing functions of selling, buying, transporting, storing, standardization and grading, financing, risk-bearing, and securing market information. He used both his own and others' vessels, handled a broad commodity line (e.g., see Table 1.2), and in these ways differed little from thousands of "sedentary merchants" of his and earlier days.[8]

Morgan's partners in these sailing ventures were men much like himself—Connecticut and New York born, and reared to shipping on the quarterdeck or in the countinghouse. He obviously preferred to minimize his risk through co-operation within a small, experienced, investment group, which drew heavily on fellow Connecticut men: twenty-nine of Morgan's forty-four co-owners in sailing vessels were Connecticut-born

7. Albion, *Rise*, pp. 1–2, 8–15.
8. Morgan conducted his business at 31 Peck Slip (1815–1819) and 37 Peck Slip (1820–1833). Carl C. Cutler, in *Queens of the Western Ocean: The Story of America's Mail and Passenger Sailing Lines*, p. 120, confuses Morgan's identity and invents a mythical "Charles Morgan, Jr." Morgan's elder brothers who had preceded him to the city died unmarried in 1815 and 1817, respectively.

and twelve were native New Yorkers; twenty-two had their business residence in Connecticut; eighteen in New York. He also preferred the regular profits of the packet lines and the relative safety of the inshore and coasting trades. But within these limitations, Morgan certainly moved in the highest of shipping circles.

Morgan was a major investor in "Charleston's most celebrated and important packet line, 'The Ship Line.' " He was, for example, part owner of *Franklin,* which set the early record of seventy-seven hours, New York–Charleston, in 1820, and was also an owner in 1833 when *Henry Allen* set the all-time sailing record of sixty-seven hours for the same route.[9] There is no evidence that he imported or exported cargoes in this line, but his large interest and regular profit-taking are unquestionable. He was involved in thirteen vessels of the "Ship Line" between 1819 and 1837: seven as part-owner–husband; six as part-owner (see Table 1.1). His exact share of ownership in these or in other vessels cannot be stated, as fractional shares were not consistently shown in customs documents until the 1850s.

Morgan was more likely to ship cargoes in the numerous tramp coasters that he owned and operated with Archibald Hubbard and with former schoolmates from Killingworth. Their names and prime trades appear in Table 1.1. With Benjamin Aymar & Co., New York's leading West India house and Morgan's neighbor on the East River waterfront, he sponsored lucrative voyages to such neutral free ports as Swedish St. Bartholomew and Danish St. Croix. Here sympathetic Scandinavians and pragmatic businessmen could unsnarl the Anglo-American diplomatic tangles which often blocked American vessels from the British West Indies.[10] As the British West Indies were opened to Americans, the Connecticut-born Aymars and Morgan successfully adapted by entering ships on runs to Barbados and Jamaica, and, on October 5, 1831, they established the first packet line from New York to Kingston.[11]

9. Cutler, *Queens,* pp. 124–125, 178–179, 465–466; and Robert G. Albion, *Square-Riggers on Schedule: The New York Sailing Packets to England, France, and the Cotton Ports,* pp. 53–55.

10. Lynch and Aymar Papers (New York Historical Society and Columbia University); Albion, *Rise,* pp. 175, 181, 230, 263; and "Barrett" [Scoville], *Old Merchants,* III, 69–79.

11. For the Caribbean situation, see F. Lee Benns, *The American Struggle for the British West India Carrying Trade, 1815–1830.* Morgan's relationships to the

In these ventures with others and on his own account, Morgan at first glance seems quite typical of his contemporaries. Only in his preoccupation with enterprises generated by maritime trade, his preference for the West Indies and the South, and the limitations these imposed are there any hints of specialization.

Morgan came to excel, however, in some business functions more typical of transportation than of trade. He was occasionally a procurer and quite frequently a manager of the vessels in which he invested. He had connections among Connecticut builders and arranged the construction of at least five of the thirty-three sailing vessels in which he held equity. More important, he served as "ship's husband" or managing partner for nineteen of the same thirty-three. In this capacity he was responsible for outfitting, maintenance, freight and passenger procurement, ship deployment, and accounting. In one case, that of the "Jamaica Line" of packets, he served as line manager—charged with the integrated operation of his own and others' vessels in joint venture.[12]

By the 1830s it was very unlikely that Morgan could be found shipping cargoes on his own account; as a budding specialist in ship-owning, agency, and management, however, he had few peers. He was moving into that circle of Americans who were increasingly divorcing transportation and trade and concerning themselves solely with the ownership and management of vessels, regardless of the commodities those vessels carried. In short, they were evolving as America's first common carriers—her first specialists in transportation.

As Ralph Davis has tellingly shown, specialists in ship-owning and agency existed in the eighteenth century. Yet their incidence in the New York of the early nineteenth century is more likely of lasting importance in their evolution. The high sophistication of sailing ventures and the great number of businessmen concentrated in the small area of New York City permitted specializations to an unprecedented degree—Jacob

---

Aymars and the West Indies trades have been reconstructed from New York customs registers and enrollments in the National Archives and from entrances, clearances, and relevant advertising appearing in the New York *Shipping & Commercial List*.

12. Cutler accurately describes these lines' major characteristics as "cooperative management and regularly scheduled service." *Queens*, p. 131. It should be noted that a man might serve as both husband of several vessels in their individual capacities *and* as agent of these and other vessels in the joint capacity as a "line."

Barker, Charles H. Marshall, Elisha E. Morgan, William Whitlock, Jr., and Robert Kermit clearly reflect a trend toward owner-specialists.[13]

Specialists in ships' agency were increasingly numerous, especially within the packet lines, which required specialists to manage the regularity and continuity such service demanded, and within the emerging steamboat lines. Since early American steamers subordinated freight to passengers, their managers were understandably further removed from the ownership of cargoes. For Cornelius Vanderbilt, who began in ferryboats, the evolution to transportation specialist was natural. For Charles Morgan, schooled in the tradition of the merchant-generalist, the specialization was more difficult, but no less complete. Increasingly after 1831, he restricted his business activities to the ownership and management of vessels and not to the ownership or resale of their cargoes.

Morgan's obvious fascination with the possibilities of steam packets accelerated his transition from merchant-generalist to transportation-specialist. Perhaps his interest dated from a youth spent on Long Island Sound near the Connecticut River, where so many early experiments with steam vessels occurred. More likely he was simply in step with his times. Truly, the steamboat was catching the nation's fancy. From the 78-ton *Clermont* of 1807, the American steam marine had grown by 1832 to 90,814 gross tons. While most of this tonnage was employed on inland or protected waters, trials to adapt steamships to oceanic and coastal navigation were underway. John Stevens's deepwater experiments with *Phoenix* in 1809 were soon followed by concrete achievements. A steam-packet line between New York and Charleston was proposed as early as 1815; *Savannah* had spanned the Atlantic by 1819; and at least five steamships had made the coastal journey from eastern ports to New Orleans by 1820. *Robert Fulton,* built in that year, marks the initial American attempt to construct a steamship expressly for ocean service.

The prime exponent of these coastal steamers was the New York brass-and-iron founder James P. Allaire. Morgan's senior by ten years, Allaire had opened a foundry on the East River in 1805. A close friend of Robert Fulton, Allaire cast many fittings for the inventor's steam engines and in 1816 consolidated the deceased Fulton's engine shops

13. Ralph Davis, *The Rise of the English Shipping Industry in the Seventeenth and Eighteenth Centuries*, pp. 81–109, 159–201; Robert G. Albion, "Early Nineteenth-Century Shipowning—A Chapter in Business Enterprise," *Journal of Economic History*, I (May 1941), 1–11.

with his own at 464 Cherry Street. Allaire's machinery was of high quality and design. He was an early advocate of anthracite coal as fuel and of double-cylinder, low-pressure (or "square-head") engines. His shops had produced parts and engines for the best American steamers— from *Savannah* to *Robert Fulton*. In these shops also were trained such notable marine engineers as Charles H. Haswell and John Roach.[14]

One of Allaire's long-held hopes was to establish steam-packet service between New York and the southern cotton ports. He secured the means to do so in 1832. He had built *David Brown* in that year to transport freight between New York City and his extensive iron works near Red Bank, New Jersey. But on November 11 she was shifted to commercial service on the lucrative New York–Charleston run and offered fortnightly sailings by April 1833. Challenging the reign of the sailing packets, this 136-foot, coal-burning sidewheeler made the voyage in seventy to seventy-five hours. While return on investment or other modern accounting ratios are impossible to calculate from the records available, expenses of this service initially ran only 80 per cent of gross earnings, and by September 1833 this figure had been reduced to 69 per cent.[15] More important, *David Brown* first demonstrated the feasibility of steam service to Charleston, and she was soon paired with a sister ship, *William Gibbons*. The two vessels began weekly sailings on March 1, 1834.

Charles Morgan, the Aymars, and Allaire's brother-in-law John Haggerty were intimately associated with these ventures. Indeed, their careers seemed fated to converge with that of Allaire. They had experienced the profits of the southern trade and were wise in the ways of packet management; Allaire saw the technological potential of coastal steamers. The merchants had capital and experience to invest; the engineer had designs to test and experiments to finance.

The allocation of responsibilities for the Charleston steam packets reinforced Morgan's movement toward business specialization. The vessels were run as a "line," under common management and scheduling, but not under common ownership (Table 1.3). This practice was typical

14. Hal Allaire Papers (In possession of Mrs. M. Taylor, Brielle, N.J.); *Niles' Weekly Register*, August 27, 1831; Bishop, *History of Manufactures*, III, 122–125; James S. Brown, *Allaire's Lost Empire: A Story of the Forges and Furnaces of the Manasquan;* Charles H. Haswell, *Reminiscences of an Octogenarian;* Leonard A. Swann, Jr., "John Roach: Maritime Entrepreneur."

15. Computed from reported earnings and expenditures of *David Brown*, August 1, 1832–February 1, 1833, and September 1833. Hal Allaire Papers.

of, and appropriated from, the sailing-packet lines. It facilitated continuity of management and economies of scale in administration but retained the flexibilities and limited liability historically associated with noncorporate shipowning.

The operating executive in the line was the New York agent—Charles Morgan.[16] He was compensated for his services at the usual commission rates and saw to the engagement of passengers and cargoes, the collection of passage and freight moneys, the collection and disbursement of accounts, the securance of provisions and stores, the usual "custom-house business," the selection of masters (and the delegation thereto of navigational responsibilities), and the co-ordination of schedules and advertising.

The broader "entrepreneurial" responsibilities of the owners overlay these "operating" or "managerial" functions. Chief among the former were "capital decisions" (relating to initial or subsequent capital investment, insurance, profit and loss, and breadth of ownership) and "deployment decisions" (relating to the employment of the vessel in captive, tramp, berth, or line service, its geographical and commodity preferences, and the type of operational structure to be employed—e.g., husband or commission agent; master; master-agent; or master-supercargo). These decisions were subject to the agreement of all equity holders of the particular vessel concerned and were functionally distinct from those of Morgan in his role as the operating agent. He derived his authority and decision-making framework from the equity holders and, while he might hold equity himself, his managerial function was separate and distinct.[17]

16. Before August 1833, Allaire acted as "proprietor" of *David Brown* and her master James Pennoyer acted as agent.

17. A distinction is made here and throughout between "entrepreneurial" and "managerial" decision-making. Decision-making of an entrepreneurial nature is taken to be that concerned with the definition of the enterprise's mission and role; with the institutional embodiment of that purpose; with the defense of institutional integrity; and with the ordering of internal conflict.

In this sense, the "entrepreneur" is the source of all formal authority for the organization and is primarily concerned with goal determination, planning, and fund allocation. The "manager" thus becomes more associated with the routine activities of the enterprise and those tasks delegated to him from above. As Hartmann states, "It does not matter . . . whether the entrepreneur actually delegates part of his authority or decides to monopolize it, for management is defined not by its reception of delegated authority but by not being its source." Heinz Hartmann, "Managers and Entrepreneurs: A Useful Distinction?," *Admin-*

Despite the degree of co-ordination achieved through the agency system, the steam-packet line persisted in many ancient commercial ways. Accounts were kept in the name of each vessel and by "trips" (ventures). Expenses were met through contingency funds deposited with the New York agent or by assessments (cash or sixty- to seventy-five–day notes) on the relevant owners. Profits were not pooled for the line but were distributed by shares, by vessel, through the agent. In June 1834 these arrangements were semiformalized with the erection on paper of the "New York and Charleston Steam Packet Company," the conversion of ownership increments to "stock," and the designation of profit distributions by the New York agent as "dividends." This was not a corporation in any modern sense of charters, annual reports, limited liability, etc., but rather "a written agreement in conformity with mercantile usage." The corporate form was not characteristic in the coastal steam trades until the mid-nineteenth century.

Thus to his co-agency of the Jamaica packets Charles Morgan added the day-to-day responsibilities of America's first coastal steam-packet line. Morgan increasingly subordinated his chandlery and his occasional trading ventures, and in 1833 the chandlery was sold out. He moved his offices to 31 South Street, then to 65 Washington in 1834, and concentrated on shipowning and agency.

The steamers to Charleston were his major concern. Their speed cut sailing records and attracted profitable cargoes of passengers and light freight. Despite a lack of heavy freight—which sought the larger capacities of sailers uncluttered by machinery—the steamships claimed profits of $1,000 to $2,000 per trip (after expenses; before interest on investment). Flushed with success, Allaire, Haggerty, and Morgan added the new steamship *Columbia* to the line on March 21, 1835. A United States Mail contract for weekly service, New York–Charleston, was negotiated by Morgan at $7,200 per year, and newspaper advertising was increased in size, frequency, and eye-appeal. A steamer of the line now left Pier 3, North River, New York, and May's Wharf, Charleston, each Saturday. *David Brown* had run temporarily to Norfolk in April but by June had

---

istrative Science Quarterly, III (March 1959), 439 n. See also, Philip Selznick, *Leadership in Administration: A Sociological Interpretation;* and Alfred D. Chandler, Jr. and Fritz Redlich, "Recent Developments in American Business Administration and their Conceptualization," *Business History Review,* XXXV (Spring 1961), 20–27.

rejoined the line, leaving New York every other Wednesday so as to provide alternately two steam-packets per week to Charleston.[18]

Public confidence, however, is necessary for successful passenger service, and the steam-packet line was plagued by well-publicized accidents. Although reinforced around the paddleboxes, these early "coastal" steamers were ill fitted for ocean service, especially on the treacherous waters off the Carolina capes. A vessel's engines often proved inadequate to keep it off a lee shore; while if steam power failed, the auxiliary sails were found wanting. Paddlewheels posed a dual problem: if under steam, they had to be protected from flotsam by alert maneuvering of the vessel; if not under steam, they constituted a colossal drag on the ship's sailing abilities. Errant sparks which might ignite the wooden vessels or their sails and the ever-present threat of boiler explosions (although lessened by the use of Allaire's low-pressure engine) gave steamship travel added risks.

The Charleston steam-packets were no exceptions. *David Brown* and *William Gibbons,* in particular, were repeatedly damaged or detained by such occurrences; and in October 1836 *William Gibbons* ran aground and sank near New Inlet, South Carolina—a total wreck. Widely circulated charges of drunkenness and looting against the crew and navigational ineptness against the captain added considerable loss of prestige for the line to the physical loss of the vessels themselves.[19]

The line's operations were reorganized late in 1836. With the loss of *William Gibbons* and the sale of *David Brown* to West Indian parties, the Aymars passed from the scene, leaving Allaire, Haggerty, and Morgan as partners. They set about completing two larger steamers for the line. Although the financial problems of a panic year delayed their fitting out, *New York* and *Home* finally joined *Columbia* on the Charleston run early

18. *New-York As It Is in 1833,* p. 140; *ibid.* (1834), p. 150; Norfolk (Va.) *American Beacon,* April 16, 25, May 8, 15, 29, June 12, 1835; Norfolk and Portsmouth (Va.) *Herald,* April 24, June 19, 1835; New York *Shipping & Commercial List,* May 20, 1835 ff.; *Niles' Weekly Register,* December 8, 1832, August 9, 1835; "Contracts for Carrying the Mails, 1838," *Senate Exec. Docs.,* 25 Cong., 3 Sess., No. 254 (Serial 341), 532–533.

19. Norfolk and Portsmouth *Herald,* July 8, August 26, 1833, October 28, 31, November 14, 1836; *American Beacon,* January 28, October 18–19, 1836; *Niles' Weekly Register,* January 30, February 6, October 22, November 5, 12, 1836; Thomas Ewbank, "Account of the Explosion of the Boiler of the Steamboat *Wm. Gibbons,*" *Journal of the Franklin Institute,* N. S., XVII (May 1836), 298–302.

in 1837. With three first-class steamers in operation, several short-term government charters to transport troops to and from the Florida Indian wars, and the annual mail subsidy, the line weathered its financial and publicity crises of 1836.[20] Then disaster struck again—this time to the pride of the line.

Home cost $89,708 and was supposed to usher in a new generation of coastal steamers. Lavishly appointed, with berth and stateroom accommodations for 120 passengers, she set a record time of sixty-four hours on only her second passage to Charleston. In but two coastwise voyages and several excursions around New York harbor she netted some $3,000 for her owner. On October 7, 1837, she cleared New York on her third voyage, well-patronized because of her growing reputation for elegance and speed. Her gala departure was marred by a four-hour grounding in the lower harbor, but the ship sustained no visible damage. Once at sea, *Home* had smooth steaming until heavy weather was encountered north of Cape Hatteras. The sea carried away her three life boats and stove in her larboard stateroom windows. A leak in the machinery spaces soon extinguished the boiler fires, despite frantic bailing by passengers and crew. Waterlogged and under sail alone, the ship grounded, then broached during an attempt to beach her. Ninety-nine passengers and crew perished in the surf.[21]

Sinking of *Home* was a serious setback for the proprietors of the Charleston line. Only $35,000 of insurance was carried on the vessel, and $10,000 of this was not collected until 1841.[22] But financial losses dwindled before the terrible toll of lives (among those lost was Allaire's

20. Erik Heyl, *Early American Steamers*, I, 95, 211, 281, 293; Hal Allaire Papers; "Contracts, War Department, 1836," *House Exec. Docs.*, 24 Cong., 2 Sess., No. 99 (Serial 303), 35, 36, 41, 44–45; *Ibid.*, 1837, *House Exec. Docs.*, 25 Cong., 2 Sess., No. 174 (Serial 327), 36; *Army and Navy Chronicle*, March 31, April 7, June 2, 9, 16, 23, July 14, 21, August 4, 11, September 22, 29, October 6, 13, 1836; April 20, July 27, October 12, 1837.

21. New York *Herald*, September 1, 20, October 4, 16, 18–20, 23–25, 27, 31, November 10, December 16, 1837; New York *Shipping & Commercial List*, September 2, 6, 20, 23, October 4, 7, 1837; Hal Allaire Papers; New Orleans *Bee*, October 23, November 3, 1837; [Carleton White], *Narrative of the Loss of the Steam-Packet Home, Carleton White, Master, on a Voyage from New York to Charleston, with Affidavits Disproving the Charges of Misconduct against the Master*, pp. 3–36; S. A. Howland, *Steamboat Disasters and Railroad Accidents in the United States*, pp. 13–37.

22. *Allaire v. American Insurance Co.* (N. Y. Super. Ct., March 15, 1841), reported in *Shipping & Commercial List*, March 20, 1841.

namesake nephew) and loss of confidence in the line. The *Home* tragedy became front-page news throughout America as charges and counter-charges of negligence rebounded among master, owners, builders, insurers, and passengers:

She was lost on her third trip off Cape Hatteras, through disobedience of orders given by Mr. Allaire to his Captain Carleton White.[23]

. . . the captain escaped, of course. . . . It's a horrid affair altogether. So utterly unseaworthy was she, though only on her third trip, that at every swell the bow and stern were lifted three feet from their proper position, what they call hogging, I believe. Her fault was too great length in proportion to her width and her solidarity.[24]

. . . no blame attaches itself to the captain. . . . The blame here rests with the owners or builders . . . [Allaire] was no boat builder himself, nor knew any thing of the business. He merely furnished his own and other boats with boilers and engines.[25]

. . . the most shameful negligence and culpable mismanagement which unhappily mark the progress of steam navigation in our country.[26]

Captain Carleton White and Allaire were spared from criminal charges, but the losses in lives and property were irreparable. Destruction of *Home*, followed by several closely spaced accidents to other steamers —notably *Pulaski* in June 1838—provoked federal legislation in 1838–1839 enforcing safety regulations on board "vessels propelled in whole or in part by steam."[27] But in its immediate effect, *Home* meant hard times for Morgan and his partners. As if the line had not enough trouble, the master of *New York* was roasted by the press for poor seamanship in attempting to rescue survivors of *Pulaski*.

The *Home* tragedy spurred a second reorganization of the line—in the fall of 1837. Morgan and Haggerty's *New York* was kept on the Charleston run in commercial and government service, and an arrangement was made to pair her with *Neptune*, a large new steamship then being outfitted by *David Brown*'s old master Captain James Pennoyer. Morgan

23. Memoranda by Allaire's son in Hal Allaire Papers.
24. Allan Nevins and Milton H. Thomas (editors), *The Diary of George Templeton Strong, 1835–1875*, I, 76.
25. New York *Herald*, October 20, 1837.
26. Allan Nevins (editor), *The Diary of Philip Hone, 1828–1851*, I, 334–335.
27. "Steam-Engines," *House Exec. Docs.*, 25 Cong., 3 Sess., No. 21 (Serial 345); New York *Herald*, July 7, 1838; William C. Redfield to Lewis Warrington, January 25, 1842, *Journal of the Franklin Institute*, XII (July 1846), 3–7.

continued the agency for *New York,* while Pennoyer would handle *Neptune.* Allaire, having lost *Home,* was increasingly preoccupied with his engine and iron works and relinquished his share in *Columbia,* and thus in the Charleston line, to Haggerty and Morgan—the latter becoming the managing partner of both *Columbia* and *New York.*[28]

Firmly in control, Morgan pressed on with another plan begun even before the *Home* disaster—the exploration of alternative deployments for his steamers. The possibility of extending service to the Gulf of Mexico may have been considered by the partners as early as 1835 and *Columbia* sent on a voyage to New Orleans and Galveston.[29] *David Brown* definitely tested the Gulf trades early in 1836, being detached from the Charleston line and running for three months between Havana and New Orleans, via Key West.[30] There is also evidence that *Home* might have ultimately been intended to establish a New York–New Orleans service.[31]

Although Morgan and his associates considered regular steam-packet service connecting New York and New Orleans, they apparently abandoned the idea, which was not realized for another decade. The 1,711-mile passage to New Orleans offered such extremes in navigational conditions and demanded such exceptional seamanship that insurance rates to European ports were less than those to the Gulf.

Navigation of the lower Atlantic coast was of primary concern. Here the narrow and swift Gulf Stream sweeps northward through a maze of

28. New York *Herald,* June 29, September 2–3, October 2, 17, November 2, 16, 31, December 18, 1837. For Allaire's chronic indebtedness to Haggerty, see Brown, *Allaire, passim,* and *Haggerty v. Allaire Works,* 5 Sanford (N. Y. Super. Ct.) 230 (1851).

29. Although recorded by Stanton, *Account,* p. 10, this voyage does not appear in the following contemporaneous sources: New Orleans *Price Current,* 1835–1836; *Bee,* 1835–1836; New Orleans *Commercial Bulletin,* 1835–1836; New York *Sun,* 1835; *Shipping & Commercial List,* 1835–1836; Galveston Custom House Records, 1835–1836 (Rosenberg Library, Galveston); Bureau of Customs, *Quarterly Abstracts of Passenger Lists of Vessels Arriving at New Orleans,* 1820–1875 (17 rolls, National Archives Microfilm Publication M–272), I; Bureau of Customs, *Passenger Lists of Vessels Arriving at New Orleans,* 1820–1902 (93 rolls, National Archives Microfilm Publication M–259), XII–XIV.

30. *Bee,* August 24, December 18, 1835, January 13, 18, February 3, 6, 24, 29, March 4, 21, 25, April 11, 14, 1836. Fruit was the staple cargo on these voyages; a few passengers were also carried.

31. *Home*'s final insurance policy, taken in August 1837, was a time policy for one year and specified "the boat to run between New-York and New-Orleans, and of course to the intermediate ports." *Allaire v. American Insurance Co., loc. cit.*

islands and reefs. Southbound ships sought the "Hole in the Wall" via the Providence Channel northeast of Nassau in order to gain the coast once again. Thence the curving Florida Strait guarded the entrance to the Gulf. Poor charts and navigational aids made sailors fear both passages, while illicit "wreckers" among the Florida Keys were known dangers.[32]

The excellent schedules maintained by the sailing packets also hindered development of a steam service to New Orleans. It was not until the late 1840s, when larger, swifter, and more seaworthy steamers appeared, that the square-riggers began to lose their grip on the New York–New Orleans run.[33]

Steam navigation within the Gulf itself, however, held more interest for Morgan and his partners. A host of small ports could be linked to the great entrepôt of New Orleans on a more regular basis. The New Orleans–Texas trade looked especially promising. That republic, having recently achieved independence from Mexico, was naturally interested in encouraging immigration and expanding her commerce. American shipping, formerly harassed by both the Texan and Mexican navies, was assured by May 1836 that it was safe to enter Texas ports. Commerce expanded rapidly and by May 1837, 480,000 tons of cargo had been carried to and from the Republic by some forty vessels. All save two or three Texan ships were of United States registry.[34]

Morgan and his partners were surely aware of these developments. Haggerty had traded to and from New Orleans for years and was already speculating in Texas lands. Morgan had invested in sailing packets to New Orleans for at least a decade. Both reflected the general interest of the New York business community in the Texas situation.[35]

32. *American Coast Pilot* (11th ed.), pp. 140–179; James K. Greer (editor), "Journal of Ammon Underwood, 1834–1838," *Southwestern Historical Quarterly*, XXXII (October 1928), 125–126; Dorothy Dodd, "The Wrecking Business on the Florida Reef, 1822–1860," *Florida Historical Quarterly*, XXII (April 1944), 171–199.

33. Albion, *Square-Riggers*, pp. 56–76, 134–137, 253–272.

34. A. M. Clopper to Nicholas Clopper, January 2, 1836, *Quarterly of the Texas State Historical Association*, XIII (October 1909), 130; *Bee*, May 10, 1836; Henry M. Morfit to John Forsyth, September 4, 1836, "Condition of Texas," *House Exec. Docs.*, 24 Cong., 2 Sess., No. 35 (Serial 302), 29–30; Joseph T. Crawford to Charles T. O'Gorman, May 13, 1837, in Ephraim D. Adams (editor), *British Diplomatic Correspondence Concerning the Republic of Texas, 1838–1846*, pp. 7–8.

35. James E. Winston, "New York and the Independence of Texas," *Southwestern Historical Quarterly*, XVIII (April 1915), 368–385; Robert T. Thompson,

Thus the *Home* disaster accelerated a decision already in the making. In September 1837, Morgan had negotiated an arrangement to shift *Columbia* to the Gulf trade with the prominent New Orleans commission merchant, James Reed.[36] Her arrival at New Orleans on November 18, 1837, and her inaugural voyage to Galveston on November 25 marked Charles Morgan's entrance into the economic life of the Gulf of Mexico. For the man and for the region, the union was permanent and profitable. A Connecticut Yankee, toughened in the commercial world of Manhattan, would find his destiny on the warm waters of the Mexican Sea.

Colonel James Neilson: A Business Man of the Early Machine Age in New Jersey, 1784–1862, pp. 62–69.

36. *Bee,* November 8, 18, 21, 27, 1837. For the Reed arrangement, see New York *Herald,* October 2, 1837, and Galveston *Daily News,* May 28, 1878.

2

SERVING THE TEXAS REPUBLIC,
1837–1846

WITH some twenty years of experience, Morgan was no neophyte in assessing the risks of his business environment. He had proven his abilities in a very competitive business specialization and in the most competitive of American cities. Yet entry into the Gulf economy was to tax his skill and willingness to bear risk as never before.

As areas for investment in 1836–1837, New Orleans and her sphere of influence were like waves cresting into the turbulence of surf. A population increase and a remarkable flurry of canal, railroad, and banking expansion had occurred since 1830. Influenced by increasing downriver trade, a rising British demand for cotton, and an influx of foreign capital, twenty-five railroad companies and twelve banks were chartered by the Louisiana legislature in the boom years before the financial panic of 1837. Upriver trade seemed secure, and coastwise sailings to Gulf and Atlantic ports were increasing annually. A wholesale-price rise of 68 per cent for all commodities reflected the prosperity occurring between 1830 and 1836.

Yet flaws existed in Louisiana's economic structure. Too many of her railroads were erratically planned or poorly subscribed and contributed little to the solution of her transportation needs. While some $39,943,832 in paid-up banking capital was created by 1837, much of it was consumed in short-term real-estate and cotton speculations, and little found its way into growth investments. The complacency of the New Orleans businessmen in their geographic position obscured the fact that their position as gatherers of upriver output and as redistributors of domestic and foreign goods was already declining.[1]

The New Orleans economy proved tremendously unstable. In early 1836 the *Bee* cockily urged New York merchants such as Morgan to "locate among us [for] . . . a capital of $10,000 can in a few years here realize $100,000." Between March and December of the following year, however, in the wake of the financial crisis, 2,800 bankruptcy suits were filed in Orleans Parish alone.[2] Yet in the midst of this chaos Charles Morgan and his partners committed a major investment of their capital to New Orleans and the Gulf. Their decision resulted in part from their bad luck on the Atlantic. More likely they were attracted by the great expectations of the vigorous young Republic of Texas. It was Galveston as much as New Orleans that drew their attention.

Galveston Island in 1837 was far from impressive. Twenty-seven miles long and barely three wide, it separated the rough waters of the western Gulf of Mexico from a more placid bay. A maximum elevation of nine feet and a dearth of vegetation did little to shield the settlement straggling along the island's bayshore from autumn's tropical storms or the buffeting of winter "northers." Yet the commerce carried across the planks of a single wooden wharf made this the principal port-of-entry for the Republic of Texas.

Irregular trade routes radiated from Galveston to other nascent Texas ports: across the bay to Anahuac at the mouth of the Trinity River or to Lynchburg, Harrisburg, and Houston, via Buffalo Bayou; to Velasco, at the mouth of the Brazos, where a good anchorage in thirty feet of water permitted discharge of passengers continuing up the river; to Matagorda, a bustling settlement near the mouth of the Colorado, eighty-two miles down the coast; to Aransas Bay, forty miles farther south, where vessels drawing eight feet might enter; or northward fifty miles to the mouth of the Sabine.[3]

1. Merl Reed, "Boom or Bust—Louisiana's Economy during the 1830's," *Louisiana History*, IV (Winter 1963), 35–54.
2. New Orleans *Bee*, May 13, 1836; Reed, "Boom or Bust," p. 50. Morgan and Haggerty were not the only northern shipowners lured to the Gulf. Between 1830 and 1839, 14 new sailing packet lines were formed from New York, Boston, Philadelphia, and Baltimore to New Orleans; 10 to Mobile. Cutler, *Queens, passim.*
3. *City of Galveston Island, in Texas, with a History of the Title of the Proprietor and a Brief Account of All Its Advantages; Accompanied with a Plan*

Under the command of John T. Wright, *Columbia* inaugurated steam-packet service to the Texas Republic, beginning regular sailings between New Orleans, Galveston, and Velasco in November 1837.[4] Since *Columbia* is traditionally considered the first vessel of the Morgan Line, Morgan's financial interest in her during these early years is significant. *Columbia*'s agent in New Orleans, from her arrival there on November 25, 1837, through her twenty-sixth voyage to Galveston in January 1839 was James Reed & Co. Reed purchased shares in the vessel in September 1837 to bring her to the Gulf. The exact division of ownership in *Columbia* after that sale is unknown, but Reed's interest has been estimated as high as $50,000, Charles Morgan's as low as $15,000. After October 31, 1838, however, Reed ceased to have any financial interest in *Columbia*. Her owners then were only Morgan and John Haggerty of New York—the apportionment of shares not known. In the light of Haggerty's passive role in former enterprises, it is likely that Morgan was again the dominant partner. Thus *Columbia* was largely a Morgan venture until the two New Yorkers sold her on January 14, 1840.[5]

Columbia completed twelve round-voyages to Galveston and Velasco by June 8, 1838, when she was joined in the trade by *Cuba*—an unsuccessful New Orleans–Havana steamer then owned and operated by the Crescent City firm of Bogart & Hawthorn. The vessels formed a "New

---

of the City and Harbor, and a Map of Texas, Showing the Commerical Channels with the Interior through Which the City Is to Derive Its Extensive Trade, pp. 1–8; Andrew F. Muir (editor), *Texas in 1837: An Anonymous, Contemporary Narrative,* pp. 1–10, 180–182; Crawford to O'Gorman, May 13, 1837, Adams (ed.), *British Correspondence,* pp. 5–7; *Bee,* November 13, 1837; William R. Hogan, *The Texas Republic: A Social and Economic History,* pp. 5–9, 53–80.

4. One earlier attempt to establish scheduled steamboat service to the Texas Republic has been found. Between April 1837 and March 1838 William Bryan of Texas and New Orleans advertised *Constitution* and *Convoy* as a "New Orleans and Texas Steam Boat Line," but regular schedules were not maintained. Other independent steamers made sporadic voyages throughout 1836–1837 but none in the highly organized and well-advertised fashion of *Columbia*. New Orleans *Commercial Bulletin,* 1836–1838; Survey of Federal Archives (La.), *Registers and Enrollments of New Orleans, Louisiana, 1804–1870,* III, 48–49 (hereafter cited as *Registers, NOLA*); Galveston Custom House Records, Record Book I. The connection of Morgan with these earlier vessels recorded in "Morgan Lines," *The Handbook of Texas,* II, 234–235, is garbled and incorrect.

5. New York *Herald,* October 2, December 18, 1837; New Orleans *Price Current,* December 2, 1837–January 19, 1839; *Bee,* November 21, 1837–January 14, 1839; Galveston *Daily News,* May 28, 1878; *Registers, NOLA,* III, 44.

Orleans and Texas Line" and thereafter offered weekly sailings between Louisiana and the Republic.[6]

The Texas "line" thus organized was a traffic pool and differed from the original Allaire-Haggerty-Morgan Charleston "line." Morgan and Haggerty and their agent, Reed & Co., owned no interest in *Cuba;* Bogart & Hawthorn none in *Columbia.* There was no common managing partner or agent, yet the steamers definitely ran in conjunction with each other— rates of passage and freight were standardized and sailings and advertising integrated. Profits and losses were not pooled but accrued to each vessel on a venture basis—in short, the arrangement was the same as the one then prevailing on the Charleston run between Morgan's *New York* and Pennoyer's *Neptune.* The partners and the public accepted as utilitarian the fact that the *Columbia–Cuba* pool monopolized existing steamship services in the western Gulf.[7]

Contrary to her experiences on the Charleston route, *Columbia* proved well-suited for the peculiarities of the New Orleans–Texas trade. A steamship encountered fewer of the delays which plagued sailers on the Mississippi below the Crescent City. Of shallower draught than most sailing vessels, she could more easily cross the shifting sand bars at the river's mouth. Coming upriver, her engines eliminated the sailing ship's need for elaborate tacking against the current or expensive towing by steam tugs. In Texas waters, her light draught, speed, and maneuverability permitted safer and more predictable navigation of the Republic's narrow passes and shallow bays.[8]

The elegance of *Columbia* and *Cuba* balanced their utility. The steamship disasters on the Atlantic coast showed passenger comfort and safety

6. Except for a refitting voyage to New York by *Cuba,* July 14–October 25, 1838. *Price Current,* December 2, 1837–June 9, 1838; *Commercial Bulletin,* January 6, March 26, April 12, May 26, June 8, 1838.

7. For ownership of *Cuba* see: *Commercial Bulletin,* May 26, 1838, and *Registers, NOLA,* III, 55–56. For evidence that *Columbia* and *Cuba* were considered part of the same "line" see: *Commercial Bulletin,* May 26, June 8, 23, 1838, January 15, June 19, 1839; Thomas F. McKinney to Samuel May Williams, November 3, 1838, Samuel May Williams Papers (Rosenberg Library, Galveston); R. A. Irion to J. Pinckney Henderson, November 28, 1838, George P. Garrison (editor), *The Diplomatic Correspondence of the Republic of Texas,* III, 864–866.

8. *Commercial Bulletin,* March 26, 1838, June 17, 1840; *Bee,* January 24, 1839; *American Coast Pilot* (14th ed.), pp. 262–266, 267–271; Walter Mc. Lowrey, "Navigational Problems at the Mouth of the Mississippi River, 1698–1880."

to be the best advertisements for a line, and Morgan and his associates certainly recognized this truth by 1838. Perhaps the shock of seeing Galveston after the luxury of the steam-packets accounts for some of the dreary views of that settlement. *Columbia* soon established a reputation as "one of the best and safest sea-boats in the United States," while *Cuba* was considered "equal to the *Columbia* in all the qualities of a sea boat. Superior in size & elegance of finish."[9]

One early passenger, Mary Austin Holley, writing with a lady's eye for decor, described *Columbia*'s interior: she slept on "the finest and whitest linen;" was attended by "a lady-like chamber maid;" dined with "silver forks, or what looks like silver" and "ivory knives" at the Captain's table. The meals were prepared by a "French cook" and served by "White waiters," on this, "the most perfect boat . . . the best I have ever seen."[10] *New York*, placed by Morgan on the Texas run in 1839, exceeded *Columbia* in elegance. Mrs. Holley, after a voyage on *New York*, pictured herself as Cleopatra at rest on her fine stateroom couch. The main cabin glistened with polished mahogany set off by white satin damask and dimity draperies. Stained-glass windows decorated with the arms of Texas overlooked a dining table replete with fine white porcelain (decorated with "a blue device . . . representing the New York at Sea with the Texas eagle hovering over her"), engraved silver, and crystal. Again Mrs. Holley mentions her pretty, white chambermaid and the "curly-headed, rosey-cheeked Irish waiters," always at her service.[11]

But not all passengers could sample the luxury of the main cabin. "Uncle Jimmy" Smith and his family came to Texas in 1840 in steerage (on *New York*), "since this . . . was much cheaper than Cabin Passage—And much more Comfortable than Deck Passage." The steerage itself was below decks and curtained off into berths for sleeping, while during the day the passengers were allowed the freedom of the awninged decks. The family slept in "Good Berths" but had to "find" and prepare their own meals until Smith persuaded Captain Wright to allow him to pay for preparation by the regular cooks. Deck and steerage travelers

9. *Commercial Bulletin*, March 15, 26, June 8, 1838; New Orleans *Daily Picayune*, June 26, October 26, 1838.

10. Mary Austin Holley to Mrs. William M. Brand, December 19, 1837, as quoted in William R. Hogan, "A Social and Economic History of the Republic of Texas," p. 6. Used by permission.

11. Holley to Brand, November 12, 1840, *ibid.*, pp. 6–7.

were requested to control their "loud discourse" for fear of disturbing their more affluent fellows in the cabin.[12]

The steam-packets again excelled the sailers in speed. Their voyages to Texas required but thirty-five to forty hours, while a schooner might consume two weeks in beating around the coast. In 1838, *Columbia's* longest and shortest runs were forty-eight and thirty-three hours, while *Cuba* varied from fifty-four to thirty-six hours. Such service led one New Orleans paper to conclude that steamships were undoubtedly the "kind of vessel best calculated" for the trade, "on account of the quickness of their voyages, as the most profit is made by carrying passengers, and they always give the preference to celerity of motion."[13]

Passenger traffic did constitute the steady income of the New Orleans and Texas Line as it had on the Charleston run. Businessmen, soldiers, immigrants, and diplomats found the steamers well suited to their needs. Cabin passage to Galveston was $30 ($5 above schooner rates), deck or steerage usually $15. To Velasco, where passengers were landed for transit up the Brazos River, passage from New Orleans was $35. All fares were payable in advance and only in specie or current New Orleans city banknotes—a reflection of general American currency disorders of the time. *Columbia* and *Cuba* were seldom taxed to capacity by travelers, but the traffic was consistent, as indicated in Table 2.1.[14] Comparison of these figures with the price of passage and projection of the product for the full number of voyages indicate significant gross receipts for Morgan and associates.

Freight carriage by *Columbia* and *Cuba* is more difficult to estimate from the partial manifests available. Freight consigned to Texas via the steamers before 1840 consisted of emigrants' effects, light merchandise, and provisions. Goods were taken mostly to Galveston (some being lightered at Velasco) until service was extended to other ports in the

12. "Memoirs of James Norman Smith (1789–1875)," III, 115–121. Used by permission of Dr. William R. Hogan, New Orleans.

13. *Commercial Bulletin*, January 8, 1838. For passage times, see: *Daily Picayune*, January 12, February 13, 27, March 28, 1838; *Bee*, April 13, May 14, 26, June 12, 25, July 2, 12, 26, August 14, 28, September 13, October 1, 27, November 12, 23, December 1, 1838; *Commercial Bulletin*, April 28, June 18, 1838. Faster runs were usually made westward because of prevailing Gulf currents. *Daily Picayune*, May 27, 1874.

14. *Columbia* carried an estimated 700 passengers to Texas by March 1838. *Commercial Bulletin*, January 8, February 7, March 26, 1838.

1840s. From Texas the primary exports were cotton and hides. The manifest of *Columbia*, New Orleans to Galveston, December 17, 1838, is typical: "1 hhd. sugar, 45 bbls. do., 1 hhd. hams, 16 bbls. flour, 11 bbls. whiskey, 2 tierces rice, and an assorted cargo of brandy, nails, wine, dry goods, coffee, loaf sugar, clothing, saddlery, candles, gin, onions, brandy, fruits, oil, varnish, butter and dry goods."[15]

In general, this trade reflects the Texas tariffs of the period which encouraged importation of foodstuffs, lumber, and immigrants' effects. There is little doubt, however, that cargo was secondary to passengers in producing steamers' revenue in these early years. The *Commercial Bulletin*, for example, repeatedly implied that "the most profit is made by carrying passengers;" yet it was also said of *Columbia* that "she generally carries down freight sufficient to pay fuel & other charges."[16]

The trade evidently satisfied its promoters and the public. *Columbia*'s net receipts were characterized as "handsome" in January 1838, and by March "her immense & increasing profits" were reputedly "clear of all expenses, $12,000." The New Orleans press continually agitated for more steam-packets for "the vast and multiplying intercourse" with Texas, and persons like young John Herndon, who recorded "Considerable heaving and much groaning" among his fellow passengers on *Columbia*, were chided "to regard the trip as an excursion of pleasure on which the comforts and elegant conveniences would be amply provided." The Texan government reciprocated these optimisms and encouraged steam navigation by exempting steam packets from tonnage duties from December 1837 to January 1839.[17]

Morgan had thus again been able to search out a profitable area for investments of the type he preferred. Indeed, developments in the Gulf were welcome news to him and Haggerty, contrary to the news from the Atlantic coast. Although Pennoyer's 221-foot *Neptune* had joined *New York* on the Charleston run in January 1838, all was not well.

15. *Price Current*, December 22, 1838.
16. H. P. N. Gammel (editor), *Laws of Texas*, I, 988, 1011–1014, 1207–1208, 1286–1287, 1313–1319, 1422; II, 209–225; *Commercial Bulletin*, January 8, February 7, March 26, 1838.
17. *Commercial Bulletin*, January 8, March 26, April 12, 30, May 26, June 18, 1838, January 24, 1839; Andrew F. Muir (editor), "Diary of a Young Man in Houston, 1838," *Southwestern Historical Quarterly*, LIII (January 1950), 282; Gammel (ed.), *op. cit.*, I, 1428–1429, II, 40–41.

On *Neptune*'s maiden voyage, "the majority of captains employed in the North River line of steamboats took passage . . . to share any risk that might occur and to encourage others by their example." Yet despite an "ostentatious display of safety belts and all other imaginable contrivances against drowning in case of ship-wreck," *Neptune* and *New York* were obviously losing their share of the Charleston trade. There was a general falling-off of travel during the depression year, and a line of larger and swifter steamers inaugurated by Baltimore and Charleston interests in October 1837 was more successful than the Morgan vessels in obtaining what traffic there was. Most likely, the reason for the decline was reflected in traveler Charles Daubeny's opinion that, "the fatal accident that occurred [to *Home*] . . . must be present in the minds of those who undertake the voyage for some time to come;" or, as James Gordon Bennett's *Herald* bluntly put it, "for the present, the public have had quite enough of Charleston steam packets."[18]

As a result, the old Allaire-Morgan-Haggerty Charleston line was terminated in mid-1838. *Neptune* shifted her allegiance to the Baltimore–Charleston line, and Allaire severed any remaining interest in *New York*. The $7,200-per-year mail contract held by Morgan was forfeited, and *New York*, unable to match the schedules maintained by her competitors on the Atlantic, was finally shifted to the Gulf in January 1839.[19]

Actually, Morgan and Haggerty had considered this shift as early as April 1838.[20] It was part of a major reassessment by Morgan which increased his degree of business specialization and permanently committed his major capital investment to the Gulf states.

Charles Morgan at forty-three was no longer the clerk from Connecti-

18. New York *Herald*, June 29, July 1, September 2, 3, December 18, 1837, January 24, February 27, 1838; Charles G. B. Daubeny, *Journal of a Tour through the United States and in Canada, Made during the Years 1837–38*, pp. 122–123.

19. New York *Evening Post*, January 31, February 14, 27, March 5, April 14, May 8, 19, 28, June 21, 25, July 9, 21, October 8, 19, December 24, 26, 1838; *Herald*, December 18, 1837, January 24, March 8, 12, July 7, September 17, 1838; "Contracts for Carrying the Mails, 1838" (Serial 341), 532–533; *Registers*, NOLA, III, 154; Alexander C. Brown, "An Early American *Neptune*," *American Neptune*, XII (April 1952), 148–149; John H. Morrison, *History of American Steam Navigation*, p. 438.

20. *Commercial Bulletin*, May 14, 1838; Irion to Henderson, November 28, 1838, Garrison (ed.), *op. cit.*, III, 866.

cut but an experienced businessman who had most recently weathered the Panic of 1837. He was managing-owner of two excellent steam-packets (in partnership with one of the richest men of New York) and still owned interests in a dozen sailing ships. He had held a large U.S. Mail contract and several government charters for shipments of military personnel and supplies. In 1838, as one-third partner in T. F. Secor & Co., he helped establish a machine and engine-building shop at Ninth Street and East River, known in later years as the Morgan Iron Works. His family was healthy, his eldest daughter about to marry one of his promising young clerks, and he would become a grandfather for the first time in November 1840. No man to plunge recklessly into far-off ventures at middle age, Morgan maturely weighed the hazards and prospects of the Gulf trades and found them acceptable.[21]

Certainly there were hazards in the Gulf trades. Pirates and belligerent warships were not unknown to Morgan's vessels. In November 1837, *Columbia*'s passengers witnessed the capture of the pirate schooner *Blooming Youth* by a United States revenue cutter. Captain John T. Wright sighted the schooner, put in at Mobile, and then led the cutter to her prey. In February 1838, two Mexican naval vessels harassing Texan commerce fired upon *Columbia*. As a passenger described the incident, Captain Wright demanded an explanation and "They replied: 'We want your papers.' Capt. W. rejoined: 'Come aboard and get them, and —— you, if you fire another shot at me I'll blow you to h--l.' " The Mexicans then fired upon him with muskets "loaded with buck and slug," but at that moment *Columbia*'s engineer let off the vessel's steam with a roar. The Mexicans took cover, *Columbia* veered off, "and we proceeded on our way without being searched."[22]

Problems of climate, capital, and control were more chronic than these melodramatic incidents. Seasonal employment of vessels was familiar to

21. *Herald*, October 9, 16, 1837; "Contracts for Carrying the Mails, 1838" (Serial 341), 532–533; "Contracts, War Department, 1836" (Serial 303), 35, 36, 41, 44–45; *ibid.*, 1837 (Serial 327), 36; *ibid.*, 1839, *House Exec. Docs.*, 26 Cong., 1 Sess., No. 89 (Serial 365), 25, 40; Bishop, *History of Manufactures* (3rd ed.), III, 130–132; Morgan, *Genealogy*, pp. 154–155.

22. Journal of James S. Lauderdale, 1838, in *Saturday Review* (Galveston), I (October 9, 1897), 8. See also: *Commercial Bulletin*, March 28, May 15, 1838; *Bee*, March 28, 1838; "Attack on Steamboat *Columbia*," *House Exec. Docs.*, 25 Cong., 2 Sess., No. 360 (Serial 330); "The Capture of Mitchell the Pirate," *Bee*, November 18, 1837.

Morgan, who had been weaned on tropical importing, cotton packets, and ice closures of New York's harbor. The Gulf climate was an equally important consideration in his business planning.

The southern commercial year began on October 1, but little business was transacted after June. The heat, fevers, the seasonal nature of the cotton crop, and the high incidence of tropical storms—causing higher insurance rates between July 15 and October 15—combined to diminish the Gulf trades during the summer months. Morgan reacted predictably during these slack times by curtailing sailings or withdrawing his vessels (see Table 2.1).[23] He was thus content to relinquish his monopoly to other steamers and sailers for at least a portion of the year.

Morgan's preference for refitting his vessels in New York rather than in the limited shipyards of New Orleans also contributed to the withdrawals. Steamship operating expenses in the Gulf nearly matched those of New York, with cheaper labor balancing higher fuel costs. Repair and construction costs, however, as well as quality of craftsmanship, were superior in New York. Throughout the 1830s and 1840s New York thus remained Morgan's residence and center of capital, construction, and repair, while New Orleans became the locus of his vessels' operations.[24]

Legal residence in New York, which Morgan maintained throughout his lifetime, had other advantages. The high taxes on personal property typical of the southern states and municipalities could thus be avoided to some degree but, more important, litigation involving business ventures was ensured the comparative advantage of original jurisdiction within the federal and New York courts rather than wthin the state and local courts of the South.

Geographical separation of policy-making and operations had disadvantages, however. Since Morgan preferred to remain in New York, the

23. For insurance rates, see: New York *Shipping & Commercial List*, February 25, 1840. For withdrawals, see: *Daily Picayune*, May 1, June 16, November 3, 1840, June 18, 25, August 28, November 6, 1841, July 6, 1842; *Price Current*, November 4, 1843, July 20, November 6, 1844, June 25, October 15, 1845; Charles Eliot to Aberdeen, August 14, 1842, and William Kennedy to Aberdeen, July 29, 1844, Adams (ed.), *British Correspondence*, pp. 93–94, 350–352.

24. As late as 1870, another northern steamship owner could testify: "A vessel in the neighborhood of Galveston or New Orleans might almost as well be given away as to undertake to pay the cost of repairs in those ports. It was generally found cheaper to float her back to Philadelphia." Henry R. Edmunds, in "Causes of the Reduction of American Tonnage," *House Reports*, 41 Cong., 2 Sess., No. 28 (Serial 1436), 153.

securance of adequate representation in New Orleans became a perennial problem.

For the duration of the 1830s, Morgan solved his problem of control in a most traditional mercantile manner. While he depended upon and received considerable allegiance and service from trustworthy captains—like John T. Wright or John Wade, who had served him on the Atlantic—Morgan consigned more and more of the commercial and non-navigational responsibilities of his vessels to independent agents resident in the Gulf ports.

Unlike New York, where the specialist in ship-agency had already appeared, New Orleans ship agents were more often factors or wholesale or retail merchants as well—hence more likely to divide their loyalties between personal interests and those of the vessels within their charge. Particularly if agents owned no share in the ships they represented were their loyalties divided, as was the case with the agents of *Columbia* and *New York*. Retention of ship ownership allowed flexible selection of agents, and Morgan relied upon the usual rates of commission in compensating his representatives.

Throughout 1839 and for years following, Morgan searched for the right New Orleans representative. A quarrel with James Reed removed *Columbia* from his agency in January 1839. *Columbia* was also withdrawn from the traffic pool with Bogart & Hawthorn's *Cuba* and placed with the New Orleans firm of Smith & Voorhees. *New York*, however, was placed with Bogart & Hawthorn upon her arrival in the Crescent City and replaced *Columbia* in the line with *Cuba*.

Morgan thus combined old and new ways. He clung to the ancient concepts of venture-accounting and ship-operation under different commercial representatives. Yet the degree of operational integration achieved was certainly suggestive of more "modern" shipping-line management. His philosophy of management remained pragmatic, however.[25]

Pragmatism was evident in the assignment of *New York*. Although sent to the Gulf to run in the Texas trade, the vessel was almost shifted to a

---

25. Based on: *Registers, NOLA*, III, 44, 55–56, IV, 207; advertisements in *Bee*, 1838–1840 and *Commercial Bulletin*, 1838–1840; *Daily News*, May 28, 1878. Suggestive but not conclusive on the degree of specialization of New Orleans businessmen is Robert E. Roeder, "Merchants of Ante-Bellum New Orleans," *Explorations in Entrepreneurial History*, First Series, X (April 1958), 113–122.

Cuban run when a flurry of interest in a New Orleans–Havana steamship line swept the Crescent City in early 1839. On February 14, Maunsel White & Co., owners of the steam-packet *Merchant,* proposed to open regular service to the Cuban port, but by February 25 the project had been abandoned due to heavy expense and lack of patronage. Three days later Morgan's *New York* took up the plan, proposing to inaugurate the service on March 8, "if a sufficient number of passengers should offer to justify her making the trip." She could not attract enough travelers for even the initial voyage, however. The idea was forgotten and *New York* remained on the Galveston run.[26]

The break with James Reed precipitated another inevitable problem for Morgan and Haggerty—competition in the Gulf. Reed quickly associated with Morgan's old employee and former partner, Captain James Pennoyer of New York, in plans for an opposition line from New Orleans to Texas. Pennoyer and Reed fitted out the steamship *Charleston* by early January 1839 and brought her to New Orleans on March 11. *Charleston* proved no threat to Morgan, however, for, after her subsequent clearance for Galveston, it was revealed she was intended for the Texas Navy and soon became the steam warship *Zavala.* More serious was Reed's purchase into Pennoyer's *Neptune* in May 1839 and their announcement to enter her in the Texas trade.[27]

In June, to ready *New York* for the anticipated fall competition, Morgan and Haggerty took advantage of the slack summer season to return her to New York City for refitting. *Columbia* remained in the Gulf and unexpectedly inherited the entire steam service to Texas when *Cuba* was wrecked in Galveston Bay's east pass on June 12. *Columbia* ran unchallenged through October 1839, advertising departures from New Orleans on the first and fifteenth of each month and from Galveston on the eighth and twenty-second. *New York* returned to the Gulf on November 4 and four days later re-entered the Texas trade, again under the agency of Bogart & Hawthorn; *Columbia* continued her schedules as

26. *Bee,* February 14, 21, 25, 27, 28, 1839; *Daily Picayune,* February 14, March 2, 3, 12, 1839; *Registers, NOLA,* III, 144.

27. *Herald,* August 18, December 7, 1838; *Commercial Bulletin,* February 1, March 11, May 11, 1839; *Bee,* March 4, 11, May 11, 1839; *Daily Picayune,* March 5, 19, 1839; *Registers, NOLA,* III, 154; Forrest R. Holdcamper (editor), *Merchant Steam Vessels of the United States, 1807–1868: The "Lytle List,"* pp. 30, 37, 53, 138.

before, represented by Smith & Voorhees. This Morgan-Haggerty monopoly was short lived, for on November 7 *Neptune* arrived from New York to activate the Reed-Pennoyer opposition line.[28]

Neptune's maiden voyage to Galveston on November 20 meant stiff Gulf competition for Morgan and Haggerty, whose vessels had faced no concerted opposition before (although they had reduced freight rates by 25 per cent in February, probably to meet the challenge of more commodious sailing vessels). *Neptune* was larger and faster than *Columbia* or *New York*, and the reputation of her owner-master, Pennoyer, was equal to that of any mariner of his day. *Neptune* initiated biweekly sailings to Galveston, leaving New Orleans on the eighth and twenty-second and Texas on the first and fifteenth of every month. *Columbia* and *New York* countered with similar schedules; the former left New Orleans on weeks alternate to *Neptune*'s, while *New York* directly opposed the Reed-Pennoyer entry by advertising identical sailing dates.

By chance or arrangement, however, this head-on competition soon ended. The schedules of the three steamers had been adjusted by December 16 to give each her own departure day at each port: *Neptune* now left New Orleans on the fifth and twentieth of each month, Galveston on the twelfth and twenty-seventh; *Columbia* departed the Crescent City every first and fifteenth, Galveston every seventh and twenty-second; *New York* cleared New Orleans each tenth and twenty-fifth, Galveston each seventeenth and thirty-first. Evidently there was enough traffic to go around and competition was reduced to niceties—*Neptune* accepted Texas money at fifty cents on the dollar while her competitors still required specie or New Orleans bank notes, for example.[29]

A more lasting result of this rivalry was the extension of the Morgan-Haggerty passenger and freight service from Galveston and Velasco to Matagorda Bay in November 1839. This settlement of 1,000 persons, some eighty miles south of Galveston, was reached by negotiating Paso de Caballo, a tricky approach across a shallow bar. At low water this bar admitted ships drawing less than nine feet, but it sometimes changed,

28. *Commercial Bulletin*, June 10, 15, 19, July 6, September 10, 17, November 5, 8, 1839; *Bee*, June 19, 22, November 8, 1839; "Account of Arrivals Comg. January 1st 1839," Galveston Custom House Records, Record Book I, 112–130.

29. *Commercial Bulletin*, February 16, 17, October 17, November 5, 6, 8, 21, December 3, 16, 1839, January 3, 1840; "Account of Arrivals Comg. January 1st 1839," *loc. cit.*

allowing larger ships to enter. The usual practice for ships of any size was to lie offshore and have their cargo lightered to the beach, a custom prompted by the vagaries of Paso de Caballo and a general distrust of the pilots at Decrow's Point near the pass. Morgan and Haggerty initially sent *New York* to Matagorda, but repeated delays because of bad weather at the pass caused them, by 1841, to offer only connections with smaller steamers at Galveston for Matagorda.[30]

In view of the challenge presented by *Neptune*, Morgan and Haggerty's sale of *Columbia* to her master Henry Windle in January 1840 is difficult to explain.[31] *New York*, the one remaining ship of their Gulf fleet, now faced both *Neptune* and *Columbia*. In retrospect, however, Morgan and Haggerty's action seems reasonable. *Columbia* had been in continuous service since her launching in 1835, and during the preceding twenty-six months had completed forty-six round voyages to Texas. Unquestionably, her replacement by a newer vessel would be desirable, and such a steamship, *Savannah*, was then available in the East. While the immediate loss in business to *Columbia* was unmistakable, the slack summer season was near, and with *Savannah* to join *New York* in the fall, long-term profits from the transaction were likely.

Neptune returned to New York for refitting in April, and *New York* was withdrawn from the Gulf for the summer on June 16, leaving the Texas trade to *Columbia*. The partners began preparations for the fall season. They purchased the 160-foot steamship *Savannah* (built in 1838 for the New York–Liverpool trade, but thereafter running in Carolina waters) and refitted her for the Gulf. Morgan must have had his eye on this vessel for some time, for she contained the first marine engines built by T. F. Secor & Co., of which he was a partner. After refurbishing at New York, *Savannah* was dispatched to the Gulf, arriving at New Orleans on October 15, 1840. She was joined by *New York* on November 2, and once again Morgan and Haggerty had two first-class steamers in the Texas trade.[32]

New York and *Savannah*, placed with *New York*'s old agents Bogart &

30. *Bee*, November 13, 1837; *Daily Picayune*, November 4, 1838, December 17, 26, 29, 1839, March 27, 1840, February 12, 17, 1841; *Commercial Bulletin*, November 5, December 16, 1839; *American Coast Pilot* (14th ed.), pp. 268–269.

31. *Registers, NOLA*, III, 44.

32. *Commercial Bulletin*, October 16, November 5, 1840; Redfield to Warrington, January 25, 1842, *Journal of the Franklin Institute*, XII (July 1846), 7–8; Bishop, *loc. cit.*

Hawthorn, maintained weekly schedules to Galveston throughout the 1840–1841 season—*New York* was being recalled on June 25, 1841, *Savannah* on August 27. Competition had slackened since sale of *Columbia* to Cuban interests in November 1840 removed her from the Gulf, but James Reed again brought out *Neptune* to run in the trade (through June 1841). A newcomer to the Gulf was *Kingston* (which New Orleans interests entered on the Galveston run during the summer of 1841), but because of the slack season she garnered little patronage. The real rivalry remained *New York* and *Savannah* against *Neptune*.

Again by chance or arrangement, the arrival and clearance dates of the three vessels were staggered so that seldom were two loading in the same port at the same time. *Neptune*'s size and her willingness to cut rates gave her a slight edge in the freight business, but the Morgan-Haggerty steamers' frequency of service attracted more passengers. For many voyagers it mattered not which vessel they chose, for as George Wilkins Kendall portrayed his seasick fellow travelers on *New York* in May 1841, "some of them asserted, very positively, that if they could once set foot upon shore, they never would be seen out of sight of it, while others said they cared but little whether they ever saw land again."[33]

Viewing this successful 1840–1841 season, Morgan and Haggerty had good reason to anticipate the reopening of the trade in the fall. *New York* was back in the Gulf by November 4, and *Savannah* cleared for the South twenty days later. Then came a double blow. Two days following *Savannah*'s clearance from New York, a fire destroyed the engine shops which provided Morgan a steady income as one-third partner in T. F. Secor & Co. The $10,000 loss was covered by insurance, but the task of rebuilding the shops probably consumed much of Morgan's attention during the remainder of 1841.

More serious was the sinking of *Savannah* off Cape Hatteras on November 28. The loss of eight passengers and the vessel was a severe setback to Morgan and Haggerty's plans. They had gambled on *Savannah* and lost, for, to inspire public confidence, no insurance had been carried (a practice in which Morgan persisted). Obviously the loss of the vessel did not ruin either partner; Haggerty was one of the richest men in New York, and Morgan continued to derive income from the Secor engine shops and his West Indian sailing business. But loss of *Savannah* did

33. George W. Kendall, *Narrative of the Texas Santa Fé Expedition*, I, 19.

equalize the Gulf trade, eliminating the one-ship advantage Morgan and Haggerty had enjoyed. From November 1841 to November 1845 with one short exception, Morgan and Haggerty had but one steamship in the Gulf—the most pronounced lull that would occur in their activities. Throughout these doldrums, however, Morgan was slowly accumulating capital for the tremendous expansion of his operations after 1846.[34]

With *Savannah* sunk, *New York* and *Neptune* competed on even terms in the Gulf. During the three seasons following the disastrous 1841 autumn, the Morgan-Haggerty entry recorded forty-two voyages to Galveston and four to Mobile. *Neptune,* still sailing for Reed, compiled thirty-seven and two voyages respectively over the same period, sharing the passenger business equally with *New York.* Third parties attempted no concerted opposition to either steamship, although New Orleans-owned steamers picked up the trade during the slack summer months when the regular packets were withdrawn—*Kingston* in 1841, *Merchant* in 1842, and *Sarah Barnes* in 1843. But the pattern was broken in the summer of 1844.

On July 18, 1844, the first new Morgan steamship in almost three years arrived in New Orleans. Obviously intending to establish year-round service to the Republic of Texas, Morgan purchased *Republic* on June 8 and shortly thereafter cleared her for the Gulf. A small steamer (262 tons compared to *New York's* 365 or *Neptune's* 745 tons), *Republic* was a nautical and financial experiment. She was also the first steamship owned solely by Charles Morgan.

Unlike the Morgan-Haggerty vessels, which were side-wheelers fitted with auxiliary sails, *Republic* operated her canvas and steam machinery simultaneously. Her hull was trimly devoid of paddlewheels and fitted instead with screw propellers of the John Ericsson design. The Ericsson vessels, introduced into American in 1839, were much in vogue in the East by 1844, but Morgan was the first to test their application in the Gulf. John R. Crane, then master of Morgan's sailer *Emily,* influenced Morgan's choice. A veteran of the coasting trade and former captain of Morgan's *John W. Cater* in the West Indies, "Mad Jack" Crane had won greater fame as master of the tiny, thirty-five-ton *Robert F. Stockton* on

34. *Commercial Bulletin*, November 5, 19, December 13–14, 1841; New York *Daily Tribune*, May 5, November 25, 26, December 8, 1841; S. A. Howland, *Steamboat Disasters and Railroad Accidents in the United States,* pp. 275–278; Holdcamper (ed.), *op. cit.,* p. 221.

her inaugural voyage London to New York in April and May 1839. This was the first Atlantic crossing by a screw steamship (although only her sails were used) and the first arrival of an Ericsson ship in America.[35] In keeping with the experimental nature of the venture, Morgan placed *Republic* with the New Orleans agency of Williams, Whitman & Co. rather than with *New York*'s handlers Hawthorn & Woods.[36]

Republic completed four voyages to Galveston through November 7 when *New York* joined her, again placing two Morgan-owned and managed steamers in the Gulf. Apparently *Republic* proved unsatisfactory, however, for, after only three more voyages to Texas, her owner recalled her to New York in February 1845 and sold her. *New York*, again the sole Morgan-Haggerty steamship in the Texas trade, faithfully finished out the 1844–1845 season, completing fifteen trips to Galveston. *Neptune* was no longer a threat, having failed to return to the Gulf in the fall of 1844, but *John S. McKim*, which entered the trade in December 1844, provided stiff competition.[37] *McKim*, Texan-owned and exempt from certain dues now levied by that Republic on foreign steamships, could offer rates 10 per cent lower than could *New York*. Another competitor entering the trade in March 1845 was the New Orleans-owned steamer *Marmora*.

After *New York*'s annual withdrawal, *McKim* shared the route with the former New Orleans–Havana steam-packet *Alabama* and with a former New Orleans–Mobile–Charleston steamer, *Cincinnati*, throughout the summer of 1845. The sudden appearance of this variety of steamships on the Texas route, however, reflected more the increased governmental charter work involved in the movement of General Zachary Taylor's army to Texas than planned opposition to Morgan and Haggerty. Table 2.1 graphically shows the primacy of Morgan's vessels in the Texas trade throughout the period of the Republic.

35. *Herald*, May 29, 1839; William C. Church, *The Life of John Ericsson*, I, 101–175.

36. *Commercial Bulletin*, June 11, 1844; *Bee*, July 19, 1844; *Daily Picayune*, July 24, August 4, 29, September 5, 12, 1844; "Report and Manifest of Cargo laden on board the Steamer Republic," August 29, 1844, Bureau of Customs, *Passenger Lists, New Orleans*, XXIII, 60.

37. *McKim* is often called "the first commercial steamer in the United States to be driven by a propeller." Morgan's *Republic* has better claim to this unprovable title and was certainly the first Ericsson vessel in the Gulf. For *McKim*, see Heyl, *American Steamers*, I, 227–228 and Frank O. Braynard, *Famous American Ships*, pp. 56–58.

Indeed, Morgan was in the thick of things. *New York* had resumed her station in the Texas trade by October 1845, advertising cabin passage at $15, with only one night at sea. On November 26, the new 548-ton side-wheeler *Galveston* joined her, and the two vessels quickly re-established weekly service between New Orleans and Texas.[38]

Thus 1846 dawned a New Year in many ways for Charles Morgan. Entering his fifty-first year and already thrice a grandfather, he was still active in business and still gaining in experience and wealth.[39] In shipping, he was part owner of *New York* (the fourth steamship he so held) and sole owner of *Galveston* (the second so held). His commitment to steam became complete as he divested himself of the last of his sailing vessels in favor of further investment in T. F. Secor & Co. His interest prospered as the firm constructed marine engines for such vessels as *Savannah*, 305 tons (1838), *Troy*, 724 tons (1840), *Empire*, 936 tons (1843), *Thomas Powell*, 585 tons, *T. F. Secor*, 210 tons, *Isaac Newton*, 1,332 tons, *Perry*, 256 tons, *Atlantic*, 1,112 tons, and *John Stevens*, 686 tons (all 1846).[40] Gulf prospects were promising. The annexation of Texas eliminated many complicated and expensive tariff restrictions and duties of the former Republic and stimulated increased trade with the new state.[41] In addition, there was now the possibility of a U.S. Mail contract for Gulf service.

From the inception of the Republic, attempts to establish ocean mail service between New Orleans and Texas had been futile.[42] Early in 1846,

38. *Daily Picayune*, June 8, 1845; *Price Current*, November 26, 29, 1845; *Registers, NOLA*, IV, 106–107.

39. Morgan's eldest child Emily Ann, now Mrs. Israel C. Harris, gave birth to Emily Frances Harris, November 3, 1840, and Charles Morgan Harris, April 21, 1845. His second daughter, Frances Eliza, married George W. Quintard of New York City, February 15, 1844, and gave birth to the first of three children, Frances Louise Quintard, November 10, 1845. Morgan, *Genealogy*, pp. 154–155.

40. Bishop, *loc. cit.*; Heyl, *op. cit.*, II, 77–78, III, 21–22, 279–280, 327–328; Holdcamper (ed.), *op. cit.*, pp. 13, 57, 102, 150, 172, 183, 186, 189; *Journal of the Franklin Institute*, XLII (November 1846), 335.

41. Asa K. Christian, "The Tariff History of the Republic of Texas," *Southwestern Historical Quarterly*, XX (April 1917), 315–340; XXI (July 1917), 1–35. The changeover date from Texan to United States laws was December 31, 1845.

42. Gammel (ed.), *op. cit.*, I, 963–977, 1226–1238, II, 248–262, 756–757, 831–832, 863–864, 867–868, 1212; R. G. Dunlap to James Webb, May 29, 1839, Dunlap to Amos Kendall, May 20, 1839, Kendall to Dunlap, May 25, 1839, Dunlap to Kendall, May 27, 1839, Kendall to Dunlap, May 29, 1839, Garrison (ed.), *op. cit.*, I, 390–394; C. A. Wickliffe to James Reily, May 18, 1842, Reily to

however, the United States Post Office Department absorbed the Texas postal system. Morgan's *New York* and *Galveston* received contracts to transport the mails, New Orleans to Galveston and back, every five days from November 1 to July 1. For such service, Morgan was paid 75 per cent of postages at Galveston.

Unfortunately, the coming of the Mexican War hindered Morgan's fulfilment of the contract: *Galveston* was often diverted to carry troops and supplies to the Rio Grande, slowing delivery of civilian mails. Loss of *New York* in September 1846 was also a factor: aboard was Daniel J. Toler, formerly Postmaster General of Texas, returning from Washington with complete instructions for the operation of the new service. In the wreck these official papers were destroyed, while Toler barely escaped with his life. To augment the faltering Morgan service, the Postmaster General made special short-term contracts with other shippers, but in his words, "The facts of the case did not seem to warrant an annulment of so favorable a contract as the one with Mr. Morgan, who, it is expected, will, at no distant day, supply the place of *New York,* and cause the service to be again regularly performed."[43] The Postmaster General was acknowledging eight years of dependable service. The contract was not revoked and Morgan earned $8,033 in 1847, $5,000 in 1848, and $12,378 in 1849 for service under its provisions.[44]

The annexation of Texas marked the end of Charles Morgan's initial business ventures as a shipping specialist and steamship owner-operator. He had experimented with vessel types, schedules, and management arrangements. He had met and coped with competition. He had established a route, a routine, and a reputation for his steamships. He was well on his way to the successful application of his business specialization to the Gulf trades. The era of the war with Mexico brought him continuing and abundant advancement toward that goal.

Anson Jones, May 21, 1842, Jones to Reily, June 7, 1842, *ibid.,* 560–563; *Commercial Bulletin,* April 6, 1838; Galveston *Civilian and Galveston Gazette,* February 1, 1843; "Mails to Texas: Arrangement Respecting Postage," *House Exec. Docs.,* 27 Cong., 3 Sess., No. 146 (Serial 421).

43. "Report of the Postmaster General, 1846," *Senate Exec. Docs.,* 29 Cong., 2 Sess., No. 1 (Serial 493), 684, 703; *Price Current,* March 7, 1846; *Daily Picayune,* March 22, 27, 1846.

44. "Report of the Postmaster General, 1847," *Senate Exec. Docs.,* 30 Cong., 1 Sess., No. 1 (Serial 503), 1339; *ibid.,* 1848, *House Exec. Docs.,* 30 Congs., 2 Sess., No. 1 (Serial 537), 1268; *ibid.,* 1849, *House Exec. Docs.,* 31 Cong., 1 Sess., No. 1 (Serial 569), 843.

PART II

"Supr. men, as honest as the day. . . .
The Texas trade is monopolized by
them, out of wh. they are coining
money. . . . one of the most profitable
lines in the U.S. & prob. in the world."

Dun & Bradstreet credit reports
on Morgan Line, 1852–1857

3

THE ERA OF THE MEXICAN WAR, 1846–1849

THE initial lure of the New Orleans–Galveston trade had been the obvious need for fast and regular transportation and communication between the principal port-of-entry of Texas and the entrepôt of the Gulf. As Vanderbilt and Drew had linked New York and Albany; as the Portland, Providence, Stonington, and Fall River lines served the northern Atlantic Coast; so Morgan's steamships served the western Gulf. He had recognized the need, calculated its hazards, and succeeded in establishing and maintaining control of the situation. Indeed, this trade formed the major continuing justification for Morgan's Gulf enterprises and for their profitability—as New Orleans and Galveston were not linked by railroad or telegraph until 1880.[1]

But the Gulf economy involved more than Galveston and New Orleans—it bordered the endless southwestern frontier and the developing republics of Latin America. Other ports and other trades came to demand Morgan's attention and alter the geographic and competitive frameworks of his business decision-making. The process was not new, as growth and redeployment were basic to survival in nineteenth-century shipowning.

---

1. The essence of the situation was caught by a Galveston resident of the 1860s: "Without telegraphic connection, news reached the State only by the weekly steamer from New Orleans or Brashear; so that, though we stagnated in dull and apprehensive ignorance for six days at a stretch, we got our information by wholesale when it did come." John W. Ames, "Leaving Texas," *Overland Monthly,* XII (February 1874), 131.

But for Morgan, the problems seemed to expand and accelerate as the annexation of Texas spread its political and economic ripples across the Gulf.

The cessation of diplomatic relations with Mexico on March 31, 1845, began three years of war for the United States. The Texas question, smoldering for a decade, burst into open flame once more, to blaze on until the final settlement of Guadalupe Hidalgo became effective in May 1848.

Immediately obvious was the strategic importance of the wilderness between the Nueces River and the Rio Grande in southern Texas. This disputed, but almost deserted, frontier must be securely in American hands before any effective military defense of the new state could be sustained. If an offensive against the Mexican homeland were contemplated, a base of operations in lower Texas would be a necessity. With these considerations certainly in mind, troops under General Zachary Taylor had encamped on the Nueces by July 1845.

Equally obvious in the maturing crisis was the importance of New Orleans, the leading Gulf port, as a marshaling center and embarkation point for troops and supplies destined for Texas or Mexico. Possessors of sea transportation facilities between the Crescent City and Texas inevitably stood to gain—none more than Charles Morgan.

Unlike such New York business contemporaries as George Griswold, Stephen Whitney, Moses Taylor, Philip Hone, or William H. Aspinwall, Morgan had not participated in public demonstrations of antiexpansionism or moral indignation concerning Texas and Mexico.[2] In part, his inaction reflects a lifelong aversion to politics, but the fact that he had a personal stake in the success of "manifest destiny" in the western Gulf of Mexico is unmistakable. Having achieved almost a decade of successful steam-service to Texas, with the new U.S. Mail contract guaranteeing a base income on the route for the next four years, Morgan was already ahead of the field. Without endowing him with any prescience, one must conclude that the Mexican War provided the New Yorker a great financial opportunity of which he took considerable advantage.

Morgan's opportunistic approach to the situation in the Gulf is appar-

2. Philip S. Foner, *Business & Slavery*, pp. 16–19; Winston, "New York and the Independence of Texas," *Southwestern Historical Quarterly*, XVIII (April 1915), 368–385.

ent in his willingness to ignore agreements with one government agency to negotiate with another. *New York* and *Galveston,* although contractually committed to the New Orleans–Galveston U.S. Mail route, were quickly made available for military service. *New York* was chartered for $2,196 on April 29, 1846, to transport troops to the newly established U.S. Army depot at Brazos St. Iago, Texas. In May 1846 *Galveston* was retained for $7,000 to transport additional men and stores over the same route. Between April 29 and September 16, 1846, the two steamships, through various military charters, grossed almost $80,000 for their owner.[3] This intense military activity naturally interfered with regular schedules, and civilian service suffered. But despite public protestations against Morgan's sporadic service between New Orleans and Galveston, the New Yorker suffered no deductions in pay from his mail contract.[4]

A serious loss to Morgan's operations, however, was the sinking of *New York* between Galveston and New Orleans, September 7, 1846. Eighteen lives were lost in the tragedy.[5] As a consequence, from then until March 1847 *Galveston'*s participation in military work diminished. Presumably, fear of losing the more permanent mail contract and business concerned with the New Orleans–Galveston trade prompted Morgan to withhold her from further army charters, unless in conjunction with the regular route.[6]

Yet the lure of government gold was irresistible, and 1847 became a key year in the expansion of the Morgan fleet. Five new ships flying the red-white-and-blue Morgan pennant were placed in Gulf service. The steady accumulation of profits from his steamships and engine works and the sudden rush of new capital from government work prompted the New Yorker's decision: To maintain regular civilian service *and* reap the windfall created by the war, more ships were needed—and more came.

3. For sixteen charters, Morgan earned $78,480. A seventeenth has been estimated at $1,500. "Contracts, War Department, 1846," *House Exec. Docs.,* 29 Cong., 2 Sess., No. 46 (Serial 499), 31, 32–33, 35–36, 38–39, 41–42; *ibid.,* "1847," *House Exec. Docs.,* 30 Cong., 1 Sess., No. 29 (Serial 516), 3, 6.

4. "Report of the Postmaster General, 1846" (Serial 493), 684. J. W. McMillen to Williams, June 8, 1848, and August 15, 1848, Samuel May Williams Papers, indicate the effects of the war on mail service.

5. [M. Bonzano] Diary, 1845–1846 (Archives, Howard-Tilton Library, Tulane University), entries for September 5–9, 1846; New Orleans *Price Current,* September 12, 1846.

6. *Price Current,* September 12, 1846–April 1, 1847; "Contracts, War Department, 1847" (Serial 516), 70–71.

Charles Morgan took delivery on the magnificent new steamship *New Orleans* in January 1847. Built by William H. Brown, with powerful 700-horsepower engines by Morgan's partners, T. F. Secor & Co., the $120,000 vessel cleared New York for Charleston, Havana, and New Orleans on January 12. The 225-foot, 869-ton steamer could accommodate 150 first-class passengers and was fitted with 32-foot paddle wheels, well calculated to "keep her off a lee shore in the hardest gales." Although intended to run as a regular mail packet between New Orleans and Galveston, she was instead immediately chartered to the army. *New Orleans* collected $33,000 transporting troops and stores in the Gulf for the next three months. Morgan, however, soon converted the vessel into ready cash to aid in further expansion of his line. On May 7, 1847, he sold the new steamship to the U.S. Government for $125,000. In only five months of service under the Morgan flag, *New Orleans* thus earned for her owner considerably more than her construction price.[7]

A more permanent addition to Morgan's fleet was *Palmetto* (533 tons). Built in 1846 for Atlantic coastal service, this steamship entered the Gulf later that year under the able command of her owner, Captain Jeremiah Smith of New Orleans. Smith sold all but a fractional interest in the vessel to Charles Morgan in March 1847 and became a trusted investor-employee of the Morgan lines. *Palmetto* was immediately chartered for three months of government service, grossing $27,000 for her new owner. Upon termination of this contract and after a return to New York for refitting, she resumed a Galveston run, alternating with *Galveston,* until rechartered by the army in June 1848 for sixty days at a rate of $9,000 per month.[8]

Yacht became the third new ship of the line. Built in 1844 and purchased by Morgan and Jeremiah Smith in April 1847, she reached the Gulf on April 27. A small steamer (249 tons) only 140 feet in length and drawing but 8 feet, 4 inches, she easily navigated the shallow bays of

7. New York *Tribune*, January 11–13, 1847; New Orleans *Daily Picayune*, January 31, February 2, May 8, 1847; "Contracts, War Department, 1847" (Serial 516), 54; *ibid.*, 1848, *House Exec. Docs.*, 30 Cong., 2 Sess., No. 44 (Serial 541), 36; Enrollment No. 5, N.Y., January 11, 1847 (RG 41, NA).

8. *Price Current*, October 24, November 25, December 5, 16, 1846, January 2, 16, February 3, 20, March 10, 20, May 29, June 26, July 17, 31, November 6, 1847; *Daily Picayune*, March 4, 7, 1847; "Contracts, War Department, 1847" (Serial 516), 60; *ibid.*, 1848 (Serial 541), 72; *Registers, NOLA*, IV, 220.

Texas. In an obvious attempt to maintain regular Galveston service, *Yacht* joined *Galveston* on the run in May 1847 and in July 1847 held her only diversionary charter throughout the war.[9]

Morgan acquired at this time another small steamer, *Portland* (445 tons). This 163-foot side-wheeler was built in 1835 and intended for the service maintained between Portland, Maine, and Boston by the Cumberland Steam Navigation Company. She later served as connecting steamer for railroads at Portland and Bangor. Morgan purchased her in late 1847 from the New York steamboat operator Isaac Newton. She was moved to the Gulf in November and chartered to the army. *Portland* cleared New Orleans with troops and supplies for Tampico and Vera Cruz, arriving December 15 after weathering severe storms en route—a hundred horses belonging to the First U.S. Dragoons had been jettisoned to prevent swamping. Upon termination of this contract, *Portland* was placed in civilian service on the Galveston route until rechartered to the government at $8,000 per month in June 1848.[10]

Globe (481 tons), a 200-foot steamer built in 1842 for service on the Connecticut River, was the final 1847 addition to Morgan's fleet. Arriving in New Orleans in December, she was placed in the regular Galveston service and held no government charters during the war.[11]

Thus by rapid expansion of his line in 1847, Morgan was able to maintain regular passenger, freight, and mail service on the contract route to Galveston and yet participate in the bonanza created by the Mexican War. Only six nongovernment voyages to and from Galveston were made by Morgan ships from June through December 1846. The forty-one such voyages in 1847 indicate the influence of the new ships in maintaining regular service in addition to military charters. Government contractors preferred steamships for their speed and maneuverability.

9. *Tribune*, April 14, 1847; *Price Current*, April 28, May 1, June 21, August 7, September 11, October 30, December 11, 1847; *Daily Picayune*, April 28, 1847; "Contracts, War Department, 1848" (Serial 541), 38; *Registers, NOLA*, IV, 302; Enrollment No. 30, N.Y., April 7, 1847 (RG 41, NA).

10. *Tribune*, November 11, 1847; *Daily Picayune*, November 14, 25, 26, 1847; *Price Current*, November 27, December 4, 1847, January 5, February 9, 1848; "Contracts, War Department, 1849," *House Exec. Docs.*, 31 Cong., 1 Sess., No. 38 (Serial 576), 26; *Registers, NOLA*, IV, 234; Heyl, *American Steamers*, I, 335.

11. *Daily Picayune*, November 14, December 19, 30, 1847; *Price Current*, December 22, 1847, January 4, 1848; *Registers, NOLA*, IV, 116.

Too often becalmed sailing transports delayed the arrival of essential troops. Steamers too large to enter the shallow bays of Texas and Mexico (thus necessitating dangerous transfers to lighters) were equally unpopular; but the shallow-water navigational abilities of Morgan's steamships suited them to the needs of the military.[12]

The end of hostilities was not the end of Morgan's windfall. His ships were among those chartered to bring troops home. In all, from August 1845 to June 1848, Morgan held thirty-four government charters which yielded him more than $400,000. In W. W. Rostow's term, the profits of the Mexican War initiated the "take-off" period in the fortunes of Charles Morgan.[13]

But the return of peace to the Gulf also brought problems to the New Yorker. The Galveston route, although profitable, could not hope to support the five ships Morgan now had in the Gulf. With government activity curtailed, he naturally sought some other profitable disposition for his vessels. The next five years became years of expansion, both for Morgan and the areas he served.

Morgan's service to the Texas Republic had concentrated on the ports of Galveston, Velasco, and, briefly, Matagorda. Troop movements during the Mexican War, however, had demanded voyages to other settlements on the Texas coast. After the war, using the idle steamers at his disposal, Morgan continued service to some of these budding ports, augmenting the well-established Galveston line. In the years before 1850, Brazos St. Iago, Port Lavaca, and Indianola became permanent ports-of-call for the Morgan lines (see Map 3.1).

Brazos St. Iago was created by the Mexican War. A small settlement had existed near the tip of Padre Island, ten miles north of the mouth of the Rio Grande, for some years before the war. A pilot station was maintained on the bar guarding the approach to Matamoras, and small sailing vessels plied to and from that Mexican town. This trickle of commerce surged to a remarkable crest in the war years. From 1845 to 1848 several thousand government-contract military supplies destined for

12. Luther Giddings, *Sketches of the Campaign in Northern Mexico*, pp. 25–26; Emma J. Blackwood (editor), *To Mexico with Scott: Letters of Captain E. Kirby Smith to His Wife*, pp. 16–17.

13. "Contracts, War Department, 1845," *House Exec. Docs.*, 29 Cong., 1 Sess., No. 51 (Serial 482); *ibid.*, 1846 (Serial 499); *ibid.*, 1847 (Serial 516); *ibid.*, 1848 (Serial 541); *ibid.*, 1849 (Serial 576); *Price Current*, June 17, 24, July 8, 15, 1848; Heyl, *op. cit.*, I, 335.

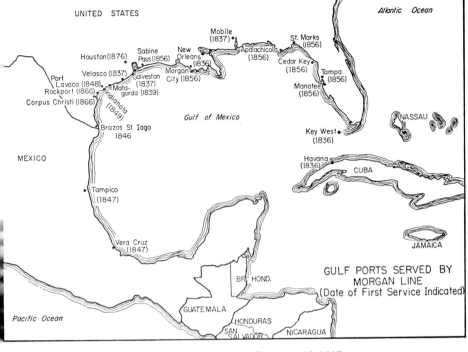

Map 3.1. Gulf of Mexico Ports, 1835–1885.

the armies in Mexico poured through the hamlet. A new port was born.[14]

Despite its strategic location, Brazos St. Iago left much to be desired. One Indiana soldier in his "whole recollection of Brazos St. Iago" remembered not "one single pleasant incident." Lt. George B. McClellan, fresh from the parade ground of West Point, felt sure that "Brazos is probably the very worst port that could be found on the whole American coast. . . . nothing more than a sand bar, perfectly barren, utterly destitute of any sign of vegetation." The passage of the shallow bar was unusually dangerous in any sea, and often steamers ran aground, to remain for hours awaiting a higher tide. To young John W. Audubon,

14. William Kennedy, *Texas: The Rise, Progress, and Prospects of the Republic of Texas*, I, 54; *American Coast Pilot* (14th ed.), 267, 269; Blackwood (ed.), *op. cit.*, pp. 20, 62, 100–103; "Contracts, War Department," 1845–1848, *loc. cit.* The town was originally named Brazos de St. Iago, which was shortened to Brazos St. Iago and ultimately corrupted to Brazos Santiago.

there was "not a landmark more than ten feet high," only "miles and miles of breakers, combing and dashing on the glaring beach" lettered with "dark weather-stained wrecks." [15]

Accepting the uncertainties of the route, Morgan initiated civilian service to Brazos St. Iago. *Globe* began the 550-mile run from New Orleans in February 1849, leaving each port fortnightly. At Brazos St. Iago she made connections with small steamboats for Brownsville, Matamoras, and the interior Rio Grande. *Portland* and *Yacht* extended service from Galveston to the Rio Grande area in June, and the three ships had made twelve New Orleans–Brazos St. Iago circuits by September 30.

The usual route was direct from New Orleans, but occasionally a trip was made via Galveston or perhaps the Matagorda Bay area, depending upon cargo consignees.[16] While flour and foodstuffs contributed the regular imports to Brazos St. Iago, that port had a particularly attractive export—specie. During 1849 and 1850, Morgan vessels transported over $1,650,000 in specie to New Orleans from this southernmost Texas port of entry. Wool and hides made up the remainder of Brazos St. Iago's exports.[17] Morgan's service to the port was standardized on a weekly basis by July 1, 1850, with the negotiation of a four-year, $15,000-per-year, U.S. Mail contract.[18]

Besides this increased service to the tip of Texas, Morgan resumed and expanded his operations to ports near the center of the curving shore of the western Gulf. Settlement in this Lavaca–Matagorda bay area dated from La Salle's attempts to found a French colony in Texas. Years later, about 1830, a settlement known as Linnville was in existence near what is

15. Graham A. Barringer (editor), "The Mexican War Journal of Henry S. Lane," *Indiana Magazine of History*, LIII (December 1957), 388; William S. Myers, *The Mexican War Diary of George B. McClellan*, pp. 8–9; Frank H. Hodder (editor), *Audubon's Western Journal, 1849–1850*, pp. 50–51.

16. *Price Current*, February 7, June 30, July 14, 21, 28, 1849; *Daily Picayune*, March 21, 1849; "Commerce of the Port of Brazos de St. Iago," *Senate Exec. Docs.*, 31 Cong., 1 Sess., No. 69 (Serial 562), 3–8.

17. Cargo manifests as published in *Price Current*, 1849–1850. The specie was for specific consignees in New Orleans: bankers, merchants, and corporations, and was *not* for the New Orleans Branch Mint, as is so often stated. This specie, presumably Mexican silver, was a vital source of solid capital for New Orleans businessmen, and it conveniently entered the United States at Brazos St. Iago after the latter was made a port of entry in 1849. U. S. Senate *Journal*, 30 Cong., 2 Sess. (Serial 528), 194, 312, 315, 323–324.

18. "Report of the Postmaster General, 1850," *Senate Exec. Docs.*, 31 Cong., 2 Sess., No. 1 (Serial 587), 439.

now Port Lavaca. Morgan had indirectly served Linnville through connections with a small steamer at Matagorda in early 1841. When the settlement was destroyed by Indians in the middle 1840s, the new town of Lavaca was founded nearby, and by 1846 Port Lavaca was the bustling county seat of newly formed Calhoun County.[19]

Morgan steamers began serving Port Lavaca in 1848 as an extension of the Galveston route and later to break the voyage to Brazos St. Iago. *Yacht* met the larger vessels at Galveston and continued on to the Lavaca and Matagorda bays. "At least once a week," wrote a Texan in 1848, "the two large steamboats *Palmetto* (J. Smith, captain) and *Galveston* (J. E. Haviland, captain) leave from Galveston for New Orleans, carrying United States mail, passengers and freight. Making connection with these steamers, a small steam yacht [*sic*] runs from Galveston to Paso de Caballo, Indian Point, and Port La Vaca twice a week. The . . . *Galveston* and the *Yacht* have combined, and, by registering passage for the entire trip, cabin fare on both vessels from New Orleans to Port La Vaca costs only twenty-five dollars [only $10 more than by sail]." At Port Lavaca connections could be made by wagon or biweekly stagecoach to Victoria, San Antonio, and points west.[20]

The "Indian Point" mentioned by Bracht was founded as a landing place for immigrants of the Society for the Protection of German Immigrants in Texas. This group, directed by Prince Karl Solms-Braunfels, selected the site on Matagorda Bay opposite Paso de Caballo to serve as a suitable harbor to disembark for the interior. A settlement known as Karlshafen was founded about 1844 and formed the nucleus for towns successively named Indian Point and Indianola.[21]

Indian Point nestled on a mile-wide peninsula thrusting three miles into Matagorda Bay. Protected from the Gulf by the larger Matagorda Peninsula, the settlement was separated from the mainland by Powder Horn Lake. Morgan began service to the area in 1848 when the Galveston

19. *Indianola Scrap Book: Fiftieth Anniversary of the Storm of August 20, 1886*, pp. 159–162; *Price Current*, February 17, 1841; John J. Linn, *Reminiscences of Fifty Years in Texas*, pp. 338–344.

20. Charles F. Schmidt (editor and translator), *Texas in 1848 by Viktor Bracht*, p. 83. See also *Daily Picayune*, December 28, 1847, January 13, May 30, 1848, March 27, 1849.

21. Rudolph L. Biesele, *The History of the German Settlements in Texas, 1837–1861*, pp. 83, 108–110; Alice F. Fluth, "Indianola, Early Gateway to Texas," pp. 31–34.

route was extended to Port Lavaca. Initially, passengers and cargo were lightered ashore at Indian Point, but before the year's end, Morgan had constructed a small pier into the bay. Over this landing and one built by the local merchants Runge and Poole, the commerce of the port was carried—commerce consisting of cotton and cattle exported to New Orleans in return for flour, whiskey, and provisions, the staples of the Texas trade. Because of its excellent overland connections with the West, Indian Point rapidly became the loading port for ranchers, farmers, and military units located in interior Texas. Again Morgan was there to serve and benefit.[22]

When Port Lavaca's city commission increased their channel and dockage fees in 1849, Morgan shifted the bulk of his business to Powder Horn, a new settlement near Indian Point (now "Old Town"), which offered deeper water and better wharf locations. Morgan shortly furnished Powder Horn, soon popularly known as Indianola, with weekly service from New Orleans via Galveston under terms of a four-year $12,000-per-year U.S. Mail contract.[23]

Thus by July 1, 1850, Morgan had standardized his service to Texas. The two mail subsidies he received ($12,000 per year for weekly service from New Orleans to Galveston and Indianola; $15,000 per year for similar service to Brazos St. Iago) over the next four years put him far ahead of any competitors. Although he was fined frequently for delays and failure of the mails, he maintained sufficiently regular service to renew the four-year contracts in 1854. The fact that a New Orleans–Galveston segment was common to both mail routes, allowing Morgan to collect two subsidies for one voyage, was either unknown or ignored by the Postmaster General.[24] In any case, the added security to Morgan's profit picture given by these subsidies became an important element of his success.

22. *Daily Picayune*, May 30, 1848, March 27, 1849; *Price Current*, February 2, March 15, September 10, 1850; *Indianola Scrap Book*, pp. 23–24, 28, 95, 101, 172; Charles S. Potts, *Railroad Transportation in Texas*, pp. 17–19.
23. "Report of the Postmaster General, 1850" (Serial 587), 439.
24. "Fines and Deductions, Mail Contractors, 1851," *House Exec. Docs.*, 32 Cong., 1 Sess., No. 56 (Serial 643), 900–901, 912–913, 979, 986, 1008; *ibid.*, 1853, *House Exec. Docs.*, 33 Cong., 1 Sess., No. 22 (Serial 717), 8–9, 52–53, 142–143; *ibid.*, 1854, *House Exec. Docs.*, 33 Cong., 2 Sess., No. 92 (Serial 790), 4, 13, 22, 36, 63, 76. For Morgan's pursuit of the mail contracts see Cornelius B. Payne (for Harris & Morgan) to Williams, September 3, 1848, Samuel May Williams Papers.

Morgan's expansion of service and profits during the Mexican War was accompanied by another key development in his business evolution—the selection of new Gulf agents for his steamships late in 1847. Since his entry into the Texas trade in 1837 and because of his own preference for residence in New York, Morgan had relied upon established New Orleans and Galveston commission merchants to represent his vessels. It was also customary for a vessel's master to act as her agent on occasional voyages to allow him a share of the profits. In view of the control difficulties these arrangements bore, however, it is not surprising that in the general reorganization of his enterprises after the Mexican War, Morgan secured more reliable New Orleans representatives.

In resolving his problems of agency, Morgan reverted to the ancient ways of family partnership. In December 1847, shortly after a personal inspection of Gulf ports by Charles Morgan himself, the firm of "Harris & Morgan" opened its doors at 79 Tchoupitoulas Street, New Orleans, and assumed control of Morgan's Gulf fleet. The firm, which became synonymous with Gulf steamships, was a partnership composed of Morgan's eldest son-in-law Israel C. Harris and his twenty-year-old second son Henry R. Morgan.

In Harris, who had married his eldest daughter Emily Ann, Morgan found perhaps his most trusted lieutenant. The consumptive death of their beloved daughter and wife at thirty-seven in 1856, only seemed to bind them closer. It was Harris who carried the routine burden of the Morgan lines for some twenty years.[25]

Young Henry was another matter, indeed. His stay in New Orleans was shorter than Harris's, but he was the perfect complement to his partner. He married a New Orleans belle, Miss Laura Malard, on June 1, 1854, and became in every way a social and business asset to the firm. Returning to New York in the late 1850s, Henry engaged in shipping and mining ventures of his own—being badly taken in mines—and died a premature death at forty-seven in 1874. His partnership in Harris & Morgan was his initial assignment in his father's employ, but he acquitted himself admirably.[26]

25. *Daily Picayune*, August 5, 1856, February 7, 1866; New Orleans *Daily Crescent*, April 1, December 27, 1867.

26. *Daily Picayune*, August 15–16, 1874; New Orleans *Republican*, August 16, 1874; Morgan, *Genealogy*, 211; *Morgan v. Skiddy, et al.*, 62 New-York Reports 319 (1875).

It is of some interest that it was Morgan's second, not his elder, son who entered the family firm. The elder boy, Charles W., had preferred the grocery trade in New York, opening a business in 1849. Married to a New York girl and independent of his father, Charles W., too, died an early death—at thirty-eight, in 1863. He seems never to have participated in his father's enterprises but undoubtedly drew prestige to his own through his father's name and reputation in New York. As will be seen, it was Morgan's sons-in-law and not his sons who were most often associated with his maritime activities.[27]

Between 1848 and 1856, the partnership of Harris & Morgan owned shares in all Morgan vessels in the Gulf, saw to their commercial management, and engaged in the commission business on their own. The division of ownership in the vessels of the line illustrates the chain of command and the allocation of profits. In each vessel, the firm of Harris & Morgan owned two eighths. Eighths in selected vessels were allocated among senior captains of the line—partially for seniority; partially for their services as marine superintendents in New York and New Orleans. On only two occasions were outside investors admitted; Morgan himself always held the remaining four to five eighths. Under this arrangement, Charles Morgan never lacked interested representation in Gulf ports.[28]

With the reorganized and expanded Gulf fleet in the trusted care of his son-in-law and son and with no competitors on that business horizon, Charles Morgan turned his personal attention to other areas of the maritime sector of the American economy—particularly the Atlantic and Caribbean coasts. Here a series of events, triggered by threats of British domination of the oceanic steam-lanes but intensified by the discovery of gold in California, presented Morgan another opportunity for expansion and profit.

By the end of the Mexican War, the United States found herself far behind Great Britain in the expansion of deep-sea steam navigation. A greater industrial capacity, the needs of European commerce and of a far-flung empire, and willing governmental assistance had combined to

27. Morgan, *Genealogy*, 211; *Doggett's New-York City Directory* (1850), p. 359; *Rode's New York City Directory* (1850), p. 367.
28. For the relationship among owners, masters, and agents, see *The Merchant's and Shipmaster's Guide* (3rd ed.), pp. 64–148 and Albion, "Early Nineteenth-Century Shipowning," pp. 1–11. For Harris & Morgan, see: *Price Current*, December 25, 1847; *Cohen's New Orleans Directory* (1849), pp. 75, 119; *Registers, NOLA*, IV, 106–107, 116, 141, 167, 220, 234, 302; V, 43–44, 48–49, 178–179, 199–200, 207, 252–253; D. & B., La., vol. 9, p. 164; vol. 10, p. 544.

push English steamers ahead. Four great subsidized lines were in operation by 1845: the Peninsular and Oriental Steam Navigation Company, serving the Mediterranean and the Orient; the Royal Mail Steam Packet Company to the West Indies and Latin America; the Pacific Steam Navigation Company, serving the western coast of South America; and, most galling to Americans, the Cunard Line, which dominated trans-Atlantic service.

To many Americans these British lines increasingly posed challenges of naval preparedness, commerce, and prestige. A reaction was inevitable; it began in 1845. In March, Congress authorized the Postmaster General to contract for carriage of foreign mails; similar powers were granted the Secretary of the Navy in 1847; and by 1850 subsidized American steamship lines were in operation in many areas of world commerce, notably to Le Havre, Liverpool, and Bremen. The California gold discoveries in late 1848 gave greater stimulus to this expansion of American service. These events of the late 1840s were welcome news to the shipbuilders and engine-makers of New York—of whom T. F. Secor & Co. and Charles Morgan were no exceptions.

With this increased demand for steamships during and after the Mexican War, the Secor shops had prospered. Their plant was enlarged in 1846 to cover a block and a half along the East River between 8th and 10th streets and employed some 700 men at full strength. Between 1847 and 1849 (inclusive) marine engines were completed for such ocean and coastal steamers as *Antelope* (424 tons), *Crescent City* (1,291 tons), *Empire City* (1,751 tons), *Georgia* (2,727 tons), *Goliah* (333 tons), *New Orleans* (869 tons), *New World* (1,312 tons), *Ocean* (658 tons), *Ohio* (2,432 tons), *Ontario* (832 tons), *Queen City* (906 tons), and *United States* (1,857 tons).[29]

Morgan, as a passive but equal partner, shared the profits of these ventures, but he was simultaneously laying plans to secure complete control of the Secor shops. His associate in these endeavors was another son-in-law, George W. Quintard.

Quintard's youth had resembled Morgan's own. Born in Stamford,

29. Bishop, *History of Manufactures* (3rd ed.), III, 130–131; Augustus C. Rogers (editor), *Sketches of Representative Men, North and South*, pp. 445–447; Heyl, *op. cit.*, I, 27–28, 117–118, 141–142, 177–178, 315–316, 321–322, 431–432; III, 265–66; John H. Kemble, *The Panama Route, 1848–1869*, pp. 214, 223, 224–227, 229, 236, 239–240, 250–251; Holdcamper (ed.), *Merchant Steam*, pp. 10, 42, 57, 75, 77, 137, 138, 143, 144, 145, 158, 193.

Connecticut, on April 22, 1822, he had moved to New York at fifteen to enter the grocery trade. At twenty-one, he married Morgan's second daughter, Frances Eliza, and the same year opened his own grocery and ship chandlery. Quintard entered the firm of T. F. Secor & Co. in 1847, and, with Morgan's prestige complementing his own ability, rose quickly in the financial department of the shops. By February 1850, Morgan and Quintard had purchased the entire factory and changed its name to Morgan Iron Works.[30] Thus in another segment of the maritime industries of the United States did Charles Morgan expand in the late 1840s. He secured a thriving enterprise riding a rising market. And again, he ensured trusted, family representation, as he gave Quintard the reorganized iron works to manage.

Quintard served as chief operating executive of the works from 1850 to 1867, while Morgan's roles in the enterprise were as sole owner and supplier of capital, credit, and prestige—he made up any deficiencies in operating funds, supplemented reinvested earnings, absorbed large capital expenditures, endorsed the notes and paper of the firm, posted contract bonds, and generally sustained the works "in any case of emergency."

The only exception to this pattern of ownership and control lasted from May 1, 1857, to May 1, 1861, while a second Morgan son-in-law, Charles A. Whitney, joined the firm as part owner and co-manager. To sustain this partnership, Morgan conveyed the works to Quintard (2/3) and Whitney (1/3) in April 1857 for $250,000. To secure working capital they mortgaged the property for $67,500 and successfully operated the firm on their own account until Whitney's withdrawal to assume the New York agency of the British steamship *Great Eastern*. The Whitney-Quintard partnership was dissolved, the mortgage paid off by Morgan, and the property resold to him for $250,000. The works remained under his ownership and Quintard's management until 1867.[31]

With Harris and Morgan managing his Gulf steamers and Quintard

30. Frederick Q. Boyer and Herbert A. Poole (compilers), "The Quintard Family in America," *New England Historical and Genealogical Register*, CIX (October 1955), 260; Henry Hall (editor), *America's Successful Men of Affairs: An Encyclopedia of Contemporaneous Biography*, I, 529–532; *Doggett's New York City Directory* (1847), pp. 293, 334, 365; *ibid.* (1848), pp. 293, 334, 364; *ibid.* (1850), advertisement between pp. 358–359, 359, 411.
31. D. & B., N.Y., vol. 316, pp. 48, 83, 16, 1W.

taking over the new Morgan Iron Works in New York, Charles Morgan reconsidered a lifelong ambition. It is obvious that a New York–New Orleans line of steamships was always in the New Yorker's thoughts. Passengers had been carried with some success on the annual northward voyages of his Texas line ships. The trip was made in nine days in 1839, eight in 1840, and seven in 1841. Family staterooms were available, but no freight was carried. The usual fares had been $60 for saloon or staterooms, $50 for lower cabin berths; a few deck passengers were also accommodated. No stops were necessary, as the ships carried twelve days' fuel, but passengers were landed at Key West and Charleston when required.[32]

The idea of New York–New Orleans steam service had languished through the early 1840s with the continued excellence of sailing-packet schedules and preoccupation with the Mexican War. After 1845, however, with the government's increasing willingness to contract for mail service, a new boom in coastwise steam navigation began. In 1848, subsidized lines were opened from New York to Charleston and Savannah, and another contract was let for a New York–New Orleans route. Charles Morgan joined this rush in 1848.

Crescent City, a sidewheeler of 1,291 tons with engines by T. F. Secor & Co., was launched in December 1847. Her construction had been financed by Isaac Newton of New York, who (with her sister ship *Empire City* still on the ways) intended to open the People's Line of Steamships between New York and New Orleans. Sometime in 1848, however, part-ownership and control of both vessels passed into the hands of Charles Morgan. Presumably heartened by the experience of others on the New Orleans run, Morgan implemented service to the Crescent City via Charleston and Havana throughout the latter months of 1848, but his lack of a mail subsidy and the lure of the newly opened Central American transit seem to have prompted removal of *Crescent City* to a New York–Chagres, Panama, run in December 1848.[33]

The year 1849 thus found Charles Morgan at another milestone in his business career. Now fifty-three, he had seen his two elder daughters

32. *Daily Picayune*, May 1, June 16, November 3, 1840, June 18, 25, August 28, November 6, 1841, January 22, July 6, 1842, July 8, 1845.
33. *Price Current*, December 25, 1847, June 10, 17, August 12, 19, September 12, 30, November 29, December 2, 1848; *Tribune*, December 25, 1848; *American Railroad Journal*, XXII (February 3, 1849), 66–68; Heyl, *op. cit.*, I, 117.

marry well and had provided for their spouses—Israel Harris in New Orleans, George Quintard in New York. His sons Charles W. and Henry had been established in business under the watchful eyes of their father. Only sixteen-year-old Maria Louise remained at home with her parents.[34]

One might expect such a man to be complacent, merely enjoying advancing age. Not so Morgan. His engine business was flourishing and his seven steamships were serving New York, Havana, Chagres, New Orleans, Galveston, Port Lavaca, Indianola, and Brazos St. Iago.[35] The era of the Mexican War had brought him new capital, new ships, and new ports-of-call, as well as new managers. These and the national awakening to developments in California broadened his economic and geographic horizons. The stage was set for further expansion which would propel Morgan to the foremost of entrepreneurial circles.

34. Morgan, *Genealogy*, pp. 154–155, 211.
35. *Jerry Smith* (159 tons) joined *Galveston, Palmetto, Yacht, Portland, Globe,* and *Crescent City* in 1849. *Price Current,* April 25, 1849; *Registers, NOLA,* IV, 141.

4

THE CALIFORNIA ROUTE:
ECONOMIC WAR IN
CENTRAL AMERICA
1849–1860

On January 24, 1848, gold was discovered on the American River in California. Reports of the strike had reached San Francisco by February; by June, Salt Lake City; by August, New York. Official notice was received in Washington on September 16 and confirmed by President Polk in his annual message to Congress on December 5. The gold rush was on!

As in the Mexican War, owners of transportation facilities again foresaw prosperous advantage. And once more shipowners led the field, for news of the discoveries reached the eastern seaboard in late 1848, just before overland routes west were closed by winter storms. Until spring's thaw, a sea voyage remained the quickest alternative for the anxious prospector.

Yet the natural passage from New York to San Francisco stretched 14,194 nautical miles around Cape Horn; from New Orleans, the distance—14,314 nautical miles—was even greater. The alternate route—4,992 nautical miles, New York to San Francisco—involved an overland segment crossing the Isthmus of Panama. The longer routes, though fiercely demanding, were more reliable, since the whole voyage could be made in one ship; Panama was quicker if proper connections could be made (see Map 4.1)

Gold seekers in their clamor for passage ignored the hazards and cost

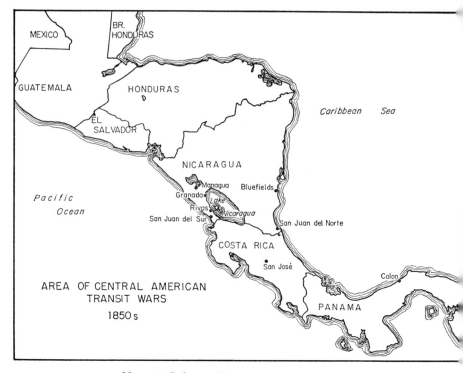

MEXICO

BR.
HONDURAS

GUATEMALA

HONDURAS

EL
SALVADOR

Caribbean   Sea

NICARAGUA

Managua   Bluefields
Granada Lake
Rivas Nicaragua
San Juan del Sur

San Juan del Norte

Pacific

Ocean

COSTA RICA

San José

Colon

AREA OF CENTRAL AMERICAN
TRANSIT WARS
1850 s

PANAMA

Map 4.1. Isthmian Transit Routes in the 1850s.

of the voyages, however. Ninety vessels cleared Atlantic ports for California during the first month of 1849, and seventy more advertised departures. Ships of all types were pressed into service yet could not meet the demand. The Cape Horn passage would spawn the majestic freight and passenger clippers and their less glamorous but more numerous sailing sisters. On the Central American route it was the ocean steamship that came into her own; in both instances, ships were built to answer the needs of transit to California.[1]

The sea routes to the West differed in another detail. The Cape Horn

1. Ralph P. Bieber, "California Gold Mania," *Mississippi Valley Historical Review*, XXXV (June 1948), 3–28; Raymond A. Rydell, "The Cape Horn Route to California, 1849," *Pacific Historical Review*, XVII (May 1948), 149–163; John H. Kemble, "The Gold Rush by Panama, 1848–1851," *ibid.*, XVIII (February 1949), 45–56.

passage was made almost entirely in international waters with few questions of right-of-way. Not so the Central American route. A portion of this journey passed over foreign soil; problems of territorial sovereignty fostered intrigue, corruption, and bloodshed as titans of transportation waged ruthless economic war for the prized concession of isthmian transit. Charles Morgan was in the thick of the fight.[2]

The idea was not new, as trans-isthmian schemes have agitated Central America since antiquity, but the 1840s saw the realization of several projects to link the Atlantic and Pacific oceans at the waist of the Western Hemisphere. In 1840 the British-owned and subsidized Pacific Steam Navigation Company opened service to the Pacific side of the Panamanian isthmus, and in 1846 the Royal Mail Steam Packet Company extended its London–West Indies route to include Chagres on Panama's northern shore. Steamers of the two British companies were linked by canoe and mule across the isthmus and by 1848 offered a through passage, London to Valparaiso.

Stirred by these British activities (although they were directed more toward Pacific South America than northward), by the advantageous settlement of the Oregon boundary question in 1846, and by the communications needs of her post–Mexican War westward expansion, the United States, too, turned her attention to the Central American transit.

Three congressional acts of March 3, 1845, and March 3, 1847, authorized the Postmaster General and the Secretary of the Navy to contract separately for American ocean mail routes, and by early 1849 one crossing was in operation via Panama: under a Navy Department contract assigned September 3, 1848, the United States Mail Steamship Company on December 1, 1848, dispatched *Falcon* from New York to New Orleans and Chagres. The Pacific Mail Steamship Company, chartered by New York on April 12, 1848, and holder of a Navy contract assigned on November 19, 1847, provided a Pacific connection with *California, Oregon,* and *Panama,* all on a Panama–San Francisco run by June 1, 1849.

2. The purpose of this chapter is to document more fully Charles Morgan's relationship to the Central American transit wars of the 1850s. It is intended to supplement, not supplant, the large body of analysis already extant on the general Central American situation. Several sources not appearing in that literature are utilized, however. The best of the general histories are the works of Kemble, Scroggs, Wiltsee, Lane, Hutchins, Lewis, and Carr, as cited in the bibliography.

Conceived in 1847, these companies had been an uncertain gamble until the California gold discoveries dealt them a royal flush.[3]

This existing Panama transit was instantly jammed with passengers to California. A lack of ships on the Atlantic side, high prices, and uncertain promises concerning the regularity of the isthmian crossing could not stifle the flow. Competition for the subsidized Panama route was inevitable and immediate. In both of the major opposition lines Charles Morgan played a prominent role.

Crescent City, owned in large part by Morgan, but under the agency of J. Howard & Son of New York, opened direct service New York–Chagres on December 23, 1848, and reached Panama within a week after the U.S. Mail Steamship Company's *Falcon*. Although possessing no guarantee at the time, Morgan and Howard assured travelers that a Pacific connection with their vessel would always be available. This quick and bold decision identified Charles Morgan with the first Atlantic competition offered to the established isthmian mail companies.[4]

Success on the Panama run with *Crescent City* over the next six months prompted Morgan to abandon the New York–New Orleans service begun by the vessel under Isaac Newton's direction. He also purchased from Newton *Crescent City*'s sister ship, then still on the ways, and spent over $300,000 on her price and outfitting. *Empire City* (1,751 tons) was completed at the yard of William H. Brown in July 1849 and entered the Panama trade. Beautifully appointed in zebra, rose, and satin woods, with inlaid panelings, rosewood chairs, and luxurious sofas and divans, the splendid vessel featured carvings and paintings in each stateroom and a specially constructed iron safe to carry gold from California. Owned by Morgan and represented by Howard & Son, the sister ships formed the Empire City Line, New York to Chagres.[5]

---

3. "Information in Relation to Contracts for the Transportation of the Mails by Steamship between New York and California," *Senate Exec. Docs.*, 32 Cong., 1 Sess., No. 50 (Serial 619); "Mail Steamers," *House Exec. Docs.*, 32 Cong., 1 Sess., No. 91 (Serial 644); Kemble, *Panama Route*, pp. 3–38.

4. Morgan bought into Isaac Newton's *Crescent City* in late 1848 or early 1849. J. Howard & Son, her agents since launching, retained their husbandry and some undetermined interest in her ownership. New York *Tribune*, December 14, 25, 1848, January 11, 1849; *American Railroad Journal*, XXII (February 3, 1849), 66–68; Heyl, *American Steamers*, I, 117.

5. *Tribune*, October 20, 1848, March 10, 12, June 20, 28, July 11–12, 16, 1849.

Morgan and John T. Howard also negotiated to offer through service to San Francisco, to compete more evenly with the mail companies. *Sarah Sands,* an iron screw-steamship of British construction was chartered by Howard and cleared New York for the Pacific on December 13, 1849. *New Orleans* (formerly Morgan's vessel) and *Northerner* (1,193 tons) were purchased and both dispatched to join *Sarah Sands* on the Panama–San Francisco run. Contracts were made with Perrine, Patterson & Stack of Williamsburg, New York, and the Morgan Iron Works for construction of *San Francisco* (1,875 tons) and *Brother Jonathan* (1,359 tons) to join the Empire City Line. Thus by September 24, 1850, the Morgan-Howard line had two vessels under construction, two operating on the Atlantic, and three on the Pacific—the latter five connecting at Panama.[6]

Seeking additional revenue for their line and a counterbalance to the subsidies of their competitors, Morgan and Howard attempted to gain a New York–Chagres mail contract in November 1849. Under the act of March 3, 1845, empowering the Postmaster General to contract for foreign mail service, a bid of $110,000 for semimonthly service was submitted. But the offer was refused (although half the sum the Navy was paying to the U.S. Mail company) stating the Postmaster General could no longer contract for such foreign mails. Thus the Empire City Line's try for government subsidization failed.[7]

Yet throughout the remainder of 1849 and for most of 1850, Morgan and Howard's Empire City Line fought the mail lines for the Panama business. The Empire City Line continued its reliance on *Crescent City* and *Empire City* on the Atlantic and *Sarah Sands, New Orleans,* and *Northerner* on the Pacific. On both routes, Morgan and Howard opposed companies now squabbling between themselves. Each of the mail lines interpreted their contract to extend only to mail carriage, and entered non–mail-carrying vessels on the other's route. By October 1850 George Law's U.S. Mail Steamship Company was operating *Falcon, Ohio* (2,432 tons), and *Georgia* (2,727 tons) on the Atlantic and *Isthmus* (339 tons),

6. *Ibid.,* November 8, 30, 1849, January 4, May 3, June 15, October 2, 1850; New York *Herald,* November 7, December 13–14, 1849; John T. Howard to Joseph S. Williams, November 11, 1856, *House Exec. Docs.,* 35 Cong., 2 Sess., No. 30 (Serial 1004), 108–109.

7. Kemble, *Panama Route,* p. 48. Private mails were carried, however, by the line to Kingston, Jamaica, and Central America. John Bigelow, *Jamaica in 1850,* p. 183.

Columbus (460 tons), *Republic* (852 tons), and *Antelope* (424 tons) on the Pacific. Howland & Aspinwall's Pacific Mail Steamship Company had added *Unicorn* (650 tons), *Tennessee* (1,275 tons), *Carolina* (544 tons), and *Columbia* (777 tons), to *California, Oregon,* and *Panama* and had entered *Cherokee* (1,244 tons) on the Atlantic, to be joined in November 1850 by *Philadelphia* (897 tons).[8]

Morgan and Howard were the first to abandon this intense rivalry. In October 1850 the Pacific Mail company assumed the charter of *Sarah Sands* and purchased *Northerner* on the Pacific and *Crescent City* and *Empire City* on the Atlantic. Howard & Son continued as agents for the latter two vessels (now representing Pacific Mail) while retaining part-ownership and agency of *New Orleans* (and several subsequent steamers) on the Pacific. The two vessels under construction for Howard and Morgan (*San Francisco* and *Brother Jonathan*) were sold to Richardson, Watson & Co. and to Edward Mills respectively for service on other sea lanes. From scanty evidence, it appears that while the Howards continued the Empire City Line under that name until 1852, Charles Morgan disassociated himself from its operations late in 1850.[9]

Thus by 1851 Morgan had removed himself from the Panama route. On January 21 the U.S. and Pacific Mail companies formed an agreement to pool mail, freight, and passenger service via Panama—effective April 1.[10] But there was no lull in opposition to this monopoly, and Morgan was intimately involved—now, with two new names on the already complicated isthmian scene: Cornelius Vanderbilt and Nicaragua.

While the earliest interest of Americans in Central America was directed toward Panama, the Nicaragua crossing 500 miles northward soon came under equal scrutiny. Wider than Panama (175 miles to 55), Nicaragua was broken by the 120-mile Rio San Juan and lakes Nicaragua and Managua. If these waterways could be navigated, only a short overland journey remained to the Pacific. A Nicaragua route would shorten the distance from New York to San Francisco by more than 500 miles.

With these considerations in view, international venture capital, seeking transit concessions, moved into Nicaragua soon after the California gold discoveries. An agent of the British Pacific Steam Navigation Com-

8. Kemble, *Panama Route,* pp. 38–57.
9. *Tribune,* October 2, 30, 1850, January 1, 1851; Howard to Williams, November 11, 1856 (Serial 1004), 108–109; Kemble, *Panama Route,* pp. 48–49, 51.
10. *Tribune,* March 12, 1851; Kemble, *Panama Route,* pp. 51–52.

pany had signed a preliminary agreement for transit privilege with the Nicaraguan *encargado de negocios* in London by February 16, 1849, but ratification by the Nicaraguan government had not materialized.[11]

Two American companies were also on the scene. David T. Brown, representing Willard Parker, Simeon H. Ackerman, Asher Kursheadt, and J. Howard & Son of New York, negotiated a transit concession from Nicaragua on March 14, but his principals did not ratify its provisions. They acted in cognizance of the displeasure of the State Department which opposed their contract as illegally pledging the faith of the United States to a treaty proposed to accompany the concession.[12] It remained for another wily New Yorker, Cornelius Vanderbilt, to pluck the rich fruit of a Nicaraguan concession.

Fresh from his steamboating triumphs in the East and attracted by the success of the Panama companies, Vanderbilt had investigated possibilities for a ship canal or transit across Nicaragua early in 1849. He chose as his negotiators the prominent and well-connected attorneys, Joseph L. White in Washington and David L. White in Central America. With the encouragement of President Zachary Taylor, Secretary of State John M. Clayton, and the aid of the newly appointed U.S. chargé d'affaires in Nicaragua, E. George Squier, a liberal charter of privileges was secured from the Nicaraguan government.[13]

Under articles signed at Leon on August 27, 1849, the "American Atlantic and Pacific Ship-Canal Company" (composed of Vanderbilt, Joseph L. White, Nathaniel J. Wolfe, "and their Associates," but not incorporated) bound itself to construct an interoceanic canal via Nicaragua within twelve years of ratification by both parties.

For her concessions of exclusive right-of-way, construction materials, convict labor, customs exemption, and eight sections of land for coloniza-

11. *Artículos entre* Francisco Castellon *y* William Wheelwright, February 16, 1849, *Artículo Adicional*, June 12, 1849, *House Exec. Docs.*, 31 Cong., 1 Sess., No. 75 (Serial 579), 247–249; E. George Squier to John M. Clayton, October 10, 1849, *ibid.*, p. 207.

12. Agreement between Nicaragua and Nicaragua Steam Company of New York, March 14, 1849, *ibid.*, pp. 141–145; Elijah Hise to James Buchanan, February 8, Squier to Clayton, April 16, June 10, August 20, 1849, *ibid.*, pp. 137, 153.

13. Clayton to Squier, May 1, 1849, Squier to Clayton, June 6, June 23, August 20, September 10, 1849, *ibid.*, pp. 118–130, 133–138, 147–149, 151–158, 168–173.

tion, Nicaragua was to receive $10,000 upon her ratification of the contract, $200,000 in canal stock when issued (with a sixty-day option on $500,000 more), $10,000 per year during the canal's construction period, 20 per cent of the canal's annual net profit for the first twenty years of its operation, and 25 per cent of the same thereafter.

After eighty-five years of operation by the company, Nicaragua would assume the assets and property of the canal and pay its former operators a percentage of its profits for ten or twenty years thereafter (depending upon the gross worth of the company at the time of surrender of its holdings).

During construction of the canal, the company would be permitted to operate a temporary transit via river, road, lake, or railroad upon payment of 10 per cent of such a route's annual net profit. Further, an escape clause allowed the substitution of "a rail road or rail and carriage road, and water communication between the two oceans," should a canal prove unfeasible. Thus Vanderbilt ensured an alternative concession on the same terms but independent of the construction of a canal.[14]

With the personal endorsement of Chargé Squier (who wrote at least four of its articles), the contract was ratified by Nicaragua on September 22, 1849. To protect the American company's interests, Squier signed commercial treaties and protocols with Nicaragua on September 3 and with Honduras on September 28—the latter agreement temporarily ceding Tigre Island (which guarded the likely Pacific terminus for a canal) to the United States.[15]

International repercussions followed the signing of these agreements. Great Britain, established on the Caribbean shore of Nicaragua through support of the Indian kingdom of the Mosquito Coast and in possession (since January 1, 1848) of the natural eastern outlet for a canal (Grey-

14. The original contract was ratified by Nicaragua on September 22, 1849, and by the "Company" on September 26. Several amendments were made on April 11, 1850, ratified on April 12, 1850, and are included in the present analysis. *Charter and Act of Incorporation of the American Atlantic and Pacific Ship Canal Company and Treaty of Protection Negotiated between the United States and Great Britain*, pp. 3–22.

15. Squier to Clayton, September 10, October 10, 1849, in William R. Manning (editor), *Diplomatic Correspondence of the United States: Inter-American Affairs, 1831–1860*, III, 360–374, 393–408; New York *Tribune*, November 17, 1849.

town or San Juan del Norte at the mouth of the Rio San Juan), was in a position to harass any transit project of which she disapproved.

England's zealous commercial agent in Central America, Frederick Chatfield, responded to Squier's Nicaraguan treaty by signing one with Costa Rica (supporting her long-asserted claim to the northern bank of the Rio San Juan), and to the Squier-Honduran agreements by seizing Tigre Island on October 16, 1849. Jealous of her commercial domination of Central America and traditionally opposed to United States Pacific expansion, Britain was thus a factor to be satisfied in American plans for interoceanic communication via Nicaragua.[16]

The diplomatic solution for these differences was the Clayton-Bulwer Treaty signed April 19, 1850. The Squier and Chatfield treaties were scrapped and replaced by an Anglo-American pledge of neutrality for any Central American canal.[17]

The prospect of British investment in a transit scheme attracted the Vanderbilt group to the Clayton-Bulwer solution, and many persons (including Squier) considered them obnoxious in their support of the diplomats.[18] But Vanderbilt ignored his detractors. His strategy appears twofold: to seek financial assistance from his American "associates" in establishing the temporary transit allowed by his contract and to attract American and foreign investors for his canal scheme.

To attract investors, he planned to begin canal surveys and establish his good faith, meanwhile maintaining pressure on the State Department for amicable settlement of diplomatic affairs on the isthmus—with the encouragement of British investment in the canal a desired byproduct of negotiation. In seeking American aid, Vanderbilt found willing assistance from many, but none was more aggressive than Charles Morgan.

Morgan's interest in the isthmus drew him naturally to Vanderbilt. On

16. See the works by Naylor, Van Alstyne, Williams, Stansifer, and Rodriguez, as cited in the bibliography.

17. The essential documents are in: "Tigre Island and Central America," *House Exec. Docs.*, 31 Cong., 1 Sess., No. 75 (Serial 579) and "Clayton-Bulwer Treaty and the Monroe Doctrine," *Senate Exec. Docs.*, 47 Cong., 1 Sess., No. 194 (Serial 1991). The negotiations are described and analyzed in the works by Williams, Travis, Perkins, and Russel, as cited in the bibliography.

18. Squier to Clayton, May 8, 1850, in Mary W. Williams (editor), "Letters of Ephraim George Squier to John M. Clayton, 1849–1850," *Hispanic American Historical Review*, I (November 1918), 429–431.

December 14, 1849, the two boarded Morgan's *Crescent City* for Central America and a firsthand inspection of the transit. Morgan was still deeply involved with the Empire City Line and Vanderbilt had only recently received his Nicaraguan concession, but their mutual aspirations are unmistakable and must have been discussed on the voyage. Unfortunately, *Crescent City* developed engine trouble three days out of New York and had to trans-ship her passengers to sailing vessels and put into Charleston for repair.

Although the Vanderbilt-Morgan trip thus came to naught, the incident provides a unique glimpse of how two of the foremost financiers of their day coped with adversity. After a day's attempt at sailing the disabled *Crescent City*, the schooner *Sarah A. Smith* of Belfast, Maine, and the brig *Roscoe* of Boston were hailed. Morgan and Captain Stoddard boarded the schooner but encountered some "down East" stubbornness, for Stoddard reports that, after discussion, "Mr. Morgan bought the cargo, which consisted mostly of lumber, and chartered her to go to Chagres with as many passengers as she could." Not to be outdone, "Mr. C. Vanderbilt went on board [*Roscoe*] and made arrangements for himself, Mr. Morgan," and eight others to sail to Havana.

Two such men of action quickly recovered: Vanderbilt returned to New York on *Ohio*, arriving January 9, 1850, while Morgan went on to New Orleans for a short visit, returning to New York in the repaired *Crescent City* on February 18.[19]

The *Crescent City* fiasco actually strengthened the Vanderbilt-Morgan liaison. As Vanderbilt set his plans for the canal survey and the temporary transit, Morgan was prominently mentioned as one of the "right kind of men" associated with the enterprise, and he may have been one of the eight original "associates" in the canal partnership.[20]

To implement the agreement of August 27, 1849, the tax-free, infinitely capitalized American Atlantic and Pacific Ship-Canal Company was incorporated by Nicaragua on March 9, 1850. Stock was issued, and orders were placed with Jeremiah Simonsen of New York for two shallow-draught steamers to operate on Nicaragua's lakes and river and for an

19. *Tribune*, December 14, 17, 1849, January 5, 9, February 18, 1850.
20. *Herald*, April 25, 1850; *Tribune*, April 27, 1850. New York *Tribune*, March 26, 1852, states there were eight original partners in the American Atlantic and Pacific Ship-Canal Co., but only three are identified in its contract: Vanderbilt, Joseph L. White, and Wolfe.

ocean steamship, later christened *Prometheus,* to run from New York to Nicaragua.

Pending completion of *Prometheus* and her anticipated sisters, arrangements were made for Morgan and Howard's Empire City Line to call at Nicaragua's Caribbean and Pacific ports while making their Panama runs. Surveying crews under Col. Orville W. Childs were dispatched to Nicaragua in July, and a careful search for an immediate transit route and the canal's ultimate location began.[21]

Vanderbilt and his associates were less successful, however, in attracting foreign investment or government aid. A personal mission by the Commodore and Joseph L. White garnered only a promise of English financial aid—pending completion of the Childs survey.[22] A $180,000 bid for twice-monthly mail service via the Nicaragua route, New York to San Francisco, was turned down by the United States Navy Department, although far below the $389,000 then paid the Panama companies.[23]

Disappointed, Vanderbilt temporarily set aside the canal project and concentrated on the water-land transit across Nicaragua. The route would run from San Juan del Norte up the Rio San Juan by shallow-draught steamers to San Carlos. There, on the shores of Lake Nicaragua, larger steamers would continue to Virgin Bay on the lake's western shore. Thence, a road would be cut to San Juan del Sur, twelve miles west on the Pacific.

By July 1851, the entire route of Vanderbilt's New and Independent Line for California via Nicaragua was in operation: from New York to San Juan del Norte, ran Vanderbilt's *Prometheus* (1,207 tons), *Northern Light* (1,767 tons), and the vessels of the Empire City Line; from New Orleans ran Charles Morgan's new steamship *Mexico* (1,043 tons); in Nicaragua, *John M. Clayton* and *Sir Henry Bulwer* navigated the Rio San Juan connecting with *Director* on the lake; from Virgin Bay to the Pacific, travel was by muleback and thence via Vanderbilt's *Pacific* (1,003 tons), *Independence* (1,376 tons), or *North American* (1,440

---

21. *Charter and Act of Incorporation . . . (1850)*, pp. 22–24; *Tribune*, April 15, 25, 27, May 25, June 15, July 12, 1850.

22. London *Times*, February 13, 1849, October 14, 15, 17, 19, 1850; *Herald*, October 14, November 15, 1850; *Tribune*, October 29, 1850.

23. "Information in Relation to Contracts for the Transportation of the Mails by Steamships between New York and California" (Serial 619), 162–164, 206. Vanderbilt tried again early in 1852, bidding $250,000 per year for semimonthly service, but was refused. *Tribune*, January 28, 1852.

tons) to San Francisco—the whole journey supposedly to consume twenty-five days, New York to California.[24]

To operate the "temporary" water-land route a new tax-free corporation was formed "distinct and separate" from the canal company (but "comprised of the same members" as the latter). The canal and transit enterprises were separated on August 14, 1851, and the newer company, styled the Accessory Transit Company of Nicaragua, assumed the transisthmian privileges and liabilities of its parent. The original eight partners of the canal company received 38,400 $100 shares in the new company and, to many observers, the canal seemed more distant than ever—nothing more than "making some twenty Indians work a few months at twenty-five cents a day; indeed . . . the most clever speculation which ever came into a Yankee's head."[25]

Others were more optimistic, and canal-company shares, which had entered the market at $800, were being traded as high as $3,600.[26] Colonel Child's report, dated March 9, 1852, upheld the feasibility of a Nicaraguan canal but at questionable cost—$31,538,319.55.[27] A new commission was dispatched to seek British aid but again returned with only promises—to take one half of a $30,000,000 joint Anglo-American canal company if Americans would subscribe the other half first! The

24. *North American* was purchased in June and entered the Pacific line on October 10, 1851. Vanderbilt (by D. B. Allen) to William A. Graham, August 13, 1851 (Serial 619), 162–163; *Tribune*, July 12, August 3, October 1, November 23, 1850, January 1, February 10, 25, May 10, 21, 27, June 18, 1851; *Herald*, July 9, December 26, 27, 1850, July 3, 4, August 13, 1851.

25. *Charter and Act of Incorporation of the American Atlantic & Pacific Ship Canal Company, As Amended; Also, Treaty of Protection Negotiated between the United States and Great Britain; and Charter Granted by the State of Nicaragua to the Accessory Transit Company*, pp. 25–28; Julius Froebel to Editor, August 13, 1851, *Tribune*, September 5, 1851. For stock split, see *Tribune*, September 24, 26, October 7, December 2, 1851, March 26, 1852.

26. *Tribune*, March 30, April 1, 3, 10, 14, 1852.

27. Orville W. Childs and John D. Fay, *Report of the Survey and Estimate of the Cost of Constructing the Inter-Oceanic Ship Canal from the Harbor of San Juan del Norte on the Atlantic to the Harbor of Brito on the Pacific in the State of Nicaragua, Central America; Made for the American Atlantic and Pacific Ship Canal Co. in the Years 1850–51*. To appraise the risk more accurately, Childs also computed the canal's cost if built in New York State—$13,243,099.47. Childs, *Engineer's Report of the Cost of Constructing the Ship Canal of Nicaragua As Estimated at New York Prices*.

canal project was dead; its shares had plummeted to $750 by August and soon disappeared from the exchange.[28]

Unlike its faltering parent, the Accessory Transit Company became "the most buoyant fancy" on the market, fluctuating erratically under heavy trading and the uncertainties caused by such events as the sinking of *North American* on February 27, 1852.[29]

By July, however, *Brother Jonathan* (1,359 tons) and *S. S. Lewis* (1,103 tons) had been added by purchase to the Pacific line, and *Daniel Webster* (1,035 tons) and *Star of the West* (1,172 tons) had joined the Atlantic fleet. A $132,000 contract for planking the transit's twelve-mile overland segment had been let, and seven steamers were in operation on Nicaraguan waters by the end of the year. On June 1, the company's "aggregate earnings" since charter had been reported at $400,000, and a dividend of $2.00 per share was declared on the entire $3,840,000 capital stock.[30]

But *"sick Transit,"* as the company was known to Wall Street wags, had problems. British officials at Greytown harassed vessels of Vanderbilt's Atlantic line, creating an unsolved diplomatic tangle which culminated in a British warship's shelling *Prometheus* late in 1851. A British apology settled the matter, but the transit company moved its piers and shops at considerable expense across the river to Punta Arenas, in an attempt to avoid further conflict.[31]

Vanderbilt's interest in the company was also waning. Loss of his newest steamship *Pioneer* (1,833 tons) on her maiden voyage to San

28. Abbott Lawrence to Daniel Webster, February 17, 1852, Webster to Lawrence, May 14, 1852, Lawrence to Webster, June 8, 1852, Lawrence to Lord Malmesbury, June 16, 1852, Malmesbury to Lawrence, June 30, 1852, Lawrence to Malmesbury, July 2, 1852, Lawrence to Webster, August 13, 1852, in Manning (ed.), *op. cit.*, VII, 76–77, 453–454, 462–465, 467, 481–482; *Tribune*, April 3, June 1, August 13, August 20, 23, 1852.

29. Accessory Transit Co. opened on the New York Stock Exchange on January 2, 1852, at 24. From that date, through December 31, 1852, over 100,000 shares were traded at prices between 19 and 50. *Tribune*, 1852.

30. *Tribune*, October 23, December 15, 1851; March 26, April 16, June 2, 7, 1852.

31. "Information in Relation to the Firing into and Seizure of the American Steamship *Prometheus* by a British Vessel of War," *Senate Exec. Docs.*, 32 Cong., 1 Sess., No. 6 (Serial 614); "British Correspondence in Relation to the Attack on the American Steamer *Prometheus* by the British Brig-of-War *Express*," *ibid.*, No. 30 (Serial 618).

Francisco was a severe setback. Again denied a mail contract in early 1852 and unsympathetic to the stock speculations of his fellow directors, he resigned his presidency on September 13. On December 24, he proposed to sell his connecting steamers to the company and become only a company bondholder and its general agent. The company accepted, purchasing *Prometheus, Daniel Webster, Northern Light, Star of the West, Pacific, Brother Jonathan,* and *S. S. Lewis.*

Vanderbilt's terms were high: $1,200,000 cash; $150,000 in 20 per cent bonds of the company due January 1, 1854; the general agency of the line, at 2½ per cent commission; 20 per cent of passage moneys on the isthmian crossing; and payment out of the first earnings of the steamships for coal and coal-hulks surrendered to the company ($180,337.67). The cash payment was met by an issue of 40,000 new shares of transit-company stock sold privately to insiders at $30 per share—a neat paper profit, as the market price for previously issued stock was then $39.25.[32]

It was the issuance of the 40,000 additional shares and Vanderbilt's abdication of his presidency that catapulted Charles Morgan to the fore of the transit company. Still the intimate of Vanderbilt, Morgan had been a prime investor in transit stock since its appearance on the market; he now joined the Commodore on the company's directory on February 14, 1853—during a successful purge of Joseph L. White's now anti-Vanderbilt faction.

But Morgan's allegiance to the Commodore was short lived. On June 7, 1853 (just after Vanderbilt and his family departed for a European holiday on their new steam yacht *North Star*), Morgan was elected to replace Vanderbilt as general agent of the transit company without the Commodore's prior consent. Vanderbilt's name was stricken from the company's advertisements, and company offices were moved to Morgan's

---

32. Vanderbilt to Editor, September 14, 1852, September 25, 1852, *Tribune*, September 16, 27, 1852; Vanderbilt to A.T.C., December 24, 1852, *ibid.*, January 7, 1853; Resolution of Directors of A.T.C., December 27, 1852, *ibid.*; James De P. Ogden to Stockholders of A.T.C., January 3, 1853, *ibid.* See also: *Tribune*, September 2–9, 14, 25, December 28, 30. Vanderbilt had also been plagued by litigation regarding alleged poor service on the transit during 1852, and this probably reinforced his decision to relinquish its operation. *Briggs v. Vanderbilt*, 19 Barbour (N.Y.) 222 (1855); *Bonsteel v. Vanderbilt*, 21 Barbour 26 (1855); *Quimby v. Vanderbilt*, 3 Smith (N.Y.) 306 (1858); *Williams v. Vanderbilt*, 1 Tiffany (N.Y.) 217 (1863).

address at 5 Bowling Green. Morgan, attuned to the politics of the transit company, had abandoned the absent Commodore and cast his lot with the White faction. His reward came quickly. On July 18, 1853, White and his sycophants recaptured the directory, and Charles Morgan was elected to the still-vacant presidency of the Accessory Transit Company.[33]

Morgan's most fruitful liaison, however, was with the recently appointed San Francisco agent of the transit company. Like Morgan, Cornelius K. Garrison was a self-made man. Born in upstate New York in 1809, he had begun as cabin boy of a Hudson River sloop, taken three years of engineering and architectural study in New York City, and worked for the Upper Canada Company—all before 1833. By 1840 he and two brothers had moved to St. Louis and formed Garrison & Brothers Company—a machine shop and foundry supplying public-works projects and riverboats. "C. K." participated in the firm, but was better known as a steamboat captain and "the best euchre player on the river, and for much besides which that term implies."[34]

When gold was discovered in California, Garrison migrated to Panama and with an old river-days crony—Ralph Stover Fretz of Fretz & Brother, New Orleans—established a forwarding and commission business on the isthmus. The partners engaged in a variety of activities from travel agency, through shipowning and agency, to mercantile banking. In 1851, the firm expanded to include William Chapman Ralston—formerly a clerk on the Mississippi to both Garrison and Fretz; now a steamship captain on the San Francisco–Nicaragua run; ultimately to become the president of the famed but ill-fated Bank of California.

Garrison's Panama business was as famous for its principal's three-card–monte tables and dueling as for its profits. Yet it was this very combination of gambler and businessman that attracted Cornelius Vanderbilt to Garrison, and at the former's insistence "C. K." moved to San Francisco in early 1853—as agent of the Accessory Transit Company at a salary of $60,000 per year and with letters of credit to transport $1,000,000 per month in gold to eastern firms.

33. *Tribune*, February 15, 17, May 19, 30, June 9, July 22, 1853.
34. *Tribune*, May 2, 1885; Cecil G. Tilton, *William Chapman Ralston: Courageous Builder*, pp. 25–41; Henry Clews, *Twenty-eight Years in Wall Street*, pp. 346–348; H. W. Howard Knott, "Cornelius Kingsland Garrison," *D.A.B.*, VII, 167–168.

Garrison was a tremendously aggressive man, elected mayor of San Francisco six months after his arrival. He well deserved an admirer's dubious compliment that it took "twenty men to watch him." Under Morgan and Garrison the transit company entered the most colorful period of its existence.[35]

The new agents of the Nicaraguan line pressed their competition with the Panama steamers. They purchased *Cortes* (1,117 tons) for $225,000 and chartered *Sierra Nevada* (1,246 tons) from her owner (C. K. Garrison!) for the Pacific run—replacing *North American, Independence,* and *S. S. Lewis,* which had sunk during 1852 and 1853. The contest drove first-cabin rates from $300 to $100; second-cabin to $75; steerage from $150 to $50. The rivalry was heated but profitable, and the Nicaraguan company reported "net earnings" of $535,410.48 for the second half of 1853.[36] Its end-of-year financial statement seemed to indicate further profits ahead (see Table 4.1).

Insiders knew otherwise. The statement of December 31, 1853, left unrecorded two of the company's major liabilities: its 78,400 shares of capital stock—sodden with water—and its unsquared accounts with Cornelius Vanderbilt. During Vanderbilt's absence Morgan and Garrison refused to honor drafts on the former agent which the company had agreed to assume in the settlement of January 1853. Furthermore, they withheld payments against Vanderbilt's claim on 20 per cent of gross receipts from the transit crossing, alleging there had been no profits on that segment of the route and that even if there had, Vanderbilt's indebtedness to the company had to be settled first. The *Herald* had predicted "trouble . . . upon the return of Commodore Vanderbilt," and trouble came.[37] On his return to New York in September 1853, Vanderbilt reputedly informed Morgan and Garrison:

35. Isaac J. Wistar, *Autobiography,* pp. 161–162, 300–301; Frank Soule, John H. Gihon, and James Nisbet, *The Annals of San Francisco,* pp. 744–747; O. T. Shuck, *Representative and Leading Men of the Pacific Coast,* pp. 143–164; Wiltsee, *Gold Rush,* pp. 112–118.

36. "To the Stockholders of the Accessory Transit Company of Nicaragua, Statement of the Affairs of the Company . . . 31st December, 1853," *Tribune,* January 6, 1854. The same statement is reprinted in Wiltsee, *Gold Rush,* pp. 340–346.

37. Vanderbilt to Editor, September 26, 1853, *Herald,* September 28, 1853; Ogden to Public, September 28, 1853, *Tribune,* September 30, 1853; *Herald,* June 10, July 29, 1853.

Gentlemen:
You have undertaken to cheat me. I won't
sue you for the law is too slow. I'll ruin you.
Yours truly,
C. Vanderbilt[38]

The Commodore fought hard. On September 20, 1853, he announced formation of an "Independent Opposition Line," composed of Edward Mills's *Uncle Sam* and *Yankee Blade* on the Pacific and Vanderbilt's former yacht *North Star* on the Atlantic. A three-way rate war followed among the Vanderbilt-Mills, Morgan-Garrison, and U.S.–Pacific Mail lines and by June, first-cabin and steerage accommodations had fallen to $100 and $35. The inevitable settlement was announced September 1, 1854: Morgan and Garrison, for the transit company, purchased *Uncle Sam* and *Yankee Blade* for $500,000; the mail lines gave $300,000 for *North Star* and agreed to pay Vanderbilt $40,000 per month "blackmail" for his promise never again to compete against them in the California passenger trade.[39]

With Vanderbilt removed, rates increased again. Morgan and Garrison negotiated with Pacific Mail for alternate weekly sailings, but the arrangement ended in January 1855. A similar agreement of March 1855 (which included equal division of gross receipts during the first quarter of the twelve-month period of concert as a bonus to the smaller Nicaraguan line), was broken after three months. Competition stiffened with completion of the Panama Railroad in January 1855, which gave the mail lines a swifter isthmian connection. The result was a new agreement in September 1855 between Morgan and Garrison and the mail companies. Rates were set at $225, $200, and $100 for first-cabin, second-cabin, and steerage, with a $25 surcharge on eastward crossings. The line carrying more passengers than the other would reimburse the lesser company at rates of $75, $50, and $25, respectively, per excess passenger— retroactive to July 1, 1854. The total due the Accessory Transit Company

38. No contemporaneous report of this letter found. Appeared in Vanderbilt's obituary, New York *Times*, January 5, 1877.
39. *Herald*, January 6, 11, 20, February 2, 20, 28, May 18, June 6, September 1, 1854; Kemble, *Panama Route*, pp. 70–72; Wiltsee, *op. cit.*, pp. 127–142.

by October 6 came to $114,263.32, of which $101,949.62 had been paid.[40]

Morgan and Garrison matched this settlement with the mail companies by making one with Vanderbilt. Besides operating his opposition line, the Commodore had continually harassed them throughout late 1853 and 1854: he threw blocks of transit stock on the market forcing Morgan to purchase it to retain control of the company; he attempted to attach the company's steamers; he sued for claims under his former agency. Coupled with the loss of *Yankee Blade* in November 1854 and continued uncertainties with the British at Greytown, these events pushed transit shares as low as 15. Yet Morgan and Garrison weathered the storm, declaring a dividend of $3 per share in July and, in December 1854, settling Vanderbilt's "claims of every sort" for $115,000—$60,000 cash, the remainder on account.[41]

With these negotiations concluded, the Accessory Transit Company rendered a new statement of affairs covering the period July 1, 1854, to October 5, 1855. Assets totaling $2,749,684.70 were reported including: *Northern Light* and *Star of the West,* running New York–Nicaragua; *Daniel Webster* and *Prometheus,* running New Orleans–Nicaragua; *Brother Jonathan, Cortes, Pacific,* and *Uncle Sam,* running on the Pacific; four lake and ten river steamers on the isthmus; depots and the transit road. Gross receipts for the period had been $1,688,452.39 of which $1,149,235.15 had been passage and freight payments. Cash on hand in New York totaled $13,901.64, in San Francisco, $27,000; cash due and anticipated, $71,063.70; debts through 1856 were estimated at $259,853.[42]

Most prominent among the debts of the transit company were unsatisfied claims of Nicaragua. The transit company had pledged Nicaragua 10 per cent of its annual net profit plus a $10,000 annual "bonus." The annuity was paid regularly until 1855, when payment was enjoined in the courts of New York by other creditors of Nicaragua. No percentage of transit profits, however, was ever acknowledged as received by that government. A succession of Nicaraguan commissioners had sought ad-

40. *Tribune,* September 13, October 11, November 21, 1855; Kemble, *Panama Route,* pp. 70–72.
41. *Tribune,* September 1853–December 1854, November 21, 1855.
42. Statement, Accessory Transit Co., *ibid.,* November 21, 1855. Also: *ibid.,* October 16, 1855.

justment of this account (questioning dividends declared by the company in 1852 and 1854), but negotiations repeatedly foundered upon the amounts due or the credentials of the Nicaraguan representatives. Arbitration before a bipartisan commission was pending in 1855 when a new personality disrupted the already complex transit situation: William Walker, the American filibuster.[43]

Pressed for control of the transit stock by Vanderbilt and harried by their Nicaraguan creditors, Morgan and Garrison saw in Walker the means to wipe the slate clean. In Nicaragua since June 1855 as military commander of the Patricio Rivas *junta*, Walker had secured *de facto* control of the country's affairs by October 23. Although he had sought Garrison's financial support before leaving San Francisco for the isthmus, Walker was refused and later denied charges that Morgan and Garrison sponsored his entry into Nicaragua. But his immediate involvement with the transit managers after his arrival in Central America is unquestionable.[44]

On October 3, 1855, Charles J. Macdonald arrived in San Juan del Sur as confidential agent of Morgan and Garrison. Macdonald was not an official representative of the transit company, but acted solely for his principals as private individuals through a power of attorney from Garrison. Attaching himself to Walker's staff through a mutual friend, Macdonald accompanied the filibusters in their victorious campaigns against Virgin Bay and Granada. He or his friend, Col. Charles Gilman, kept Walker informed on the power "struggle in the [transit] company . . . [in which] the agents in New-York and San Francisco were acting together," and when the Rivas-Walker faction achieved governmental control by treaty on October 23, Macdonald was there offering aid.[45]

What he offered in the name of his employers was gold. Macdonald extracted $20,000 from specie in transit across the isthmus, giving drafts on Charles Morgan in New York to its shippers. Short of funds, Walker accepted the "loan," pledging "repayment with interest and securing the

43. José de Marcoleta to A.T.C., November 5, 1852, *Tribune*, November 18, 1852; Ogden and Isaac Lea to Editor, November 18, 1852, *ibid.*, November 19, 1852; Charles O'Conor, F. B. Cutting, and J. Prescott Hall to A.T.C., November 26, 1852, *ibid.*, November 29, 1852; Vanderbilt to William L. Marcy, March 26, 1856, *Senate Exec. Docs.*, 34 Cong., 1 Sess., No. 68 (Serial 822), 80–83.

44. William Walker, *The War in Nicaragua*, pp. 86–87, 146.

45. *Ibid.*, pp. 127–128, 148–149; *Macdonald v. Garrison and Morgan*, 2 Hilton (N.Y. Common Pleas) 510 (1859).

debt by pledging dues from the Accessory Transit Company." Morgan honored the drafts, and Garrison further demonstrated the agents' interest by supervising (as he had done as early as October 6) shipments of supplies to Walker. The forcible use of transit steamers for military purposes by the filibusters was also ignored by Morgan and Garrison. Thus encouraged, Walker commissioned A. Parker Crittenden of San Francisco to seek more aid from the transit agents. He hoped for assistance in enlisting 500 recruits for his army; he received a staggering counter-offer.[46]

Meeting with Walker's friends Crittenden and Edmund Randolph, Garrison proposed the revocation of the existing transit charters and their assignment to a new company, which he and Morgan secretly headed. This offer was conveyed to Walker by Garrison's son (W. R. Garrison), Randolph, and Macdonald who arrived in Nicaragua on December 17, 1855. As a gesture of trust, Garrison sent more than 100 men to Walker on the same steamer and "promised that as many as possible" would follow—"Garrison advancing to the State the price of their passage." What transpired at Granada is best told in Walker's words:

> . . . the agreement of Crittenden with Garrison was . . . at that time, the only means, for carrying out the policy of the Rivas administration. . . . After Randolph and Walker had agreed on the terms of a new transit grant, a copy was sent up to Garrison at San Francisco [carried by] Macdonald. . . . W. R. Garrison went to New-York for the purpose of informing Charles Morgan of the arrangements which had been, and were about to be made. . . . Nothing was said to Rivas of the new transit contract.[47]

Rivas was not alone in his ignorance of these secret negotiations. Morgan saw to it that nothing was said to Vanderbilt or any other of his fellow transit company directors. To all appearances Morgan was merely going about his normal duties as president and general agent. On November 30 he increased the debts of the company but added needed working capital by mortgaging *Northern Light* and *Star of the West* to secure an issue of 120 $1,000 bonds (with interest payable at 7 per cent beginning

46. Walker, *op. cit.*, pp. 109–110, 127–128, 149; William V. Wells, *Walker's Expedition to Nicaragua: A History of the Central American War*, pp. 63–69, 84–87; *State of New York, Supreme Court, David Colden Murray, Receiver of the Accessry [sic] Transit Company, Plaintiff against Cornelius Vanderbilt, Defendant. Deposition of Joseph N. Scott*, pp. 33–40, *et passim*.
47. Walker, *op. cit.*, pp. 150–152.

May 31, 1856). Early in December, he established a new $20 "emigrant" rate from New York to Nicaragua to encourage increased passenger traffic. Payment of passage for those traveling on this special rate was charged to Nicaragua pending final arbitration of her claims against the transit company.[48]

Still apparently amicable with Vanderbilt, Morgan deferred to the latter's wish to reassume active control of the company. On December 21, 1855, Morgan agreed to resign his presidency and agency, effective December 31. Vanderbilt assumed the general agency on January 3, 1856, and was elected president on January 30. Under these developments transit stock opened 1856 at 18, peaked at 24½ on January 4, and remained "firm" for the rest of the month.

In secret, however, Morgan was planning his "killing." He was fully briefed on the Walker-Garrison agreement by *at least* January 12 and gave it his approval. Randolph and Walker had meanwhile drafted a "decree of revocation" and a new grant of exclusive transit rights to "Randolph and his associates." The conspirators then awaited a favorable moment for the actual coup. Time was needed for Garrison and Morgan to arrange for connecting steamships to replace those which would surely be withdrawn once the Accessory Transit Company's charter was canceled.[49]

Morgan also took aim on Vanderbilt in New York. Throughout January and February, he sold his and Garrison's stock holdings in the company and went heavily short at prices ranging from 20 to 23. The Vanderbilt group willingly purchased over 20,000 Morgan and Garrison shares as they pyramided their holdings to more than 68,000 of the company's 78,400 shares. Transit company stock closed at 22½ on March 12, and the New York *Tribune* reported "a very general impression that there is a large advance impending in this stock."

Nothing could have been further from the truth. The crash came on March 13, when the text of the revocation decree signed by Rivas on February 18 reached New York. The order annulled the grants and charters of the American Atlantic and Pacific Ship-Canal and Accessory

---

48. *State of New York, Supreme Court, David Colden Murray, Receiver of the Accessory Transit Company, against Cornelius Vanderbilt. Complaint*, pp. 15–18; "Documents and Correspondence Relating to the Government of Nicaragua," *Senate Exec. Docs.*, 34 Cong., 1 Sess., No. 68 (Serial 822), 80–83, 120–121.

49. Walker, *op. cit.*, pp. 152–155.

Transit companies on grounds of nonpayment of the 10 per cent of their net profits supposed to accrue to Nicaragua. Rivas (as Walker's front man) appointed commissioners to seize the financial and physical assets of the transit company in Nicaragua, to appraise their value toward payment of the sums allegedly due Nicaragua, and to negotiate for the continued operation of the transit under new management. On the New York Stock Exchange, the resulting "stampede in Nicaragua" drove the price of transit shares to 18½ by dusk and to 13 by March 14.

Morgan's actions of the past three months suddenly snapped into focus. Vanderbilt, who had purchased 118 of the 120 bonds issued under the mortgage of November 31, 1855, now saw the interest on those securities due May 31, 1856, as unlikely to be paid. Further, he now saw that Morgan's "emigrant" rate of December had merely provided free transportation for some 1,000 travelers (many of them mercenaries) only to cement the Walker-Morgan-Garrison alliance. Worse, at the deflated prices current on the exchange, Morgan had easily covered his short position and turned a substantial profit at the expense of Vanderbilt and his friends.[50]

The war was on again. On March 14, Vanderbilt withdrew his ocean steamers from the Nicaraguan route, and on March 17, he was vested with "full powers to conduct all . . . negotiations, and do such acts as in his judgment might be necessary" to restore the Accessory Transit Company's rights in Nicaragua.[51] Meanwhile, Morgan and Garrison scrambled to consolidate their position.

Since Randolph's charter signed by Rivas on February 19 granted only the transit *privilege* for a period of twenty-five years, his "associates" (i.e. Morgan and Garrison, who stoutly protested their ignorance of the whole matter to the press) concentrated on opening the connecting steamship lines from New York and San Francisco which Randolph's contract required within six months. On March 28, Morgan's *Orizaba* under the agency of his youngest son-in-law, Charles A. Whitney (formerly agent of the U.S. Mail Steamship Company), was advertised, New York to Nicaragua. By her departure on April 9, her advertisements offered a connection via Nicaragua with Garrison's *Sierra Nevada* on the Pacific. Morgan subsequently shifted *Calhoun, Texas,* and *Tennessee* from his Texas line

50. *Tribune*, November 27, December 17, 22, 24, 1855, January 1, 5, 8, 13, 22, 25–26, 28, February 4–5, 9, 14, 19, 23, 25, March 3, 5, 7, 11–15, 1856; *Herald*, March 14–18, 1856.

51. *David Colden Murray . . . Complaint, op. cit.,* p. 13.

to the Nicaragua run, while *Orizaba* was moved to the Pacific. By June rates via the new monthly Nicaragua line were $175, $125, and $90 for first-cabin, second-cabin, and steerage.[52]

The appraisal of transit assets in Nicaragua was complete by late July. The commissioners appointed by Walker offered the seized property (under the decree of February 18) "to such responsible persons as may make application . . . upon their executing a bond in a sum one fourth greater than its appraised value." The purchasers: Charles Morgan and C. K. Garrison; the price: a complicated swapping of liabilities typical of the whole "transit war." Morgan and Garrison's previous cash advances to Walker ($20,000 in October 1855 and $10,000 in January 1856) and some $70,000 of steamer-fare advances were credited at the inflated value of $500,000. In satisfaction of this "debt," the transit company (valued at $400,000) and $100,000 in 10 per cent Nicaraguan bonds were exchanged. The absurdity of the whole transaction is clear when compared to the valuation of $537,621 placed on the property in the company's statement of October 6, 1855—a statement Morgan had prepared![53]

In the open at last, Morgan and Garrison purchased Randolph's charter of privileges on August 6. Under this grant, the "company" agreed to pay Nicaragua one peso for each passenger and for each ton of freight carried to or across her boundaries.[54] Pending establishment of a monthly line of steamships to Nicaragua, they pledged "to send men and supplies to you [Walker], either by Steamer or sailing vessel at any time." To encourage passengers, they also agreed to accept land in lieu of passage money from prospective homesteaders in Nicaragua—66⅔ acres per single man or 133⅔ acres per family—as part of a general land-grant scheme offered by Walker's New York agent Appleton Oaksmith.[55] Morgan and Garrison

52. *Tribune*, March 15, 28, 29, April 9, 1856; *Deposition of Joseph N. Scott*, *loc. cit.*, 40–47, 60–67, 111; Affidavit of David Ogden, November 25, 1862, "Claims against Costa Rica under the Convention of 1860" (RG 76, National Archives).

53. *Tribune*, November 21, 1855; *Herald*, September 7, 1856; Lane, *Vanderbilt*, p. 122; Scroggs, *op. cit.*, pp. 156–158; Wiltsee, *op. cit.*, pp. 184–209.

54. Oaksmith to Randolph, August 7, 1856, Oaksmith to Walker, August 9, 1856, Appleton Oaksmith Papers (Manuscript Division, Duke University Library). Incredibly, and perhaps unknown to Morgan, Randolph and Garrison had offered the privilege to Vanderbilt for $300,000, on June 26, but were refused. Randolph to Vanderbilt, June 26, 1856, Vanderbilt to Randolph, undated, *Tribune*, November 22, 1856.

55. Morgan to Walker, August 9, 1856, quoted in Pierre F. Mancosos to Oaksmith, September [?], 1856, Emigration Agreement, August 30, 1856, Oaksmith Papers.

had elaborate plans and ordered a new steamer from Jacob Westervelt, but other events soon closed the Nicaraguan transit forever.

Vanderbilt had never ceased his efforts to reinstate the Accessory Transit Company. Twice he demonstrated sufficient solvency to avoid receivership for the company (from which Morgan as a trustee of certain mortgages of the company would have gained).[56] In March 1856 he secured a renewal of his previous guarantee of $40,000 per month from the Pacific Mail and the United States Mail companies if he would *not* compete with their lines (from which he collected $1,200,000 over the next thirty months). This gave him the freedom to concentrate on "ruining" Morgan and Garrison. In July he offered Walker $250,000 to restore the transit company's franchises and property, but the offer was rejected.[57] Turning to the courts, the Commodore was equally unsuccessful—losing a $500,000 suit alleging fraud against Garrison in October, and having a $2,000,000 action against Morgan, Garrison, and Walker refused by a U. S. Circuit Court in December.[58]

Vanderbilt was more successful in the rough-and-ready world of the isthmus. Costa Ricans under President Juan Rafael Mora had been fighting Walker for the transit route since February 1856, and the Commodore had served them well by public endorsement of their struggle for territorial adjustments and expulsion of the Nicaraguan filibusters. In November he took a more active role by introducing his own filibusters into the battle.[59] William R. C. Webster and Sylvanus H. Spencer joined the Costa Ricans and with the financial aid of Commodore Vanderbilt succeeded in seizing the river segment of the transit—Punta Arenas and four river steamers on December 23, 1856; San Carlos and two lake steamers on January 3, 1857.[60]

56. *Hamilton v. Accessory Transit Co.*, 26 Barbour (N.Y.) 46 (1857). See comment on this case and on *Patten v. Accessory Transit Co.* in *Tribune*, October 9, 10–18, November 4, December 25, 27, 1856, January 5, 8, 9, March 21, 1857.

57. *David Colden Murray . . . Complaint, op. cit.*, pp. 13–14, 23–24; Domingo Goicouria to Walker, August 2, 1856, Walker to Goicouria, August 20, 1856, *Tribune*, November 22, 1856.

58. *Vanderbilt v. Garrison*, 5 Duer (N.Y. Superior) 689 (1856); *Tribune*, October 8, 20, December 22, 1856.

59. Rafael Obregon Loria, *La Campaña del Transito, 1856–1857*; *Tribune*, February, 1856 ff.; Depositions of Sylvanus H. Spencer, July 21, 1857 and July 25, 1860, "Claims against Costa Rica under the Convention of 1860" (RG 76, National Archives); *Deposition of Joseph N. Scott, loc. cit.*, pp. 91–99.

60. Protest of I. C. Harris, January 7, 1857, Deposition of A. C. Hutchinson, January 8, 1857, *Tribune*, January 26, 1857.

Morgan's attitude toward these Central American "wars" is suggested in a letter to Walker's New York agent in September:

The large expenditures made to organize a line to California via Nicaragua, together with the many other business calls for money, must necessarily have involved large amounts; which facts together with the knowledge that our business has not, & for some time will not be remunerative, should lead you to the conclusion that in order to carry successfully through the Nicaragua Line, we need all we have & all we can get. . . . others, interested in the cause, should put their shoulders to the wheel, leaving us to push forward the arrangements for steam communication, which we deem the most essential aid that can be required of us.[61]

With the transit closed, Morgan and Garrison's steamers carried fewer paying passengers and increased their vulnerability to charges of transporting only arms and recruits.[62] Walker's position was tenuous at best, and within three months after the overland and lake transit closure, Morgan and Garrison terminated their connecting steamship lines. Walker's cause was doomed, and he surrendered his army on May 1, 1857. He admitted he had expected Morgan and Garrison "to remain faithful . . . only as long as their interest required fidelity; he expected them, however, to show more commercial nerve and sagacity than they displayed."[63]

Regardless of Walker's opinion the Nicaraguan transit remained closed. Three rival groups bid before the new government for the franchise: the old American Atlantic and Pacific Ship-Canal Company, Vanderbilt's Accessory Transit Company, and Morgan and Garrison. The latter were the first to withdraw. Effective April 1, 1858, they "disposed" of their Nicaraguan properties to Vanderbilt. Morgan also made another settlement with the Commodore. As part of the battle, Vanderbilt had opened a line of steamships in the Gulf in opposition to Morgan. He now sold these to Morgan for cash and a promise to stay out of Nicaragua. In return, Vanderbilt purchased *Ocean Queen*, then in construction in New York, and a half interest in two Pacific steamers, *Orizaba* and *Sierra Nevada*. The "War of the Commodores" was over.[64]

61. Morgan to Oaksmith, September 22, 1856, Oaksmith Papers. Also see Morgan to Oaksmith, September 20, 1856, Alexander C. Lawrence to Oaksmith, November 12, 1856, *ibid.*

62. Passengers across Nicaragua declined from 22,311 in 1854 to 658 in 1857. Kemble, *Panama Route*, pp. 253–254.

63. Walker, *op. cit.*, pp. 398–409.

64. *Herald*, January 27, May 1, 6, 29, 1857; *Times*, April 10, 1858; C. K. Garrison to Joseph N. Scott, April 20, 1858, *Deposition of Joseph N. Scott, loc.*

Vanderbilt never reopened the Nicaraguan transit, although he was granted the privilege on March 8, 1858. He also thoroughly milked the Accessory Transit Company for its remaining assets and abandoned it into receivership on May 31, 1858.[65] He then used his Nicaraguan franchise to "blackmail" the Pacific Mail lines into increasing to $56,000 his monthly "bonus" to stay out of competition. Meanwhile he and Morgan, once again an acceptable partner, hatched a new scheme.

By September 1859, all the original contracts for mail via Panama had expired. The U.S. Mail Steamship Company retired from the field leaving it open to Pacific Mail and Vanderbilt and Morgan. The latter formed the Atlantic and Pacific Steamship Company, and obtained the ultimate contract for semimonthly mail, New York and New Orleans, to San Francisco, by way of Panama. For this they were paid $187,500 per annum. They did not derive income from the isthmian transit itself, however, as that was operated by Pacific Mail's Panama Railroad.

This resumption of competition via Panama ended in compromise in February 1860. Vanderbilt and Morgan retained control of the Atlantic side and sold their four Pacific steamers to the mail company for 5,000 shares of its stock and $250,000. Future gross receipts of the combined lines would be divided 70–30 in favor of Pacific Mail. Morgan and Vanderbilt maintained his arrangement until September 1865, when they sold their interests to the newly formed Atlantic Mail Steamship Company and withdrew.[66]

The record of Charles Morgan's participation in these isthmian schemes is admittedly fragmentary. Initially, he attempted his own isthmian line. He then became a trusted intimate of Vanderbilt and reaped his share of the early profits of the Commodore's Central American ventures. Morgan then cast his lot with a man he exceeded in wealth but whom he was unable to match in cunning and deception—C. K. Garrison. Several of the Morgan-Garrison enterprises were legitimate and conventional—notably the banking house of Garrison, Morgan, Fretz & Ralston, which operated ethically and profitably in San Francisco and New York between December 1, 1855, and July 14, 1857. The firm was the usual

---

cit., p. 260; "Information Concerning Nicaragua Transit," Charles A. Gulick, Jr. and Winnie Allen (editors), *The Papers of Mirabeau Buonaparte Lamar*, IV, Pt. III, 137–138; Chapter 5, below.

65. *David Colden Murray . . . Complaint, op. cit., passim.* . . . .

66. Kemble, *Panama Route*, pp. 77–100.

sort of mercantile bank and catered especially to the California–New York gold trade.[67]

Behind the legitimate façade of Morgan's reputation, however, he and Garrison participated intimately in one of the most ruthless episodes of American financial history. Morgan's role and responsibility are shadowy because of a lack of personal records. Garrison seems to have been the instigator of most of the schemes, but Morgan was always there with money and assistance. While a profit-and-loss analysis of the activities of such men as Vanderbilt, Garrison, or Morgan is impossible, it is clear that Morgan was willing and able to hold his own in the rough-and-tumble business world of the 1850s. It added much to his wealth but little to his prestige.

Yet with all its dash and fire, the transit war denied Morgan a lifetime investment. This he found where it had always waited for him, in the Gulf of Mexico.

67. Leroy Armstrong and J. O. Denny, *Financial California: An Historical Review of the Beginnings and Progress of Banking in the State*, pp. 115–116; Tilton, *op. cit., passim.*

5

EXPANSION IN THE
GULF OF MEXICO, 1850–1860

ALTHOUGH much of the personal energy of Charles Morgan was expended in the "war" for the isthmian transit, his shipping interests elsewhere did not languish. The decade before the Civil War became the most active period of expansion for the Morgan lines serving the Gulf of Mexico. A solid financial foundation for those services was achieved, and they survived and prospered long after the Nicaraguan "fancy" had passed.

The potential of the Gulf region was unmistakable by 1850. The opening of the Southwest after the Mexican War and the discovery of gold in California multiplied the traders and emigrants using the markets and shipping points of Alabama, Louisiana, and Texas. Increased patronage dictated enlargement of transportation facilities to meet the demands of the expanding Gulf Coast economy.[1]

The prospects of Texas continued to impress businessmen. Her vast hinterland, her numerous natural harbors, and her navigable rivers gave her special attractions for settlers and trade. The commerce of the western Gulf was steadily increasing and diversifying. Receipts of cotton at Texas ports jumped from 39,744 bales to 62,433 in the four years after 1848. By 1856 this figure climbed to 116,078 bales, and the 193,963 bales received in 1860 set an ante bellum record. Besides cotton, Texas was producing and exporting increasing quantities of sugar, cattle and

1. "Great Commercial Advantages of the Gulf of Mexico," *De Bow's Review*, VII (December 1849), 510–523.

hides, lumber, pecans, and wool. Morgan, having firmly established himself as master of the New Orleans–Texas trade by 1850, increased his
service in proportion to this new prosperity.[2]

His first chore, and that of his agents Harris and Morgan, was the
refurbishing of his older vessels. The Morgan steamers had all seen
service in the Mexican War and showed it. *Galveston* and *Palmetto* were
advertised as the flagships of the line, and Morgan strove to maintain
first-class accommodations on them. *Galveston* "was fitted up with the
choicest of woods, birds'-eye maple and rose, and the decorations of the
saloon were really beautiful," wrote a passenger in 1849. But the vessel's
long, narrow construction made her topheavy, causing considerable motion in heavy weather. Even so hardy a seaman as Mrs. Matilda Houstoun
described this tendency as "most disagreeable . . . owing as much to the
above causes as to the drunkeness of the captain, who was in a state of
intoxication the whole time we were on board." Her opinion of the
Morgan Line decreased further after an "odious" breakfast of "corn
bread, salt butter, 'Boston crackers,' and sticky molasses."[3]

Conditions on the small steamers purchased hurriedly during the war
were worse. In 1847 Morgan assured the public that *Globe* was "fitted up
expressly for this trade [hence] passengers may rely upon a degree of
comfort and convenience such as is seldom experienced at sea." Yet by
1851 Mrs. Teresa Vielé described *Globe* as "an old disabled shell that had
been already condemned as unsafe . . . our old, leaky vessel." She spent
her passage across the Gulf in the "ladies cabin" where "a shelf a foot
wide" served for a bunk amidst a "scene of dreadful squalor and confu-
sion." Emigrant families lay about on trunks and boxes and their children
"cried, screamed, and were seasick incessantly." But at least, in contrast
to the commander of *Galveston*, Captain Thompson of *Globe* "was a
splendid specimen of the rough and fearless sailor, a genuine hero of the
sea [concealing] . . . a soft heart under a rough jacket."[4]

2. "Inducements to Settle or to Invest Capital in Texas," *ibid.*, XI (November
1851), 533–537; "Growth of Galveston, Texas," *ibid.*, XXIII (November 1857),
554–555; "Commerce of Galveston," *ibid.*, XXV (December 1858), 710–711;
"Commerce of Galveston, Texas, 1860," *ibid.*, XXIX (October 1860), 529.

3. Matilda C. F. Houstoun, *Hesperos; or, Travels in the West*, II, 97–99. For
Mrs. Houstoun's qualifications as a sailor, see Houstoun, *Texas and the Gulf of
Mexico; or, Yachting in the New World*.

4. New Orleans *Daily Picayune*, December 30, 1847; Teresa Vielé, "*Following
the Drum:*" *A Glimpse of Frontier Life*, pp. 76–89.

To offset this deterioration of his older steamers Morgan embarked on an ambitious construction program. Between May 1850 and November 1852, five new vessels flying the red-white-and-blue Morgan pennant rolled off the ways of New York shipbuilders: *Louisiana* (1,056 tons) and *Perseverance* (827 tons) completed in 1850 and 1852 by Westervelt and Mackay, with engines by the Morgan Iron Works; *Mexico* (1,043 tons), *Meteor* (542 tons), and *Texas* (1,151 tons), launched in 1850 and 1851 by William Collyer, and also supplied with Morgan engines. To round out his reorganized fleet, Morgan purchased *Jerry Smith* (159 tons) from the United States government in April 1849 and *Cincinnati* (276 tons) from New Orleans interests in June 1852. The firm of Harris & Morgan owned a small share (⅛ to ¼) in each vessel, but Charles Morgan himself paid their construction price and held the majority share.[5]

This expansion was not without setbacks. The treacherous western Gulf with its shifting currents and depths continually levied its toll on Morgan's steamers. *Palmetto* was stranded and abandoned in Matagorda Bay, January 9, 1851, and *Globe* wrecked on the bar at Brazos St. Iago, June 17. On November 25 *Galveston* was beached on Ship Island, Mississippi, and on April 29, 1852, *Meteor* was snagged and abandoned off Paso de Caballo. Thus in a period of sixteen months Morgan lost four steamers valued at $250,000, and, as was his custom to promote passenger confidence, all were self-insured. The loss of *Meteor* resulted from the negligence of the pilots at Paso de Caballo, and thenceforth Morgan employed his own pilots to navigate the approaches to Texas ports.[6]

Morgan was solvent enough, however, to absorb these losses of 1851 and 1852. His income from his New York iron works, the mail subsidies he held, and his Nicaraguan investments supplied ample funds for rebuilding, and in 1853 and 1854 four new vessels were launched in New York for his fleet: *Charles Morgan* (1,215 tons), *Nautilus* (898 tons), *Tennessee* (1,149 tons), and *Orizaba* (734 tons).[7]

5. New Orleans *Price Current*, April 24, 1849, May 11, 1850; New York *Tribune*, June 15, October 1, 25, December 9, 1850, January 1, September 24, October 23, December 27, 1851, April 15, October 14, 18–19, 29, 1852; *Registers, NOLA*, IV, 141, 167; V, 48–49, 160, 178, 207, 252–53.

6. New Orleans *Daily Crescent*, April 29, 1852; *Daily Picayune*, March 29, 1854; Holdcamper (ed.), *Merchant Steam*, pp. 224, 227, 230, 240.

7. *Registers, NOLA*, V, 44–45, 188, 199–200, 268; *Tribune*, June 18, 1853; *Daily Picayune*, April 3–5, May 5–7, July 31, August 1, 1854.

With these new steamers Morgan maintained service on his established Texas lines and opened a new route as well. By 1854, semiweekly service to Galveston and Matagorda Bay was a reality, employing four large steamers on the circuit. Smaller steamers continued occasionally to extend the line to Brazos St. Iago offering connections with steamboats plying the Rio Grande.[8] But the new area of service was Mexico itself.

Communication with Vera Cruz and talk of a Mexican isthmian connection were logical outgrowths of the Mexican War and the Gold Rush. Numerous proposals to open mail service to Mexico's leading port had been made to the U.S. Congress, but nothing was accomplished until 1852. In that year concrete steps were taken to establish mail service to Mexico, and Charles Morgan was associated with the scheme.

In July 1852, Albert C. Ramsey of Pennsylvania, the holder of a yet-unfulfilled contract of August 31, 1850, from the Mexican government to establish mail service between Vera Cruz and Acapulco, received "a renewal and extension of the grant." Ramsey obligated himself to carry only through mails for fifteen years commencing January 1, 1853, and to pay Mexico 20 cents per pound on letters and 20 cents per 100 pounds on periodicals so transported. Ramsey also received various grants for the construction of roads, ferries, and bridges, as necessary, from the states of Guerrero and Puebla. The obvious intention of the American contractor was to operate this overland segment as part of a through route from Atlantic or Gulf ports of the United States to California.[9]

To give the over-all project corporate form, Ramsey and investors from New York and New Orleans, on January 1, 1853, incorporated as the Mexican Ocean Mail and Inland Company. Organized for twenty years and with a capital stock of $1,500,000, the New York–domiciled corporation's "specific objects" were quite grandiose:

building . . . equipping, furnishing, fitting, purchasing, chartering, navigating and owning vessels, to be propelled solely or partially by . . . steam . . . for the transportation of passengers, freight and mails . . . be-

8. *Daily Picayune*, March 9, June 15, 20, July 27, August 3, September 23, 1852, November 5, 1854; Herbert Davenport, "Notes on Early Steamboating on the Rio Grande," *Southwestern Historical Quarterly*, XLIX (October 1954), 288–289.

9. *First Annual Report of the Mexican Ocean Mail and Inland Company*, pp. 27–30.

tween . . . New Orleans, Tampico, and Vera Cruz . . . Acapulco, Sihua-
tanejo, Petacalco and San Francisco . . . with the intention of connecting
with, running or establishing . . . mail passenger or freight lines . . . between . . . any of the above ports, or the port of New York and other ports
of the United States, Havana, the . . . West India Islands, Zacatula, Monterey,
San Diego, or other Mexican ports, and the ports of Polynesia, China, Cochin
China and Siam . . . and . . . ports of the Russian or British Possessions.

Significantly, too, the corporation's charter empowered it "to purchase,
hold, take and use any or all . . . of all grants, contracts, authority,
franchises, powers, privileges or exemptions already or hereafter to be
derived by Albert C. Ramsey" or others from the federal or state governments of Mexico for the "transportation of mails, passengers, freight, or
other property" across Mexico. With this understanding the stock of the
company was sold to "under forty" investors at $1,500 per share, and
Ramsey of Pennsylvania, Simeon Draper, George L. Schuyler, Elihu
Townsend, Robert G. Rankin, Edward H. Carmick, and Robert B. Coleman of New York, and James Robb and Morgan's son-in-law Israel C.
Harris of New Orleans were elected from among the stockholders to form
a managing board of directors with Rankin as president.[10]

To begin its operations, the company (through Ramsey and Carmick
as agents) on February 15, 1853, signed a contract with Postmaster
General S. D. Hubbard for a Vera Cruz–San Francisco mail service. A
separate agreement for service on the New Orleans–Vera Cruz segment
was signed March 3. The contract of February 15 bound the corporation
to establish and perform twice-monthly mail service from Vera Cruz to
San Francisco and return, via Acapulco. The company would be paid
$420,000 annually for four years upon ratification of the contract by
Congress. The second contract promised thrice-monthly service from New
Orleans to Vera Cruz via Tampico for five years at $69,750 per annum.
No congressional ratification was required for this second agreement.[11]

Without waiting for congressional approval, the company dispatched
agents to Mexico to establish a daily line of stagecoaches from Vera Cruz,
to Puebla, and to Acapulco (see Map 4.1). At Acapulco connections were
to be made with a weekly line of steamers then being operated between

10. Quotations from *ibid.*, pp. 3–4, 22, 31–36; see *Daily Picayune*, March 11,
1853, for other details.
11. Conditional Contract between U. S. and Ramsey and Carmick, February 15,
1853, *House Exec. Docs.*, 35 Cong., 2 Sess., No. 30 (Serial 1004), 160–165;
"Report of the Postmaster General, 1853," *Senate Exec. Docs.*, 33 Cong., 1 Sess.,
No. 1 (Serial 692), 722–724, 744, 779.

Panama and San Francisco by the Pacific Mail Steamship Company. To establish a Gulf connection, Charles Morgan was retained for "a part" of the $69,750 subsidy and on April 14, 1853, Morgan's *Texas* opened the first segment of the proposed route. Semimonthly service was offered (omitting Tampico) with cabin fares set at $50 from New Orleans; $25 for steerage; freight, 30 cents per cubic foot.[12]

By June 30 *Texas* had carried only $630.84 worth of mail and by October had yet to perform the third monthly trip via Tampico as required. Passengers were scarce as the overland segment was not completed. Post coaches, wagons, horses, and mules had been delivered in June, and by July, some private mail was being carried on the 384-mile land route. It appeared, however, that the service would not be in full operation until December 1853. Yet Morgan went ahead with construction of *Orizaba,* which was conceived as a sister ship to *Texas* on the New Orleans–Vera Cruz line—both embracing an investment of "nearly $300,000" on that portion of the route.[13]

The New Orleans–San Francisco service via Mexico never materialized. The Pacific Mail Company altered its schedule of arrivals at Acapulco, disrupting connections with the stagecoach line and with Morgan. Worse, a new Postmaster General, economy-minded James Campbell, disapproved of the route as too expensive and persuaded Congress to reject the contract of February 15, 1853. The company petitioned for reconsideration, then for redress and damages totaling $98,000. It was eventually awarded $69,750 in 1858, but that sum was later revoked by an Attorney General's ruling. Thus the company never formally opened its route from Vera Cruz to San Francisco.[14]

Despite the troubles of the Mexican Ocean Mail Company, Morgan

12. New Orleans *Daily Picayune,* May 1, 1853; Rankin to James Campbell, June 15, 1853, M.O.M. & I.C. and Morgan to same, October 26, 1853, William H. Aspinwall to Harris and Morgan, October 28, 1853, Harris and Morgan to Campbell, October 29, 1853, Campbell to Harris and Morgan, November 3, 1853, Rankin to Campbell, November 23, 1853 (Serial 1004), 165–171, 173–184; *Report, M.O.M. & I.C.,* pp. 8–14.

13. *Ibid.; Tribune,* June 18, 1853; New York *Herald,* September 28, 1853. For a passage on *Texas* see Robert A. Wilson, *Mexico and Its Religion, with Incidents of Travel in That Country during Parts of the Years 1851–52–53–54,* pp. 15–16.

14. "Ramsey and Carmick Contract," *House Exec. Docs.,* 33 Cong., 2 Sess., No. 47 (Serial 783); "Case of Carmick and Ramsey," *ibid.,* 35 Cong., 2 Sess., No. 30 (Serial 1004); Leonard V. Huber and Clarence A. Wagner, *The Great Mail: A Postal History of New Orleans,* pp. 89–90.

provided good service to Vera Cruz. In 1854 twenty-four round trips from New Orleans earned him $37,200 in mail subsidies. This service earned $34,000 for the shipper in 1855. These figures represent receipts for mail carriage after approximately $8,000 per quarter had been deducted for noncompliance with the original contract for thrice-monthly service via Tampico.

By 1857 the Ramsey and Carmick agreement had lapsed, and a temporary arrangement between the Post Office Department and Morgan (and his current partner Garrison) was substituted. Under this instrument Morgan vessels carried twice-monthly mails from New Orleans to Vera Cruz at $1,210.93 per voyage through June 30, 1858. After that date no formal mail contracts were negotiated for the Vera Cruz route until after the Civil War. But under special agreements authorized by a congressional act of June 14, 1858, Morgan's *Tennessee* continued to carry occasional mails. In fiscal 1859 she made fourteen round trips for $2,810.73. Eight outward and six inward mail voyages earned Morgan $1,911.15 during fiscal 1860, and $4,370.08 was received for trips completed during fiscal 1861.[15] The Mexican route had become an integrated part of the Morgan service and Vera Cruz a regular port-of-call for his steamers.[16]

While Morgan's Mexican line was being established, his older Texas route was encountering its first opposition since the Mexican War. As Morgan's four-year mail contracts lapsed again in 1854, spirited bidding over their renewal arose. Prominent among new bidders for the service was Cornelius Vanderbilt. Incensed at Morgan because of the Nicaraguan battle then in progress, the Commodore sought to weaken Morgan's steady source of income in the Gulf. For Route 7851 (the four-year

15. "Report of the Postmaster General, 1853" (Serial 692), 760–761; *ibid.*, 1854, *Senate Exec. Docs.*, 33 Cong., 2 Sess., No. 1 (Serial 757), 628, 646; *ibid.*, 1855, *Senate Exec. Docs.*, 34 Cong., 1 Sess., No. 1 (Serial 812), 330–332, 349; *ibid.*, 1856, *Senate Exec. Docs.*, 34 Cong., 3 Sess., No. 5 (Serial 876), 789; *ibid.*, 1857, *Senate Exec. Docs.*, 35 Cong., 1 Sess., No. 1 (Serial 921), 969, 1021; *ibid.*, 1858, *Senate Exec. Docs.*, 35 Cong., 2 Sess., No. 1 (Serial 977), 753; *ibid.*, 1859, *Senate Exec. Docs.*, 36 Cong., 1 Sess., No. 2 (Serial 1025), 1437; *ibid.*, 1860, *Senate Exec. Docs.*, 36 Cong., 2 Sess., No. 1 (Serial 1080), 452; *ibid.*, 1861, *Senate Exec. Docs.*, 37 Cong., 2 Sess., No. 1 (Serial 1119), 676; "Fines and Deductions, Mail Contractors, 1855," *House Exec. Docs.*, 34 Cong., 1 Sess., No. 112 (Serial 859), 60, 82.

16. *Daily Picayune*, April 2, December 15, 1854; *Daily Crescent*, March 14, 16, 1859; New Orleans *Daily Delta*, September 29, 1860; *Mygatt and Co.'s Directory* (1857), p. 60; *Gardner's New Orleans Directory*, p. 389.

contract, New Orleans to Indianola, 540 miles, once a week from October 1 to July 1), the Postmaster General received the following bids, in order of arrival:

Harris & Morgan	$45,000 per annum
Cornelius Vanderbilt	$40,000 per annum
William C. Lacy	$50,000 per annum (3 weekly trips to Galveston, October–July, 2 thereafter)
William C. Lacy	$45,000 per annum (same service)
Harris & Morgan	$30,000 per annum

What prompted Harris & Morgan's second bid is unknown, but its late nature would suggest they had some knowledge their first bid was too high. Their second bid, $15,000 less than before, offered no decrease in service, implying perhaps some duplicity. In any case, the second Morgan offer was accepted May 10, 1854, to expire June 30, 1858. The second Lacy offer was also accepted but was transferred to Harris & Morgan on September 15, when Lacy failed to begin service.

Under the terms of these contracts Morgan vessels were rescheduled to leave New Orleans every Sunday and Thursday at 8 A.M., arriving at Galveston every Tuesday and Saturday by 10 A.M. Morgan steamers departed Galveston for Indianola each Wednesday and Saturday at 4 P.M., arriving the next day by noon. On the return voyage vessels left Indianola every Saturday and Wednesday at 2 P.M., arriving in Galveston the next day by 10 A.M. New Orleans–bound steamers were to leave Galveston every Sunday and Tuesday at 4 P.M., arriving every Tuesday and Saturday at 4 P.M. The additional trip, added from October 1 to July 1, would leave New Orleans every Tuesday at 8 A.M., arriving at Galveston on Thursday by 10 A.M. The return voyage would depart every Friday at 4 P.M., arriving in New Orleans on Sunday by the same hour.[17]

Morgan service to Brazos St. Iago, in contrast, was faltering and had been abandoned in October 1853 due to lack of patronage. Over $10,800 was deducted from Morgan's mail subsidy for failures of service, and before his contract expired in June 1854, the Postmaster General opened bidding on a new arrangement.

But no competitors appeared to bid for Route 7853 (the new four-year contract, New Orleans to Brazos St. Iago, 550 miles, twice-monthly by steamship). The route was reluctantly let to Harris & Morgan again by

17. "Contracts for Carrying the Mails, 1854," *House Exec. Docs.*, 33 Cong., 2 Sess., No. 86 (Serial 789), 484.

contract of May 10, 1854, at $20,000 per annum. Service began July 1, with steamers leaving New Orleans the first and third Thursday of each month at 8 A.M., arriving in Brazos St. Iago the following Monday by the same hour. On the return trip vessels left Brazos St. Iago the second and fourth Monday of every month, arriving at New Orleans by the following Monday at 4 P.M.[18]

As his activities in Nicaragua and Mexico increased between 1854 and 1858, Morgan's Texas service again became irregular. Ships were diverted to the more lucrative transit routes, and the prestige and receipts of the Morgan Gulf lines suffered. During the last three months of 1855, for example, the New Orleans–Galveston mail failed seventeen times. Over forty failures were recorded the following year with appropriate deductions from Morgan's subsidy. Even when the passage was made, it could consume two days and often was somewhat unpleasant. In 1855 Amelia Murray journeyed from New Orleans to Galveston in thirty-six hours on *Louisiana,* and while "not positively ill," was "rather uncomfortable," the "majority of passengers [being] unhappy" because of the swell.[19]

Under these demands for increased service, capital, and competition, Morgan finally incorporated a portion of his Gulf shipping interests for the first time under the name of the Southern Steamship Company of New Orleans. Organized for twenty-five years under a general Louisiana incorporation law of March 14, 1855, the company's purpose was stated in its charter of May 9, 1856:

to transport for compensation passengers, freight, mails, and all personal property by steamships between the ports of New Orleans, Galveston, and Lavacca Bay [*sic*], and between such other ports, foreign or domestic, as this corporation may determine, and for the purpose of sea navigation by steam or otherwise, and to maintain steamships, and for all other purposes, belonging and incidental to navigation.[20]

18. *Ibid.,* p. 485; "Fines and Deductions, Mail Contractors, 1854," (Serial 790), 22, 36, 76.

19. *Ibid.,* pp. 4, 13, 22, 36, 63, 76; *ibid.,* 1855 (Serial 859), 60, 69, 82, 96; *ibid.,* 1857, *House Exec. Docs.,* 35 Cong., 1 Sess., No. 81 (Serial 956), 18, 37–39, 62; Amelia M. Murray, *Letters from the United States, Cuba, and Canada,* p. 291.

20. Charter of the Southern Steamship Co. of New Orleans, May 9, 1856. Act before William Christy, N.A. (Orleans), recorded in Mortgage Office (Orleans Parish, La.), Society Book III, 414 (May 12, 1856), hereafter cited as M.O. (Orleans).

With a capital stock of $400,000, provided by 4,000 shares of $100 each, the company was dominated by Charles Morgan. He personally subscribed for 500 shares; Harris & Morgan (in which he remained the silent partner and financial angel) purchased 890 shares and Cornelius B. Payne, a third partner in that firm since 1853, took 250. E. J. Hart & Co., the largest grocery firm in New Orleans and an old friend of Morgan's, subscribed for 500. The remaining shares in smaller blocks were held by various investors in Louisiana, New York, and Texas.[21]

Executive powers of the company were vested in a board of four "managers" appointed to serve until February 1862 and to be elected thereafter every five years. Harris, Henry R. Morgan, Payne, and Hart filled these positions initially at a compensation of 5 per cent on freight receipts, $2\frac{1}{2}$ per cent on disbursements, and $2\frac{1}{2}$ per cent on other receipts. This group subsequently elected Hart "president," but significantly, three fourths of the board of managers were partners in the firm of Harris & Morgan.

To implement its charter the corporation purchased (to be delivered on June 10, 1856) the following items from Charles Morgan for the sums indicated:

Charles Morgan	$120,000
Louisiana	80,000
Mexico	80,000
Perseverance	60,000
Tools, iron, furniture, etc.	525
New Orleans–Galveston–Indianola Mail Contract	46,875
Eight Negroes	8,800
Total	$396,200

A coal contract with R. and J. Watson negotiated by Harris & Morgan was also assumed for 170 shares of stock.

The board of managers was further given power to

invest . . . one-half, but not more, of the profits of the company in loans, secured by mortgage on improved and unincumbered real estate, situate within the parishes of Orleans and Jefferson, in this State; and in every case the property mortgaged must be worth twice the amount loaned thereon.

21. *Ibid.* Edmund J. Hart was the leading grocer in New Orleans and had purchased small shares in Morgan vessels as early as 1854. *Registers, NOLA,* V, 188.

They may also invest the cash or surplus profits of the company in the purchase of any bonds or stocks created by or under the laws of the United States, or of any of the States . . . or by corporations of any of the States . . . and may make loans of such cash or surplus profits on pledge of any of the aforesaid securities, bonds or stocks.[22]

To provide for growth, the capital stock of the company could be increased by a majority vote of the shareholders, and under these terms, the corporation began its operations on June 10, 1856.

As can be seen from its charter, the Southern Steamship Company did not purchase all the assets of Charles Morgan. His iron works and his Nicaraguan interests were separate, and he operated several ships independently. *Cincinnati* had been lost off Brazos St. Iago on May 23, 1853, and *Portland* had been dismantled in 1854.[23] *Texas, Orizaba,* and *Tennessee,* being utilized in Nicaragua and Mexico, remained outside the new corporation. Likewise the Brazos St. Iago mail contract and *Nautilus* were not included. Morgan's basic Gulf service from New Orleans to Galveston and Indianola was actually all that had been incorporated. But in the midst of this birth of the Southern Steamship Company, other events matured which subsequently made it the most important of Morgan's ante bellum enterprises.

"Let New-Orleans awake before too late," wrote an engineer in 1851, "she sleeps in her purple pomp, with a poinard at her breast."[24] This was but one expression of a growing awareness of a "crisis" in New Orleans's western trade. By the 1850s there was a strong possibility that her monopoly of the Mississippi Valley would slip behind the bustling canal and western railroad projects of competing regions. This concern expressed itself in many ways, but in the decade prior to the Civil War a railroad to the Pacific became the dream of a large segment of the population of the Crescent City. Such a road would serve as an aid in collecting and distributing goods and thus complement the trade of the Mississippi.[25]

22. This power was revoked in 1858. Amendment to Charter of the Southern Steamship Co. of New Orleans, July 2, 1858. Act before William L. Poole, N.A. (Orleans), M.O. (Orleans), Society Book IV, 168–173 (July 5, 1858).
23. Holdcamper (ed.), *op. cit.*, pp. 339, 347.
24. "Thoughts on a Rail-Road System for New-Orleans," *De Bow's Review*, X (February 1851), 181.
25. Erastus P. Puckett, "The Attempt of New Orleans to Meet the Crisis in Her Trade with the West," Mississippi Valley Historical Association, *Proceedings for the Year 1920–1921*, pp. 481–495; E. Dale Odom, "Louisiana Railroads, 1830–1880: A Study of State and Local Aid," pp. 44 ff.

Promoted by James Robb, Buckner H. Payne, and others, a railroad westward from New Orleans was well under discussion in 1851 and on March 12, 1852, a provisional corporation, christened the New Orleans, Opelousas, and Great Western Railroad Company (N.O.O. & G.W.), was formed to raise money and complete surveys. Capital stock of the provisional company was fixed at $3,000,000 and among many prominent investors were Harris and Morgan and Cornelius B. Payne.[26] Upon completion of promising surveys in 1852, the railroad was permanently chartered by the Louisiana legislature on April 23, 1853, as a $6,000,000 corporation.[27] Its ambitious construction program was as long as its name:

from Algiers, on the opposite bank of the Mississippi River from New Orleans, westward near Thibodeaux, across Berwick's Bay to Washington in the Parish of St. Landry; thence to a point on the Sabine River, most favorable for the purpose of constructing said Road through the State of Texas to El Paso . . . thence to the Pacific Ocean. The road to be made on such a scale as to serve for the main trunk of railway between New Orleans and the Pacific States.

The westward construction of the N.O.O. & G.W. is beyond the scope of this study. At times the financial and engineering problems involved in laying track across the swamps of southwestern Louisiana taxed the very existence of the company. But the able leadership of President William G. Hewes and the skill of Chief Engineer G. W. R. Bayley and others held the corporation together, and by April 12, 1857, eighty miles of single track had been completed from Algiers to Berwick's Bay, Louisiana (see Map 5.1).[28]

Unexpected costs of constructing this initial section of the road halted plans for its extension to Texas and the Pacific. To gain additional funds

26. Buckner H. Payne, *Report on the Algiers and Opelousas Railroad;* Charter of the New Orleans, Opelousas, and Great Western Railroad Co., March 12, 1852, M.O. (Orleans), Society Book II, 411–426 (May 5, 1852).

27. A. G. Blanchard, *Report of the Preliminary Survey of the Algiers and Opelousas Railroad; Louisiana Acts* (1853), pp. 115–123, 141–142; Amendment to Charter of the N.O.O. & G.W., March 2, 1853, M.O. (Orleans), Society Book III, 46–62 (April 25, 1853).

28. Aside from the reports of the company (published annually after 1853), the best accounts of this construction are the works of Prichard, Thornburgh, Reed, and Odom, as cited in the bibliography. The corporate records of the N.O.O. & G.W. are held by the Southern Pacific Company (Texas and Louisiana Lines), Houston, Texas, and were not used in these studies. The present study is the first to use these vital records. Hereafter cited as N.O.O. & G.W. Records.

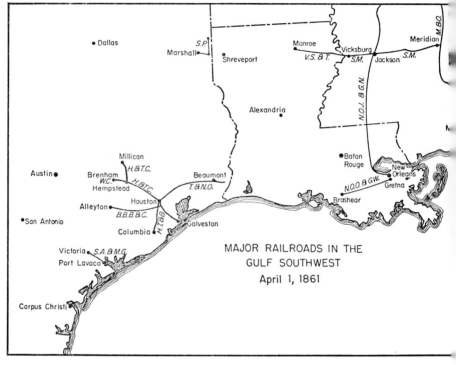

Map 5.1. Gulf Coast Railroads, 1830–1861.

for construction to add to state, parish, and municipal aid, the directors sought to build up freight and passenger traffic over that portion of the road already completed.[29]

Unfortunately the railroad did not go anywhere. The solution proposed was to arrange steamship service directly from the terminus of the N.O.O. & G.W. at Berwick's Bay to Texas, counting on a share of the profits of the Texas trade to provide new capital for completion of the road. Such a combined rail-water route would be popular since it would shorten the distance from New Orleans to Galveston some 160 miles and would avoid the unreliable Mississippi River. Unable to build or purchase steamers of its own, the railroad entertained proposals from shipmen. The two who responded were those two combatants then locked in the Nicaraguan struggle—Charles Morgan and Cornelius Vanderbilt.

Morgan offered the services of one steamer from Berwick's Bay to

29. *Fifth Annual Report of the President and Directors of the New Orleans, Opelousas, and Great Western Railroad Company* (1857), pp. 1–9.

Galveston to begin on October 1, 1856, and reserving the right to stop at Sabine Pass. He proposed to pay the railroad $2,000 per year from his New Orleans–Galveston mail contract for weekly mail service via Berwick's Bay. He would pay the expenses of through freight and passengers over the railroad segment, but at 33.3 per cent discount. In addition he demanded the privilege of lowering his rates by sea if competition required (thus, implicitly, the railroad must lower theirs). In effect, Morgan offered co-operation only as long as it did not interfere with his regular routes by sea.[30]

The directors of the railroad were not pleased with the Morgan proposal but accepted it as the best available. They expressed three principal objections: First, they feared Morgan would always favor his established sea route since "every passenger over the road cost [him] $2." Second, the right to stop at Sabine Pass and the offer of only weekly service would lengthen the voyage to Galveston and thus deprive the railroad of its advantage of a shorter trip to Texas. Finally, the railroad objected to Morgan's reservation of the right to change the rates of his sea route if he desired. The directors felt this gave the shipper the means to force them out of business through a rate war. That the railroad accepted Morgan's terms indicates the New Yorker's bargaining power—power obtained by his domination of steamship service in the Gulf of Mexico.[31]

But the railroad soon found a willing and able challenger to Morgan, whose contract never went into effect. On September 18, 1856, Vanderbilt opened negotiations with the road's board of directors proposing to run steamers semiweekly, triweekly, or daily ("according to the exigencies of the trade"), from Berwick's Bay to Texas. In return, he asked for the powers to fix through rates and to receive 80 per cent of gross passage receipts, 50 per cent of freights, and 80 per cent of any mail contract negotiated.[32]

The company preferred Vanderbilt to Morgan and willingly accepted the high price of such co-operation. Morgan's contract was canceled on thirty-days' notice, and on April 1, 1857, Vanderbilt's new steamship *Galveston* (945 tons) opened service from the railroad terminus to Galveston and Indianola. By May, the Commodore had added *Opelousas*

30. Harris and Morgan to Hewes, August 7, 1856, *ibid.*, p. 29; Minute Book No. 1, Board of Directors, N.O.O. & G.W., 113–116 and Minute Book No. 1, Stockholders, N.O.O. & G.W., 140–142, N.O.O. & G.W. Records.
31. *Fifth Annual Report . . .* , pp. 5–6.
32. Minute Book No. 1, Board of Directors, N.O.O. & G.W., 123–186.

(944 tons) and had *Magnolia* (843 tons) and *Matagorda* (616 tons) under construction in New York to add to his line. *Suwanee* (494 tons) was placed on the "outside route" to Galveston in December to compete further with Morgan, and rates fell as low as $10 for cabin passage.[33]

Vanderbilt's moves in the Gulf were part of his plan to oust Morgan from the then current Nicaraguan transit war. By campaigning on a second front, the Commodore hoped to divide and conquer Morgan's opposition. The opening salvo of their Gulf conflict had been Vanderbilt's unsuccessful bids for the mail contracts in 1854. He followed with his N.O.O. & G.W. contract and in late 1857 made another try at outbidding Morgan for the Texas mail contracts which would expire in 1858. The creation of new mail routes via Berwick's Bay increased the rivalry.

Morgan's Southern Steamship Company was able to retain the "outside" New Orleans–Indianola route with no trouble. The company agreed to provide biweekly service for four years at $55,000 per annum on the following schedule: leave New Orleans every Sunday and Thursday at 8 A.M., arrive Galveston each Tuesday and Saturday by the same hour; depart Galveston for Indianola every Saturday and Tuesday at 4 P.M., arriving by noon on Sundays and Wednesdays. On the return voyage, Galveston vessels would leave Indianola each Thursday and Monday at 8 A.M., arriving within twenty-four hours. For New Orleans, vessels would depart every Friday and Tuesday at 10 A.M., arriving by 4 P.M. on Sundays and Thursdays.

Route 8502, New Orleans to Brazos St. Iago, direct, attracted more spirited competition. W. C. Templeton, agent for Vanderbilt, received the contract signed April 24, 1858, with a bid of $15,950 for bimonthly service, defeating Morgan's offer of $25,000. This was the only steamship-mail contract to Texas ever lost by the latter. Morgan laughed last, however, assuming the service in August 1858, after his final settlement with the Commodore. Under a four-year agreement, retroactive to July 1, 1858, he thereafter provided vessels from New Orleans on the first and third Tuesday and from Brazos St. Iago on the second and fourth Tuesday of each month. But the three new routes offered from Berwick's Bay to Galveston, Indianola, and Sabine Pass attracted the most intense bidding.

33. *Ibid.*, 223–273; *Tribune*, March 10, 1857; *Daily Picayune*, March 29, April 1, May 10, 18, 25, 1857; Indianola *Indianolian*, July 18, 1857; *Registers, NOLA*, V, 98, 174, 247; VI, 193–194.

The Southern Steamship Company successfully won the Brashear–Galveston mail contract signed April 24, 1858. For biweekly service via Sabine Pass from July 1 to November 1 (with an additional trip, November to July), the company would be paid $45,000. The Morgan company, sole bidders for this route, coerced the government into accepting a stop at Sabine by making a second bid of $100,000 for direct Brashear–Galveston service. This prohibitive price forced the Postmaster General to choose the cheaper but slower route via Sabine.

The Indianola route from Brashear also attracted Vanderbilt. He offered three proposals: $40,000, twice-weekly; $60,000, thrice-weekly; $70,000, for his own schedule. All of these bids were withdrawn, however, in a settlement with Morgan, who used his position as sole bidder to advantage. Offering direct, thrice-weekly service, Brashear to Indianola, at the prohibitive price of $75,000, he forced acceptance of his second bid of $45,000, for biweekly service via Galveston. Again he had been able to mold government contracts to meet his existing service.

For the biweekly Sabine route both Morgan and Vanderbilt offered service in connection with other contracts and, as described, the service was melded into Morgan's Galveston route.[34]

As implied above, Morgan and Vanderbilt settled their Gulf differences in early 1858. The Commodore had lost *Opelousas* in a collision with *Galveston* in November 1857, and on April 1, 1858, "for value received" transferred his contract with the railroad to Cornelius B. Payne and the Southern Steamship Company. The latter by July also purchased *Galveston, Magnolia, Matagorda,* and *Suwanee,* and Vanderbilt ended his try at "ruining" Charles Morgan in the Gulf.[35]

With Vanderbilt removed, Morgan negotiated a new agreement with the railroad company. Its terms well illustrate the strength of his position by 1858. He agreed to run two steamers per week from Berwick's Bay to Indianola via Galveston, and one per week to Galveston via Sabine Pass. For this service Morgan was to receive 80 per cent of gross receipts from passage, New Orleans to Galveston and Galveston to New Orleans; 50 per

34. "Contracts for Carrying the Mails, 1858," *House Exec. Docs.,* 35 Cong., 2 Sess., No. 109 (Serial 1013), 236, 244, 267–268.
35. Assignment of Contract by Vanderbilt to Payne, April 1, 1858, attached to Abrogation of Contract between N.O.O. & G.W. and Payne, July 4, 1858. Act before Selim Magner, N.A. (Orleans); *Registers, NOLA,* V, 98, 174, 247, VI, 193–194.

cent of gross freight receipts on the same route; and 100 per cent of passage and freight receipts between Galveston and Indianola. Supplies for Morgan's steamers were to be carried to Berwick by the railroad at a 50 per cent reduction and "suitable and ample wharf accommodations, store rooms and convenient fuel depots" at that terminus were to be built *at railroad expense*. Rates of passage via the combined route were to be no lower than by Morgan's "outside" line, but the latter reserved the right to reduce his "outside" fares "when necessary . . . to meet opposition." The eight-year agreement took effect on the date of cancellation of Vanderbilt's contract, July 4, 1858.[36]

Just before the Morgan–N.O.O. & G.W. contract became effective, the Southern Steamship Company was reorganized to centralize control of its expanding operations. The board of four "managers" was replaced by a single individual elected from and responsible to a seven-man board of directors. The purposes of the company were revised to read "transporting passengers and freight and mails by steamship for compensation between the Port of New Orleans and Ports in the States of Texas and Florida, and . . . other ports," the provision for investing up to one-half the company's profits in real estate omitted, and the manager's tenure governed by annual election.[37]

Cornelius B. Payne was elected manager of the reorganized company and to simplify Morgan's relations with that corporation, a procuration to Payne was signed on June 3, granting the latter

full power and authority . . . to conduct, manage and transact [Morgan's] . . . affairs in . . . Texas, or the State of Louisiana . . . [especially] in relation to the steamships or vessels belonging to him and running under the name of the Southern Steam Ship Company and all steamships or vessels . . . employed in conformity with a contract [between Morgan] . . . and the New Orleans, Opelousas, and Great Western Rail Road Company . . . to place and replace or displace any of the employees of said vessels, to collect all amounts of freight or passage money and make all settlements.[38]

36. Contract between N.O.O. & G.W. and Morgan, June 1, 1858. Act before Magner, N.A. (Orleans); Minute Book No. 1, Board of Directors, N.O.O. & G.W., 446–477, N.O.O. & G.W. Records. In comparison, similar water-rail agreements in New England were more favorable to the latter, giving railroads "approximately a third of the joint returns." Edward C. Kirkland, *Men, Cities, and Transportation: A Study in New England History, 1820–1900*, II, 142–143.

37. Amendment to Charter of the Southern Steamship Co. of New Orleans, July 1, 1858. Act before Poole, N.A. (Orleans), M.O. (Orleans) Society Book IV, 168–173 (July 5, 1858); *Daily Picayune*, July 2, 1858.

38. Procuration, Morgan to Payne, June 3, 1858. Act before Magner, N.A. (Orleans).

The Morgan railroad route to Texas, managed by Payne, opened in July 1858, advertising itself as twenty-four hours faster than the "outside" route, managed by Harris & Morgan. The trip over the "Applesauce," as the Opelousas railroad became known, began at Jackson Square in New Orleans where passengers crossed to the west bank of the Mississippi by ferry. Thence, from Algiers, the railroad ran westward to Des Allemands, Lafourche, and finally to Brashear, traversing many miles of "crocodile or alligator swamp . . . covered with water and heavy timber, and a thick undergrowth of cane, Spanish daggers and dwarf palm." From Brashear, Morgan's steamers continued down the Atchafalaya River, across the bay of the same name to the Gulf, then on to Texas.[39] The route was popular, as 16,261 passengers utilized it to Texas in 1859 and 28,783 in 1860.[40]

Actually, despite his scrupulous concern for maintaining parity between his "outside" routes and the lines via Brashear, Morgan was obviously aware of certain advantages of the latter service—particularly as the 1850s progressed. Brashear, a new, raw, railroad town, allowed the steamship line more latitude in physical facilities than did the always crowded New Orleans waterfront. Also, the railroad company pledged in the contract of June 1, 1858, to furnish at *its* expense "suitable and ample wharf accommodations" for Morgan's vessels. Moreover, at Brashear, the New Yorker could avoid the property taxes and port fees of New Orleans.[41] State taxes still had to be paid in Brashear, but one particularly irritating set of New Orleans levies could be avoided.[42]

39. *Daily Crescent*, July 1858 ff.; Thomas North, *Five Years in Texas; or, What You Did Not Hear During the War*, pp. 52–53; Thomas L. Nichols, *Forty Years of American Life*, pp. 140–141, 148–149.

40. *Ninth Annual Report of the President and Directors of the New Orleans, Opelousas, and Great Western Railroad Company* (1861), p. 20. Floods halted regular railroad service from late July to October 1858. *Sixth Annual Report . . .* (1858), p. 16.

41. The Southern Steamship Co. was assessed for New Orleans city taxes in 1857 on $223,400 "capital in business" and on $20,000 estimated annual income, "the excess over $1,000." The capital assessment was raised to $320,000 in 1858. Both sets of figures are rather low considering the corporation was capitalized at $400,000. New Orleans Real Estate Assessment Rolls (New Orleans Public Library), 1857; II, 7–8; 1858: II, 1–2. See also *Brief for Defendants: New Orleans v. Southern Steamship Co.*

42. Morgan attempted to avoid payment of state taxes on the steamship portion of his company's capital stock in 1857, arguing it was not defined as taxable property under the applicable Louisiana statute (no. 346 of 1855) but lost his case. *State v. Southern Steamship Co.*, 13 Louisiana Ann. 497 (1858).

Under a Louisiana act of March 15, 1855, the port officers of New Orleans were empowered to collect $5 (in addition to their regular fees) from every vessel arriving in that port—whether called on to perform any services or not. Morgan challenged the validity of this statute, alleging it to be an illegal regulation of commerce by a state. It seriously affected his vessels since they were regularly engaged in trade in and out of the port. But prior to the Civil War he received no relief, losing his plea in the Louisiana Supreme Court.[43] Undoubtedly this expense, added to the usual high pilotage fees on the Mississippi, was among those factors considered by Morgan and his agents in establishing the alternate Brashear connection for their steamship company.

Although organized to give corporate form to Morgan's lines between New Orleans and Texas, the Southern Steamship Company also opened a new Morgan route. In September 1856 when the original contractors failed to perform service, Morgan had assumed a contract to provide biweekly mail service between New Orleans and Key West. For the remaining three years of its duration he had received $70,000 per annum for service via Pensacola, Apalachicola, St. Marks, Cedar Key, Tampa, and Manatee. On June 11, 1859, through the Southern Steamship Company, Morgan renewed the four-year contract at $59,000 per annum, adding Key West to his growing list of regular ports of call.[44]

Thus 1860 found Charles Morgan operating six regular steamship lines in the Gulf through his agents Harris and Morgan or through the Southern Steamship Company managed by Payne: New Orleans to Galveston and Indianola (twice-weekly); New Orleans to Indianola and Brazos St. Iago (fortnightly); New Orleans to Vera Cruz (twice-monthly); New Orleans to Key West (twice-monthly); Brashear to Galveston and Indianola (twice-weekly, July 1 to November 1; thrice-weekly otherwise); Brashear to Sabine Pass and Galveston (every third trip in conjunction with the preceding route).[45]

43. *Master and Wardens of Port of New Orleans v. Charles Morgan,* 14 Louisiana Ann. 595 (1859). This decision reversed by *Southern Steamship Co. v. Master and Wardens of Port of New Orleans,* 6 Wallace (U.S.) 31 (1867).

44. "Contracts for Carrying the Mails, 1853," *House Exec. Docs.,* 33 Cong., 1 Sess., No. 125 (Serial 735), 688; *ibid.,* 1859, *House Exec. Docs.,* 36 Cong., 1 Sess., No. 86 (Serial 1057), 291; "Report of the Postmaster General, 1856" (Serial 876), 862; *ibid.,* 1857 (Serial 921), 1081; *ibid.,* 1858 (Serial 977), 777; "Fines and Deductions, Mail Contractors, 1857" (Serial 956), 21; *Daily Picayune,* June 3, 1857.

45. *Galveston Directory for 1856–7,* p. 43; *Gardner's New Orleans Directory* (1858), p. 389; *Texas Almanac for 1860,* p. 306; *Galveston Directory for*

Such extensive service dictated skillful deployment of vessels, and Morgan and his agents continued their well-established methods of rotation and replacement of steamships. Especially were they pressed to replace three large vessels lost in 1856 and 1857. *Nautilus* was wrecked on Last Isle (L'ile Dernière) in the famous hurricane of August 10, 1856, with twenty fatalities. *Perseverance* burned to the waterline at Indianola on October 3, 1856, fortunately without casualties. Far more serious was the explosion of *Louisiana* in Galveston Bay, May 31, 1857, in which sixty-six persons perished. Galveston's lack of any organized rescue service increased the toll of lives. Shocked by the tragedy, the city subsequently organized the Galveston Life Boat Association to aid in future emergencies. For Morgan, however, each vessel was a severe loss, as all were self-insured.[46]

To replace these vessels Morgan purchased *Atlantic* (623 tons) and *Calhoun* (508 tons) in October 1856 and placed them in Gulf service. His purchase from Vanderbilt of *Galveston, Suwanee, Magnolia,* and *Matagorda* has been noted, yet because of conflicting schedules or minor accidents he was occasionally forced to charter additional vessels to maintain his lines, vessels such as the schooners *Charity* and *Brazos,* or the steamer *Robert Waterman.*[47]

In addition to their increased responsibilities in ship deployment, maintenance, and replacement, Morgan's agents also worked constantly to improve their access to Gulf ports and to secure more convenient repair arrangements in the South. In the 1850s they were successful in strengthening their position in both Galveston and New Orleans.

In the 1830s and 1840s, waterfront facilities in Galveston were all privately owned and operated by a score of individual wharf and warehouse companies and, seeking comparative advantage, Morgan dealt with all at one time or another. On the whole, however, he took things in Galveston pretty much as "given." By the late 1850s things were changing.

On February 4, 1854, the Galveston Wharf and Cotton Press Company was chartered for the express purpose of consolidating all Galveston

1859–60, p. 83; *Texas State Register,* p. 46; Indianola *Courier,* November 3, 1860.

46. *Daily Picayune,* August 14–25, October 12, 1856, June 2, 1857; *Galveston Directory for 1859–60,* p. 47; Holdcamper (ed.), *op. cit.,* pp. 237, 242, 247.

47. *Daily Picayune,* October 8, 1856, July 7, 1857; *Registers, NOLA,* V, 22, 23, 37, 43.

wharves under common, quasi-public ownership and control. One third of the stock of this new company was taken by the city and the remainder by private investors. Over the next two decades, the company achieved its goal and absorbed all of the wharves and waterfront warehouses in the port area.[48]

The wharf company was to become Charles Morgan's nemesis in the 1870s, but throughout the 1850s his relations with it remained amicable. Morgan was a desirable customer, and as long as the wharf company lacked a monopoly of the waterfront, he was able to secure preferential treatment. In return for regular use of the company's facilities, Morgan, on November 7, 1858, received "(for a nominal sum) the exclusive privilege of landing at the front of Central Wharf." He was also given permission to build a warehouse on the wharf, but the wharf company retained its right "of collecting wharfage on all articles landed or shipped by such vessels as may occupy the front, or any other part of said Central Wharf." Goods placed in the Morgan warehouse would be subject to storage charges payable to the wharf company only if they remained there overnight.[49]

While Morgan thus agreed to pay wharfage *in principle*, in practice the rates he paid were usually below those charged others and were subject to rebate—particularly after Morgan's commission agent in Galveston, E. B. Nichols, became president of the wharf company in 1859. There is no doubt that the wharf company coddled the Morgan Line prior to the Civil War. On April 13, 1861, their relations were formalized by an agreement in which the company was to charge the line only one half the "regular" wharfage rate on such freight as the steamers "may land on the wharf for reshipment to the West" and none at all on "freight transferred from one boat to another" (as, say, from the New Orleans boat to the Indianola boat).[50] Since the vast proportion of Morgan's freight business at Galveston *was* in transit either west or south, the wharf company's concessions to him were substantial indeed. Of course, war soon interrupted all arrangements made.

48. "Historical History of the Galveston Wharf Company" (MS in possession of The Galveston Wharves, Galveston, Texas); Minute Books Nos. 1–4, Board of Directors and Stockholders, Galveston Wharf Co., 1854–1926 (*ibid.*).
49. Minute Book No. 1, Board of Directors, Galveston Wharf Co., 23–24, 30–31, 36–37.
50. *Ibid.*, p. 73.

In New Orleans, the efforts of the Morgan agents were directed toward better repair facilities and improved service and maintenance of the ships of the line. Members of the Southern Steamship Company were among the leading incorporators of the Louisiana Dry Dock Company No. 2, formed in April 1856. This corporation, located in Algiers across the Mississippi from New Orleans, thereafter was able to provide shipyard service for Morgan steamers at 10 per cent below prices charged other patrons.[51]

Of more lasting importance, however, during this period of physical expansion in the late 1850s, was the initial employment of Harlan and Hollingsworth and Company of Wilmington, Delaware—the firm which built most of his later steamers.[52] Between 1856 and 1861 Harlan's launched four steamships for the New Yorker: *General Rusk* (417 tons), *Arizona* (578 tons), *Austin* (603 tons), and *William G. Hewes* (747 tons). These vessels varied in length from *Austin*'s 198 feet to *Hewes*'s 233; in beam from *Rusk*'s 25 feet, 3 inches to *Austin*'s 35; in draught from 8 feet, 6 inches to 16 feet, 8 inches. All had compartmentalized iron hulls and single vertical-beam engines. *Hewes,* the largest, cost about $150,000, and her 50-inch-diameter cylindrical engine consumed about 1,680 pounds of coal per hour in turning her 30-foot iron paddlewheels. The performance of these iron steamers convinced Morgan of their advantages of strength, durability, and safety from fire, and with few exceptions, Harlan's built all of his future steamships of similar design.[53]

Thus in the 1850s the Morgan Line continued its dominant role in the coasting trade of the Gulf. A healthy, if traditional, rival in the person of Vanderbilt was overcome, and the newer threat of railroad competition was emasculated. Morgan and his managers expanded his line and broadened its capital base through newer and larger steamships, increased government service, and partial incorporation.

51. Charter of the Louisiana Dry Dock Co., No. 2, April 3, 1856. Act before Richard Brenan, N.A. (Orleans), M.O. (Orleans), Society Book III, 422 (May 16, 1856). Of 80 shares of $1,000 each, Harris and Morgan subscribed for 15; Payne for 5; Hart for 5.
52. *Semi-Centennial Memoir of the Harlan & Hollingsworth Company,* pp. 244–260, 376–389.
53. *Daily Picayune,* April 1, 1857; New Orleans *True Delta,* January 30, 1861; Plans of Vessels Built by Harlan and Hollingsworth, 1849–1896 (Mariners Museum, Newport News, Va.), III, 5; "Particulars of the Steamer Wm. G. Hewes," *Journal of the Franklin Institute,* N.S., XLI (April 1861), 270.

Probably, Morgan would have been unable to raise the capital necessary for expansion without the Southern Steamship Company, since his personal investments were divided among New York, Nicaragua, Mexico, and the Gulf. Yet through Harris, Henry Morgan, and Payne, Morgan kept close rein on the partnership and the corporation he had created. Payne served as liaison between Morgan and the company until April 24, 1860, when he was replaced (because of poor health) by Harris. The latter, granted "full power of authority" by Morgan "to conduct, manage and transact his affairs in the States of Louisiana or Texas . . . [especially] in relation to the steamships or vessels belonging to him and running to or from New Orleans and Brashear," continued the operation of the Morgan Line through the decade of the 1860s.[54]

Yet the carefully constructed and vigilantly defended shipping empire of Charles Morgan was soon to suffer stresses beyond the control of its creator. The era of the Civil War affected him as personally as it did any businessman of his day.

54. Abrogation of Power, Morgan to Payne, April 24, 1860. Act before Magner, N.A. (Orleans) ; Procuration, Morgan to Harris, April 24, 1860. *Ibid.*

PART III

"Who stood to gain?"

Cicero, *Pro Milone.*

6

THE ERA OF THE CIVIL WAR

CHARLES MORGAN entered the 1860s in his sixty-fourth year, advancing in age and wealth, yet retaining many of the traits of the young New York merchant of years before. His personal vigor showed no diminution and his avoidance of the political and social arenas remained steadfast. As always, his family and his ships consumed the bulk of his time and affection.

But Morgan's family life brought him sadness as well as joy in the 1850s and 1860s. His two youngest children married in 1853 and 1854—Maria Louise, barely twenty-one, to a promising young New York shipping agent, Charles A. Whitney; Henry to the socially prominent Miss Laura Malard of New Orleans—and by 1860 these unions had blessed Morgan with five more grandchildren. Yet he felt keenly the death of his beloved eldest child Emily Ann Harris in 1856, and his grief was compounded by the loss of his ten-year-old grandson Chapman in 1861, his eldest son Charles and his eighteen-year-old granddaughter Frances Louise Quintard in 1863.

His greatest sorrow, however, had come at the dawn of his most prosperous years. In 1850, Emily, Morgan's wife for twenty-three years, died. She did not live to know her youngest children's spouses or eight of her twelve grandchildren.[1]

1. Morgan's grandchildren were: Emily Frances Harris (1840), Charles Morgan Harris (1845), Frances Louise Quintard (1845), James W. Quintard (1848), Chapman Harris Morgan (1851), Richard Jessup Morgan (1852), Laura Adele Quintard (1852), Charles Morgan Whitney (1854), Laura Louise Morgan (1855), George Quintard Whitney (1857), Montaigu Morgan (1858), and William Henry Morgan (1860). Morgan *Genealogy*, pp. 154–155, 211, 281.

Fifty-five years old at Emily's death, Morgan was a widower for less than a year. The object of his almost immediate attention was Miss Mary Jane Sexton, a native New Yorker then in her early twenties. Short and buxom, Miss Sexton differed markedly from the angular austerity of Emily Reeves Morgan. The daughter of a bankrupt merchant, she had been educated at her maternal grandfather's expense in several of New York's better schools for young ladies and had taught French and mathematics to Morgan's youngest daughter at Dr. Schroeder's School. A quiet woman, Mary Jane Sexton's youthful interests seemed restricted to languages, flowers, and art, and to the untutored, wealthy, and widowed father of her student Mary Louise Morgan.

Morgan made young Miss Sexton his second wife on June 24, 1851, and temporarily moved her into a rented house at 22nd Street and 4th Avenue pending completion of the residence which the two occupied from 1852 to their deaths—an imposing mansion at 7 East 26th Street, fronting on Madison Square. From these surroundings, Charles Morgan faced the trying years of the 1860s.[2]

Indeed, although he sought political anonymity throughout his life, Morgan found himself directly involved in the growing sectional crisis. As a northerner with extensive investments in the southern states, he was inevitably affected. The dual problem of maintaining profitable returns yet protecting his investment throughout the war years taxed his business acumen to the limit.

Morgan's position on the sectional politics of his lifetime is difficult to document but merits speculation on available evidence. His lack of participation in anti-Texas demonstrations sponsored by fellow New York businessmen, the numerous services performed for that republic by Morgan's agents and captains, and his long economic involvement in the Texas nation suggest sympathy for such southern-expansionist causes as the Texas Revolution and the annexation of that territory to the United States.[3]

Yet Texas annexation cost him money. Morgan was one of those

2. New York *Times*, March 12, 1886; New York *Sun*, November 28, 1885.
3. Foner, *Business & Slavery*, pp. 16–19; James Reed & Co. to Henry Smith, August 4, 1837, and July 21, 1838, William Bryan to James H. Starr, March 26, April 10, May 16, June 6, 1840, William Fields to Commissioner of Revenue, May 18, 1841, Seymour V. Connor and Virginia H. Taylor (editors), *Texas Treasury Papers: Letters Received in the Treasury Department of the Republic of Texas, 1836–1846*, I, 48, 119–120; II, 425–426, 441, 472–473, 498–499, 668.

businessmen who, holding depreciated Texas treasury notes, were allowed to present claims under a state legislative act of March 20, 1848. These notes had come to him as passage and freight moneys but had decreased in value as the fortunes of the Republic waned. He registered a claim of $21,569, but no record of satisfaction of any part of this claim has been found.[4]

Morgan was not, however, among those Texas bondholders reimbursed by the federal government after 1856 as provided for in the Boundary Act of 1850, and he took no discernible part in the debate over that portion of the Compromise of 1850. But the financial returns of his participation in the Mexican War and of his isthmian "fancies" clearly linked him with the course of Manifest Destiny—unlike most of his New York mercantile brethren.[5]

Perhaps only chance accounts for Morgan's affinity for expansionism. His lines constituted the most southerly link in America's Atlantic coastwise chain of trade. His vessels, of all America's vessels on the western oceans, were most directly in contact with the frontier and most receptive to its whims. Though a New Yorker, Morgan among all his shipping fellows could most logically be expected to hearken to expansionistic sentiment.

More difficult to understand, however, for a permanent resident of New York City who spent only "a portion of the season"[6] in the South, Morgan was a more-than-casual slaveholder. Between 1846 (or earlier) and 1861, he owned at least thirty-one slaves and condoned ownership of a like number by his New Orleans agents Harris, Morgan, and Payne. Most of these Negroes were used as stevedores, deckhands, or chambermaids on Morgan's steamers, but the moral and political implications of these chattels would again seem to tie their owner closer to the southern rather than the northern democracy (see Appendix 3).

One further hint of Morgan's Democratic persuasion derives from his participation in government contract work. Although he had held postal

4. J. T. Doswell to Williams, September 6, 1849, Samuel May Williams Papers.
5. William M. Gouge, *The Fiscal History of Texas*, pp. 158–159, 167–169, 179; Holman Hamilton, "Texas Bonds and Northern Profits: A Study in Compromise, Investment, and Lobby Influence," *Mississippi Valley Historical Review*, XLIII (March 1957), 579–594; Register of Texas Debt Warrants, 1856–1861 (Record Group 39, National Archives); Untitled Workbook Pertaining to the Texas Debt of 1850 (Record Group 56, National Archives); Foner, *op. cit.*, p. 121.
6. New Orleans *Daily Picayune*, March 23, 1866.

and military contracts under both Democratic and Whig administrations, the conduct of one Morgan company regarding a series of important naval contracts in the 1850s suggests partisanship.

On July 26, 1858, Secretary of the Navy Isaac Toucey invited sealed proposals for the construction and installation of engines and machinery for seven of the eight steam sloops-of-war authorized by congressional act of June 12, 1858. Fourteen bidders submitted forty-four bids on the seven projects including seven from the Morgan Iron Works—the latter totaling $903,500. But in the ultimate allocation of jobs the Morgan firm secured the contract to construct machinery for only one of the vessels.[7] By agreement signed October 28, 1858, "George W. Quintard and Charles A. Whitney . . . doing business under the firm of Quintard & Whitney as principals, and Charles Morgan and Henry R. Morgan . . . as sureties of the first part," contracted to deliver and install appropriate machinery as per specifications within ten months in the sloop-of-war then building in Pensacola, Florida—their price to total $120,000 as proposed.[8] This was the first government construction contract ever won by the works, but created no great stir outside the firm until 1859.

On January 12, 1859, Daniel B. Allen, the son-in-law of Cornelius Vanderbilt and president of the Allaire Works—one of the unsuccessful bidders on the contracts—in a letter to Representative John Sherman of Ohio, requested a congressional investigation of the letting of these jobs and of other alleged malpractices in the Navy Department. Allen (an old-time Whig, as was Vanderbilt, the chief stockholder in the Allaire Works) charged the contracts had not been let to the lowest bidder (there was an aggregate difference of $82,000 over the seven low bids) and that Secretary Toucey, with the knowledge and prompting of President James Buchanan, had favored only Democratic firms. He also charged the existence of a letter from the President to the Morgan Iron Works suggesting a partisan subcontractor.[9]

Testimony on these charges was heard between January 20 and Febru-

7. Advertisement of Navy Dept., July 26, 1858, Quintard & Whitney by Miers Corryell to Toucey, September 7, 1858, Toucey to Morgan Iron Works, October 2, 1858, "Report of the Select Committee on Naval Contracts and Expenditures," *House Reports*, 35 Cong., 2 Sess., No. 184 (Serial 1019), Pt. III, 252–254, 257–258, 277.

8. Contract between Quintard, Whitney, Morgan, and Morgan and Toucey for U.S., October 28, 1858, *ibid.*, Pt. III, 273–276.

9. Allen to Sherman, January 12, 1859, *ibid.*, pp. 98–99; "Views of the Minority," *ibid.*, pp. 78–89.

ary 24, 1859, by a Select Committee on Naval Contracts and Expenditures of the House, headed by Sherman. Dr. William Cockcroft, proprietor of the Franklin Iron Works of New York, and the man who was alleged to have told Allen of Buchanan's letter to George W. Quintard, denied under oath that he had seen it and refused to disclose the gist of his conversation with Quintard on the matter. Cockcroft asked to be excused on the grounds that he now held the disputed subcontract from Quintard. Quintard and Miers Corryell, the superintendent of the Morgan Iron Works, testified that, although they were approached by private individuals suggesting Democratic subcontractors, no public official had ever made any overtures to them, and, in any case, the subcontract had not been let to the suggested firm.[10]

Unable to resolve the voluminous and conflicting testimony, the committee issued majority and minority reports—the former, written by Thomas S. Bocock (Dem., Va.), William S. Groesbeck (Dem., Ohio), and Charles Ready (Whig, Tenn.), discounting the charges against the firms and against Buchanan and Toucey; the latter, written by Chairman John Sherman (Rep., Ohio) and David Ritchie (Rep., Pa.), criticizing and censuring the conduct of the President and the Secretary.[11]

The testimony of Corryell and Quintard, although never explicit, seems to imply more familiarity with Democratic patronage desires than with Whig or Republican, but definitely attests to their firm's former lack of success in securing construction contracts from the government:[12]

Question: Do you know of any inducements held out by you or any of your firm to induce the giving of this Pensacola contract to you?
Answer: There were no inducements held out; on the contrary, it was very much to our surprise that we got the award; we paid no attention whatever to the matter after we delivered the bids and drawings.
Question: Why were you surprised?
Answer: We had been previously five or six times before the department with good drawings and had received no encouragement; but as we had been solicited, as was customary, to give in a bid, we did so merely as a matter of principle.

10. Testimony of Allen, February 9–10, 1859, of James Murphy, February 16, 1859, of Cockcroft, January 26, 1859, of Corryell, January 29, 1859, and of Quintard, January 31, 1859, *ibid.*, Pt. III, 75, 79, 99–100, 15–18, 21–23, 36–42. The testimony must be read in this inverted order for understanding of the charges and denials.
11. "Report," *ibid.*, pp. 1–54; "Views of the Minority," *ibid.*, pp. 55–89.
12. Testimony of Corryell, January 29, 1859, *ibid.*, Pt. III, 24.

When asked the same questions, Quintard answered: "I had no more idea of getting one of these contracts than you have. It is the first work we have ever got from the government. We have generally bid, but have never been successful before." Although not reflected in the majority report, the testimony of Allen and the minority opinion still imply that Morgan's firm was among those recipients of Democratic favoritism.[13]

But it was in the Gulf, not in Washington, that the test of Morgan's politics came. As the lower South seceded in early 1861, and the majority of New York merchants lobbied to prevent further secession and to entice the departed states back with compromise, Morgan was content to maintain his regular routes and augment civilian service with income derived from increased military activity in the Gulf.[14] Indeed, although not without denials by his agent, Morgan's vessels were made available to both secessionist and union forces. One example of this opportunism should suffice.

On February 4, 1861, three days after the Texas ordinance of secession was adopted, E. B. Nichols, Morgan's agent at Galveston, was appointed commissioner and financial representative of the seceded state. Nichols was ordered to secure funds and transportation for the movement of Colonel John S. Ford's command from Galveston to Brazos St. Iago to capture Federal encampments and supplies in the lower Rio Grande Valley.[15] Nichols secured the required funds in New Orleans and chartered Morgan's *General Rusk* for transportation. For her use the Southern Steamship Company was to receive $5,000 for ten days and $500 per day thereafter. *Rusk* was used by the Texas troops from February 16 to March 15 in their successful capture of Brazos St. Iago—at a fee (including fuel) of $14,750 to Morgan's company. Upon completion of her charter to the secessionist forces, *Rusk* was chartered on the spot for

13. Testimony of Quintard, February 1, 1859, *ibid.*, Pt. III, 43. Morgan's son-in-law Charles A. Whitney was well known in Washington, having in his younger days been private secretary to Senator Lewis Cass, now Buchanan's Secretary of State. *In Memoriam: Charles A. Whitney*, p. 18.

14. New Orleans *Daily Delta*, November 14, 20, December 4, 1860; *Daily Picayune*, February 8, 20, 25, 28, March 3, 7, 16, 22, 1861; "Contracts, War Department, 1860," *House Exec. Docs.*, 36 Cong., 2 Sess., No. 47 (Serial 1099), 23; *ibid.*, 1861, *House Exec. Docs.*, 37 Cong., 2 Sess., No. 101 (Serial 1136), 18; Foner, *op. cit.*, pp. 232 ff.

15. O. M. Roberts to Nichols, February 4, 1861, in William Winkler (editor), *Journal of the Secession Convention of Texas, 1861*, pp. 317–319; Committee on Public Safety to Ford, February 5, 1861, *ibid.*, pp. 321–324.

$12,500 by the defeated Federal commander at Brazos St. Iago to evacuate his troops to Key West![16] Morgan's son-in-law and New Orleans agent, Israel C. Harris, on hearing of the latter charter, hoped it would cast no "imputations . . . upon my fealty to the South," but accepted the contract and its retainer.[17]

The correspondence concerning these transactions produced the most explicit reference to Charles Morgan's opinion of the secession crisis. Informing Harris of the failure of the scheduled Morgan vessel to honor a proclamation of martial law in Brazos St. Iago by calling on the port commander, Nichols wrote:

but for my knowledge of your political sentiments and those of my much esteemed friend Mr. Morgan and your stockholders, your handsome treatment to me as the agent of Texas, and the fact that the *Arizona* comes to us with the flag of Louisiana at her main . . . I should feel bound to take possession of her.[18]

Morgan's acquiescence in these decisions is unquestionable, for he was in the Gulf area as late as April 5, 1861, inspecting his properties and receiving public testimonials on his behalf in Texas ports.[19] He was returning home to New York when the attack on Fort Sumter crystallized southern efforts at rebellion. President Lincoln declared a blockade of southern ports from South Carolina to Texas on April 19; the embargo had been partially effected off New Orleans and Mobile by May 26; off Galveston by July 2. The challenge of the Confederacy had been accepted.

War brought immediate problems to Morgan—a northerner with southern investments. On April 28, 1861, Governor Thomas O. Moore of Louisiana ordered seizure of *Tennessee, Texas,* and *William G. Hewes* at New Orleans as property belonging to a northern enemy. The vessels were allowed to continue some service but Louisiana troops were stationed on board "to see that [each steamer] . . . makes sure of getting to Texas and returns to this port." Texas troops took the same precautions at

16. Agreement between State of Texas and Southern Steamship Co. of New Orleans, February 13, 1861, Nichols to Harris, March 5, 15, 1861, Harris to Nichols, March 18, 1861, *ibid.,* 351–352, 359–360, 361–362; "Contracts, War Department, 1861" (Serial 1136), 18.
17. Nichols to Harris, March 5, 15, 1861, Harris to Nichols, March 18, 1861, Winkler (ed.), *op. cit.,* pp. 359–362.
18. *Ibid.*
19. New Orleans *Commercial Bulletin,* April 5, 1861.

Galveston. The New Orleans press and arguments presented to the Confederate States Congress meeting in Montgomery, Alabama, soon demonstrated to Governor Moore, however, that Morgan had recently sold the vessels to Israel C. Harris as president and manager of the Southern Steamship Company. Presumably these statements refer to Harris's *de facto* control already exercised over the vessels because of Morgan's procuration to him dated April 24, 1860. Harris and the stockholders pointed out that, except for Morgan's shares, theirs was a southern-owned company immune from such seizure. On orders from the Montgomery Congress, the vessels were released and returned to regular service by May 12.[20]

Despite hostilities, Morgan thus committed himself to retaining his vessels in the Gulf, to be managed by his openly Confederate son-in-law. Harris was an ardent supporter of Confederate loan drives and of the raising of militia companies, and he identified the Morgan lines with these sympathies. But while attuned to southern aspirations, Morgan and the Southern Steamship Company were more interested in maintaining regular service. Their desire is demonstrated by their lengthy protests over further seizures of their vessels. On May 21, 1861, General Sidney Sherman, the Confederate commander at Galveston, seized *General Rusk* and *Orizaba*. Sherman intended to use the vessels to assist in the capture of Federal troops at Indianola, a plan endorsed by Lieutenant Governor Edward Clark, but encountered a vigorous merchants' protest led by E. B. Nichols. Assured of the wish of Morgan to continue regular Gulf service, Sherman eventually compromised by retaining *General Rusk* and allowing other Morgan vessels to trade freely.[21]

As 1861 progressed, however, Morgan's attitude toward keeping his vessels in southern waters seems to have changed. In the early fall, after her release by the Galveston authorities, *Orizaba* cleared that port for New Orleans. Once at sea, however, the captain (acting, he said, under

20. *Commercial Bulletin*, April 27, 29, 1861; New Orleans *True Delta*, April 30, 1861; New Orleans *Daily Crescent*, May 1, 1861; *Daily Picayune*, May 9, 12, 1861; *Journal of the Congress of the Confederate States of America, 1861–1865*, I, 431.

21. Protest of Leon Smith, Master of *General Rusk*, May 21, 1861, Clark to Sherman, May 23, 1861, William T. Austin by order of Sherman to Nichols, May 27, 1861, Protest of Nichols, *et al.*, [May] 28, 1861, Sidney Sherman Papers (Rosenberg Library, Galveston, Texas); John A. Kennedy to William H. Seward, September 15, 1861, *The War of the Rebellion: A Compilation of the Official Records of the Union and Confederate Armies*, Ser. II, Vol. II, 67.

sealed orders from "Mr. Morgan") headed for Key West and New York. The first mate and several prosouthern passengers thwarted the plan, and the steamer was run into Berwick's Bay and turned over to Confederate authorities.[22]

It would appear that the few attractions of keeping vessels in southern waters had disappeared by late 1861. The declaration of hostilities removed the possibility of American-flag vessels benefiting from the lower Confederate tariff. Prior to March 1, when the provisional Confederate government resurrected the tariff schedules of 1857, and April 1, when the high Morill rates became effective in northern waters, there had been considerable expectation that if the South were allowed to secede peaceably, her lower tariff would divert European commerce to her ports. Among southerners and shipowners serving them, this seemed an attractive prospect, but their hope was short lived as the blockade was declared.[23]

U.S. Mail contracts were also nullified on May 31, 1861, and the threat of expensive fines for nonperformance of those contracts thereby ended. Furthermore, the most lucrative government charter work was to be had in the New York area, not from the infant Confederate States.[24] As war became a reality, any vessel in southern waters was liable to be pressed into service by the Confederate states or nation or, if not, face a constricting Federal blockade. As early as June 1861 three Morgan vessels were examined by the Confederacy to determine their potentialities as gunboats. *Mexico* and *Galveston* were declared unfit and *Tennessee* recommended for use only as an ocean dispatch vessel. While no action was taken at that time, Morgan should have recognized the inevitable. But he waited too long. By 1862 the Federal blockade of New Orleans was effective, and Morgan's ships lay idle at the city's wharves.[25]

The inevitable came on January 16, 1862, when General Mansfield

22. Kennedy to Seward, September 15, 1861, *War of the Rebellion, ibid.*

23. Foner, *op. cit.*, pp. 261–296.

24. E. Merton Coulter, *The Confederate States of America, 1861–1865*, pp. 124–125. Vanderbilt and others were chartering their vessels indefinitely for $1,000–$3,000 per day. "Contracts, War Department, 1861," (Serial 1136), *passim*; Harry J. Carman and Reinhard H. Luthin, *Lincoln and the Patronage*, pp. 144–147.

25. "Report of Board Appointed to Examine Vessels with a View to Their Conversion into Gunboats," June 27, 1861, *Official Records of the Union and Confederate Navies in the War of the Rebellion*, Ser. I, Vol. XVI, 828–829; *Commercial Bulletin*, July 18, 1861.

Lovell, Confederate commander at New Orleans, seized (under the authority of Secretary of War Judah P. Benjamin), the following vessels of the Southern Steamship Company: *Mexico, Texas, Orizaba, Charles Morgan, Arizona, William G. Hewes, Atlantic, Austin, Magnolia,* and *Matagorda. Tennessee* and *Calhoun* had been sold to private parties shortly before. Compensation for the seizures was authorized, but no record of payment has been found. Thus with one sweep Charles Morgan lost his remaining Gulf fleet. The Southern Steamship Company continued to exist in name until 1863, when its business was liquidated.[26]

During the Civil War, the former Morgan liners saw a variety of service. *Mexico* became C.S.S. *General Bragg,* assigned to the Mississippi River Defense Fleet, but was captured off Memphis, Tennessee, June 6, 1862. She finished the war as U.S.S. *General Bragg,* seeing action in the Vicksburg campaign and against the Confederate ram *Arkansas.* The disposition of *Texas* is unknown, but *Calhoun* became the Confederacy's first privateer. Later captured at New Orleans, she was used in the Federal Western Gulf Blockading Squadron.[27]

Charles Morgan, renamed *Governor Moore* of the Louisiana State Navy, participated in the battles below New Orleans, ramming and sinking U.S.S. *Varuna.* The federal fleet sank *Governor Moore* and *General Quitman,* formerly Morgan's *Orizaba,* the same day, April 24, 1862. After many months of attempting to run the blockade, *Tennessee* was captured at her New Orleans wharf on the fall of that city in May 1862 and afterward, as U.S.S. *Tennessee,* saw service in the Western Gulf Blockading Squadron. *Magnolia* was captured while running the blockade off Mobile, February 19, 1862. She then saw extensive action with the Eastern Gulf Blockading Squadron as U.S.S. *Magnolia.*[28]

Arizona, Atlantic, William G. Hewes, Austin, and *Matagorda* each made several successful blockade-runs to Havana and Nassau, but all were eventually captured. *Arizona* (C.S.S. *Caroline*) was taken under English colors October 28, 1862, off Mobile. Renamed U.S.S. *Arizona*

26. Benjamin to Lovell, January 14, 1862, Lovell to Benjamin, January 16, 1862, *Records of Union and Confederate Navies,* Ser. I, Vol. XVII, 159–160; Dissolution of Southern Steamship Co. of New Orleans, May 13, 1863. Act before Magner, N.A. (Orleans); M.O. (Orleans) Society Book V, 1 (May 13, 1863).

27. *Records of Union and Confederate Navies,* Ser. I, Vol. XXIII, 120–123, 140–141, 283–285, 296–297; William M. Robinson, Jr., *The Confederate Privateers,* pp. 37– 46, 253–254.

28. *Records of Union and Confederate Navies,* Ser. I, Vols. XVIII, 304–309, XVII, 137–141, 337–339, 449–452; XVIII, 155–159; XIX, 306–307.

and assigned to the Western Gulf Squadron, she was destroyed by fire near New Orleans in 1865. *Ella and Annie* (formerly *William G. Hewes*) was captured off Wilmington, North Carolina, November 9, 1863. Recommissioned as U.S.S. *Malvern*, she became the flagship of Admiral David D. Porter's North Atlantic Blockading Squadron.[29]

Austin (C.S.S. *Donegal*) was captured off Mobile June 6, 1864, and finished the war as U.S.S. *Donegal*. After considerable success as a blockade-runner, *Matagorda* was captured under the name *Alice*, September 10, 1864—ironically by U.S.S. *Magnolia*, her former sister-ship. Early in the war on May 14, 1861, Federal forces at Key West seized *Suwanee*, which was subsequently used as a mail steamer by the North Atlantic Squadron, while *General Rusk* was sunk by U.S.S. *Montgomery* October 8, 1862, in the harbor of Mariano, Cuba.[30]

Although the war deprived Morgan of his Gulf steamers and trades, he adapted profitably. He was able to capitalize on existing investments in the North as well as to seek out new profits for the duration. A vigorous construction program at Harlan and Hollingsworth's between 1862 and 1864 produced *St. Mary* (678 tons), *Crescent* (678 tons), *Clinton* (721 tons), *Frances* (679 tons), and *Louise* (1,351 tons). Through heavy federal charter work (see Table 6.1), these vessels became instantaneous money-makers and provided steady wartime profits for their owner.[31]

The larger share of Morgan's income during the Civil War, however, came from his ownership of the Morgan Iron Works. Under George Quintard's aggressive management, that firm had become one of America's foremost manufacturers of marine steam engines. Its specialty was medium-sized machinery for coastal and river craft, and its engines were widely used in the United States and by American steamship companies in China. From 1850 through 1860, the works had built engines for

29. *Ibid.*, Ser. I, Vols. IX, 291–296, XVII, 212–213; XIX, 208, 321–333; Ser. II, Vol. I, 38, 133; Marcus W. Price, "Ships that Tested the Blockade of the Gulf Ports, 1861–1865," *American Neptune*, XI (October 1951), 276, 280–283, 285–286, 288–289, XII (January 1952), 52–57, 59, XII (April 1952), 154–155, 158–159, XII (July 1952), 229–232.

30. *Ibid.*, Ser. I, Vols. IV, 184; VI, 586; XVII, 446–447, 755–756; XIX, 269–286; XXI, 321; Ser. II, Vol. I, 75.

31. In addition to Vessel Charter Files, Quartermaster General, U.S. Army, RG 92, National Archives, see: "Vessels Bought, Sold and Chartered by the United States, April 1861–July 1868," *House Exec. Docs.*, 40 Cong., 2 Sess., No. 337 (Serial 1346), 24, 58, 92, 141; Plans of Vessels Built by Harlan and Hollingsworth, IV, 13; *Scientific American*, VII, N.S. (August 16, 1862), 99; Samuel W. Stanton, *American Steam Vessels*, pp. 176–177.

forty-nine merchant steamers, (see Appendix 2) and it continued its output during the war years, completing machinery for twenty-three more merchantmen from 1861 through 1865.

The firm added military contracts to this civilian activity. From 1858 through 1866, the works produced the machinery for thirteen vessels of the Union navy and for one Italian man-of-war. In addition, the firm completely constructed the double-turret monitor U.S.S. *Onondaga*. Gross income from these naval construction contracts exceeded $2,275,000 (see Table 6.2).

Morgan prospered from all these northern activities, and incredibly, despite his heavy Federal charters and construction contracts, he opportunistically aided the South as well. *Frances* made at least four successful blockade runs between Havana and Gulf ports from September 1864 through the following spring. She and her owner were well known to Federal authorities, but she was never captured and earned over three times her construction price of $120,000.[32]

From the available evidence, Morgan thus appears to have played both sides of the war willingly and skilfully and to have suffered no diminution of income. Indeed, he seems to have made sizable profits which he speedily reinvested in both old and new enterprises. In the late 1860s he concerned himself with four major projects: a brace of Mexican speculations; the Morgan Iron Works; a steamship line from New York to Charleston; and the reactivation and expansion of his Gulf lines. In each case he followed his custom of working with and through his son and sons-in-law; with all he was generous with capital, credit, and advice. As always, however, he reserved the bulk of his investment and his personal attention for his Gulf services.

Morgan's Mexican ventures were a pair of steamship lines which owed their birth and their death to the career of Maximilian of Austria as "Emperor of Mexico." In part they reflected the Emperor's real interest in the economic development of his nation and as such anticipated the later opening of Mexico to American investment under the republic of Porfirio Diaz.[33] In equal part, however, the lines reflected the zeal of

32. Plans of Vessels Built by Harlan and Hollingsworth, IV, 13; Price, "Ships that Tested the Blockade of the Gulf Ports, 1861–1865," *American Neptune*, XI (October 1951), 276.

33. There is no adequate study of Maximilian's encouragement of foreign investment in his empire. A prime source for such an essay would be the

Maximilian's New York consul, Charles F. DeLoosey, in raking off commissions from the negotiation of concessions for American firms.[34]

The Mexican lines were typical Morgan family enterprises. Morgan made the initial proposals to the Imperial Mexican Government in September 1864; Quintard supplied some of the capital and part of the negotiations, but the concessionary companies that finally emerged were primarily the work of their president and agent, Morgan's youngest son-in-law, Charles A. Whitney.

Born in Hoosick, New York, in 1823, Whitney was a qualified "man of affairs." A gold-rusher at twenty-six, he had returned to become private secretary to Senator Lewis Cass and subsequently an employee of the shipping firm of Howland & Aspinwall. At the time of his marriage to Maria Louise Morgan in 1853, he was New York agent of the U.S.–Pacific Mail steamship line via Central America. From 1857 to 1860 he served as co-manager of the Morgan Iron Works and most recently had been New York agent for the British leviathan *Great Eastern*. In 1864, Whitney took over negotiations surrounding Morgan's Mexican projects.[35]

Two companies emerged: the American and Mexican Steamship Company and the Vera Cruz and New Orleans Mail Steamship Company. Both were closely held corporations given life by concessions from the Imperial Mexican Government. Both were financed in large part by Charles Morgan and operated by his "sons."

Each of the companies was chartered for ten years; the former to establish round voyages between New York and Vera Cruz via Havana twice monthly; the latter for service between Vera Cruz and New Orleans thrice monthly. The New York line was to receive a subsidy of $5,000 in gold or silver per round voyage during its first two years of operation, while the New Orleans steamers would be paid $2,000 per round trip for

voluminous papers of Charles F. DeLoosey held by the New York Historical Society. DeLoosey handled most of the negotiations regarding concessions.

34. DeLoosey's commissions on subsidy contracts ranged from 5 to 25 per cent. See, e.g., George W. Quintard to DeLoosey, January 1866 (3 letters), and DeLoosey to John S. Keeling, February 11, 1865 (DeLoosey Papers, New York Historical Society). See, also, Robert W. Frazer, "Maximilian's Propaganda Activities in the United States, 1865–1866," *Hispanic-American Historical Review*, XXIV (February 1944), 4–29.

35. *In Memoriam: Charles A. Whitney*, pp. 8, 11–12, 18; New York *Tribune*, June 1, 1852; *Daily Picayune*, June 23, 1863; D. & B., N. Y., vol. 348, p. 857.

their initial three years of service. After these initial periods, the subsidies were to be recomputed so as to stabilize "net profits" on capital invested at 15 per cent, allowing 10 per cent for depreciation.[36]

Only the New York line, which was signed into being in April 1865, ever began service. The 1,339-ton sister steamships *Manhattan* and *Vera Cruz*, built in New York City by Lawrence & Foulke, with engines by the Morgan Iron Works, opened the line in late 1865. The almost immediate sinking of *Vera Cruz* and the counter-revolution which eventually deposed Maximilian interfered with schedules, however, and the line ceased operations in May 1866. The New Orleans line, organized in early 1866, was unable to begin its service before the end of Maximilian's regime.[37]

The profits, if any, of these Mexican ventures are unknown. Most likely they were financial failures, as clauses in both contracts permitted the Mexicans to delay subsidy payments as much as one year after the opening of service. With the execution of Maximilian in 1867, the probability is that these payments were never made and that the ventures were written off as disastrous miscalculations by Morgan and his sons-in-law.

The losses in Mexico, however, were partially recouped by the fortuitous and profitable sale of the Morgan Iron Works in the spring of 1867.

The postwar history of the works is brief. Speculative overproduction of vessels during the Civil War and their postwar release from military and navy charters had glutted the American steamship market by 1866. Also, with rising costs of metals caused by "protective" tariffs and domestic shortages, new construction was being curtailed. Marine engine builders felt the pressures of a falling market (the Morgan works built only one set of marine engines in 1866) and were scrambling to survive through diversification, mergers, cutbacks, and vertical integration.[38] Morgan solved the problem by selling out which he could do profitably. Quintard's interest in the firm was flagging, and in early 1867 he and Morgan found a pigeon on whom they unloaded their iron works.

The purchaser was John Roach, then engaged in forming a monopoly

36. The relevant correspondence, conventions, and contracts are all located in vol. 22 of the DeLoosey Papers.

37. *Ibid.*; Heyl, *American Steamers*, I, 437.

38. These conclusions reached after comparative study of the credit histories of the Allaire Works, the Hogg & Delameter Works, the Morgan Iron Works, and John Roach's Iron Works (see D. & B., N.Y., vols. 316, 316a, and 317) and of Hutchins, *Maritime Industries, passim.*

of engine-building in New York City and in consolidating a vertically integrated shipping empire. Though Roach's activities are beyond the scope of this study, he did provide an escape route for Morgan to abandon engine-building.[39] Although the exact increment of gain is unknown, insiders considered the sale of the Morgan Iron Works to Roach for $450,000 to be a profit for Morgan.[40] Sale of the iron works covered some of the losses sustained in Mexico and left Morgan and his son and sons-in-law freer to concentrate on shipping. One result was the formation of the New York and Charleston Steamship Company in 1867.

A steamship line to Charleston was Quintard's idea for employing his capital and energy now that the iron works and the Mexican lines were gone, but he involved most of the Morgan family in his scheme. Charles became a prominent investor, his son Henry served as the line's agent from its inception until 1873, Quintard was president, and Whitney's steamship *Manhattan* was transferred from the defunct Mexican line to the Charleston service.

Capitalized at $300,000 under the general incorporation laws of New York, the New York and Charleston Steamship Company purchased *Champion* (1,452 tons) and *Charleston* (1,517 tons) and chartered *James Adger* (1,151 tons) to add to *Manhattan*. The four steamships ran between the New York–Boston area and Charleston (being replaced by newer vessels in the late 1870s) but never paid a dividend on their investment. The line had begun in the flush days following the Civil War, when the resumption of commerce exceeded the capacity of the South's immature and battered railroads. It perished in the late 1880s before the onslaught of larger steamships and trunk-line railroads.[41]

Morgan participated in these enterprises as financial angel and advisor, but it is doubtful that they competed seriously for his capital or time. He

39. "Investigation by the Committee on Naval Affairs," *House Misc. Docs.*, 44 Cong., 1 Sess., No. 170, Pt. 6 (Serial 1705), 236–238; Leonard A. Swann, Jr., *John Roach, Maritime Entrepreneur: The Years as Naval Contractor, 1862–1886.*

40. Roach paid $100,000 cash and signed two mortgages to Morgan to secure payment of the remainder: $100,000 (signed 10–22–67; due 1–1–68) ; $250,000 (signed 1–1–68; due 1–1–73). He defaulted on both mortgages, but Morgan did not foreclose and carried Roach's bad debts for years. The debts were paid shortly before Morgan's death in 1878. D. & B., N.Y., vol. 317, pp. 229, 300p, 300kk, 300pp, 300qq, 300ww, 300a/13, 300a/63, 300a/75.

41. D. & B., N.Y., vol. 345, p. 600a/1; vol. 371, pp. 858, 1000p, 1g; Heyl, *op. cit., passim.*

was diverted from his preoccupation with his Gulf lines as he had been in Nicaragua (but not on the same scale). Once again, when the excitement and prospects of the diversions had waned, he gradually withdrew and settled more firmly than ever in what had always been the mainstream of his business—the interstate commerce of the Gulf South. He would never be diverted again.

To rebuild his Gulf fleet was costly, but Morgan blended a balanced program of purchase and construction and found the Quartermaster and the Navy provided a bonanza of bargains.

From the Navy Department in the fall of 1865, he purchased for $230,500 *Alabama* (870 tons) and his former steamers *William G. Hewes* and *Austin*. *Matagorda* was also repurchased from the naval authorities for an unnamed price. *Clinton, Crescent,* and *St. Mary,* sold to the government in August 1865 for $495,000, were repurchased a year later for $225,000.[42] New construction at Harlan's added *Morgan* (995 tons), *Lady of the Lake* (716 tons), *I. C. Harris* (995 tons), *City of Norfolk* (1,040 tons), *Laura* (1,098 tons), *Mary* (1,096 tons), *Harlan* (1,163 tons), and *Josephine* (1,282 tons) to Morgan's fleet between 1865 and 1867. During the same period, *Agnes* (583 tons) was purchased from private parties.[43]

Returning to New Orleans in March 1866, Morgan personally supervised the reopening of the "outside" routes to Texas. Again under the management of Israel C. Harris (who with his father-in-law was widely feted for his devotion to the Gulf economy) triweekly service on a New Orleans–Galveston–Indianola route was standardized by a four-year mail subsidy of $24,429 per annum negotiated by Morgan in 1867. A Galveston–Brazos St. Iago run, via the ports of Matagorda and Aransas bays, was also reactivated under a $12,000 annual subsidy secured at the same

42. *Registers, NOLA,* VI, 6–7, 28, 54–55, 65, 193–194, 243, 290; "Vessels Bought, Sold, and Chartered" (Serial 1346), 141–142; "Naval Vessels," *House Exec. Docs.,* 40 Cong., 2 Sess., No. 280 (Serial 1343), 26–27.

43. *Registers, NOLA,* VI, 118, 140, 153, 163, 176–177, 203–204; Plans of Vessels Built by Harlan and Hollingsworth, II, 8, III, 2, IV, 23; *Semi-Centennial Memoir of the Harlan & Hollingsworth Company,* pp. 376–389; William M. Lytle, "Iron Construction in the United States," *Annual Report of the Commissioner of Navigation for 1899,* Pt. I, 219–221; David B. Tyler, *The American Clyde: A History of Iron and Steel Shipbuilding on the Delaware from 1840 to World War I,* pp. 27, 43.

time. At Brazos St. Iago connections were made with steamboats owned by King, Kenedy & Co. which plied the Rio Grande as far upstream as Roma.[44]

Morgan also resumed his Berwick's Bay connection in 1866. The New Orleans, Opelousas, and Great Western Railroad, operated by Union troops until January 31, 1866, quickly restored rail service from New Orleans to the Atchafalaya and again negotiated a contract with Morgan to extend that route to Texas.[45] Signed on May 3, 1866, the new agreement resembled the Morgan–N.O.O. & G.W. contract of 1858 and its benefits to Morgan again indicate the strength of his bargaining position.

Again, in return for twice-weekly service between Brashear and Galveston, Morgan received 80 per cent of gross passage receipts, 25 per cent of livestock-shipment revenue, and 50 per cent of all other freight revenue. Morgan's own supplies were to be carried at half price and his agents or crews free. In return, the railroad would "remove the obstructions . . . in Atchafalaya bay" and furnish "ample wharf & store house accommodations at Brashear." The mutually exclusive contract contained provisions for dividing costs of advertising and through-ticket sales geographically as before, weekly cash settlements of accounts, and assignment of liability for loss or damages to "the party at fault."

Signed by Morgan and President A. B. Seger of the railroad, the contract was secret (not recorded in Orleans Parish Mortgage Office until 1868) and would expire on March 31, 1871.[46] The contract provided for tri-weekly service (one trip via Sabine Pass) from Brashear to Galveston and Indianola and awarded two mail subsidies to Morgan in 1867: $30,000 annually for service Brashear–Galveston–Indianola; $18,000 an-

---

44. *Daily Picayune*, February 7, March 23, 1866; *Texas Almanac for 1867*, p. 356; "Fines and Deductions, Mail Contractors, 1868," *House Exec. Docs.*, 40 Cong., 3 Sess., No. 88 (Serial 1381), 20–21; *ibid.*, 1869, *House Exec. Docs.*, 41 Cong., 2 Sess., No. 289 (Serial 1426), 12–13, 28–29, 48–49; J. L. Allhands, *Uriah Lott*, pp. 2–3.

45. For the wartime operation of the N.O.O. & G.W. see *Fourteenth Annual Report of the President and Directors of the New Orleans, Opelousas, and Great Western Railroad Company* (1867), pp. 52, 59 and Odom, "Louisiana Railroads," pp. 146–147, 152–154.

46. Agreement between N.O.O. & G.W. and Morgan, May 3, 1866. Deposited with Magner, N.A. (Orleans), November 30, 1868, M.O. (Orleans), Society Book VII, 217 (November 30, 1868); Minute Book No. 2, Board of Directors, N.O.O. & G.W., April 30, June 7, 1866, N.O.O. & G.W. Records.

nually for a Brashear–Indianola direct route.[47] Morgan and his agents also negotiated separate contracts and schedules of rates between 1866 and 1868 to secure the transportation of government stores and personnel over both the "inside" (railroad) and "outside" (river) routes to Texas.[48]

This speedy resumption of his Texas services dictated enlargement of Morgan's physical assets in that state—both in his traditional ports of call and in newer cities as well. In 1867, because of the demands of his increased service, he received exclusive four-year rights to the best wharves in Galveston (the "Central" and "Brick" wharves) and to one warehouse.[49] Similar enlargements in Morgan facilities soon appeared at more southerly Texas ports. In particular, the cattle-shipping and packing centers along the shores of Matagorda and Aransas bays received increased attention.

Manifests of Morgan vessels reprinted in the New Orleans press indicate shipments of cattle from Indianola to New Orleans as early as 1849, and throughout the 1850s the New Yorker had kept pace with the growing livestock and hide industry of the Matagorda Bay area. Indianola was uniquely fitted for livestock export, draining the vast plains of southern Texas and permitting cattle to be driven directly to her harbor's shore—unlike, for example, Galveston's island port. In addition, preserved meat factories established in the 1850s swelled Indianola's exports with hides, tallow, and processed beef and turtle meats.[50] By 1870, Calhoun and Matagorda counties contained five meat packeries capitalized at $61,000 and producing an annual output valued at $256,306. For the fiscal year preceding September 1, 1867, alone, Indianola had exported

47. Richardson (ed.), *loc. cit., Daily Picayune,* 1866–1867; "Fines and Deductions, Mail Contractors, 1868" (Serial 1381), 84–85; *ibid.,* 1869 (Serial 1426), 12–13, 48–49, 70–71.

48. "Contracts, Quartermaster Department, 1866," *House Exec. Docs.,* 39 Cong., 2 Sess., No. 28 (Serial 1289), 10; *ibid.,* 1867, *House Exec. Docs.,* 40 Cong., 2 Sess., No. 35 (Serial 1330), 14; *ibid.,* 1867–68, *Senate Exec. Docs.,* 40 Cong., 2 Sess., No. 59 (Serial 1316), 5.

49. Agreement between Morgan and Galveston Wharf Co., May 13, 1867, Morgan's Louisiana and Texas Railroad and Steamship Co. Records (Southern Pacific Co.). Hereafter cited as M.L. & T.R. & S. Records.

50. Indianola *Bulletin,* October 19, 1853, May 3, July 6, 1855; Galveston *Commercial and Weekly Prices Current,* September 1, 1856; *Daily Picayune,* January 2, 1859; D.E.E. Braman, *Braman's Information about Texas, Carefully Prepared,* pp. 67–71; T. J. Cauley, "Early Meat Packing Plants in Texas," *Southwestern Political and Social Science Quarterly,* IX (March 1929), 473–475; E. C. Barksdale, *The Meat Packers Come to Texas.*

(foreign and coastwise) 18,000 head of cattle, 50,410 hides, 55,000 goat skins, and 2,100 bales of sheep skins as opposed to 13,391 bales of cotton, and 2,544 bales and 5,917 bags of wool. These shipments of "sea lions," as the cattle were known, and their byproducts were carried almost exclusively by Morgan's steamers.[51]

The shipper's involvement in this growing Texas industry included an abortive attempt to export beef under refrigeration. In February 1869, Texas and Pennsylvania investors formed the United States and West Indies Fresh Meat and Fruit Company to utilize a refrigeration process patented by Wilson Bray of New York. The process permitted shipment of fresh meats from Indianola throughout the Gulf and Caribbean. Morgan's steamer *Agnes*, equipped with the cooling device, was chartered and in July carried Texas' first export-cargo of refrigerated meat from Indianola to New Orleans. Although the refrigeration process was successful and Morgan's service satisfactory, the company endured for only two years, falling before financial difficulties, the opposition of New Orleans butchers, and competition from eastern firms. Yet again, Morgan had been a pioneer.[52]

The Texas cattle industry drew Morgan's attention to still another area after the Civil War—Aransas Bay. There had been some coastwise shipments of cattle, hides, and tallow from this area (roughly 180 miles south of Galveston) as early as 1854. The consolidation of large ranches and the establishment of beef and turtle packeries after 1865 increased the area's export potential.

Dealing primarily with the leading packer, W. S. Hall, and stockmen John M. and Thomas Henry Mathis, Morgan agreed to extend service to Aransas Bay in 1867. He contracted with Hall and other packers to carry $1,000 worth of hides and tallow every ten days and placed two steamships on a weekly route between the newly founded town of Rockport and New Orleans. With the Mathis brothers, who owned the largest herds in the area and who became his agents, Morgan constructed warehouses, wharves, and pens. Morgan could boast by 1869 that he carried the bulk

51. *Manufactures of the United States in 1860* (*Eighth Census of the United States*, III, 1865), 580–591; *The Statistics and the Wealth and Industry of the United States* (*Ninth Census of the United States*, III, 1872), 735–736; *Daily Picayune*, January 18, 1868.

52. *Daily Picayune*, July 13, December 2, 1869, February 17, July 17, 1870; *Commercial Bulletin*, July 14, 1869; Barksdale, *Meat Packers*, pp. 21–23.

of the 1,198,254 pounds of dried hides, 1,183,298 pounds of wet salted hides, 1,726,507 pounds of wool, 395,135 pounds of tallow, 90,109 pounds of salted beef, and 33,000 pounds of bones shipped by sea from Aransas Bay. Another new port was born.[53]

But Morgan's postwar extension of service in the Gulf was not restricted to Texas. The New Orleans–Mobile trade also drew his attention. Since the opening of the Pontchartrain Railroad in the 1830s, a variety of vessels had connected that road's lake terminus at Milneburg with Mobile. Throughout the ante bellum period Morgan had made no attempt to enter the route. In mid-1865, however, he opened daily service, Milneburg to Mobile, connecting with the railroad. By 1866 Morgan had three steamers on the run, representing a capital investment of $585,000 and subsidized by a U.S. Mail contract for $25,000 per annum.[54] Yet, still dissatisfied, he soon took steps to eliminate competition on this route.

On April 17, 1866, Morgan and the Pontchartrain Railroad signed a five-year agreement on rates, New Orleans–Mobile, allocating 75 per cent of through freight receipts to Morgan. As other ships in the trade made similar arrangements with the railroad, spirited competition resulted, driving freight rates from 50 to 15 cents per barrel and passage from $4 to 50 cents per person. One of Morgan's competitors charged that in seeking to eliminate competition, Morgan absorbed losses totaling over $33,000 in the summer of 1867 alone. Unsuccessful, on November 1, 1867, Morgan "loaned" the railroad company $250,000 for a contract at special lower rates. Reduced to writing on January 20, 1868, the favored agreement succeeded in driving out any regular competition on the route.[55]

Taken to court, the railroad argued its duty "to carry for a reasonable compensation" but also its right "to make special bargains with every freighter that presents himself." The arrangement with Morgan had been

53. Log Books, Mustang Island Pilot Station, Aransas Bar, Texas, 1866–1881 (In possession of Mrs. Robert A. Mercer, Aransas Pass, Texas), II, 197–198; Rockport *Transcript*, February 12, 1870, March 28, 1874; *Daily Picayune*, January 1, 5, 1870; Cauley, *op. cit.*, pp. 468–469, 472–473, 477–478; Dorothy L. Nims, "History of the Village of Rockport," pp. 26, 33–44; A. Ray Stephens, *The Taft Ranch: A Texas Principality*, pp. 8–9.

54. *Daily Picayune*, July 4, 1865; "Contracts for Carrying the Mails, 1871," *House Exec. Docs.*, 42 Cong., 2 Sess., No. 191 (Serial 1513), 676; *Answer of Defendants, April 29, 1871: Eclipse Towboat Co. v. Pontchartrain Railroad Co.*, pp. 12–15.

55. *Appeal by Plaintiffs, April 17, 1871: Eclipse Towboat Co. v. Pontchartrain Railroad Co.*, pp. 1–18.

necessary since from "a third to a half of the freight from New Orleans to Mobile was controlled by the Morgan line," and his vessels were the largest and swiftest on the route. Agreeing it unfortunate that smaller vessels had failed in their attempts to compete, the railroad still maintained that by 1868 "making money [on any Mobile line] was out of the question . . . the question was not what profit could be made; but whether the competing lines could survive the struggle"—and only Morgan had survived. The Louisiana Supreme Court agreed with the railroad, ruling:

There was nothing illegal and giving rise to damages in the contract made between the Pontchartrain Railroad Company and Charles Morgan, whereby they agreed to "pro rate" the charges on freight from New Orleans to Mobile, and were to charge the regular tariff to the public.[56]

It was not until the completion of a railroad from Mobile to New Orleans in 1870 that Morgan again faced serious competition on this route.

Despite his advancing age, Morgan thrived on the expansion of his lines in the four years following Appomattox. His prestige in the South was not harmed by his prompt but conservative donations to southern relief associations, and even his critics grudgingly admitted his enterprise and stamina.[57] Indeed, it was not Morgan but his agent and son-in-law Israel C. Harris who proved less able to endure the strain of postwar enlargement of the Morgan lines. On April 1, 1867, because of "continued ill-health," Harris announced his retirement from active management of the lines. Thus ended the twenty-year existence of the firm Harris & Morgan—young Morgan having resigned to pursue his personal investments during the Civil War. Harris sought to regain his health by travel but died in New York on Christmas Eve.[58]

Saddened by Harris's death, Morgan did not allow it to affect the operation of his steamers, as he had taken adequate precautions for succession to Harris's agency in April and May 1867. Once again he had drawn upon his immediate family to receive his trust. Skipping over Quintard and his son Henry who were now engaged in financial enter-

56. *Answer of Defendants, April 29, 1871: Eclipse Towboat Co. v. Pontchartrain Railroad Co.;* 24 Louisiana Ann. 1 (1872); New Orleans *Republican,* December 19, 1871.
57. *Report of the New York Ladies' Southern Relief Association,* p. 2.
58. *Daily Crescent,* April 1, December 27, 1867; *Daily Picayune,* December 27, 1867, August 15–16, 1874; *Republican,* August 16, 1874.

prises of their own, Morgan selected Charles A. Whitney to inherit Harris's mantle. An intense Episcopalian of portly physique and sporting enormous mutton-chop whiskers, Whitney was unemployed because of the failure of the Mexican lines. With kinship, experience, and availability, he fitted Morgan's needs.

Alexander C. Hutchinson, a man equal in experience but of no relation to Morgan, joined Whitney in the newly created firm of "Charles A. Whitney & Co., New Orleans." Brusque and remote when compared to the courtly Whitney, "A.C." had come up through the ranks of Morgan's enterprises. Born in 1832, he had foregone all but minimum schooling to learn mechanics and shipbuilding in the yards of his native Brooklyn.[59] Hutchinson had attracted the attention of Morgan and Vanderbilt, and he had been placed in charge of the river and lake steamers in Nicaragua during the 1850s. After further seasoning in the Morgan Iron Works, it was said of Hutchinson "there was nothing that he did not know about a vessel" and he, Miers Corryell (long superintendent of the Morgan Iron Works), and Captain James Lawless (Morgan's supervisor of construction at Harlan's) probably contributed most to the structural excellence of Morgan's steamers. Sent to New Orleans in 1866, Hutchinson married a local girl, Miss Josephine P. Thomas of Algiers, and a year later joined Whitney in managing Morgan's New Orleans agency.[60] Whitney and Hutchinson's conduct, as had Harris's before them, soon lent further strength to Morgan's public image—an image well characterized by a later admirer: "Select the right man for the right place, then proceed."[61]

Morgan invested Whitney and Hutchinson with the necessary powers of attorney in April and May 1867 and leased, at $600 per month, a spacious brick building at 50–52 Camp Street, between Gravier and

59. As late as 1883 (and worth several millions of dollars), the self-made Hutchinson could still be attracted by such works as G. A. Gaskell, *Gaskell's Compendium of Forms, Educational, Social, Legal and Commercial, Embracing a Complete Self-Teaching Course in Penmanship and Bookkeeping and Aid to English Composition, together with the Laws and By-Laws of Social Etiquette and Business Laws and Commercial Forms, a Manual of Agriculture, Mechanics, and Mining and a Complete Encyclopedia of Reference.* Copy inscribed "A. C. Hutchinson, New Orleans, 1883" (Howard-Tilton Library, Tulane University).

60. *Daily Picayune,* July 23, 1866, December 8, 1902; New Orleans *Times-Democrat,* December 18, 1902; *Semi-Centennial Memoir of the Harlan & Hollingsworth Company,* p. 256.

61. "Charles Morgan: His Courage Helped Build an Empire," *Southern Pacific (Texas and Louisiana Lines) Bulletin,* VIII (May 1936), 4.

Natchez, to serve as their offices. The partners were granted "full power and authority" to manage all Morgan's affairs "relating to any and all steamships or other vessels owned by him, inclusive of the steamers known as the 'Morgan Line of Steamships' plying between [New Orleans] . . . and Texas and across the Lake." Whitney and Hutchinson were to make any or all contracts or charters, employ or discharge officers and crews, and handle all "Customhouse business."[62] Under this secure and trusted agency, the affairs of the Morgan lines entered the last years of the 1860s—years of the utmost significance to Morgan and his future operations.

62. Procuration, Morgan to Whitney and Hutchinson, April 29, 1867. Act before Magner, N.A. (Orleans); Procuration, Morgan to Whitney and Hutchinson, May 28, 1867. *Ibid.*; Agreement between Wright R. Fish and Morgan, July 13, 1868. Act before George W. Christy, N.A. (Orleans).

7

RETROSPECT AND PROSPECT

DESTRUCTION and interruption of Morgan's prewar economic way of life had challenged his ability to sustain his profits through the Civil War years. He was equal to the task, although playing both sides, and re-established his traditional Gulf lines by 1867. But as became increasingly apparent, Federal victory and the advent of Congressional Reconstruction accelerated revolutionary changes in the framework of his business decision-making. The rapidity of these changes only underscored their magnitude.

Before considering Morgan's postwar environment, however, it is useful to review his ante bellum goals, to assess their risks, and to gauge his achievement of business purposes. With these conclusions in mind, the dimensions of the new environment which the seventy-year-old Morgan faced in 1865 become more evident and meaningful.

Broadly stated, Morgan's prewar business goals were concentration of his capital in American-flag vessels engaged in common carriage in the coasting and inshore trades; steamliner service between New Orleans and all significant ports of the Gulf of Mexico; monopolization of his chosen routes; power to turn windfall profits in shipping; and growth through reinvestment of earnings rather than through equity-dilution or debt-financing.

In retrospect, and relative to alternative or subsequent possibilities, these were modest goals involving manageable risks. Furthermore, Morgan was consistently able to cope with the uncertainties that did arise. For example, he remained solvent during the depression of 1837–1843 and moved his steamers from the Atlantic Coast to the booming Texas trade.

In 1857 he was at his ante bellum peak of prosperity in shipping and engine-building and remained so until the Civil War. Besides his own skill and efficiency in management, other factors—environment, concentration in short-haul steamers, and the nature of competition—accounted for his success.

The nature of Morgan's market environment was an important consideration. At no time before the Civil War did intrusions of foreign capital or competition threaten the rigorously protected coasting trades that he favored. As opposed to investment in foreign carriage, the coasting trades proved to require less capital—smaller ships and crews and quicker turnaround—and less risk—as insurance rates testify. Morgan was able to keep his acquisitions of ships on a cash basis by carefully setting aside earnings in "Construction" and "Purchase" accounts; thus he merited an A-1 credit rating. His vessels were always self-insured by reserves earmarked for that purpose. He felt the quality of his ships, his crews, and his agents to be a better hedge against loss than insurance policies. On the whole he was correct, but natural calamity remained his most implacable foe.[1]

Concentration in short-haul line steamers and the intra-Gulf trades proved prudent and possible. None of the commodities to which Morgan's liners catered suffered market obsolescence, and the demand for the nature and pattern of his services grew steadily. Morgan had wisely deferred on the longer coastal routes to the capacity (even over-capacity) of the sailing-packet lines. Within the Gulf, however, in the absence of competitive land transport, his steamers demonstrated their technical advantages and the short-haul superiority of steam over sail in terms of speed, draught, and maneuverability.

Morgan had also coped with competition quite well. His challengers, his strategies, and his tactics changed over time, but two ante bellum periods can be identified and compared. Two factors must be recalled,

1. "Cash" in the custom of marine purchases usually meant $\frac{1}{3}$ to $\frac{1}{4}$ down and $\frac{2}{3}$ to $\frac{3}{4}$ upon delivery. Among numerous sources reflecting Morgan's C.O.D. preference and ability is a credit statement of May 1852: "they [the Morgan lines] never build a ship or purchd. an interest in one without they had thr. *own* money in hand to pay for it." D. & B., La., vol. 9, p. 164. Also see, *ibid.*, N. Y., vol. 341, pp. 162, 200a/54. Self-insurance was thoroughly respectable, but little done. "Marine Insurance," *Report of the Commissioner of Corporations on Transportation by Water in the United States*, I, 339–365; Solomon S. Huebner, *Marine Insurance*.

however—the long dependence of the port cities and hinterland of the western Gulf of Mexico on water transportation for access to their primary markets and the disappearance of this dependence through the development of land transport. Through the 1870s these factors set the contours of Morgan's business environment.

During the initial period of his Gulf activities, which prevailed from the 1830s into the 1850s, with concentration on the Texas trade, a number of environmental factors conditioned his actions. First, the Texas ports were so spaced by nature and their rudimentary system of internal transport as to minimize overlapping of their hinterlands: Galveston commanded the region north and east of the Colorado River; Matagorda, Port Lavaca, and Indianola served the backlands between the Colorado and Nueces rivers; and Brazos St. Iago supplied the Rio Grande Valley. There were, of course, rivalries, but in general these ports did not seriously compete at interior points before the coming of the railroad. Second, during this early stage of Morgan's operations the commerce of Texas flowed mainly to and from New Orleans. Third, the lack of effective land-transport between Texas points and the Crescent City placed the bulk of commerce on the decks of water carriers.

Given these conditions, Morgan directed his efforts to domination of the sea lanes from New Orleans. His steam packets and liner service specialized in passengers, mail, and goods more sensitive to speed, consignment-size, frequency of voyage, and care in handling than to freight rates. His rates were high, but the convenience of his liners merited their premium over alternative means of transport.

To sustain his position, Morgan competed strenuously against all comers, but generally he arranged to co-operate with those competitors he could not drive away. The size, speed, safety, and luxury of his vessels were competitive weapons, and he regularly used the traditional liner-techniques of rate-cutting, rebates from shippers and waterfront facility operators, increased or alternative sailings, and blacklisting of shippers using competitors. He was even accused of sabotage! These practices, in addition to some slight cost advantages because of efficient management and economies of scale, plus the possession of all of the water-mail contracts to Texas, enabled him to drive off most aspirants to his position.

In a number of cases—notably with the owners of *Cuba* and *Neptune* in the 1830s and 1840s and with Vanderbilt in the 1850s—Morgan preferred co-operation to competition. Co-operation usually took the forms of pooling of advertising, staggering of sailing dates, and equalized rates. These early agreements show no evidence of traffic allocation or pooling of revenues, but these ends were met to some degree through staggered sailings and equalized rates.

Thus, before the 1850s, competition among the Gulf steamship operators conformed to the classic model of liner competition: rate competition was less frequent than monopoly (through price-service victory) or duopoly (through price-service compromise). Rates were sensitive to what the traffic would bear and to the presence (or lack) of alternative transport; not to costs of carriage. Also, the only competing railroad to appear, the N.O.O. & G.W. had been neatly emasculated by Morgan.

A final characteristic of Morgan's competitive policies in this initial era was his and his fellow water carriers' lack of concern with the costs and channels of interior trade. He influenced inland shippers through his credit extensions and rebates, but he interfered very little with either the means or the prices of transport to and from the seaboard. Goods were received or delivered in the historic way—"at end of ship's tackle"—and that was that.

Morgan's success in applying these strategies and favorable environmental factors made his ante bellum Gulf lines sound and safe investments. The chance that New Orleans might lose her dominant position among Gulf ports was unthinkable, as was any notion that some day coastal shipping lines would cease to radiate from her wharves. Indeed, there were many indications to the contrary as Morgan enmeshed newly developing ports within his personal system and New Orleans' trading network. On the whole, he achieved his business goals profitably, with high risk appearing only at the beginnings of new enterprises and in his windfall ventures in Central America and Mexico.[2] Underlying all was the basic safeguard of the water carrier: the ability to move his capital equipment about and to redeploy it for maximization of profit and minimization of risk.

2. Curiously, Morgan does not appear in any of the well-known listings of wealthy New Yorkers compiled by Moses Yale Beach (See Henrietta M. Larson, *Guide to Business History*, p. 157). Reuben Vose, in *Wealth of the World Displayed*, lists him at $2,000,000 and in *The Rich Men of New York, Series 4*, at $1,000,000. Dun & Bradstreet commented on Morgan and son-in-law Harris in May 1866: "Have any amount of means. Morgan is a Millionaire." D. & B., La., vol. 10, p. 544. A report of December 1874, estimated Morgan "wor. 15 or 20 millions." *Ibid.*, vol. 12, p. 324.

His competitive position began to change, however, as a second stage in the transportation history of the Gulf emerged. This second stage began in the 1850s and lasted through the 1870s and was characterized by a number of environmental changes. The Texas ports were increasing their volume of trade through greater productive capacity and demand within the state and by improving and extending their lines of interior transport. The latter brought Texas ports into greater competition in the hinterland. For example, beginning in the 1850s and resuming activity in the 1870s, railroads began to overlap the traditional backlands of Galveston and Indianola.

This interport rivalry initially meant little to Morgan as he continued to dominate the trade of the Texas ports by his control of the route to New Orleans. But the primacy of that route was changing too. The increased commerce of Texas was both a cause and an effect of direct contact with more external market cities—notably New York through the extension in the 1850s of sailing lines and, after 1865, steam lines from the East. As the number of water carriers available in the Texas trade increased, shippers became much more sensitive to alternative market prices for their goods and to the charges for freight and associated services. The price elasticity of demand for liner service thus increased. While no competing land route had yet developed, Gulf water carriers—and particularly Morgan since he represented the old order—were forced to become more rate-conscious and competitive among themselves.

These trends were only begun by 1861. But after the war's close, they accelerated. This became an era of competition, not of co-operation, and a new strategy was increasingly employed. For the first time in the Gulf, and largely because of their inability to compromise matters at sea, water carriers began systematically to influence, develop, and co-operate with lines of transport radiating inland from the seaboard. They also began to take a more active role in port development as they jockeyed for position along crowded waterfronts. The strategy was to guarantee a flow of goods from hinterland to port to water carrier in order to offset competition at sea—in short, to push competition inland.

Morgan was to become the champion of this strategy in the Gulf. Witness, for example, the change in affairs at Indianola between 1866 and 1871:

It was the uniform custom with the owners of this line [Morgan's], and well known to, and acquiesced in by, the community, to discharge the cargoes of these vessels on the wharf, immediately on their arrival in port. . . . It was also customary for the goods landed on the wharf to be left there till called for by the owners and consignees. In that case they were covered over with tarpaulins by the agent of the carrier. The wharf was the warehouse of this line of steamers, but no charges were made by the owners of the line for storage or services in taking care of the goods until their delivery.[3]

As matters stand now, it is emphatically Charles Morgan from New Orleans to Victoria. Of course, then to make a living, we must follow our master (for such he is) of draymen, warehousemen, and commission merchants. Indianola as well as Lavaca must go to Victoria to keep up with the business. The commission merchants of both places have been compelled to move up and build temporary warehouses in order to hold their customers; and it is evident that as soon as the road will reach the next point they will all have to pack up and move again. . . . when the road reaches San Antonio . . . Indianola, with chagrin, will sit hunched up and gaze wistfully upon Mr. Morgan's steamers, coming up the bay and Landing at Mr. Morgan's wharf, and Mr. Morgan's cars going down, and Mr. Morgan's men rolling the freight off the steamers right on the cars; passengers likewise stepping off the steamer right on the train; off she goes to San Antonio.[4]

Contrasting with his prewar record of political and economic stability and success, Morgan's postwar interaction with his environment was to be laced with uncertainty, risk, and frustration. Severe new environmental pressures were everywhere: the political and economic disruptions of Reconstruction and Redemption; the construction of railroads which paralleled his port-to-port steamship lines; the building of railroads perpendicular to the coastline and to the port cities he served; and the increased technological and economic feasibility of long-haul coastal steamships.

As we have seen, some of these developments had ante bellum antecedents, but it was their confluence and interaction after the Civil War that affected competition among carriers, intercity rivalries, and the traditional patterns of trade. The intensity and speed of their effects forced Morgan into a major reappraisal and redirection of his purposes. The results were important new policies directed toward basically modified business goals. In the process both Morgan's enterprises and their economic environment were significantly altered.

Increased interaction with government at all levels was one of Mor-

3. *Morgan v. Dibble & Seeligson*, 29 Texas Reports 108–121 (1867).
4. Samuel H. Canfield, Port Lavaca, to Editor, December 18, 1871, *New Orleans Republican*, December 31, 1871.

gan's new, postwar facts of life. The location of his enterprises plunged them into the political and economic rivalries of Reconstruction and Redemption and involved Morgan whether he liked it or not. The situation was worst in Louisiana, his center of operations, where Radical politicians and competing northern businessmen suspected his southern sympathies. In Texas the situation was generally better and was eased further by Morgan's subscription to $650,000 in state bonds during the depression of 1874, yet again difficulties arose.

Overlying the general problems born of civil and political disorder were new postwar taxes directed against transportation enterprises. These were the result of municipal, county, state, and federal attempts to broaden their tax base in support of the expenses of war, the restoration of the South, and a myriad of actual and planned internal-improvements projects. Businessmen, who both contributed public revenue and received public aid, were intimately concerned with the evolution of complicated and sometimes paradoxical attempts at the redistribution of income.

In the transportation sector, the picture was especially blurred. Some transportation companies exempted by their charters from taxation (partially or wholly for varying time periods) also received liberal public aid. Other companies that received public aid were still liable to taxation upon capital, property, and/or receipts. Still others were taxed and received no public aid. The profusion of taxing powers—be they municipalities, counties, states, or the federal government—added to the upset.[5]

The deep involvement of Morgan's steamship and railroad enterprises in the rationalization of these conflicts was certainly an undercurrent in much of his postwar decision-making. A summary of his tax difficulties provides a prologue to other developments.

A barrage of tax levies was laid upon transportation companies in the years following the Civil War. Some were new and some were old techniques; all had to be synthesized under the Constitution.[6] For example, state capitation taxes on passengers, which had been prohibited in the foreign trade in 1849, were not voided in reference to interstate com-

5. For Morgan's bond subscription, see New Orleans *Daily Picayune*, August 17, September 20, December 28, 1874, April 4, 1875. For general conditions, see the works by Goodrich and Stover cited in the bibliography.

6. The cases relevant to the following points of law are admirably summarized in: *Report of the Commissioner of Corporations on Transportation by Water in the United States*, I, 368–382.

merce until 1867.[7] Similarly, state taxes upon interstate freight shipments were not definitely outlawed until a series of Supreme Court decisions in 1872.[8] There was also the question of a state's power to tax the gross receipts of interstate corporations, upheld in an 1872 case but voided in 1887.[9]

The protracted resolution of even such basic issues as these conditioned the decision-making of individuals engaged in transportation. Should one comply with questionable state and municipal acts, or should one resist and fight them out in the courts? In most cases, Morgan took the latter course.

One of his earliest contributions to clarifying the tax situation had been the suit of the Southern Steamship Company against the Masters and Port Wardens of New Orleans. This case, brought in 1855 and decided in Morgan's favor in 1867, became a landmark in prohibiting state taxation or interference with the right to navigate public waters.[10]

Other irksome burdens were the tonnage duties and wharfage charges that some Reconstruction governments imposed upon shipping. The most flagrant levies were made in a major area of Morgan's operations—Alabama and Louisiana—and he participated in a number of joint actions designed to test the legality of these measures. As a steam-packet operator, whose stock in trade was regular service by large vessels, these taxes were particularly burdensome to him. And while the ultimately decisive cases were not always in his name, Morgan was intimately involved in identifying the problems, in resisting taxes, in instigating litigation, and pressuring for judicial interpretation.

The effect of these suits on state tonnage taxes was the 1870 federal rejection of Alabama acts of 1866 and 1867 levying a tax of $1 per ton (registered tonnage) "on all steamboats, vessels, and other water crafts plying in the navigable waters of the State."[11] The federal Supreme Court

7. *Passenger Cases,* 7 Howard (U.S.) 282, 408 (1849); *Crandall v. Nevada,* 6 Wallace (U.S.) 35, 44, 46 (1867).

8. *State Freight Tax Cases,* 15 Wallace (U.S.) 232, 273, 281, 282 (1872).

9. *State Tax on Railway Gross Receipts,* 15 Wallace (U.S.) 284, 295, 296 (1872); *Philadelphia and Southern Mail Steamship Co. v. Pennsylvania,* 122 U.S. 326, 338, 342 (1887).

10. *Steamship Co. v. Port Wardens,* 6 Wallace (U.S.) 31, 34, 35 (1867). See also *Moran v. New Orleans,* 112 U.S. 69, 74, 75 (1884).

11. *State Tonnage Tax Cases,* 12 Wallace (U.S.) 204, 213, 214, 217, 218, 224, 225, 226 (1870).

voided municipal tonnage taxes levied by New Orleans in 1874.[12] Wharf-age charges, as distinguished from tonnage duties, were continually up-held by the courts, however, and were a constant burden, especially in New Orleans.[13]

Morgan also challenged quarantine fees when levied by the states. In a Texas case decided in 1873 he successfully voided such fees when levied according to the tonnage of vessels involved. His company lost a Louisiana case in 1886, however, when it was proven that the fees were devoted wholly to quarantine expenses and were not levied on a tonnage basis.[14]

Property taxes on vessels, as distinguished from tonnage duties, were another gambit of Reconstruction governments. Morgan was instrumental in clarifying this situation in a clash with the City of Mobile discussed more fully in Chapter 8.[15] He also became involved in several cases concerning state and local taxation of railroad companies. He never challenged the taxes as unconstitutional; he merely claimed the right of inheritance for the tax exemptions originally granted to the N.O.O. & G.W., which he purchased in 1869. The U. S. Supreme Court, however, ruled in 1876 that tax benefits "did not attach to the property of the corporation so as to follow it into the hands of third parties."[16]

Morgan's tax liability was thus much greater after the Civil War than ever before. A profusion of new taxes and the courts' slowness in sorting out their constitutionality caused this, rather than any change in his business policies. His tax difficulties reflect some of his problems under Reconstruction governments, and his consistent and intense involvement in their resolution indicates the importance of these challenges to his enterprises. Much more important, however, was the other side of Mor-gan's postwar dealings with government—his role, for him un-precedented, as applicant for, and recipient of, public aid. Besides his mail subsidies and military contracts (discounting the Nicaraguan aberra-tion), the chartering of the Southern Steamship Company and a few wharfage and port-fee exemptions were his only examples of receiving

12. *Cannon v. New Orleans,* 20 Wallace (U.S.) 577, 580 (1874).
13. *Ouachita Packet Company v. Aiken,* 121 U.S. 444, 447, 448, 450 (1887).
14. *Peete v. Morgan,* 19 Wallace (U.S.) 581 (1873); *Morgan's Steamship Co. v. Louisiana Board of Health,* 118 U.S. 455, 463 (1886).
15. *Morgan v. Parham,* 16 Wallace (U.S.) 471 (1873).
16. *State v. Morgan,* 28 Louisiana Ann. 482 (1876); *Morgan v. Louisiana,* 3 Otto (U.S.) 217 (1876).

public assistance before the Civil War. He actively sought public funds after the war, however, because of increased availability and because of basic changes in his business goals. The circumstances of this change bear brief notice here.

At the federal level Morgan continued to seek and win mail subsidies and military charter work that remained important parts of his business receipts. In bidding for these franchises, however, he experienced increasingly serious competition from parallel rail lines and had to relinquish several short-haul routes to them. To lose to rival water carriers had once been his major fear; now an entirely new competitor had appeared.

A more basic result of the railroad's presence in the Gulf States was its intensification of intercity rivalries and its scrambling of traditional land and water trade routes. Morgan's reactions to these developments included his "coming ashore" to engage in railroads himself and embarking on an ambitious program of port development and rail-water integration. This involved him more than ever in federal, state, and local politics and finance affecting transportation. He sought various forms of public aid in Louisiana and Texas but gained a minimum of support relative to his own efforts and accomplishments.

This summary underscores one basic change in Morgan's postwar activity—an increased, more fluid, and more uncertain inter-relationship with government. At one time he might be an active litigant able to expedite crucial issues to the federal courts by virtue of his personal proprietorship and interstate operations. Or, as an interested party, he might lend his name and prestige to the suits of others. He might openly defy the law by resisting taxation[17] and yet petition for public assistance in his enterprises. He was seldom passive, however, and it was his interaction with his environment which produced change and helped remold each.

These political and fiscal difficulties and the legalities they involved

17. Morgan was constantly resisting one city or state tax or another. For example, he owed the following amounts in New Orleans taxes as of the dates shown: $2,000 (7/31/71); $2,750 (7/31/72); $8,685 (7/31/73); $20,570 (7/31/74). On 8/12/73 he was listed as owing $129,041.50 in back Louisiana state taxes. Most of these sums were resolved one way or the other by the lawsuits cited above. See also: *Republican*, July 11, 1869, March 26, August 13, 1871, August 22, 1872, April 24, 29, August 5, 12, 1873, August 4, 1874, May 22, June 3, 1875; Protest by Morgan, February 18, 1870. Act before George W. Christy, N.A. (Orleans).

were overlaid and intertwined with the coming to the Gulf of railroads and long-haul steamships. They all impinged on Morgan at different times and in varying patterns, but all were basic factors affecting the course of his postwar business strategy. The next three chapters consider the major ways in which these problems clustered and illustrate Morgan's adaptive path to ultimate rationalization of the situation.

Figure 1. Charles Morgan (1795–1878), from painting about 1835. Note *Columbia* in background.

Courtesy, Mrs. Charles Bailey.

Figure 2. Emily Reeves Morgan, Charles Morgan's first wife.

Courtesy, Mrs. Charles Bailey.

Figure 3. Advertisement for Morgan Iron Works, 1850.

Figure 4. Columbia, built 1835, Morgan's first wholly owned vessel. She opened the Texas trade in 1837.

Figure 5. Neptune, chief competitor for Morgan's Texas trade.

Figure 6. Waterfront facilities at Indianola, port of call second only to Galveston. Note rails and handcars on wharves (*ca.* 1850).

Figure 7. Calhoun, purchased 1856, was typical of the steamships used in the intra-Gulf trade in the 1850s.

Figure 8. Empire City, pride of Morgan's Empire City Line, 1849–51, was typical of the type of steamship used by Morgan, Garrison, and Vanderbilt in the Central American transit wars. Note sidewheels and "clipper" bow.

Figure 9. Cornelius Vanderbilt, Morgan's chief competitor for the Central American trade.

Figure 10. C. K. Garrison, Morgan's ally in the Nicaragua transit wars.

Figure 11. Morgan City, built 1876, one of Morgan's first New York–Gulf long-haul screw steamships.

Figure 12. Aransas, built 1877, was a special screw steamer built expressly for the shallow Texas coast. She was an important innovation in marine architecture for her day.

Courtesy, The Mariners Museum, Newport News, Virginia.

Figure 13. Cutaway drawing of *Chalmette*, a typical Morgan screw steamship of the 1880s.

Figure 14. Saccharine, one of three inland vessels owned and operated by the Morgan Line to connect Bayou Teche, Louisiana, with its railroad.

Courtesy, Mrs. J. J. Lamperez.

Figure 15. "Christopher Adams," built for the N.O. & G.W.R.R. by Rogers in 1853, later to become M.L. & T. No. 15. This photograph taken at the old passenger station in Algiers, around 1865.

Figure 16. M.L. & T. No. 27, a "Forney" Type engine built by Baldwin in 1879. It was a special engine used in moving railroad cars on and off car ferries in New Orleans.

Figure 17. Stock certificate in Morgan's Louisiana & Texas Railroad and Steamship Company.

PART IV

"Not houses finely roofed or the stones
of walls well-builded, nay nor canals
and dockyards, make the city, but men
able to use their opportunity."

Alcaeus, quoting Aristides, *Rhodian Oration.*

8

STEAMSHIPS VERSUS RAILROADS,
1867–1877

MORGAN'S first real test in the postwar Gulf economy resulted from the projection of railroads east and west of New Orleans. Since these lines would parallel his services to Mobile and Texas, they vitally threatened his interest. One rival was an old one, his "partner" on the "inside" route to Texas—the New Orleans, Opelousas, and Great Western. A newer and more formidable opponent was the New Orleans, Mobile, and Chatanooga. Each elicited a different response from the steamship operator; each basically altered his business system and goals.

Despite interruptions of service by crevasses and quarantines in 1866 and 1867, prospects of the "Opelousas" were promising after Federal troops relinquished her on January 31, 1866. Gross receipts for 1866 totaled $414,000; 1867 receipts, $378,199. Plans to extend the road beyond Brashear to Houston or Dallas continued, and $343,452 was expended in 1866 alone for surveys, grading, and land purchases toward extension.[1]

But the railroad was far from prosperous. Of its $6,000,000 authorized capital, two thirds had been subscribed by the end of 1868, but not more than one third was actually paid up. Of a $2,000,000 first mortgage on the Algiers to Brashear section, negotiated April 1, 1859, $1,987,000 of

1. *Fourteenth Annual Report of the President and Directors of the New Orleans, Opelousas, and Great Western Railroad Company* (1867), *passim; Fifteenth . . .* (1868), *passim.*

the twenty-year bonds had been sold by January 25, 1869. However, overdue 8 per-cent-interest coupons totaled $606,600 on October 1, 1868, with $80,000 more coming due on April 1, 1869. An effort to fund these maturing coupons with a $1,000,000 second mortgage of March 1, 1867, had not attracted investors—only $34,000 being subscribed by January 25, 1869, with overdue interest coupons already totaling $4,080. Other debts of the road on January 25, 1869, totaled $54,977.83, including $34,011.59 balance due, with interest on $113,770 for rolling stock and rails purchased from the War Department when the railroad had been relinquished by the military authorities.[2]

Prospects for federal or state aid were bleak. Provisions of 1856 for a federal land grant had never been implemented and expired in 1866,[3] and the Republican legislature of Louisiana "was not likely to give any aid to a notoriously Confederate railroad."[4] The loss of most of the "Texas freight business" to Morgan's "outside" route also dimmed hopes of future revenue. Unquestionably, a lack of freight receipts, due to the inconvenience of transshipping twice (at Algiers and Brashear), cut deepest into the railroad's financial expectations.[5]

The plight of the railroad became worse on June 10, 1868, with the filing of a suit against it in U. S. District Court in New Orleans. The action, brought by the Illinois Central Railroad, requested bankruptcy proceedings against the Opelousas, alleging nonpayment of ten first-mortgage-bond coupons totaling $400. The "southern ambitions" of Illinois Central were well known and such a railroad as that to Brashear

2. Mortgage, N.O.O. & G.W. to Edmund J. Forstall, April 1, 1859. Act before Magner, N.A. (Orleans) ; Agreement between N.O.O. & G.W. and Forstall, April 1, 1859. *Ibid.*; Contract between N.O.O. & G.W. and Forstall and Louisiana State Bank, October 25, 1859. *Ibid.*; Second Mortgage, N.O.O. & G.W. to Samuel Smith, March 1, 1867. *Ibid.*; *Sixteenth Annual Report of the President and Directors of the New Orleans, Opelousas, and Great Western Railroad Company* (1869), *passim.*

3. "The New Orleans, Opelousas and Great Western Railroad Company received in 1856 a land grant aggregating 719.193 acres from the United States Government. Of these lands, 175 acres were sold for the sum of $1,044.75. Expenses incident thereto amounted to $14,653.40, resulting in a net loss of $13,608.65. By an act of Congress, approved July 14, 1870, the unsold part of the grant was declared forfeited to the United States Government." 36 ICC Val. Rep. 662.

4. Odom, "Louisiana Railroads," pp. 182–183.

5. *Fifteenth Annual Report . . .* , 20–21.

would have provided a springboard from New Orleans to the West.[6] Citizens of the Crescent City followed the suit closely; none watched more closely than Charles Morgan.

Morgan had been interested in the N.O.O. & G.W. from its inception, first as a competitor, then as a partner and investor. Throughout the Civil War, he had purchased bonds and interest coupons of the railroad, initially as an investment of growth potential, but gradually with a view toward incorporating the railroad-steamship service to Texas under his own flag. There were definite advantages, too, in the Brashear connection. The railroad had provided ample accommodations for his steamers and expended some $10,000 in clearing a seaway through Atchafalaya Bay. With his ships based at Brashear, Morgan would enjoy better physical facilities, cheaper municipal taxation, lessened port fees, and avoid the lengthy and costly navigation of the lower Mississippi River. The *Picayune* commented in 1869 that the "expenses to which ships coming to this city [are put] for pilotage, towage, wharfage and other port charges, are positively frightful," and in 1875, reminisced, "the wharfage dues, and the port-warden's fees and the harbormaster's tax, and all the rest of the miserable afflictions that are slowly cutting our commercial throat, drove Mr. Morgan with his fleet and the various attendant industries away from New Orleans to build a city on Berwick's Bay."[7] Brashear, described in 1863 as "a big mud hole with a few houses stuck up on stilts," would soon become the thriving hub of the Morgan Line.[8]

Morgan got his first inside glimpse of the railroad's plight in March 1868. Acting upon a resolution of their board of directors, "to secure the services of some individual to aid in the prosecution of this great enterprise whose ability and widespread reputation will command the attention of capitalists," three representatives of the road sought his aid. His response was noncommittal.

He first learned of the threat of legal proceedings against the N.O.O. & G.W. in April. On April 23, twenty-six first-mortgage bondhold-

6. These attitudes of the I.C. are implicit in John F. Stover, "Southern Ambitions of the Illinois Central Railroad," *Journal of Southern History*, XX (November 1954), 499–510.

7. New Orleans *Daily Picayune*, January 30, December 9, 1869, July 29, 1875.

8. Leo M. Kaiser (editor), "The Civil War Diary of Florison D. Pitts," *Mid-America*, XL (January 1958), 47.

ers of the road, led by William S. Pike of New Orleans, proposed an agreement to file suit seeking judicial sale of the road. Morgan, as "a large holder of the first mortgage bonds" of the company, was approached to join but declined, and the suit was abandoned. Before alternative action could be taken, the Illinois Central action against the Opelousas intervened.[9]

Yet Morgan was not diverted from his alternate idea. Meeting with Pike in New York in early September 1868, he proposed (provided the railroad's directors would agree) to

Lease the right of way and franchise of the railroad from Algiers to Sabine River, or as far as they exist, with all its privileges and property of every kind, for a term of 99 years, on condition that the lessees pay all the indebtedness of the company, and also pay $5,000 per annum to keep up the organization of the company; and also on condition that they extend the railroad to Sabine River . . . within four years after the signing of the lease. The lease to include the ferry rights and privileges and property between New Orleans and Algiers.[10]

Pike and associates of his choosing were to assume one third of the cost of the enterprise, Morgan, two thirds.

Returning to New Orleans, Pike subsequently declined Morgan's offer because of a lack of funds and his opinion that other railroad bondholders would not relinquish their securities at the 40 to 50 per cent discounts Morgan was willing to pay. Morgan accepted Pike's refusal with "good wishes" but expressed the opinion that the "road will probably now get into bankruptcy."[11] That is, unless it could be prevented. Spurned in his lease plan, Morgan turned to the courts. He employed Miles Taylor of New Orleans as counsel with instructions to institute such suits as Taylor deemed advisable "for the enforcement of his rights . . . and to join the counsel of the [railroad] company in resisting the application [of Illinois Central] . . . pending . . . to put the road into bankruptcy."[12]

Taylor immediately brought suit against the Opelousas company in the

9. Minute Book No. 2, Board of Directors, N.O.O. & G.W., March 5, 1868, N.O.O. & G.W. Records; Miles Taylor to Public, *Daily Picayune*, May 25, 1869.

10. Memorandum of Conditions Written and Delivered to Me [Pike] by Chas. Morgan, Esq. [no date], *Daily Picayune*, May 28, 1869; Morgan to Pike, September 10, 1868, *ibid.*

11. Pike to Morgan, September 20, 1868, Morgan to Pike, September 25, 1868, *ibid.*

12. Taylor to Public, *Daily Picayune*, May 25, 1869.

Sixth District Court of Orleans Parish "for foreclosure of mortgage *via executiva . . .* on $219,000 of coupons past due," and speedily obtained an order of that court for the seizure and sale of the railroad. Illinois Central checked Morgan's gambit, however. An order of the federal District Court enjoined the order of seizure and sale pending that court's decision on the application to have the company adjudicated a bankrupt.[13]

Morgan had instituted his counteraction because of the widespread rumor that the Opelousas would lose its case to Illinois Central, and as a large bondholder of the former, he might thus lose a sizable investment. Hence he took immediate steps to circumvent the injunction of the District Court. Under an agreement signed December 18, 1868, in which Morgan secured the consent of twenty-four other bondholders, Taylor discontinued the enjoined suit and turned from the state to the federal courts.[14] On February 23, 1869, he filed a petition for executory process in the U. S. Circuit Court, District of Louisiana. Entering the suit in Morgan's name, Taylor later recalled, "I deemed it more advantageous to carry on the litigation in that court; and as he was a citizen of the State of New York, by using his name alone that court would have jurisdiction of the cause." But as the caustic *Republican* put it, the Opelousas railroad, "with that 'old man of the sea,' Charles Morgan, on its back . . . has been ridden by him into the Bankrupt court."[15]

Yet it was not bankruptcy which Morgan sought for the road. His petition to the Circuit Court identified himself as holder of 840 first-mortgage bonds of the Opelousas and of 7,921 overdue interest coupons—a total claim against the railroad of $316,840. He requested an order of payment be issued to the railroad under threat of seizure and sale by the court.[16]

The railroad thus faced two creditors in two courts: Illinois Central seeking bankruptcy proceedings; Morgan requesting a mortgage foreclosure. The key was Judge E. H. Durell who, as District Judge, was

13. *Ibid.;* New Orleans *Republican,* January 31, 1869.
14. New Orleans *Commercial Bulletin,* January 7, 14, 19, 22, February 1, 1869; *Daily Picayune,* January 16, 1869; *Republican,* January 28, 1869; New Orleans *Daily Crescent,* January 30, 1869.
15. Taylor to Public, *Daily Picayune,* May 25, 1869; *Republican,* March 17, 1869.
16. U. S. Circuit Court, District of Louisiana, *Record in Suit No. 5788: Charles Morgan v. New Orleans, Opelousas, and Great Western Railroad Co.,* pp. 1–11.

presiding at both suits. On March 29, in a surprise decision, he dismissed the Illinois Central petition, ruling the bonds and coupons of railroad companies not within the meaning of "commercial paper" as defined in the Bankruptcy Act of 1867 and further, held no acts worthy of an adjudication of bankruptcy had been committed by the railroad. Even the conservative, Old Whig *Commercial Bulletin,* was amazed (for Opelousas stock had plummeted under the general impression that Durell would declare them bankrupt), commenting, "somebody has made a 'nice thing' by the change that came o'er the spirit of the judicial mind." In any case, the decision eliminated the Illinois Central threat and isolated Morgan and the Opelousas as the remaining combatants.[17]

Morgan, who had been in the Crescent City since January, "watching with his eagle eye the first flushing of the quarry," and, ignoring rumors linking his name with various other speculators on the scene, pressed home his suit.[18]

Judge Durell responded on March 30, ordering payment of Morgan's claims plus court costs within three days under threat of seizure and sale, the price of the sale to be payable in two installments: cash to fund at par all past-due interest coupons outstanding as of January 25, 1869; the remainder payable on April 1, 1889, and carrying 8 per cent interest, payable semiannually. The writ was served on March 31, the railroad seized by the U.S. Marshal on April 5, and advertised for sale on the following day. The auction was scheduled for May 25.[19]

The railroad's managers, although unable to pay the amounts ordered, took immediate countermeasures. Their plan was twofold: first, the filing of a bill-in-chancery with the Circuit Court praying an injunction against the sale, pending preparation of a proper defense; second, an appeal to the public to subscribe further funds for the completion of the railroad. Their petition for injunction was entered April 5, and by May 4 they had their new prospectus before the public. They proposed a bond-stock combination subscription, offering with each $1,000 of second-mortgage bonds forty shares of common stock. Prompt public acceptance, they felt, would allow them to pay past-due coupons, build on to Vermillionville

17. *Commercial Bulletin,* January 7, March 30, 1869; *Republican,* January 28, 31, 1869; *Daily Picayune,* March 30, 1869.

18. *Commercial Bulletin,* January 14, 22, February 1, 1869; *Republican,* January 31, April 16, 1869; *Daily Crescent,* January 30, 1869.

19. U. S. Circuit Court, Dist. of La., *Record in Suit No. 5788,* pp. 11–15.

(now Lafayette) within two years, and with income thereby derived, pay current and future interest on their first- and second-mortgage bonds.[20]

Morgan's action and the railroad's reaction sparked intense public debate. The press supported the railroad's propositions in varying degrees, but the *Commercial Bulletin* most realistically characterized them as "suppositions, potentialities and felicitous contingencies and sequences, stated with logical skill in picturesque rhetoric." Opinion regarding Morgan ranged from the vitriolic attacks of the *Republican* to the watchful waiting of the *Picayune* and the other more southern journals.

The *Republican* was unrelenting in its criticism. It charged [correctly] that George Pandely, who had been appointed Deputy Marshal in charge of the seized Opelousas, was in the pay of Morgan as Superintendent of the Pontchartrain Railroad in which Morgan held stock. Pandely was also rebuked as chairman of a railroad committee of the New Orleans Common Council which endorsed the seizure and sale. The *Republican* argued that Morgan netted "$1,000 a day" from his Brashear steamers and would never extend the railroad, and piled personal invective on his name:

are there no men here capable of ridding us of this incubus? . . . Why should we be afraid of him? He is only worth eight hundred thousand dollars. . . . If he were a Vanderbilt or a Stewart, with more than a paltry million of dollars to back him, there might be some excuse for us in backing down before him. Charles Morgan knew the selection of a spot for his schemes when he chose New Orleans for the place of operations; for in no other city of this country possessing one-fourth the resources of our own could he be allowed to so hamper and check commerce and bind the citizens hand and foot.[21]

Unlike the pro-Radical *Republican*, the *Commercial Bulletin* and the other hallowed ante bellum journals took a more realistic view:

it does not follow necessarily that Mr. Morgan, in case of his purchasing the properties sold under his mortgage, would . . . use his new position to prevent the further extension of the road. This gentleman must know that the time has come when railroad connection between New Orleans and Texas, by *some* route, can not be long postponed. If this connection should be effected by a rival line . . . the event would work against his interests both as a railroad and as a steamship proprietor. . . . The vessels he might send into some other trade, but his railroad property would prove about as dead an investment as a capitalist ever stumbled into. It is plain . . . that if Morgan

20. *Ibid.*, pp. 27–35; *Daily Picayune*, April 3–4, 6, 26, May 2, 1869.
21. *Republican*, April 16–17, 20, 22, 27–28, 30, May 4, 6–7, 1869.

shall . . . be influenced by a rational conception of his own interests, he will be disposed to forestall rival enterprises by completing connection with Texas by the Opelousas route at the earliest day.[22]

What the *Picayune* and the southern press urged was a co-operative stock subscription *with* Morgan—"put your own shoulder to the wheel when you call on Hercules."[23]

Both plans of the railroad management, however, were doomed: by May 22 only about one-half of the expected $1,000,000 subscription had been reserved, and on May 24, Judge Durell denied their petition to stay sale of their road.[24]

The long-awaited sale took place at noon, May 25, on the steps of the New Orleans Custom House. "Mr. Morgan, who was present, kept in the background, though his representative was near the stand." Bidding opened at $1,000,000 and progressed in $500,000 increments to $2,000,000 bid by Jules A. Blanc, representing other bondholders of the road. Then after one or two calls came Morgan's response, via Charles A. Whitney: " 'Two millions and fifty thousand dollars.' " As the U.S. Marshal's gavel closed the sale, Morgan's friends besieged him with congratulations, "though he did not seem to regard his purchase as a very low one." His only statement was "he would now show the people of New Orleans how to build a road."[25]

Morgan immediately presented his plans for the railroad to Texas. His four objectives, one implicit, three explicit, were carefully outlined to the public. His first desire was to dispel any rumors that he was unwilling to extend the road. On the morning of May 25, even before the auction, he published in the New Orleans press his correspondence with Pike of the previous year, which underscored his desire to participate in projects to lengthen the road. On May 27, again in a public letter, he testified affirmatively to that cause. His candid but eloquent statements swayed even the hostile *Republican* to commend "this far-seeing financier." Morgan also pledged himself to secure final title to that portion of the railroad he had purchased and to place it "in the most perfect order."[26]

22. *Commercial Bulletin*, April 26, 28, May 8, 1869.
23. *Daily Picayune*, May 2, 6–13, 15–16, 18–19, 22–23, 1869.
24. *Ibid.*, May 22, 25, 1869; U.S. Circuit Court, Dist. of La., *Record in Suit No. 5788*, pp. 36–40.
25. *Daily Picayune*, May 26, 1869, January 29, 1870.
26. Taylor to Public, *Daily Picayune*, May 25, 1869; Morgan to Public, May 26, 1869, *ibid.*, May 27, 28, 1869; *Commercial Bulletin*, May 27, 29, 1869; *Republican*, May 27, June 1, 1869.

More important was Morgan's fourth objective. Severely critical of the mortgage-bond method of financing conducted by the Opelousas, he proposed the formation of a new corporation based on $4,000,000 capital stock, subscribed in cash, "in advance." This company would then dedicate itself to acquiring from the Opelousas management their franchises and improvements west of Brashear and then to completing the railroad to Texas. Morgan promised to subscribe up to $2,000,000 of the stock in cash if the public of Louisiana and Texas would purchase the remainder. His bond would be his word and his reputation, having "been engaged for the last forty years . . . carrying on a business in the city of New Orleans . . . [and spending] the greater portion of my time during that succession of years . . . in this city in the management of my business."[27]

His first two objectives were speedily achieved. His frank statements to the press had left little doubt of his positive intensions; he also soon secured title to his railroad. The purchase price of $2,050,000 was applied to the costs of the suit and to funding (plus 8 per-cent-per-annum interest from date of default) all first-mortgage coupons of the Opelousas overdue on April 1, 1869. A portion of the sum was also applied to pro rata funding of the bonds themselves, payable April 1, 1889, and carrying 8 per cent interest from May 25, 1869. These terms netted creditors only $29.36½ per $40-coupon and $742.70 per $1,000-bond, but yielded Morgan the railroad.[28] The Opelousas company contested the foreclosure and sale in an appeal to the U.S. Supreme Court. That court, however, upheld the Circuit Court's dismissal of the company's petition for retrial, confirming Morgan's *de facto* possession in an opinion rendered November 14, 1870.[29]

The New York businessman had purchased eighty miles of single-track railway with right-of-way, roadbed, bridging, depots, and rolling stock. Its eastern terminus was a forty-acre freight yard fronting 370 feet on the Mississippi River opposite New Orleans. From this Algiers station, the line ran westward through Jefferson, Terrebonne, and St. Mary parishes

27. Morgan to Public, May 26, 1869, *Daily Picayune*, May 27, 1869.
28. Marshal's Sale, N.O.O. & G.W. to Morgan, July 31, 1869. Recorded in Conveyance Office (Orleans Parish, La.), Book 97, pp. 208–214 (September 16, 1869), hereafter cited as C.O. (Orleans); Receipt, F. J. Herron, U.S. Marshal to Whitney & Co., September 16, 1869, M.L. & T.R. & S. Records; *Daily Picayune*, December 12, 1869.
29. U. S. Circuit Court, Dist. of La., *Record in Suit No. 5788*, pp. 17–27, 41–42; *New Orleans, Opelousas, and Great Western Railroad Co. v. Morgan*, 10 Wallace (U.S.) 256 (1870).

to a complex of wharves, warehouses, cattle landings, and coal yards fronting over 330 feet on the Atchafalaya at Brashear. Since Morgan's purchase price had funded both the stocks and bonds of the old Opelousas company, he was now the road's sole proprietor. Renamed Morgan's Louisiana and Texas Railroad, the line was placed by procuration under the management of Whitney & Co.[30] Although Morgan, a New York resident, retained ownership, the headquarters of the road became the handsome office of Whitney and Hutchinson at Magazine and Natchez streets, New Orleans—a building owned by Morgan, in which he maintained a "desk," and from whence he assumed the reins of management when in the Crescent City.[31]

The immediate task of Morgan and his managers was to improve upon what had been purchased. They had acquired no property or franchises west of Brashear for extension, and only a pedestrian ferry connected the railroad's eastern terminus with New Orleans. The correction of these deficiencies, so necessary to westward extension of the line, became the New Yorker's goal. At every turn he met apathy and adversity, controversy and competition.

Morgan's challenger was the New Orleans, Mobile, and Chattanooga Railroad Company, a corporation chartered by the Alabama legislature in acts of November 24, 1866, and February 12, 1867. This railroad—a project of New York and Boston investors, including Oakes Ames, James A. Raynor, Henry J. Gardner, and Peter Butler—was projected from Mobile to New Orleans and Chattanooga, having secured appropriate charters from Mississippi and Tennessee in 1867 and from Louisiana in 1868.[32] In its Louisiana charter, an extension from the Crescent City to Texas was added to the railroad's prospectus, and increasingly that route supplanted the Chattanooga segment in importance.[33] Planning a route

30. Procuration, Morgan to Whitney and Hutchinson, September 16, 1869. Act before Charles Nettleton, Commissioner for La. in N.Y., M.L. & T.R. & S. Records.
31. Morgan had purchased the former City National Bank building for $55,000 in March. Sale, City National Bank to Morgan, March 6, 1869. Act before Joseph Cohn, N.A. (Orleans), C.O. (Orleans), Book 94, p. 547 (March 8, 1869).
32. *Charter of the New Orleans, Mobile, and Chattanooga Railroad Company and Laws Relating Thereto*, pp. 7–26, 28, 30–45, 79–91.
33. Articles of Association, South Western Co., May 3, 1867. Act before Henry C. Banks, Commissioner for La. in N.Y., M.O. (Orleans), Society Book VI, 423 (May 11, 1867); Articles of Association, New Orleans, Mobile, and Chattanooga Railroad Co. of La., May 3, 1867, *ibid.*, 469 (August 5, 1867); *Louisiana Acts* (1868), pp. 28–38.

from Mobile to Texas via New Orleans, the New Orleans, Mobile, and Chattanooga officials were obviously interested in Morgan's steamers to Mobile and in his aim to extend his railroad to Texas. On both fronts, this interest soon turned into obstructionism and competition.

Morgan's May 27 publication of his plan for extending his railroad had received general endorsement by the press—even the *Republican* made proposals for allocating the $2,000,000 subscription among wealthy citizens of New Orleans. Hence on June 29, the New Yorker took concrete steps to implement his proposals by issuing a prospectus for a corporation to be called the Berwick's Bay and Texas Railroad Company. The company would be capitalized at $4,000,000 to construct and operate a railroad west from Brashear to Texas by the "most eligible route" with branches to the Red River area. It would operate provisionally until a state charter was secured, but would begin its corporate existence once $1,000,000 was subscribed. As evidence of good faith, Morgan immediately subscribed for $2,000,000 (at 2½ per cent down) and seventeen other investors contracted for $100,000. With this positive move, Morgan turned to other objects while awaiting public subscription of the remaining $1,900,000 and the reconvening of the Louisiana legislature.[34] He also precipitated his first serious controversy with the Chattanooga railroad.

On June 29, to secure adequate ferry connections between Algiers and New Orleans, Morgan petitioned the New Orleans Common Council for permission to purchase Square 27A at the foot of Girod Street with riparian rights and exclusive ferry privileges on a 600-foot river frontage extending from 135 feet below Girod, to 135 feet above Notre Dame, and back to Water.[35] He offered to relinquish the antiquated Opelousas ferry at the foot of St. Ann Street and construct a modern New Orleans depot and railroad-car ferry on Square 27A and on two contiguous squares (16A: Delta–Water–Girod–Notre Dame; 5A: Delta–Girod–Notre Dame–Front) which he had purchased for $47,000 earlier in the year.[36]

34. Prospectus, Berwick's Bay and Texas Railroad Company, June 29, 1869, *Daily Picayune*, June 29, 1869; Whitney & Co. to Public, June 29, 1869, *ibid.*

35. *Daily Picayune*, June 30, 1869; *Commercial Bulletin*, July 2, 1869.

36. Sales, Philip M. Betz, Jane M. Roe, Marx Kaufman and Colman Hirsch, and George P. Bowers, April 13, 1869. Acts before Magner, N.A. (Orleans), C.O. (Orleans), Book 97, p. 7 (April 16, 1869), Book 94, pp. 625–626 (April 17, 1869); Sale, Henry Bidwell to Morgan, June 25, 1869. Act before Magner, N.A. (Orleans), C.O. (Orleans), Book 94, p. 769 (June 26, 1869).

These properties were ideally located immediately below the 900-foot Julia Street wharf at which Morgan's "outside" steamers landed and adjoined the new depot of the Pontchartrain Railroad at the intersection of Delta and Girod. Thence rail connections via the levee to Elysian Fields Avenue, the lake, and Morgan's Mobile steamers were available.[37]

Morgan's petition was recommended by the Council's Streets and Landings Committee and passed the Board of Assistant Aldermen on July 6. During the intervening week, however, while consideration by the whole Council pended, the Chattanooga railroad and its journalistic sympathizer, the New Orleans *Republican* loosed a storm of protest. Possessed of conflicting levee grants (which included Square 27A) from city and state acts of 1867 and 1868, the railroad secured an injunction from the Fifth District Court of Orleans Parish restraining the proposed sale to Morgan. The Council was assailed for bartering away a valuable landing and square merely to increase Morgan's domination of the riverfront, and the railroad's claims were pressed before the court, the aldermen, and the public.[38]

Despite the growing controversy, on July 15 the Council, with but one dissenting vote, approved Ordinance 1492, N.S. Square 27A and the desired 600 feet of river frontage, with exclusive ferry and landing privileges, were to be sold to Morgan for $54,000 and his release of the old St. Ann ferry. The only restriction placed on the sale was that the Chattanooga company's injunction must first be "dissolved or set aside according to law." Morgan formally accepted the ordinance on July 12, but the fight was just beginning.[39]

Within two months three new injunctions blocked the proposed sale of Square 27A. The railroad and the state, again arguing the precedence of state grants to the railroad over the city's grants to Morgan, obtained more comprehensive orders from the Fifth District Court. A third suit, entered in the Seventh District Court by J. T. Burdeau representing the New Orleans Chamber of Commerce and several barge lines, protested

37. The Pontchartrain Railroad had extended its tracks along the levee from Elysian Fields and Peters to Delta and Girod in 1867.

38. *Daily Picayune*, July 7, 1869; *Republican*, July 10–13, 1869; *Charter of the New Orleans, Mobile, and Chattanooga*, pp. 46–78, 133–142.

39. *Republican*, July 14, 1869; *Daily Picayune*, July 14, 16, 1869; Acceptance of City Ordinance 1492, N.S. by Morgan, July 17, 1869. Act before Magner, N.A. (Orleans).

the deprivation of wharfage they would suffer if Morgan's grant was approved. Arguments in the various suits dragged late in 1869, delaying transfer of those lands and rights granted provisionally by Ordinance 1492, N.S.[40]

Pending the outcome of this litigation, Morgan postponed his plans for a Girod Street ferry and concentrated on enlarging the existing ferry at the foot of St. Ann. He expended over $100,000 fitting out *Porter*, *Lucretia*, and *Sarah* as railroad-car ferries and for ramps and turntables to permit switching cars directly from the various railroads in the city. Up to ten loaded cars per trip could be carried by the car ferry which opened between Jackson Square and Algiers on February 19, 1871. This landing was enlarged after August 23, 1871, by the addition of 700 feet of batture between Marigny and Barracks streets granted to Morgan by the city for ten years. Although denied the Girod Street square he preferred, Morgan thus made suitable alternate arrangements.[41]

As "the great batture case" dragged on, Morgan faced a new threat from the New Orleans, Mobile, and Chattanooga. Initially ridiculed as "a swindle. . . . laughed at by some and damned by others," the Chattanooga road soon demonstrated its vigor. Drawing upon $5,000,000 (of $25,000,000 authorized) of stock issued by its board on May 3, 1867, a $4,000,000 first mortgage executed to Oakes Ames and E. D. Morgan on January 1, 1869, and a $4,000,000 second mortgage to Henry J. Gardner and Peter Butler on March 8, the railroad began construction from Mobile on November 9, 1869, reached New Orleans on October 29, 1870, and formally opened on November 21.[42]

The completed railroad between Mobile and New Orleans was unbeatable competition for Morgan's steamers. The trains ran thrice daily to his one steamer and undercut his fare of $10 by half. In January 1871 Morgan reduced his fares to $2, berths and meals extra, and cut freight insurance rates by 50 per cent. The railroad responded in February with

40. *Daily Picayune*, July 16–18, 24, August 22, November 9, 12–14, 21, 23–24, 27–28, 1869; *Republican*, July 17–18, November 21, 24, 1869.

41. *Daily Picayune*, November 23, 1869, February 13, 1870, February 5, 21, June 21, 27–28, July 8, 1871; *Charter of Morgan's Louisiana and Texas Railroad and Steamship Company together with Statutes, Ordinances, By-Laws, etc. Relating to the Company*, p. 32.

42. *Republican*, July 1, 1869; *Daily Picayune*, October 8, 15, 18, November 10–11, 1869. January 7, August 21, October 29–30, November 21–22, 1870, August 17, October 5, 1873.

80 per cent reductions under Morgan's freight rates and by June had cut another 50 per cent.

Passengers preferred the swifter trains, especially after the introduction of Pullman Palace Cars on the line in March 1871. The most crushing blow, however, was the annulment of Morgan's $25,000 mail subsidy on December 19, effective December 31, 1870. While the steamers continued to attract more heavy freight shipments, the railroad by 1871 had diverted almost all New Orleans–Mobile passengers and mails to its coaches. As one of Morgan's critics had commented in 1869, "the Chattanooga Railroad promises to do all that Morgan does, but to do it better, quicker, and cheaper."[43]

A costly lawsuit with the City of Mobile added to Morgan's distress. Unlike the railroad company, whose assets were exempt from taxation under its Alabama charter, Morgan's vessels were considered taxable. Taxes levied by the city in 1866 and 1867 and resisted by Morgan brought litigation in the U. S. Circuit Court for the Southern District of Alabama in 1870. The court denied Morgan's arguments that his vessels were owned in New York, were engaged in interstate commerce, and were not "blended with the commerce and business of Alabama" and upheld the city's assessment of his vessels as personal property under Alabama law. Only after expensive and lengthy appeal did Morgan secure a reversal by the U. S. Supreme Court. The decision held in part:

The fact that the vessel was physically within the limits of the city, at the time the tax was levied, does not decide the question. . . . This vessel . . . remained the property of the plaintiff, with her home port at New York, and had never become blended with the commerce and property of the State of Alabama. . . . Whether the steamer . . . was actually taxed in New York . . . is not shown by the case. It is not important. She was liable to taxation there.[44]

Morgan proved his point and at least one advantage of his practice of nonresident personal ownership, but at cost in time and effort at a crucial point in his career. The opening of the railroad to Mobile was but one phase of a power struggle involving every segment of his operations.

43. *Republican*, July 1, 1869, January 22, February 1, March 10, June 20, 1871, May 29, 1872; *Daily Picayune*, May 1, 1870, January 15, 27, 31, February 19, April 28, May 2–3, 14, June 27, 1871; "Contracts for Carrying the Mails, 1871" (Serial 1513), 378, 676; Robert Somers, *The Southern States since the War, 1870–1*, pp. 188–191.
44. *Morgan v. Parham*, 16 Wallace (U.S.) 471 (1873).

Under its Louisiana charter of August 19, 1868, the New Orleans, Mobile, and Chattanooga had secured permission to construct a line "from its terminus . . . on or near the levee, in the city of New Orleans, . . . towards and to any point on the line . . . between Louisiana and . . . Texas." A state act of February 17, 1869, furthered that cause by guaranteeing the issuance of bonds equal to $12,500 per mile constructed. The bonds were to be delivered as each forty- (later ten-) mile segment of track was completed, the railroad being responsible only for the 8 per cent interest payments.[45] To secure the beginnings of such a railroad, the Chattanooga company sought the franchises and partially cleared road west of Brashear still held by the New Orleans, Opelousas, and Great Western. Since Morgan's Berwick's Bay and Texas company also sought this prize, the clash between the Chattanooga and Charles Morgan intensified.

Morgan won the first round in July 1869. By two suits in the Fourth District Court of Orleans Parish, he enjoined a proposed twenty-five year lease of the second division of the Opelousas by the Chattanooga company.[46] He then entered suit in U.S. Circuit Court against the Opelousas company, asking that its property west of Brashear be sold to satisfy sums due on bonds held by him and enjoining any sale or lease of the road until his claims were satisfied.[47] His plans remained twofold: to refurbish the line to Brashear and to promote the Berwick's Bay and Texas company scheme.

Despite charges that he was laying off workers in order to economize, Morgan undertook an extensive revitalization of his railroad. Chinese and Negro labor by 1870 had raised the entire grade and bridging of the road two feet to prevent flood damage. The wharves at Brashear were extended and connected by telegraph to Whitney & Co. in New Orleans. Morgan also took delivery on two new Baldwin locomotives and rebuilt two abandoned engines in his Algiers shops to add to the ten he had acquired

45. *Louisiana Acts* (1869), pp. 22–30.

46. The lease, for $2,000 per year, would have included "all the grants, franchises, privileges, railroads, roadbeds, gradings; rights of way, depots, depot grounds, rolling stock, and all other property . . . between Berwick's Bay and the Texas State Line." James A. Raynor to Stockholders, N.O.O. & G.W., July 21, 1869, *Republican*, July 22, 1869; *Daily Picayune*, July 22, 1869.

47. The sale of the first division of the road to Morgan on May 25, 1869, had funded $742.70 per $1,000 bond and $29.36½ per coupon. Morgan was now suing for the remainder. *Daily Picayune*, August 12, 1869.

with the road. He purchased thirteen new freight cars from the Southern Car Factory and two first-class passenger coaches from Harlan and Hollingsworth. The road's Algiers shops constructed one first-class passenger, four second-class passenger, and six freight cars. By the end of 1870, Morgan's Louisiana and Texas Railroad reported fourteen first-class locomotives, ten passenger, eight baggage and mail, 229 freight, and eight service cars in operation on its eighty-mile route.[48]

Morgan vigorously pursued the B.B. & T. plan. On November 12, 1869, he and others signed a notarial charter for the company; a five-man board of directors was elected with Whitney named president, and the charter was filed with $2,100,000 of $4,000,000 of stock subscribed. Morgan contracted for 20,000 shares, Whitney, Hutchinson, and Taylor for 100 each. Various New Orleans investors took the remaining $70,000, and the public was solicited to take the rest.[49] Pending this public subscription, Morgan resumed his plans to secure the Opelousas franchises through litigation. He discontinued the suit against the Opelousas company begun in U. S. Circuit Court in August and substituted new actions.

Between December 11 and 18, Morgan instituted four suits against the Opelousas company in the Seventh District Court of Orleans Parish. Two petitions in his name and one in the name of his attorney Miles Taylor were based on the pro rata settlement of the bonded debt of the railroad made in May. The proceeds from Morgan's purchase of the road had not satisfied the $10.63½ per coupon and $257.30 per bond of the first-mortgage debt, and Morgan and Taylor now sought seizure of the remaining assets of the company to satisfy residual claims totaling $359,475.75. A fourth action sued for $31,620.48, the balance and interest due the War Department, for materials sold to the road in January 1866. Morgan had purchased this lien from the government on June 26, 1869.[50] The

48. *Republican*, October 17, 1869; *Daily Picayune*, January 5, 1868, November 23, 1869, February 19, 26, 1870; Protest of Whitney & Co., January 3, 1870. Act before George W. Christy, N.A. (Orleans); *Manual of the Railroads of the United States for 1871–72*, p. 325; Gerald M. Best and David L. Joslyn, *Locomotives of the Southern Pacific Company*, pp. 53, 59.

49. Charter of the Berwick's Bay and Texas Railroad Co., November 12, 1869. Act before Magner, N.A. (Orleans), M.O. (Orleans), Society Book VII, 404 (November 25, 1869); *Daily Picayune*, October 28, November 10, 14, 19, December 12, 1869.

50. In suit No. 2248, Taylor claimed $5,320.25 and $6,432.60 as remainders due respectively on 500 coupons and 25 bonds. In suit Nos. 2249 and 2250, Morgan

intention of these suits was obvious: to force public sale of the property and franchises west of Brashear still held by the Opelousas company. Morgan would be the successful bidder. Litigation took time, however; hence Morgan resumed his search for aid for the B.B. & T. scheme. As public subscription to that plan had lagged, he turned, for the first time in his life, to the state legislature for funds. Here again he met the Chattanooga promoters.

On January 19, 1870, a bill to incorporate the Berwick's Bay and Texas Railroad Co. was introduced in the Louisiana House of Representatives. It asked legislative approval of the company's notarial charter of November 12, 1869, proposed to build a railroad from Brashear to Texas within twenty-eight months from date of passage, requested a seventy-five-yard right-of-way (to be located later), and asked for state funds to assist completion. Louisiana was to issue $1,500,000 in forty-year state bonds, bearing 8 per cent interest payable semiannually by coupon. The state would pay interest on these bonds from its general revenues. In deference to the times, the bill also assured the Republican legislature that no racial discrimination would be shown either to workers or passengers on the route.[51] Although supported by every New Orleans newspaper except the *Republican,* and by most journals along the proposed route, the bill was referred to the Committee on Railroads, and the House turned to a rival bill previously introduced by the Chattanooga company.

The Chattanooga bill, introduced on January 17, 1870, proposed in its final form to construct a railroad from the west bank of the Mississippi opposite New Orleans to Houston within forty-two months from the date of acceptance of the act by the company. To finance the road, $3,000,000 in state forty-year bonds were to be issued, bearing interest at 8 per cent, and deliverable to the company in $750,000 increments as the railroad reached Donaldsonville, Vermillionville, the Sabine, and Houston. The state would pay interest on the securities, and all previous state acts and city ordinances regarding ferry and levee rights in New Orleans were confirmed.[52]

---

claimed $106,375.50 on 9,993 coupons and $241,347.40 on 938 bonds. *Daily Picayune,* December 12–18, 1869; *Republican,* December 12–18, 1869; No. 2251, *ibid.*

51. "An Act [Proposed] Relative to the Berwick's Bay and Texas Railroad Co.," *Daily Picayune,* January 20, 1870.

52. *Daily Picayune,* January 18, 26–27, 29–30, February 1–3, 22, 1870.

The legislature favored the Chattanooga proposals from their introduction. The Republican sympathies of the directors of that road were obvious, while Morgan, although a New Yorker, was identified with more southern views.[53] The Chattanooga had also demonstrated its ability to build, as its road from Mobile was nearly complete.

In desperation Morgan journeyed to New Orleans on January 22 with an alternate proposal. In open letters to the legislature on January 25 and 27 he admitted that only "a little over $175,000" above his $2,000,000 had been subscribed to the B.B. & T., but presented a new bill containing a modified charter request. He proposed to construct a road from Brashear to Texas within three years at no cost to the state. In return the legislature would agree to grant no further bond subsidies to railroads west of the Mississippi, to grant no more parallel franchises or rights-of-way, and to confirm Morgan in possession of the property granted to him by New Orleans Ordinance 1492, N.S. He offered bond of $500,000 that he would "take all the remaining capital stock of the Berwick's Bay and Texas Railroad Company which is not taken by other persons within ten days after the passage of the act" and guaranteed the road's completion. Despite Morgan's generous offer, the legislature rejected his plan and signed the "Chattanooga bill" into law on February 21, 1870.[54]

Though defeated in the legislature, Morgan was successful in his suits against the Opelousas company. Under writs issued in his four suits before the Seventh District Court and four suits by other bondholders before that court and the Fourth District Court of Orleans Parish, the remaining assets of the New Orleans, Opelousas, and Great Western Railroad Co. were seized and sold at public auction on March 22, 1870. The only bidder was Morgan who, for $197,025.03 credit toward his various claims and $52,974.97 cash, purchased "the franchises to construct, maintain, run and operate" a railroad from Brashear to the Sabine, the right-of-way, lands, and grading for the same, and thirty-seven squares of land in the town of Brooklyn opposite New Orleans. He thus secured the rights necessary to build west of Brashear but placed himself

53. Throughout the Reconstruction period, Morgan was assailed by the Republican press as among "the enemies of Republican government" in Louisiana and endorsed by Democratic papers as "not a carpet-bagger." *Daily Picayune*, March 23, 1866, July 14, 1869, February 5, 1871; *Republican*, November 21, 1871; *Louisiana State Register*, January 6, 13, 1872.

54. Morgan to Senate and House of La., January 25, 1870, *Daily Picayune*, January 25, 1870; *Louisiana Acts* (1870), 9 ff.

in even more distinct opposition to the parallel route of the Chattanooga.[55]

Flushed with its legislative victory, the New Orleans, Mobile, and Chattanooga began construction from "West-we-go!" (now Westwego) opposite New Orleans in May 1870. By November, sixty-three miles of grading was complete to Donaldsonville, and by the end of the year forty miles of track had been laid. The line to Donaldsonville was completed on May 17, 1871, but no scheduled passenger or freight service was begun until November. The company had found state aid crucial, and the fortunes of the road fluctuated with the willingness of the legislature to issue funds.[56]

Not satisfied with racing Morgan westward from the Mississippi, impeding his ferry plans in New Orleans, and undercutting his Mobile rates, the Chattanooga company opened an opposition steamship line from New Orleans to Texas. On January 18, 1871, *Thomas Kelso*, which the railroad purchased for the purpose, began service from the Crescent City to Galveston and Indianola. With a promise of more steamers to follow, *Kelso* offered cabin passage at $12, one third less than Morgan's rate, and reduced freight charges by one fourth. She had reduced passage to $10 by February 8, and by May 28, had made six round trips to Indianola via Galveston, four to Rockport, and was hailed at all ports as healthy competition for the Morgan Line.[57]

Morgan, though a novice at railroading, knew how to meet competing steamers. He refused to lower his "card rates" and immediately doubled rates for any shipper also using *Kelso*. The "gulf shark" ignored protests from the coastal press until April 18, when passage on his steamers was reduced to $10 cabin, $5 on deck. Even so, Morgan refused to forward to or from Texas any freight handled or to be handled by the New Orleans, Mobile, and Texas—a new name the railroad company adopted in mid-1871.[58]

55. Sheriff's Sale, N.O.O. & G.W. to Morgan, April 22, 1870. C.O. (Orleans), Book 97, pp. 595–598 (April 25, 1870).

56. *Daily Picayune*, November 12, 1870; *Republican*, May 20–21, June 4–5, October 6, 25, 1871, September 8, 1874; Opelousas *Journal*, April 8, May 27, August 5, 1871; Odom, *op. cit.*, pp. 195–196, 205–207.

57. *Republican*, January 12, 14, 19, 27, February 1–2, 8–9, 12, 21, 24, March 7, 11, 22, 25, April 4, 9, 18, 20, 30, May 5, 13, 19, 30, 1871; *Daily Picayune*, January 14, 1871; Indianola *Weekly Bulletin*, January 21, 1871.

58. *Republican*, quoting Galveston, Indianola, and San Antonio papers, January 24, February 1, 8, September 16, 1871; *Daily Picayune*, April 18, 1871.

The conflict demonstrated its intensity in a meeting in Mobile on October 19, 1871, when representatives of the Morgan lines and the New Orleans, Mobile, and Texas refused to accept freight rates west of Mobile uniform with those east of that city.[59] Partially to offset criticism, Morgan made one of his infrequent trips to Texas in the summer of 1871. With vague optimism, he intimated to the press that when "the proper time arrives to put down the prices of freight and passage to a living rate" he would do so. The implication was, however, that the "proper time" had not come, since at present his investment in the Texas trade was yielding only about a 5 per cent return.[60]

Indeed, his rivalry with the N.O.M. & T. was rushing to a conclusion. The Berwick's Bay and Texas company was dissolved in July 1870, following its legislative failure, and Morgan made a last effort to secure funds for extension of the railroad west of Brashear. Morgan and investors in St. Landry Parish formed a provisional company bearing the name of the old New Orleans, Opelousas, and Great Western. The company was ceded the property west of Brashear obtained by Morgan in March 1870, and the New Yorker subscribed for $270,000 of the proposed $1,000,000 capitalization. The plan failed, however, when parish and private investors along the projected route failed to take the remaining $730,000 by a required November 1, 1871, deadline.[61]

Several suits born of the N.O.M. & T.–Morgan opposition were also nearing a climax. An action in the U.S. Circuit Court to restrain the State of Louisiana from issuing bonds to the N.O.M. & T. was decided in April 1871. The court dismissed Morgan's argument that a taxpayer could enjoin the issuance of bonds authorized by a state legislature in violation

---

59. At a meeting held October 19, 1871, in Mobile, for "the arrangement of rates from New Orleans and Mobile to interior points and to New York; also for the purpose of adopting a uniform classification," rates from Mobile eastward were established and the "New York and Savannah" classification adopted. But on the motion of Charles A. Whitney of the Morgan lines, the N.O.M. & T. and the Morgan line were allowed to name their own rates west of Mobile. Represented were: Central of Ga., Western & Atlantic, Southwestern of Ga., Selma & Meridian, South & North Ala., Mobile & Montgomery, Selma, Rome, & Dalton, Montgomery & Eufaula, Mobile & Ohio, "Girard Railroad," New Orleans, Mobile & Texas, and Morgan Line. *Daily Picayune,* October 22, 1871.

60. Indianola *Weekly Bulletin,* May 2, 1871.

61. Dissolution of the B.B. & T., July 5, 1870. M.O. (Orleans), Society Book VII, 404 (August 16, 1870) ; Opelousas *Journal,* July 1, 1871; *Republican,* July 4, November 2, 1871.

of other acts.[62] The various claims of Morgan, the N.O.M. & T., and the Pontchartrain Railroad under conflicting state and city levee grants had been consolidated in mid-1870 into a suit before the Eighth District Court of Orleans Parish styled: *New Orleans, Mobile, and Chattanooga Railroad Co. v. City of New Orleans, et als.* The voluminous testimony was completed and submitted for decision on February 17, 1871.[63] A parallel action in the U.S. Circuit Court between Morgan and the N.O.M. & T. was set June 20, 1871, to be heard in chambers on October 11.[64] The decision of either suit was expected to end the rivalry.

Before either suit was decided, however, Morgan and the N.O.M. & T. began to talk compromise. A committee of the directors of the railroad approached Morgan in New York, proffering statements of assets totaling $7,551,000 and a new capital subscription list of sixty-six names totaling $4,895,700 in recently issued stock. Morgan was solicited to combine his interest with that of the railroad. His acquiescence in an "amicable arrangement" was reported in the New Orleans *Times* as early as November 25, but the date of his decision is unknown.[65] It is conceivable that advance knowledge of the final decree in the batture suit pending in the Eighth District Court conditioned his choice. The opinion, made public on December 10, 1871, decided against Morgan's possession of Square 27A on all counts and confirmed the primacy of state levee grants to the railroad over those of New Orleans to Morgan.[66]

In any case, the rivals signed a compromise in New York City on December 12, 1871. Morgan was to exchange cash and certain properties and franchises in his possession for $1,258,000 of the securities of the N.O.M. & T.: $899,000 in first-mortgage bonds with accompanying stock certificates on the road west of the Mississippi and $359,000 of those second-mortgage bonds guaranteed by the State of Louisiana.

62. *Morgan v. Graham,* 17 Federal Cases 749 (1871).
63. State of La., Eighth District Court, Parish of Orleans, *Record of Suit No. 19: New Orleans, Mobile, and Chattanooga Railroad Co. v. City of New Orleans, et als.*
64. U. S. Circuit Court, District of Louisiana, *Record in Suit No. 6178: Morgan v. New Orleans, Mobile, and Chattanooga Railroad Co.; Republican,* June 21, 1871.
65. *Morgan v. New Orleans, Mobile, and Texas Railroad Co., et al.,* 17 Federal Cases 754 (1876) ; New Orleans *Times,* November 25, 1871.
66. "The Great Batture Case. . . . Decision of Judge Dibble," *Republican,* December 10, 1871.

As $1,082,459.50 credit toward that exchange, Morgan was to relinquish his wharves and wharf property at Mobile, the steamers *Laura* and *Frances,* his 5,078 shares (out of 7,500 total capitalization) in the Pontchartrain Railroad, and the railroad franchises and property west of Brashear which he had acquired from the Opelousas company. In addition, he was to concede all New Orleans–Mobile business to the N.O.M. & T., agree to remove his vessels from the route within fifteen days, and refrain from re-entering that trade for fifteen years. The N.O.M. & T. agreed to complete a railroad from Brashear to Vermillionville by the time of the opening of their road between Vermillionville and Houston.

To facilitate his New Orleans car ferry and steamship landing, the levee portion of the Pontchartrain Railroad between Elysian Fields and its depot at Girod was resold to Morgan for $250,000. He also received *Thomas Kelso,* ending that threat to his Texas lines. To administer the agreement, Charles A. Whitney & Co. was named agent for both Morgan and the N.O.M. & T.[67]

Morgan's purpose in signing the agreement, stated in later years, was to end "a ruinous competition . . . in the freight and passenger business between Mobile and New Orleans, and for uniting their interest in that business and in a projected railroad business between New Orleans and Texas."[68] His decision is defensible for its time but not as events matured. At the time, however, he secured a large share in a corporation well blessed with public and private aid (two commodities Morgan had been unable to acquire). In return he relinquished a trade already profitless to him because of completion of the Mobile railroad, he removed the threat to his Texas steamers posed by *Thomas Kelso* and sacrificed only franchises and preliminary grading west of Brashear.

He also improved his position from majority stockholder to sole owner of the levee portion of the Pontchartrain Railroad. Only the anticipated pro rata division of traffic receipts between New Orleans and Houston left him in a truly subordinate position, but even so, successful completion of the road would pay handsome dividends on his securities in that enterprise. His cash outlays of $175,540.50 for the N.O.M. & T. securities and

67. Agreement between Morgan and N.O.M. & T., December 12, 1871, M.L. & T.R. & S. Records.
68. *Morgan v. New Orleans, Mobile, and Texas Railroad Co.,* 17 Federal Cases 754 (1876).

$250,000 for the portion of the Pontchartrain Railroad were investments with distinct possibilities for rapid and appreciable growth.

Whitney & Co. and its principal speedily undertook their portions of the bargain. By March 30, 1872, the various property transfers had been formally completed, but long before that date, the new combination had begun its work.[69] Reversing his former position, Morgan also publicly endorsed N.O.M. & T. claims to the batture in New Orleans and urged the city to forsake appeals to the Supreme Court of Louisiana in that suit and ratify the state grants to the N.O.M. & T. by appropriate ordinances.[70]

On January 19, 1872, terms of a contract to extend the N.O.M. & T. from Brashear to the Sabine via Vermillionville were formulated in New York. By agreement signed January 31, Boynton Brothers & Bushnell were retained to begin construction within thirty days and complete the railroad by March 1, 1873; their fee: $4,500,000 in currency and securities to be drawn against according to monthly estimates.[71] Under the contract, advertisements for construction materials appeared early in February, and several hundred Chinese laborers were at work on the roadbed west of Brashear. A wharf was constructed at Berwick, opposite Brashear, and a ferry established to transport supplies until bridging could be completed. *Frances* was put in operation as a ferry at the New Orleans end of the road, between Calliope Street and Westwego.[72]

Morgan approved these positive demonstrations by the N.O.M. & T.

69. Sales, Morgan to N.O.M. & T., December 12, 1871, M.L. & T.R. & S. Records; Sale, Morgan and Mary Jane Morgan to N.O.M. & T., February 20, 1872. Act before Nettleton, Commissioner for La. in N.Y. C.O. (Orleans), Book 102, pp. 256–257 (April 18, 1872); Sale, P. R. to Morgan, March 11, 1872. Act before Pierre C. Cuvellier, N.A. (Orleans), C.O. (Orleans), Book 109, pp. 176–177 (March 12, 1872); Whitney & Co. to Gardner and Butler, June 5, 1873, *Republican*, June 6, 1873.

70. The Common Council's endless and fruitless debate and the caustic comments of the New Orleans press over Morgan's switch are found in *Daily Picayune*, December 13–17, 20, 22, 27–28, 30, 1871, January 11, 16, 1872; *Republican*, December 15–23, 27–30, 1871, January 3, April 19, 1872; Carrollton *Louisiana State Register*, December 23, 1871, January 6, 13, 1872; New Iberia *Louisiana Sugar Bowl*, January 4, 1872.

71. J. L. Macaulay to Whitney & Co., January 19, 1872, *Republican*, January 20, 1872; Contract between N.O.M. & T. and B.B. & B., January 31, 1872, M.L. & T.R. & S. Records.

72. G. W. R. Bayley to Whitney & Co., January 31, 1872, *Journal*, February 10, 1872; *Louisiana Sugar Bowl*, March 7, 21, 1872; *Republican*, April 7, May 1, 1872; *Daily Picayune*, March 6, 13, 25, April 18, 21, May 1, July 13, 1872.

and reciprocated with some of his own. In May 1872, he allowed the railroad the use of his steamer *St. Mary* to run as a packet between Donaldsonville and Baton Rouge. He also, in the summer of 1872, narrowed the gauge of his railroad to Brashear, its branch from Terrebonne to Houma, and all its rolling stock, from 5 feet, 6 inches to the 4 feet, 8½ inches used by the N.O.M. & T.[73]

Yet Morgan's relations with the N.O.M. & T. deteriorated in the summer of 1872. Work on the railroad was suspended through most of August as Morgan and the other directors quarreled over assigning priority to available construction funds: Morgan advocating completion of the road between Brashear and Vermillionville; others favoring work on the road from Donaldsonville to Houston via Vermillionville and a projected branch to Shreveport.

The N.O.M. & T. was also suffering financial difficulties. Since issuance of its state grants depended upon completion of various segments of track, the railroad tried to meet current expenses by public sales of stocks and bonds at discounts as much as 50 per cent, but with little success. Extensions of time by the legislature had also to be secured. The result was that by March 1873 only ten miles of track and thirty-one miles of grading west of Donaldsonville, two miles of grading west of Brashear, and five miles of grading west of Vermillionville had been finished. Even the ten miles of completed track west of Donaldsonville were useless, however, because of a subcontractor's refusal to release a bridge across Bayou Lafourche until a $17,000 bill was paid.

No wonder, as early as August 1872 the *Picayune* could comment that the Morgan–N.O.M. & T. agreement "had been canceled some time," or, as G.W.R. Bayley put it in February 1873, "Clap-trap will not do; something more than St. Charles Hotel rotunda railroad building is needed."[74]

Morgan was particularly distressed when two of the original "insiders," Gardner and Butler, began foreclosure proceedings as a prelude to another reorganization of the N.O.M. & T. As trustees of the road's second mortgage, Gardner and Butler brought suit in the U.S. Circuit Court in New Orleans alleging nonpayment of interest coupons due in October

73. *Republican*, May 3, July 2, 1872; *Daily Picayune*, July 7, 1872, January 26, 1873.

74. *Daily Picayune*, July 10, August 7, 18, September 25–26, 1872, February 5, 9, 16, 19, 1873; *Republican*, September 15, 20, 27–28, October 17, 20, November 14, December 13, 1872, March 12, 16, 25, 1873.

1872 and January 1873. In February, Morgan instituted an independent and antagonistic suit in federal District Court claiming $27,800 on 695 first-mortgage coupons and $14,360 on 359 second-mortgage coupons overdue since January 1.

The conflict was decided by a decree of April 13 favoring Gardner and Butler and ordering foreclosure of the road for the benefit of the second-mortgage bondholders—to be sold at auction on June 6. As expected, Morgan and Whitney & Co. immediately severed their connections as director and Louisiana agents respectively of the N.O.M. & T. On May 30, 1873, Morgan entered suit in the U.S. Circuit Court to recover the property transferred to the N.O.M. & T. under the agreement of December 12, 1871, and to enjoin the sale by the second-mortgage trustees scheduled for June 6. Despite his protest and those of the State of Louisiana and the City of New Orleans, the entire railroad and franchises westward from Mobile toward Houston were "sold" by the court from the trustees Gardner and Butler to a new combination headed by Gardner and Butler for $667,500.[75]

The N.O.M. & T. was far from operative, however, and was besieged by creditors. Its history from 1873 to 1876 comprised abortive attempts at reorganization and refunding by its various bondholders, hampered by a succession of suits by claimants to the road. Gardner and Butler divided the reorganized road into branches east and west of New Orleans and sought to secure funds for its extension by consolidation mortgages and public subscription. Unsuccessful, in December 1873 they lost the western branch to a new combination of first-mortgage bondholders headed by Frank M. Ames, son and successor as trustee of Oakes Ames.[76] The Mobile line was transferred in January 1875 to another first-mortgage bondholder group that operated it until the Louisville and Nashville Railroad leased the line on May 8, 1880.[77]

75. The various petitions and court orders involved are printed with editorial commentary in *Daily Picayune*, April 19, 1873, and *Republican*, April 20, May 30, June 6, 7, 21, 1873. See also *Financier*, III (March 8, April 19, 26, June 14, 1873).

76. *Republican*, June 6–7, 21, 1873; *Daily Picayune*, February 1–5, 1874; Deed, Gardner and Butler to N.O.M. & T. (Reorganized), October 2, 1873. C.O. (Orleans), Book 195, pp. 172–179 (December 1, 1873).

77. The road was sold to the L. & N. on October 5, 1881, for $6,000,000 and the 50-year lease annulled. Sale, Edwin D. Morgan, James A. Raynor, and Francis A. Woofley to N.O.M. & T. (Reorganized), May 8, 1880. C.O. (Orleans), Book 112, pp. 472–480 (May 21, 1880); Sale, N.O.M. & T. (Reorganized) to L. & N., October 5, 1881. *Ibid.*, Book 115, pp. 859–863 (November 17, 1881).

Ames, too, was overwhelmed with creditors on the western route, and his plans for reorganizing the road seemed perpetually enjoined.[78] Most persistent was the State of Louisiana, which in a series of suits asked forfeiture of aid granted to the road. Aroused by the N.O.M. & T.'s failure to complete trackage to the Sabine as scheduled and prompted by the economy-minded Governor William P. Kellogg, who took office in the wake of the Panic of 1873, the state seized and held the railroad for sale late in 1873 until enjoined by Ames in several countersuits in the summer and fall of 1874.

By May 1875, however, with Ames secure in possession of the road, the state agreed to drop its suits, write off those securities already issued, and void its responsibility to issue more.[79] Litigation involving over $546,000 in contractors' and subcontractors' bills also plagued the railroad. These bills were overdue until funded by stock and bond issues in late 1874.[80]

Thus Morgan was not alone in his claims against the N.O.M. & T., and his suit to recover the property transferred to the railroad was prolonged until early 1876. His petition filed May 30, 1873, had argued that the contract of December 12, 1871, had been the result of fraudulent mis-representations by the N.O.M. & T. and that, in any case, the contract had been a "commutative one"—under Louisiana law, void if one party did not comply with its provisions.

His plea was doomed. At its April 1876 term, the U.S. Circuit Court, District of Louisiana, dismissed his argument with costs. The court found no "misrepresentations of facts" by the N.O.M. & T. sufficient to void the contract of December 12, 1871, and ruled that agreement subject to New York rather than Louisiana law. The contract was made in New York and most of its provisions had been executed in that state, whose laws pro-vided for no commutation as Morgan pleaded under Louisiana practice.[81]

The decision of 1876 in favor of the N.O.M. & T. ended Charles Mor-

78. Ames's plans are found in *Daily Picayune*, December 2, 1873, January 31, 1874; *Republican*, December 2, 13, 1873, January 30, July 18, 1874.

79. *Republican*, December 3, 16–17, 1873, April 7, 16, June 30, July 18–19, 23, August 16, 19–21, September 1, October 1, 3, November 18–19, 29, 1874, January 24, February 3, May 11, 13–14, 27, June 6–8, 1875; *Daily Picayune*, December 19, 1873, July 18, November 18–19, December 28, 1874, March 2, May 11, 1875; Odom, *op. cit.*, 223 ff.

80. *Republican*, May 9, June 21, July 19, November 29, 1874.

81. *Morgan v. New Orleans, Mobile, and Texas Railroad Co. et al.* 17 Federal Cases 754 (1876).

gan's initial efforts at linking New Orleans and Texas via railroad. His hopes for a fruitful partnership with the N.O.M. & T. were smashed, and, worse, he had lost the franchises and property which would have permitted him to take up the project himself. Further, there was no prospect of securing additional franchises or state aid as long as Radical Republicans dominated the Louisiana legislature. Not until 1877 and the return of Democratic control, was he able to secure official encouragement for a railroad west of Brashear; not until 1878 did he regain the franchises and property lost to the N.O.M. & T. in 1871.

Morgan's debut as a railroad man was thus auspicious but clouded with frustration. There was no question that he lavished funds on his railroad from New Orleans to Brashear and made it physically and financially one of the soundest of postwar southern roads (see Chapter 9).

But east of New Orleans and west of Brashear Morgan learned some of the harder truths of railroading: that exclusive franchises and public aid could be crucial to success; that promises made need not be promises kept; that the laying of track was incredibly more complicated a business transaction than the opening of a line of steamers; and that on parallel short hauls, steamers would fall before trains. He had had a taste of franchise and right-of-way wars in Nicaragua, but his initial foray in Louisiana taught him much more and cost him thousands of dollars and several years of his life.

Even though now in his late seventies, his energy increased as the fight toughened. There is no greater testament to Morgan's fortitude than his ability to cope with other problems of railroad and maritime competition while his hands seemed full with the N.O.M. & T.

9

EXPANSION
AND ACCOMMODATION
IN LOUISIANA AND TEXAS,
1866–1877

MORGAN'S rivalry with the N.O.M. & T., both east and west of New Orleans, reflected both his own widening horizons and the increased competition available to thwart or modify his plans. His experiences with the City of New Orleans and the State of Louisiana also indicate the political uncertainties of his environment. Yet his personal business goals and the difficulties they encountered had other dimensions. Between 1866 and 1877 he worked hard to consolidate his few gains in Louisiana by improving his railroad between New Orleans and Brashear. He increased the number of his steamers to Texas and established a network of railway connections for them. He also opened new lines between the American Gulf ports and Havana and New York.

In all of these ventures, Morgan's primary motives were profit and a desire to consolidate gains, once made. Much of what he accomplished was on his own initiative. However, such major postwar environmental forces as Reconstruction, increased competition, changing technology, and intercity rivalries also stimulated and shaped his decision-making. Conversely, Morgan's private, profit-oriented decisions were important determinants in channeling the development of the ports and much of the commerce of the western Gulf.

Precisely this sort of dialogue between personal and public goals was the mainspring of economic growth in the Reconstruction South. Its sum was positive, but its evolution was often disjointed and contradictory. Morgan's projects and strategies are especially illustrative of the process of accommodation and advance.

The center of many of Morgan's problems was New Orleans, and his dissatisfaction was typical: "Do merchants expect capital to come to New Orleans?" asked the *Daily Picayune* of February 13, 1872. Do they expect enterprise to embark in great progressive movements here while capital is taxed to the very brink of confiscation, and enterprise is crushed and strangled?" The city's 2½ per cent *ad valorem* tax rate and its high pilotage, wharfage, and warehousing charges were only one aspect of its postwar difficulties as a business center. Its chronic tendency toward epidemic disease and resultant quarantines, the high cost of its limited amount of undeveloped land, and its political turmoil were drawbacks as well.

But because of its advantages as a center of capital, as a repair site, and as a freight-gathering point, the Crescent City had become the managerial center of the Morgan lines. On the east bank of the Mississippi were located the offices of Whitney & Co., a freight depot, levee trackage serving those wharves alloted Morgan's "outside" steamers, and the St. Ann Street ferry landing. Algiers, connected to New Orleans by Morgan car ferries capable of transferring 260 freight cars per day, held extensive machine shops for the manufacture and repair of rolling stock and of iron, steel, copper, and brass fittings. An adjoining carpenter shop could complete 130 cars per year and was supplemented by drydocks and boiler shops for marine repairs. A conservative estimate in 1873 placed Morgan's New Orleans payroll at 530 employees.[1]

Morgan's problem was to rationalize this New Orleans investment with its deficiencies and with his postwar plans for expansion. The end of his Mobile line in 1871 reduced his need for trackage on the east bank of the Mississippi River or wharfage on Lake Pontchartrain. The endless batture suit denied a favored ferry landing. Even the Louisiana Supreme

1. New Orleans Real Estate Assessment Rolls, 1868–1869: III, 13–19, IV, 14–15; 1869–1870: III, 14, 17, IV, 17–18; 1870–1871: III, 6, 9–10, IV, 12–13; Contract between Valletti Dry Dock Co. and Whitney & Co., June 1, 1868, M.L. & T.R. & S. Records; New Orleans *Daily Picayune*, January 26, 1873.

Court decision in 1874 to return Square 27A to the city did not secure transfer of the property to Morgan, and he was forced to rely on the smaller ferry at St. Ann Street.[2] Thus, the drawbacks of New Orleans as a maritime shipping point and the expense even of maintaining (much less expanding) facilities there conditioned Morgan's major decision to increase operations at his Brashear terminal. As a newer, less-urban settlement and one uniquely dependent upon his patronage, Brashear was certainly a more pliable environment. By the mid-1870s, Morgan's wharves stretched over 2,600 feet along the Atchafalaya River and employed some 800 men in the transshipment of goods or in nearby warehouses, cattle pens, coal yards, and marine ways. One traveler observed in the *Republican* of April 5, 1874, that, except for "keepers of barrooms [and] restaurants," the entire population of Brashear worked for Morgan. In 1873, the payroll on the wharves alone was $51,000 per month.[3]

Indeed, Morgan had plans for the Brashear area. On April 22, 1871, he publicly endorsed the Louisiana legislature's charter of the Atchafalaya Bay Company and became its largest stockholder and prime contractor. Authorized to dredge a seaway from the Atchafalaya River to the Gulf, the company began at once. Working day and night, three dredges cut a 100- by 12-foot channel from the river's mouth to the shell reef guarding Atchafalaya Bay. Morgan purchased $69,300 worth of dredging equipment and met all operating expenses of excavating the necessary 502,166 cubic yards, including payrolls totaling $4,278.50 per month. The channel opened on May 4, 1872. Morgan's steamers used it free, while other vessels were charged 25 cents per ton.[4]

Upon completion of the Atchafalaya channel, Morgan discontinued his

2. New Orleans *Republican*, May 20, December 2, 1873, May 5, 20, December 3–4, 1874; *New Orleans, Mobile, and Chattanooga Railroad Co. v. City of New Orleans, et als.*, 26 Louisiana Ann. 478 (1874); *idem.*, 26 Louisiana Ann. 517 (1874); Protest by Morgan, May 5, 1874. Act before George W. Christy, N.A. (Orleans); Declaration of Title by Morgan, May 29, 1874. *Ibid.*; Protest by Morgan, May 29, 1874. *Ibid.*

3. Carrollton *Louisiana State Register*, June 4, 11, 1870; *The Laws and Revised Ordinances of the Town of Brashear*, p. 20; *Daily Picayune*, January 26, 1873; Sale, Alphonse Tertrou to Morgan, December 24, 1873. Act before George W. Christy, N.A. (Orleans).

4. *Louisiana Acts* (1871), pp. 213–216; *Daily Picayune*, April 25, May 10, 21, 1871, January 26, 1873; Indianola *Weekly Bulletin*, May 8, 1872; *Republican*, December 11, 1873; *Annual Report of the Chief of Engineers to the Secretary of War, 1871*, pp. 67–68, 554–557.

"outside" routes (i.e., New Orleans–Texas, via the Mississippi River) and moved all his steamships to Brashear in the final step in a plan to upgrade his route from Louisiana to Texas. Rail-steamer integration substituted rails for ships in entering New Orleans and ships for rails in entering Texas. The most workable solution to the difficulties Morgan had encountered in linking the two areas, it made Brashear the crossroads of his growing enterprises.

Agricultural producers of western Louisiana hailed the expansion of Morgan's interests in Brashear. In return, the steamship operator worked diligently to please. He or his agents frequently visited the parishes along his railroad's route encouraging the construction of branch lines. Interested planters generously donated right-of-way and grading; Morgan reciprocated with spur trackage. The first and longest of these branches was completed over the fifteen miles from Terrebonne (now Schriever) to Houma in 1872.[5]

The railroad also maintained daily connections and through rates with independent steamboats on the waterways it crossed—bayous Lafourche, Terrebonne, Grand Caillou, Petit Caillou, Teche—and often Morgan engineers and road gangs supplied relief or protection work in times of flood. These services and courtesies won friends for the Morgan lines in Louisiana's bayou country, and few were surprised when Brashear was renamed Morgan City in February 1876.[6]

The capital investment and profitability of Morgan's railroad between New Orleans and Brashear were tremendously enhanced in the years 1866–1877. Investment and operating accounts for the period of Morgan's sole proprietorship are shown in Tables 9.1 and 9.2.

Unlike many southern railroads during the same period, Morgan's road had a remarkably serene existence. It received no government aid except in return for services rendered: an annual mail subsidy of $12,850 for six trips per week, New Orleans to the Atchafalaya (plus $764 per

5. Sale, L. Erasme Nee to Morgan, November 16, 1871. Act before George W. Christy, N.A. (Orleans); Grant, George D. Cragin to Morgan, March 21, 1872. *Ibid.*; Sale, Bernard Soulie to Morgan, May 31, 1872. Act before Eusebe Bouny, N.A. (Orleans); Sale, C. C. Williams to Morgan, June 17, 1873. Act before Christy, N.A. (Orleans); New Iberia *Louisiana Sugar Bowl*, January 18, 25, March 28, May 2, 1872; *Daily Picayune*, April 12, 1871, April 18, 28, May 5, 12, 1872; *Republican*, March 11, 1873.

6. *Louisiana Sugar Bowl*, October 19, 1871–December 30, 1875; *Daily Picayune*, May 21, 1871, April 26, 1874; *Louisiana Acts* (1876), pp. 20–24.

178 · CHARLES MORGAN

annum after 1872 for service to Houma);[7] and annual contracts for carrying Federal troops and stores from New Orleans to Texas at discounts up to 50 per cent of card rates. In 1874 there was some difficulty when Army appropriations prohibited payments for carriage of military personnel or material on land grant railroads. When ruled such (as successor to the N.O.O. & G.W.), the M.L. & T. protested and closed its line to government traffic. Congressional review upheld the War Department, but relief was granted to the Morgan road in 1880. After 1874 the exclusion of similar restrictions from subsequent appropriation bills ended further debate.[8]

The M.L. & T. also enjoyed a good press throughout its period of expansion in the 1870s. Observers recognized the social benefits inherent in Morgan's personal investments and typically commented: "If Mr. Morgan does make us pay well for our freight, he sends it through in good condition."[9] Only once did good relations turn to hostility when, in August 1875, a heated dispute between six Negro coal loaders and a Morgan wharf foreman sparked violence.

The 1875 complaint regarded not wages, but their payment in general-store scrip. The Negroes involved were discharged and jailed for disturbing the peace, but accompanying publicity forced an end to the protested practice.

Except for this incident, no report of labor demonstrations against the Morgan lines has been found. Training and promotion were from within, and Morgan agents, captains, and engineers stayed with the lines for years. A press usually receptive to the slightest hint of labor strife in Louisiana recorded only Morgan's annual company picnic and fewer than

7. "Contracts for Carrying the Mails, 1871" (Serial 1513), 631; Authorization of Mail Service on Houma Branch of M.L. & T.R., March 7, 1872, M.L. & T.R. & S. Records.

8. Contracts between U.S. and Whitney & Co., July 1, 1873, July 1, 1874, and July 12, 1875, M.L. & T.R. & S. Records; "Refusal of the Louisiana and Texas Railroad to Transport Troops," *House Exec. Docs.*, 43 Cong., 2 Sess., No. 94 (Serial 1646); *House Misc. Docs.*, 47 Cong., 1 Sess., No. 53 (Serial 2036), 469. This controversy was part of a larger debate which is covered without mention of Morgan in Norris Kenny, "The Transportation of Government Property and Troops over Land-Grant Railroads," *Journal of Land and Public Utility Economics*, IX (November 1933), 368–381 and David M. Ellis, "Railroad Land Grant Rates, 1850–1945," *ibid.*, XXI (August 1945), 207–222.

9. *New and Reduced Freight and Passenger Tariff of Morgan's Louisiana and Texas Rail Road from New Orleans to Brashear City;* (1869); *ibid.* (1872); *Louisiana Sugar Bowl*, October 5, 1876; *Daily Picayune*, May 14, 1875.

a dozen incidents of layoffs of unskilled labor. No unions opposed Morgan, and his wages were adequate for their industry and their day—$200 per month for captains and engineers; $25–30 per month for deckhands, stevedores, and trainmen. There was always considerable turnover among Morgan sailors, wharf gangs, and section crews, but the Brashear incident was his only strike. Even the national railroad strike of 1877 did not affect the Morgan Line. The "Brashear riot" is the only dissent from the more common opinion: "To be employed by Charles Morgan and to perform one's duty was tantamount to remunerative occupation for life."[10]

Since the whole purpose of Morgan's New Orleans–Brashear effort was to link the Crescent City with Texas, and since further extension of his railroad was stymied by his difficulties with the N.O.M. & T., the steamships of the Morgan Line continued to be vital links in his enterprise. Even the depression and labor unrest of the mid-seventies never stifled Morgan's desire or his ability to build ships. Replacing old vessels with ships constructed at Harlan's, he had fifteen first-class steamships running between Morgan City and Texas ports by 1876—*Agnes, City of Norfolk, Alabama, I. C. Harris, Harlan, Morgan, Austin, Clinton, St. Mary, Josephine, Mary,* and *W. G. Hewes,* joined by *Hutchinson* (1870, 1,435 tons), *Whitney* (1871, 1,338 tons), and *Gussie* (1872, 998 tons).[11]

Subsidized by mail contracts, these vessels offered a variety of services. During the four years preceding June 30, 1875, three steamers per week linked Morgan City and Galveston during the "off months" of June to December; six per week the remainder of the year. Extending the line to Indianola were two steamers per week, June to October; three per week, October to June. For these schedules, Morgan held mail subsidies totaling $60,000 per annum. The same schedules at identical sums were renewed in 1875 for the three years ending June 30, 1878. A twice-monthly route from New Orleans to Brazos St. Iago, let to Morgan in 1870 at $12,000 per year, expired in 1871, and his new bid of $20,000 was not accepted. Yet he maintained unsubsidized service from Galveston to the tip of Texas until 1875 when a three-year contract for bimonthly sailings at

10. *Republican,* July 20, 24, 1873, August 24–28, September 5, October 9, 1875; *Daily Picayune,* July 21, 1873, April 26, 1874, August 24, 1875, May 17, 1877; *Louisiana Sugar Bowl,* April 22, 1875; *Times,* May 9, 1878; Payroll, Steamer *New York,* 1876, M.L & T.R. & S. Records.
11. *Texas State Register for 1876,* p. 130.

$200 per round trip, Brashear to Brazos St. Iago, was signed. An unsubsidized line also ran between Brashear and Rockport, twice weekly, October to June; once weekly, June to October.[12]

On all of these routes, Morgan operated the only regular steamship service and charged what the traffic bore. From 1869 to 1872, passage ranged from $18 cabin and $9 deck, Brashear to Galveston, to $40 and $20, Brashear to Brazos St. Iago. In March 1873, Galveston fares were reduced to $12 and $6 and had fallen to $6 for cabin passage by 1876. Servants and children were carried at reduced prices and various inducements offered to immigrants. After 1871, emigrants to Texas from Europe, via New Orleans, were offered a $4 rate to Galveston. Reductions up to 15 per cent were offered groups of domestic emigrants numbering more than twenty in 1872; twenty-five after 1873.[13] So numerous were those availing themselves of these fares that one wag christened the steamers the *"Morgue en Line*—so called from the number of dead beats it transports to Texas."[14]

Morgan's steamships were never immune to calamity, and the increased service of the 1870s increased their susceptibility. As before the Civil War, vessels continued to be detained or destroyed by storms, collision, fire, or groundings: *Hewes* was severely damaged when rammed by another vessel in the Mississippi River in 1866; *Crescent* burned at New Orleans, December 11, 1868; *Josephine* was stranded on the Brazos St. Iago bar for six weeks in 1868 but was refloated and repaired; *Alabama* was beached at Galveston in the hurricane of 1871 but returned to service after three months; in 1875 *Morgan* was disabled for six months in a collision with *Clyde* in Galveston Bay; *Austin,* valued at $125,000 and self-insured, was sunk by a floating wreck in the Mississippi River on June 6, 1876; *Mary,* valued at $125,000, self-insured, and

12. "Contracts for Carrying the Mails, 1871" (Serial 1513), 399–400, 611; *ibid.,* "1875," *House Exec. Docs.,* 44 Cong., 1 Sess., No. 191 (Serial 1693), 502, 1297; *Daily Picayune,* September 29, 1871.

13. *Tariff of Morgan's Louisiana and Texas* [1869], pp. 1–8; *ibid.* [1872], pp. 1–9; *Daily Picayune,* October 20, 1871, March 7, 1873; *Report of the Superintendent of Bureau of Immigration of the State of Texas for the Year 1872,* pp. 12–13; *Third Annual Report of the Superintendent . . . for the Year 1873,* p. 12; *Texas Rural Almanac* (1876), p. 137.

14. *Louisiana Sugar Bowl,* October 22, 1874. For other descriptions of the Morgan route to Texas see *Daily Picayune,* March 14, 1871, October 24, 1874; *Republican,* May 15, 1872; Opelousas *Journal,* June 12, 1874; *Louisiana Sugar Bowl,* January 28, 1875; John W. Forney, *What I Saw in Texas,* pp. 28–29.

carrying cargo worth $75,000, grounded and sunk on the inner Aransas bar on November 30, 1876.[15] That these losses were absorbed by Morgan and the vessels replaced by newer steamers costing $250,000 or more apiece, offers testimony to his financial reserves. He also constructed at $15,300 each in 1875 the tugs *Restless* and *Fidget* (each 54 tons)—built at his Algiers yard for use at New Orleans and Brashear.[16]

The steamers were as likely, however, to meet adventure or humor as natural calamity. Just as the M.L. & T. in 1871 tolerated and lost a $3 damage suit for running over a rooster, Morgan's vessels had their share of the unique and the ridiculous. In 1874, the entire membership of Mechanic's Fire Company No. 6 of New Orleans and their steam fire engine were carried at excursion rates to Galveston and back again on *Josephine*. The following year two Texans boarded a Morgan steamer in Galveston, voyaged to Brashear, engaged in a duel on Louisiana soil to escape stricter Texas laws, and returned, unbloodied, to Texas the following day. *Josephine* also provided refuge for citizens of Corpus Christi, Texas, during a raid by Mexican bandits in 1875. The year before, *Clinton*, while docked at Indianola, was the scene of an episode in the famous Sutton-Taylor feud. On March 11, two Taylors boarded the steamer and murdered two members of the Sutton clan. Later arrested in Cuero, Texas, William Taylor was taken to Galveston on *Clinton* and subsequently returned to Indianola on *Harlan* to stand trial.[17]

In addition to these short-run, inshore steamers, Morgan reappraised

15. *Daily Picayune*, November 27, 1869, February 23, 1870, April 27, June 9, September 9, 14, October 6, 1871, September 14, 18, 1873, June 8, December 2, 1876; *Republican*, November 17, 21, 30, December 5, 1875; Galveston *Daily News*, December 3, 1876; Protest by Steamer *Austin*, March 15, 1867. Act before Magner, N.A. (Orleans); Protest by Steamer *Mary*, December 9, 1876, M.L. & T.R. & S. Records; Survey of Federal Archives (Louisiana), *Wreck Reports: A Record of Casualties to Persons and Vessels on the Mississippi River, Its Tributaries, on Lakes and Other Waterways of the U.S. Customs District, Port of New Orleans, 1873–1924*, pp. 32, 229; *Semi-Centennial Memoir of the Harlan & Hollingsworth Company*, p. 260; Holdcamper (ed.), *Merchant Steam*, p. 264.

16. J. A. Powers to H. M. Lull, November 2, 1935, M.L. & T.R. & S. Records; *Daily Picayune*, February 25, April 25, 1871, January 26, 1873, May 13, September 9, 1875, May 9, 1878; *Republican*, June 3, September 2, 1875; New Orleans *Times*, July 6, 1875. Some of these costs were met by sale of *Matagorda*, *Frances*, and *Laura* in 1871, *Thomas Kelso* in 1872, and *Louise* in 1874.

17. *Daily Picayune*, April 27, 1871; *Republican*, June 26, 1874, September 9–10, 1875; Mary A. Sutherland, *The Story of Corpus Christi*, pp. 44–47; *Victoria Advocate*, June 4, 1874; Walter P. Webb, *The Texas Rangers: A Century of Frontier Defense*, p. 233.

the possibilities of long-haul service between the Gulf and Atlantic coasts and built several steamships expressly for that trade.

It will be recalled that the Gold Rush had diverted him from continuance of the New York–New Orleans steamship service he had begun in 1849. He had made no attempt to re-establish that route prior to the Civil War because, during his preoccupation with Nicaragua and with Vanderbilt in the Gulf, others had secured the New York–New Orleans steamship run through federal mail subsidies.[18]

The early capture of New Orleans in 1862 had brought northern shipping into the Crescent City, and by 1865 the long-haul runs to and from the East were impossibly and unprofitably glutted with public and private carriers—long before Morgan could rebuild or recover his wartime ship losses.[19] When he did recover, however, he had chosen instead to sponsor the New York–Vera Cruz and New York–Charleston lines promoted by Quintard and Whitney.

In one sense, Morgan's daily line of Mobile steamers had been an attempt to tap the New Orleans–New York trade. At its peak the line had offered through connections by rail (via Mobile) to all major East Coast cities, but this was entirely passenger service. And even this was destroyed by the victory of the all-rail N.O.M. & T. in 1871.

Within three years, however, Morgan was engaged in a major effort to break into the long-haul trades eastward from the Gulf. His targets were the three steamship combinations then operating on the New York–New Orleans circuit: the Mallory, the Merchants', and the Cromwell lines. All had entered the trade in 1865 and were staggering from their overcapacity and the effects of the Panic of 1873.[20]

Morgan's original plan was to outflank the established lines by opening service from Brashear to New York. In 1874 he placed orders totaling $1,200,000 with Harlan and Hollingsworth for four screw steamships and opened his new service with *Brashear* (2,714 tons) on July 21, 1875. The line was to carry only freight, and its express purpose was "to furnish

18. Cutler, *Queens*, pp. 275–359.
19. New York *Herald*, May 13, 1865; Charles H. Mallory Diary, October 13, 1865, September 15, October 24, 1866, February 8, December 18, 1867, February 12, 1868, Mallory Papers (Marine Historical Assn., Mystic, Conn.). Mallory was the largest steamship operator on the New York–New Orleans run and recorded the hard times of the 1860s and early 1870s.
20. *Daily Picayune*, December 23, 1873; Charles H. Mallory Diary, September 30, 1874, Mallory Papers; *Republican*, September 7, 18, 1875.

these steamers with cargoes from Texas and to divert the sugar and molasses product of the Teche country to the New York market." The maiden voyage northward carried 25 tons of Louisiana goods and 300 tons of Texas products. In vivid contrast to the records of the New Orleans lines, the turnaround time of Morgan's new line at Brashear was thirty-six hours—"without any interference or charges on the part of harbor masters, port wardens, or other officials."[21]

It is clear that the Morgan service was formidable opposition for the New Orleans–New York lines. Morgan's reputation as a shipping manager was almost legendary by then. It is also clear that he abandoned his original plan of operation from Brashear, for by September 1875 (shortly after the Merchants' and Mallory lines abandoned their New Orleans service—the latter in preference for Galveston), Morgan moved his New York line's Louisiana terminus back to New Orleans. Even the normally critical *Republican* applauded on September 7:

Within a year, two lines of ocean steamers between here and New York— the Merchants' and the Mallory—have been discontinued. We learn also that the boats of the Philadelphia line have latterly been unable to obtain cargoes. . . . This left the field to the Cromwell line, which, it is understood, has not realized anything very handsome from the monopoly of the business.

We now see that Charles Morgan has entered the trade with four steamers . . . A weekly service may be expected. We may depend upon it that the veteran commodore is not trying an experiment. He is fully informed of the trade, and knows as well as any man can tell him the probable volume of the freight business between the two cities in the future. Furthermore, there is no doubt he will succeed, even though the managers of two other lines failed.

Such was the strength of the Morgan name, and the prediction proved valid. In 1875, *Hutchinson* and *William G. Hewes* were used on the line as well as the chartered steamship *George W. Elder,* and by the end of 1876, all of the new steamships were in operation on the weekly line: *Brashear* (renamed *Morgan City*), *Lone Star* (1875, 2,279 tons), *New York* (1875, 2,255 tons), and *Algiers* (1876, 2,279 tons).

Thus in Louisiana, despite the obstructionist tendencies of the political and economic situation in general and of the N.O.M. & T. in particular, Morgan was able to expand his intrastate trade and establish long-haul

21. *Daily Picayune,* April 21, May 13, 26, June 1, July 29, September 5, October 4, 1875; *Republican,* June 3, July 6, 9, 21, September 2, 7, 1875; *Texas State Register for 1876,* pp. 71, 142.

service coastwise to New York. He accomplished the same ends in Texas during the same period before 1878. But in the latter case the situation was infinitely more complex. It was in the Lone Star State that postwar problems of railroads and competing steamships tested Morgan's business abilities most intensely; and it was there that his actions were most important in the pattern of economic development after the Civil War.

The Civil War and Reconstruction had altered the political and economic structure of Texas as they had that of Louisiana and Alabama. But, if the political situation was less volatile than in Louisiana, the postwar investment boom, railroad expansion, and intercity rivalries were more acute in Texas. It was quite obvious that Texas would play a major role in southern redevelopment: it was an area relatively untouched by war and rich in varied resources; it served as a gateway to the great southwestern frontier. The changes and challenges were there, and once again Morgan had to adapt creatively to survive as a businessman. His problems were those specifically related to expansion of railroads and increased intraregional competition among rival cities.

At some Texas ports of call there was little postwar change, either in the type or flow of trade and, hence, no pressure to do more than re-establish traditional service. Such a port was Brazos St. Iago, where the Morgan Line continued to dominate external trade. Products of lower Texas and northern Mexico still gravitated to the sea via the Rio Grande or overland by wagon. Even the first decade of railroad building in the area did nothing but overlay traditional trade routes with track. Exporters, importers, and travelers still depended upon Morgan as their sole regular contact with other ports. Predictably and chronically they complained of their lack of choice in the matter, and Morgan responded (from his monopoly position) as the spirit moved him.[22]

A similar case was the Aransas and Corpus Christi bay area. For stock raisers, meat packing, hide and tallow, and turtle canning plants in Rockport and Fulton, Morgan provided the major external transportation link. The essence of this trade is seen in Rockport's foreign and domestic commerce for 1874: exports included 19,499 head of livestock, 846

22. *Daily Picayune*, December 1, 1869, September 29, 1871; Howard Fleming, *Narrow Gauge Railways in America*, pp. 87–88; Allhands, *Uriah Lott, passim;* Smith, Dunning & Woodward per James J. Stillman to C. A. Whitney & Co., December 22, 1869, and same to Low & Ludwigsen, February 10, 1871, in James Stillman Letterbook, 1867–1871 (Baker Library, Harvard Graduate School of Business Administration).

sheep, 200 hogs, 32,248 hides, 2,236 hogsheads of tallow, 8,550 barrels of salt beef, 101 tons of raw bones, 1,318 tons of bone meal, and 64,496 sets of horns; imports were 6,068 barrels of assorted merchandise, 199,962 board feet of lumber, 150 tons of machinery, 45,000 bricks, 521 tons of coal, 61,000 shingles, 11,744 bags of salt, and 10,393 empty barrels.[23]

Morgan's steamers carried most of this trade to and from Louisiana and Cuba. Biweekly sailings to Brashear (and thence by rail to New Orleans) carried 104,600 head of livestock alone between October 1872 and July 1878. Direct service between Rockport and Havana was opened in April 1875, with vessels leaving each port every ten days. Approximately 1,200–1,500 cattle per month were carried to the island, and by 1878 an open-end contract with the Cuban government to supply beeves at $43 gold per head earned the Morgan Line $195,890.76 in that year alone.[24]

All was not amicable between Morgan and his patrons on these routes, however. His monopoly position drew regular criticism despite his willingness to extend credits to shippers. High freight rates on merchandise and his policy of not loading cattle unless they were sold to his company added to displeasures as did the frequent problems of co-ordinating the schedules of a large shipping line with the needs of the smaller cattle drovers.[25]

The cattlemen were unable to secure alternate arrangements, however, until the arrival of railroads in the 1880s. It is true that increasing numbers of Texas cattle were moved northward to midcontinent railheads

23. *Daily Picayune*, July 21, 25, 1872, February 7, August 7, 1873, June 5, 1875, January 21, April 6, 28, May 31, 1876.

24. *Daily Picayune*, March 25, 30, April 6, 12, 1875; Rockport City Council Minute Book (City Hall, Rockport, Texas), I, 126–129; Rockport Book of Ordinances, 1870–1890 (*ibid.*), p. 17; Clarence Gordon, *Report on Cattle, Sheep, and Swine Supplementary to Enumeration of Live Stock on Farms in 1880 (Tenth Census of the United States*, III, 1883), 966, 976–977; Stevens, *Taft Ranch*, pp. 25–26; Minute Book No. 1, Board of Directors, M.L. & T.R. & S., 100, M.L. & T.R. & S. Records.

25. For a sample of criticism and rebuttal, see: William A. Cushman to M. Lefferts, October 18, 20, 25, December 8, 1868, Cushman Letterbook, 1868–1869 (in possession of author); *Daily Picayune*, September 28, 1871, September 8, 1877; *Republican*, April 5, 1874; Coleman, Mathis, & Fulton to Whitney & Co., October 12, 1876 (Coleman-Fulton Pasture Company Records. University of Texas), I, 151; Joseph G. McCoy, *Historic Sketches of the Cattle Trade of the West and Southwest*, p. 19.

in the 1870s, but Morgan's seaborne trade held up well. As late as December 7, 1876, when the Missouri and Kansas drives were at their peak, the *Daily Picayune* reported that over the year past, 75,998 head of 1871 and, upon completion of a deep-water channel to that port, began
     The Morgan lines also extended occasional service to Corpus Christi in livestock were shipped from Morgan's Rockport landing.
regular voyages in May 1874. Never as interested in Corpus Christi as in neighboring Rockport, Morgan nevertheless dominated the carriage of such trade as was available.[26]

     At the larger and more significant ports of Indianola and Galveston the re-establishment of traditional service was not enough. These towns competed actively for the richest hinterland of Texas and saw themselves as Gulf termini for transcontinental routes to the Pacific. They were, consequently, feverish projectors of railroads to the interior and were vitally interested in their proportional shares of internal and external trade. Faced with this different environmental structure, Morgan had different goals and employed techniques different from those, say, at Brazos St. Iago. His decision-making was of extreme significance to the outcome of the situation.

     In some ways Indianola was unchanged by war. Her major economic role remained the logistical support of the cattle industry and frontier forts of southern and central Texas through her ocean shipping connection, her meat-packing plants, and her stores and services. She had gained this function because of level overland routes to the interior, a well-developed harbor, and Morgan's civilian, postal, and military shipping services. Furthermore, a postwar demand for beef, hides, bone, and tallow in New Orleans and the East and wartime increases in troop movements had reinforced the dusty little cattle town's "boomer" spirit.

     Basic changes in the economic environment of Indianola were taking place, however. The town had always found its hinterland in the area west and south of the Colorado River, and its major inland shipping point was traditionally San Antonio. After 1865, this trade pattern was severely threatened by railroads probing southwestward from the Galveston–Houston axis. Columbus (on the west bank of the Colorado) was linked to Houston by rail and to Galveston by a rail-water route by 1868.

     26. *Daily Picayune*, June 27, December 15, 1871, July 14, 30, 1874, January 12, 1875, April 28, 1876; *Republican*, June 16, 1874; Coleman McCampbell, *Saga of a Frontier Seaport*, p. 29; Stevens, *op. cit.*, pp. 65–67, 77–82.

A second Houston railroad completed a branch line to Austin (farther up the Colorado) in 1871. A third line had been chartered in 1870 to link St. Louis' southwestward-building railroads with the Rio Grande, via Texarkana, Austin, San Antonio, and Laredo. All of these roads were headed toward Indianola's backland. She responded to them in kind.

The idea of railroads inward from Matagorda and Lavaca bays was not new. The area was the traditional jumping-off place for the frontier, and anyone with a map and a pencil could project a fairly straight, level, and almost bridge-free line westward, through San Antonio and El Paso to the Pacific. The San Antonio and Mexican Gulf Railway Company, for one, had been chartered by the State of Texas in 1850 to build from Port Lavaca to San Antonio via Victoria. Another line, the Indianola Railroad, was chartered in 1858 to build to Victoria and thence northwestward via the state capital at Austin.

Construction on the S.A. & M.G. began in 1856 and reached Victoria in 1861, but Confederate troops destroyed the road in 1863. No track was laid on the Indianola Railroad before the Civil War.[27] The coming of peace, the postwar boom in Indianola, and the obvious challenge of competition from the Houston and Galveston roads revived interest in both schemes. They soon became major components of Charles Morgan's business strategy.

Any possibility that rail would divert the trade of Indianola's hinterland to other points was of obvious concern to Morgan. In characteristic fashion, he challenged the challengers by plunging into railroad-building himself. On May 25, 1870, he and Henry S. McComb of Wilmington, Delaware, purchased the S.A. & M.G. and announced plans to extend it to the interior and integrate it with Morgan's steamers at Indianola.[28] The road was sold to satisfy government rebuilding claims. Morgan and McComb funded the government claim of $45,000, paid off a small floating debt, and acquired twenty-eight miles of track and equipment

27. Indianola *Indianolian*, July 6, 18, 1857; Indianola *Courier*, May 21, 1859; Contract between Indianola Railroad Co. and Warner & Fryer, November 2, 1868, Henry J. Runge Papers (Rosenberg Library, Galveston); S. G. Reed, *A History of the Texas Railroads and of Transportation Conditions under Spain and Mexico and the Republic and the State*, pp. 89–92, 115–116, 257–262.

28. Poor's *Railroads*, 1871–72, p. 434. For McComb, see John F. Stover, "Colonel Henry S. McComb, Mississippi Railroad Adventurer," *Journal of Mississippi History*, XVII (July 1955), 177–190.

and a $200,000, 8 per cent first mortgage, due in halves in 1870 and 1875.

Morgan and McComb—the latter also reorganizer of the Mississippi Central and the New Orleans, Jackson, and Great Northern railroads— journeyed to Indianola in April 1871 and with great fanfare secured the consolidation of their line with that of the Indianola Railroad. The combined resources of the two roads and general public endorsement were then thrown behind the new company christened the Gulf, Western Texas, and Pacific Railroad. The directorates of the two predecessor corporations were merged, but managerial responsibility was vested in a five-man Executive Committee dominated by Morgan, McComb, and Charles A. Whitney.

Morgan and McComb each subscribed for $450,000 of common stock and the remaining $400,000 was earmarked for public sale. The consolidation was approved by the Texas Legislature on May 19, effective June 19, 1871, and it soon embarked on its ambitious plans.[29]

The name of the new company left little doubt as to its purpose—to link the Gulf and Western Texas with the Pacific. The first task was to build backward from Port Lavaca to Indianola, the chosen Gulf terminus. This was accomplished by May 1871 with tracks laid through town and out on Morgan's pier to permit shipside transfer of passengers and freight. Track west of Port Lavaca was also renovated and through service by ship and rail between New Orleans and Victoria opened on August 28, 1871.[30]

Construction west of Victoria was the real purpose of the road, however. In planning and execution of this task, Morgan pursued a two-part strategy: he decided to aim his road for *both* San Antonio and Austin, and he chose to seek state and local financial aid for his project. In building toward both San Antonio and Austin, Morgan avoided an "airline" route to either but was able to sell the idea of a combined route via Cuero and Gonzales. What this lacked in directness it gained in its possibilities for local financial support.

To meet the initial costs of extending the G.W.T. & P., Morgan used his

29. *Daily Picayune*, March 21, April 25, 1871; Indianola *Weekly Bulletin*, March 27, April 25, 1871; Agreement to Consolidate Indianola Railroad and San Antonio and Mexican Gulf Railroad, April 22, 1871, Statement of Monies Paid by Morgan and McComb, May–September 1871, Gulf, Western Texas and Pacific Railway Co. Records (S.P. Co.).

30. *Weekly Bulletin*, May 2, 1871; *Daily Picayune*, July 20, 30, August 16, September 8, 19, 1871, February 16, 1872.

and McComb's cash reserves as well as balance transfers from other Morgan enterprises. But Morgan, Whitney, and Hutchinson worked hard to stimulate matching funds from other sources. Under Texas law, the most important of these were local bond subscriptions, private donations, and state land grants.

A general law of April 12, 1871, permitted any county, city, or town within the state to exchange its bonds for the capital stock of railroads projected through its boundaries. Interest on these bonds was divided between payments to the railroad holding them and the creation of a sinking fund for their redemption. Redemption was to follow completion of the railroad to various points within time limits specified in the bond. The G.W.T. & P. received over $864,000 in these bonds from Victoria, Caldwell, Gonzales, and Bexar counties and began construction beyond Victoria in March 1872 under pledge to reach Cuero by October 1, 1872, and San Antonio by April 1, 1873.[31]

In May 1872, Morgan purchased McComb's share in the enterprise, and Alexander C. Hutchinson was elected to the vacancy thus created on the board and committee of the road. The G.W.T. & P. became more than ever a "Morgan enterprise." Behind schedule, the railroad reached Cuero in March 1873, and daily service was opened by rail and steamer to Victoria, Indianola, and New Orleans. Five locomotives, two passenger cars, and seventy-two freight cars operated over the road's 66.8 miles, and for the year ending March 31, 1873, the railroad had netted $47,-467.17 over expenditures and interest payments.[32]

Morgan pressed on, encouraged by the railroad's completion to Cuero, a very nice plug from the internationally-known railroad journalist John W. Forney, and receipt of a meager, 448-acre state land grant in May 1873.[33] His contemporaries did not reciprocate his enthusiasm, however.

31. *Weekly Bulletin,* May 30, August 15, December 5, 1871, February 7, April 24, 1872; *Daily Picayune,* November 29, December 24, 1871, February 22, March 10, 12, 30, April 30, May 2, 14, 1872. For the history of this type of aid, see Potts, *Railroad Transportation,* pp. 86–89.

32. *Weekly Bulletin,* May 8, 29, 1872; *Daily Picayune,* July 4, 30, August 21, October 22, 1872, February 24, 28, March 23, 1873; *American Railroad Manual,* p. 402.

33. Forney, *op. cit.,* pp. 91–92. Forney's book appeared just prior to the Cuero completion and was widely quoted by those sympathetic to the G.W.T. & P. cause. A Special Act of the Legislature of May 23, 1873 (effective June 6, 1873) granted the G.W.T. & P. 16 sections of state lands per mile (28 miles) built between Victoria and Cuero (April 22, 1871–March 3, 1873). For the Texas land-grant programs, see Potts, *op. cit.,* pp. 96–105.

They criticized his failure to reach Cuero and San Antonio on schedule, and even Indianolians complained of being bypassed by his through service. Furthermore, as the Panic of 1873 spread, money and credit were tightening, and the willingness of local governments to support the enterprise waned.

Voters of Bexar County refused to extend an additional credit of $100,000 in bonds; a cash donation of $3,000 was scraped up in Gonzales but no more bonds voted there; and crucial Travis County and Austin declined to assist at all—having more interest in roads projected toward them from the northeast. Bexar County and San Antonio's September decision to switch their aid to Morgan's major competitor Thomas W. Peirce, then building west of Columbus, was even more serious. The final blow came in 1874, when legislative acts of April 22 and May 2 by the incoming Democratic Redeemers repealed the Republican local aid legislation of 1871.[34]

Under these circumstances, the initial prosperity of the G.W.T. & P. was brief. During the year ending March 31, 1874, although gross earnings totaled $242,300.54, only $14,397.56 net profit remained after operating expenses of $149,788.36 and accounts and interest were met (see Table 10.1). The following year's returns were worse. Gross earnings fell by one third to $164,454.33, no interest payments were made on the road's bonded indebtedness of $1,386,000 (inherited from its predecessors), and heavy expenses in late 1875—a $20,000 personal injury suit lost and $95,000 storm damage to wharves, shops, and records at Indianola during the hurricane of September 15–17, 1875—eliminated all working capital available for extension beyond Cuero. Though still in operation, the road was falling seriously behind Peirce's railroad in the race toward San Antonio and the West.[35]

Morgan personally inspected the G.W.T. & P. in May 1876 and decided to suspend its operations for four months. The road to Cuero had been expensive, costing $595,155.06 or $20,037.33 per mile, and prospects of reaching Austin or San Antonio ahead of competing lines were dim.

34. *Daily Picayune*, July 25, September 4, 8, 14, October 13, November 5, 25, December 2, 25, 1872, September 22, 28, 1873; Potts, *op. cit.*, pp. 86–89.
35. *Daily Picayune*, February 20, 1873, August 17, September 2, 1874, September 22, 23, 30, 1875; *Republican*, September 30, 1875; Henry Sheppard [Agent at Indianola] to Charles A. Whitney & Co., September 20, 1875, in Galveston *Daily News*, September 21, 1875; *Railroad Manual*, pp. 401–402; *Commercial and Financial Chronicle*, XX (May 1, 1875), 428.

Profits had been taken in 1874 and 1875 but at the expense of $242,550 in overdue interest coupons on the first mortgage. When the railroad reopened in October 1876, Morgan's decision was obvious: service was cut to three days per week and plans were abandoned for the road's extension to either Austin or San Antonio. Cuero remained the *de facto* western terminus of the G.W.T. & P.—with wagon and stagecoach connections to interior points.

Thus, as in Louisiana, Morgan's first venture in Texas railroading was not too successful. Again he had experienced the uncertainties of public aid and the difficulties of construction. The G.W.T. & P. did not achieve its original purpose, but it remained a part of the Morgan system. He foreclosed its first mortgage and repurchased the property for $100,000 in April 1877. A new $1,200,000 stock issue was underwritten by Morgan at a heavy discount and the road's function and route were frozen: it continued as a two-way extension of the Indianola steamers but was abandoned as an interior trunk line.[36] Morgan gave up plans to link San Antonio and Austin with Indianola. His interest in Texas railroads had shifted elsewhere and with more success—notably around Galveston and Houston.

Morgan's postwar-Galveston situation was similar to that of Indianola in that increased trade and railroad-building were new factors in his decision-making. Indeed, the two cities were persistent rivals and had many economic goals in common—especially the titles of "principal port of Texas" and "threshold of the Southwest." Because of its size and central location, however, Galveston posed more pressing and complex problems for the steamship operator.

Galveston businessmen were especially bent on lessening their traditional dependence upon New Orleans as a supplier, consumer, and re-exporter of goods. "Galveston sets the whole machinery of her commercial power in operation to prevent shipments to New Orleans and to impair those who make them," complained an inland Texas merchant in 1872, and his belief was underscored by the experiences of New Orleanians themselves: "When I lived in Texas, twenty years ago, everybody looked to New Orleans. . . . Now all this is changed, and we are practically ignored and nearly forgotten. Ask a Texan to call and see you when

36. *Daily News,* May 2, 31, 1876; *Daily Picayune,* June 7, December 7, 1876, April 5, 13, 20, August 27, 1877; Deed, Henry Sheppard, Trustee of G.W.T. & P. to Morgan, April 3, 1877, G.W.T. & P. Records.

he comes over, and he will reply, 'Certainly, if I ever go there again.' "[37]

New York, St. Louis, Kansas City, and other points north and east were where the Texans were going—or hoped soon to go. Their desire was becoming reality: with the establishment of Galveston–New York steamship service in 1865; with the great northward cattle drives; with the southern probing of Missouri and Kansas railroads toward the northward-building Texas lines. And all of these developments altered Charles Morgan's business environment and tested his ability to adapt.

Morgan had faced maritime competitors in Galveston before. Sailing packet lines from New York had been started in 1840, 1842, 1845, 1853, and 1854 with varying degrees of success.[38] They had diverted some Texas trade away from New Orleans but were never real threats to Morgan's domination of intra-Gulf shipping. Morgan's major ante bellum threat—Vanderbilt—had been beaten off.

After the Civil War, however, the Galveston–New York lines became more serious problems. Of the half-dozen steamship lines opened between the two ports in 1865, the Mallory Line had emerged the victor by 1869. The secret of its success was a result of its expertise in ship operations and, partly, Texas's growing desire to bypass New Orleans. More specifically, however, the Mallorys' success resulted from a pooling of their interests with those of the Galveston Wharf Company and with the only railroad terminating at Galveston—the Galveston, Houston, and Henderson.

Before 1870 none of the various lines of New York–Galveston steamships used the facilities of the Galveston Wharf Company (successor in 1860 to the Galveston Wharf and Cotton Press Company). Morgan remained the prime customer of the latter, while the New York steamships patronized Bean's Wharf. During the first five months of 1870, however, the Galveston Wharf Company made special efforts to improve its position vis-à-vis the New York lines. First, it entered into negotiations with the railroad to extend its lines directly to the waterfront; second, on June 2 it appointed a committee to report on the best ways "to secure the New York trade." The actions resulting from these intentions were later summarized in the minutes of the wharf company:

It became an object of the first importance to our company to get the [New York] steamships to land at our own wharves, and at the same time to

37. "Colorado," Columbus, Texas, to Editor, December 18, 1872, *Daily Picayune*, December 24, 1872; "A Ramble through Texas," *ibid.*, September 30, 1877.
38. Cutler, *op. cit.*, pp. 530–531.

get more and better vessels in the business. Negotiations were opened with Mr. Clyde and Messrs. C. H. Mallory & Co. of New York, which resulted in an agreement by the Wharf Company [on July 2, 1870] to guaranty one-fourth of the stock in four new steamships of the Mallory Line—provided their line would land at our wharves. Mr. George Ball made this enterprise a success by taking $10,000 of the stock in each ship—and against much opposition and reluctance the remainder of the one quarter of the stock guaranteed by the Wharf Company was taken by private parties here, except $20,000, which amount the wharf company now owns in stock in the Steamships *City of Galveston, City of Houston,* and *Clyde* of the Mallory line.[39]

On August 4, 1870, the state legislature granted the wharf company the right to connect its waterfront facilities with the G.H. & H., and the improvements were rapidly undertaken. The railroad and the Mallorys arranged uniform and through rates, pending completion of shipside transfer equipment and connections.[40]

Morgan's initial reaction to the appearance of the Mallorys in the Texas trade and their negotiations with the wharf company was passive. He ignored them at Galveston as he had previously ignored them at New Orleans. He was deeply involved with the N.O.O. & G.W., the N.O.M. & T., and the G.W.T. & P. during the early stages of the Mallory expansion, and the lingering postwar overcapacity on the sea routes to New York did not appeal to him. Furthermore, at Galveston he had always enjoyed good relations with the wharf company and had no knowledge or expectation that it would turn on him to support a rival.

As for the G.H. & H., Morgan had no intimate connections with that railroad and, actually, depended equally upon a waterborne link between Galveston and the interior. He had given business to the Houston Direct Navigation Company since its founding in June 1866. Organized to transship ocean commerce to and from inland points, the company connected Morgan's Galveston ships with Houston, via a fleet of shallow-draught steamers and barges plying Buffalo Bayou.[41]

These situations had radically altered by the 1870s, however. Despite a

39. Minute Book No. 1, Board of Directors, Galveston Wharf Co., 156–157, 202, 217.

40. *Ibid.*, 145–147, 149–150, 163, 203.

41. Minute Book No. 1, Board of Directors, Houston Direct Navigation Co. (1866–1896), 1–87, Houston Direct Navigation Co. Records (S.P. Co.); *The Texas Almanac* (1872), p. 147. By 1873 the H.D.N. was operating 5 passenger steamers, 22 barges, and 3 tugs between Galveston and Houston. *Daily Picayune,* February 20, 1873.

long tradition of serving Galveston, Morgan's satisfaction with that port had deteriorated. Recurrent quarantines levied by Galveston's health officers against Louisiana ports particularly annoyed him. Annually, beginning in 1870, vessels from New Orleans and Brashear were required to undergo quarantines of twenty-five days per voyage at Galveston. The practice closed commerce between Galveston and Louisiana and cut seriously into Morgan's receipts—although during periods of quarantine he charged double rates on those steamers making the voyage.

Two circumstances made the delays more irksome and suspect. It was obvious that the regulations were as much for commercial as sanitary reasons. The closure notices always came in the fall, at the beginning of the commercial year and (as Morgan and New Orleans merchants charged with some justification) were partially to allow Galveston merchants to void their shelves of leftover merchandise before new stocks came out from New Orleans. Since Galveston enjoyed direct trade with New York via the Mallory Line, there were rumors of a "New York ring" which fostered quarantines of New Orleans to insure that their goods got to Texas consumers before those of their Louisiana competitors. In addition, under a Texas statute of August 13, 1870, every vessel arriving at the Galveston quarantine station was assessed $5 per first-hundred tons and $1\frac{1}{2}\cancel{c}$ per additional ton for the benefit of the port—a tax bearing heavily on Morgan's large and regular steamships.[42]

Morgan retaliated in late 1873, filing suit in the U.S. Circuit Court for the Eastern District of Texas to restrain Galveston's health officer, George W. Peete, from collecting the quarantine fees. Granted an injunction by the lower court, Morgan's argument—that the fee constituted a tonnage tax on interstate commerce illegally levied by local authorities—was sustained on appeal to the U.S. Supreme Court. Removal of the quarantine levy was thus secured, but not the prohibition of future "health" regulations by Galveston's authorities, and friction over quarantines encouraged Morgan to seek alternate arrangements.[43]

Conditioning his dissatisfaction was a sudden increase in the rates charged him by the wharf monopoly. Rebates granted him by the Galveston Wharf Company in 1867 and in 1871 ended in 1874, however, under a new schedule which placed him at a disadvantage vis-à-vis the Mallory

42. *Republican*, September 28–29, 1871, September 22, 1872, September 4, 10, 1873.
43. *Peete v. Morgan*, 19 Wallace (U.S.) 581 (1874).

Line.[44] Interested in eliminating or avoiding these inconveniences at Galveston, Morgan was receptive to the overtures of Houstonians seeking to develop their city at the expense of Galveston. His decision to cooperate was perhaps the most important of his postwar career. It was decisive in the subsequent course of economic development in the Gulf Southwest.

Houston was actually well on its way to commercial importance when it sought Morgan's aid. Founded in 1836, the city had played second fiddle to Galveston during the Republic of Texas. By the 1850s, however, Houston had capitalized on its more central location and projected railroads to the north, west, and east.[45] Several of these efforts were bearing fruit by the 1870s.

Running westward from Houston via Harrisburg was Thomas W. Peirce's Galveston, Harrisburg, and San Antonio Railway which crossed the Brazos River at Richmond, the Colorado at Columbus, and was pushing on toward San Antonio and the Rio Grande.[46] Eastward from Houston via Liberty ran the Texas and New Orleans Railroad which headed for the Sabine River near Orange and was the target of Morgan's westward-building Louisiana railroad.[47]

Northward ran the Houston and Texas Central Railway and the Inter-

44. [S.H. Gilman], *The Tributary and Economical Relations of the Railway Systems of the United States to the Commerce of Galveston,* esp. p. 68; *Daily Picayune,* March 16, 1872, July 27, November 27, 1874; *Daily News,* January 20, 1875; Galveston Wharf Co., *Report of H. de St. Cyr,* pp. 4, 7–8.

45. *Daily Picayune,* December 24, 1871; Andrew F. Muir, "Railroads Come to Houston, 1857–1861," *Southwestern Historical Quarterly,* LXIV (July 1960), 42–63; Earl W. Fornell, *The Galveston Era: The Texas Crescent on the Eve of Secession,* pp. 157–192.

46. Chartered in 1850 as Buffalo Bayou, Brazos, and Colorado. Renamed G.H. & S.A. in 1870. Built from Harrisburg on Buffalo Bayou to east bank of Colorado River, 1851–1860; to Columbus (on west bank via Columbus Tap) in 1868; to Schulenburg and Luling in 1874; to San Antonio on February 5, 1877 (beating Morgan's G.W.T. & P.); to Rio Grande at Del Rio on November 15, 1882. Houston tied into line in 1856 via Houston Tap to Peirce Junction. A project of Boston investors headed by Thomas W. Peirce and often called the "Peirce Road." All of these were 4′8½″-gauge roads.

47. Chartered in 1856 as Sabine and Galveston Bay Railroad and Lumber Co.; renamed T. & N.O. in 1859; reached Sabine in 1861 but partially destroyed and abandoned during Civil War. Houston–Liberty segment reopened August 16, 1870, reorganized as T. & N.O. Railroad Co. of 1874 and reopened Houston–Orange service on August 1, 1876; a 5′6″-gauge road prior to 1869; 4′8½″-gauge thereafter.

national and Great Northern Railroad. The H. & T.C., which had stalled at Millican from 1860 to 1867, reached the Red River in July 1873 via Hempstead, Navasota, Bryan, Hearne, Bremond, Corsicana, Dallas, and Sherman. Its two branches probed equally inviting hinterlands, running from Hempstead to Brenham, Giddings, and Austin and from Bremond to Waco.[48] The I. & G.N. was a consolidation of several lines which by February 1873 operated trackage from Peirce Junction via Houston to Palestine; from Palestine westward to Hearne and eastward to Troup and Longview; and from Troup to Mineola. At Harrisburg, I. & G.N. cars were interchanged with the G.H. & S.A.; at Houston with the H. & T.C., the G.H. & H., and the T. & N.O.; and at Hearne with the H. & T.C.[49]

Before the Civil War and until the mid-1870s, Morgan had remained aloof from these railroads and their rivalries. His reason was simple: the roads were only lengthening and broadening the hinterlands of port cities he already served. Unlike the N.O.O. & G.W. in Louisiana and the N.O.M. & T. in Alabama, both of which threatened *to parallel* his coastwise steamers, the Texas roads ran *perpendicular* to his shipping routes and posed no competitive threat.

The crucial difference by the mid-1870s, however, was that the Texas roads had expanded sufficiently to threaten a diversion of trade from traditional hinterland-port channels. The threat to Indianola's backland has been considered. The problem in the Galveston–Houston area was the effecting of rail connections with St. Louis, Shreveport, and Kansas City—connections which might drain central Texas northeastward away from the Gulf coast and Morgan's vessels.

The threat became reality in 1873 and 1874. The Missouri, Kansas, and Texas Railway reached Denison, Texas, on December 25, 1872, and on March 18, 1873, made physical connection and interchange with the H. & T.C. at Denison. The importance of this interchange cannot be overstressed as it linked the Texas railroads with the Kansas–Missouri network for the first time and initiated a northern flow of goods which

48. Began as Galveston and Red River Railroad in 1848; renamed H. & T.C. in 1856; a 5′6″–gauge road until 1870–1871 (main line; 1877 branches).

49. Houston and Great Northern Railroad was chartered in 1866 and reached Palestine in 1873, absorbed Houston Tap in 1871 and thus linked with G.H. & S.A. via Peirce Junction. International Railroad was chartered in 1870 to build from Texarkana to Austin, San Antonio, and Laredo; roads consolidated as I. & G.N. in 1872. In 1880 the Austin line reached San Antonio. This system was all 4′8½″–gauge.

continued to grow. Through rates and service on this line were achieved by July 1873, and the co-operating roads claimed runs of 92.5 hours, Galveston to New York; 90 hours, Houston to New York; 52.1 hours, Galveston to St. Louis; and 49.5 hours, Houston to St. Louis.[50]

Other northern railroad connections soon followed. By December 1873, the Texas and Pacific Railway had trackage in operation on two east-west routes: Shreveport–Marshall–Longview–Dallas and Texarkana–Paris–Sherman. These lines were joined by a branch from Marshall to Texarkana and interchanged cars with the H. & T.C. at Sherman and Dallas and with the I. & G.N. at Longview.[51] The T. & P. was linked to St. Louis and the East on March 20, 1874, when the St. Louis, Iron Mountain, and Southern Railway reached Texarkana.[52]

Thus while New Orleans' railroads to Texas were still mired in legalities and swamps, northern railroads had penetrated the Lone Star State at two points. And it was Houston, not Galveston, that was riding the crest.

Indeed, relative to Houston's expansion was the increasing undercapacity of Galveston's only railroad—a circumstance which widened the gap. Most serious was the Galveston, Houston, and Henderson's refusal to change its gauge. While the main lines of the Houston roads were all of the standard 4′8½″ gauge by 1871, the G.H. & H. clung to its antiquated 5′6″ until July 29, 1876. This limited its through connections with the more interior roads to car-to-car transfers rather than the interchange of cars already possible on all of the Houston lines.[53]

---

50. M.K. & T. began as the Union Pacific Railway—Southern Branch and was renamed in 1870. A 4′8½″-gauge road, it paralleled the H. & T.C. between the Red River and Denison for 18 months before September 1, 1874, but thereafter shared a station at Denison, while the H. & T.C. relinquished trackage north of that city.

51. T. & P., chartered by Congress in 1871, to build from Marshall, Texas, to San Diego, California, adopted its present name in 1872 and absorbed several local companies, including: Southern Pacific; Southern Transcontinental; Memphis, El Paso, and Pacific; and Vicksburg, Shreveport, and Texas. There was a gap in the Texarkana–Sherman line, between Brookston and Nash, until August 11, 1876. T. & P. was a 4′8½″-gauge road.

52. On May 6, 1874, the S.L.I.M. & S. was formed through consolidation of: St. Louis and Iron Mountain; Cairo, Arkansas, and Texas; and Cairo and Fulton. A 5′6″-gauge road until June 28, 1879, it then standardized to 4′8½″. Until this change, it operated at some disadvantage in competition with the M.K. & T.–H. & T.C. system.

53. Before 1865, the G.H. & H. made physical connection (at Harrisburg) with only those roads which became the G.H. & S.A., but because of a difference in

Dissatisfaction with the G.H. & H. was widespread among shippers. The chartering of the Houston Direct Navigation Company in 1866 was an early response. The H. & T.C. offered in 1870 to build a third rail from Houston to Galveston (so that interchange of cars might at least take place between those points) but was refused by the G.H. & H. and the City of Galveston. As an alternative, the H. & T.C. and an I. & G.N. predecessor were even considering opening their own steamer line from Houston to Galveston by 1872.[54]

The simple fact was that geography earned a good living for the G.H. & H.'s proprietors, and they were reluctant to cut into their profits to support expansion. Net earnings for the year ending December 31, 1873, were $277,969.28 over operating expenses of $438,395.91. With the Panic of 1873 widening, they preferred to sit tight. Others did not follow their example, however. By 1873 a rival group of Galvestonians had begun the Gulf, Colorado, and Santa Fe as their city's second railroad to the interior.[55] On another front, it was Charles Morgan who took the lead.

As a carrier of goods and of much of the construction material for the Houston roads, Morgan watched their extension and interconnection carefully. In January 1873, he converted his steamers' freight tariffs to "a strictly railroad basis"—per hundred pounds rather than per barrel, per bale, etc. This must have galled the old shipping man as it marked another break with the past, but it facilitated through shipments and interchange with Texas railroads.

---

gauge could only transfer freight. In 1861 it began an extension through Houston to connect with the H. & T.C., and between 1865 and 1870 was able to interchange cars with that road. The narrowing of the H. & T.C. main line to 4'8½" during 1870–1871 ended this interchange (although H. & T.C. branches were not narrowed until 1877). No connection had been made between the T. & N.O. and the G.H. & H. before the Civil War, although both were of the 5'6" gauge. The rebuilding of the former after 1869 as a 4'8½" road precluded interchange. Physical connection with the T. & N.O. and the I. & G.N. system was made (in Houston) on January 22, 1873, but only for car-to-car transfers. The G.H. & H. did not convert to the 4'8½" gauge until July 29, 1876, following the Texas gauge standardization law of February 14, 1875.

54. Minute Book No. 1, Board of Directors, Houston and Texas Central Railway Co. (1861–1890), 207, H. & T.C. Records (S.P. Co.); Robert E. Caudle, *History of the Missouri Pacific Lines, Gulf Coast Lines and Subsidiaries, International–Great Northern*, p. 51.

55. Vernon, *Railroad Manual*, pp. 401–402; L. L. Waters, *Steel Trails to Santa Fe*.

On August 29, he agreed to a more formal arrangement and pooled his interest with the H. & T.C. and the I. & G.N. Uniform classification of rates was arranged, and through shipments between New Orleans and interior Texas points were prorated per mile by the lines over which the freight passed. Morgan accepted the liability of wharfage charges at Galveston and 200 miles as his proportional due; the railroads accepted their actual mileage as per their tariffs. Once again the shipping operator had successfully adapted to the railroad.[56]

The second stage of Morgan's reaction to the rise of Houston as a rail center was startling in the extreme. Increasingly unhappy with his Galveston situation, he plunged into a scheme to bypass it. His partner became the Buffalo Bayou Ship Channel Company.

Originally chartered on January 23, 1869, the Ship Channel Company was authorized to improve navigational conditions between Houston and Galveston and was granted a tonnage tax by Houston provided the project was completed by April 1, 1872. A question as to the legality of the original company arose, no work began before reorganization of the corporation on July 28, 1870. Capitalized at $1,000,000, the company was again granted wharfage and tonnage taxes by Houston conditional upon completion of an eight-foot-deep channel from Galveston Bay to Houston via Buffalo Bayou by January 1, 1876.[57] Construction had begun early in 1871 but stalled by 1874 because of insufficient public subscription during that depression year and the refusal of the federal government to assist beyond the deepening of Red Fish Bar in Galveston Bay. Needing funds, the company turned to Morgan.[58]

On July 1, 1874, the Ship Channel Company and the steamship proprietor combined. Morgan contracted to construct a nine-foot channel, not less than 120 feet wide, from Galveston Bay to the vicinity of Houston

56. *Daily Picayune*, January 14, 1873; Agreement among Morgan Line, H. & T.C. and I. & G.N., August 29, 1873, M.L. & T.R. & S. Records. Morgan's first equity in a Houston railroad was his purchase of 40 shares of H. & T.C. on October 28, 1875. Stock Ledger, Galveston and Red River Railroad–Houston and Texas Central Railway (1855–1884), 10/28/75, H. & T.C. Records.

57. Contract between City of Houston and B.B.S.C.C., April 3, 1869, Act Authorizing Construction of a Ship Channel from Bolivar Point to City of Houston, July 28, 1870, and Ordinance to Further Facilitate Completion of Buffalo Bayou Ship Channel, July 24, 1871, M.L. & T.R. & S. Records.

58. *Daily Picayune*, January 30, July 9, November 25, 1872, February 4, 1873; *Annual Report of the Chief of Engineers to the Secretary of War, 1870*, pp. 61–62; *ibid.*, 1871, pp. 65, 518–523, 533–537; Reed, *op. cit.*, pp. 238–240.

in return for the unissued capital stock of the corporation totaling $806,500. Payment would be made in $10,000 increments upon presentation of construction vouchers by Morgan, but the company reserved the right to repurchase up to 50 per cent of the stock so issued at par within six months after completion of the channel. Morgan's steamers would enjoy free navigation of the eventual waterway.[59]

Supervised by John J. Atkinson, formerly captain of *Matagorda*, Morgan's "dredge fleet" went immediately to work. By mid-1875, eight dredges, six tugs, and some twelve derricks and barges were working day and night excavating the channel. Despite severe storm damage in the hurricane of September 1875, a nine- to ten-foot channel was completed on April 21, 1876. The channel ran from Bolivar Channel east of Pelican Island in Galveston Bay, through the government channel at Red Fish Bar, through Morgan's Cut (named for Charles Morgan) across Morgan's Point (named for Texas' James Morgan), into the San Jacinto River to its confluence with Buffalo Bayou at Lynchburg, and thence to a steamship wharf opposite the mouth of Simm's Bayou, twelve water or six land miles from Houston. To his steamer *Clinton* went the honor of first navigating Morgan's new channel; the settlement at its western terminus was named jointly for this ship and Morgan's birthplace.[60]

Significantly, *Clinton*'s maiden cargo was railroad construction materials, for Morgan intended to link his bayou landing with the railroads radiating to the interior from Houston. Appropriating the name of a defunct corporation chartered in 1866 for similar purposes, Morgan built a railroad which he called the Texas Transportation Company from Clinton into Houston's Fifth Ward. By September 11, 1876, the 7.4-mile railroad was in operation, linking Morgan's steamers with the Houston and Texas Central, the International and Great Northern, the Galveston, Harrisburg and San Antonio, and the Galveston, Houston, and Henderson railroads. The line was capable of interchanging cars with any connecting road in the state.[61]

59. Agreement between Morgan and B.B.S.C.C., July 1, 1874, M.L. & T.R. & S. Records.

60. *Daily Picayune*, July 27, 1874, January 17, March 25, May 20, June 3, September 22, 30, November 13, 1875, April 23, May 13, July 24, 1876; *Louisiana Sugar Bowl*, March 4, April 1, June 24, September 16, 30, 1875; *Annual Report of the Chief of Engineers . . . 1875*, pp. 846–875; *ibid., 1877*, pp. 446–468; *ibid., 1878*, pp. 603–609; *ibid., 1879*, pp. 909–918; *ibid., 1880*, pp. 1236–1238.

61. *Daily News*, April 8, 21, 23, 25, July 11, August 1, 17, September 8, 12, 1876; *Daily Picayune*, May 13, July 24, August 6, 1876.

Morgan thus avoided Galveston, its quarantines, its wharf company, and its railroad and proclaimed, "Houston, not Galveston, is our terminus." Yet a final goal remained: to secure ownership of rail facilities inland from Houston which would guarantee movements to and from his steamships. This had been his hope for the G.W.T. & P. at Indianola; it was his hope at Houston as well.

Dissension within the management of the Houston and Texas Central Railway gave Morgan the chance he sought. The H. & T.C. had been Texan-owned and operated before the Civil War but had subsequently come under the control of a New York investment group headed by Moses Taylor, William E. Dodge, John I. Blair, John J. Cisco, and William Walter Phelps.[62] Through construction contracts paid in watered stock, through stock purchases, through the buying up of the road's paper and its exchange for stock, and through the underwriting of five mortgages between 1866 and 1875, the New Yorkers had a strong voice in management: Dodge became a director in 1868 and president in 1871; Taylor became a director in 1873 and Cisco in 1874; Blair held most of the road's construction contracts and became a director in 1876; Phelps was a trustee of one of the mortgages and attorney for the New York group.

By 1877 the H. & T.C. operated 343 miles of main track from Houston to Denison and 162 miles of branch line from Hempstead to Austin and from Bremond to Waco. It traversed some of the richest counties of Texas, connected with all the Houston and Galveston roads as well as the M.K. & T. and the T. & P.–S.L.I.M. & S. systems, and had demonstrated its capacity to produce respectable net earnings and meet its interest payments (see Table 9.3). Its January credit rating read: "Strongest corporation in the South & are thought perftly. safe & solvent."[63]

Under this façade of solvency, however, all was not well. As the

62. For the H. & T.C., see: Minute Book No. 1, Board of Directors, Galveston and Red River Railroad Co.–Houston and Texas Central Railway Co. (1852–1871); Minute Book No. 1, Board of Directors, H. & T.C. and Record Book No. 1, Houston and Texas Central Railway (1867–1870), H. & T.C. Records. For the Taylor-Dodge group, which was also involved in the Lackawanna, see: Lowitt, *William E. Dodge;* Moses Taylor Collection (New York Public Library), which Roland T. Ely has mined most extensively in various publications; D. & B., N. Y., vol. 417, p. 105, for Cisco; Hall (ed.), *Successful Men,* II, 91–92, for Blair who was probably the largest railroad-construction contractor in the U.S.; H. & T.C. File (Corporation Records Division, Baker Library, Harvard Graduate School of Business Administration), for copies of all mortgages, etc.

63. D. & B., Tex., vol. 15b, p. 287.

depression of the 1870s deepened, bond sales and net earnings were falling, and they became increasingly inadequate to cover the road's heavy operating costs, its new construction programs, and its interest and sinking fund payments. The New York directors favored payment of the floating debt (much of which they held through construction and operating contracts) while the Texas directors were more inclined toward maintenance of interest and sinking-fund payments at all costs.[64]

Things came to a head on March 9, 1877 ("much to the surprise of nearly every one in financial circles," reported the Mercantile Agency), when Taylor, Blair, Cisco, and Phelps filed application in the U.S. District Court for the Western District of Texas (at Austin) for appointment of a receiver for the road. Their plea was the excessive floating debt of the road, but insiders recognized "a family party" when they saw one. It was more likely a move to facilitate the consolidation of the H. & T.C. with the I. & G.N.[65] Taylor, Dodge, Phelps, and other New Yorkers had chartered the Houston and Great Northern in 1866; the International in 1870; and merged them as the I. & G.N. in 1872–1873. Their plans were known among insiders:

If the N.Y. crs. succeed in getting the order from the court it is believed that G.A. Grow of Penna. [formerly the president of the I. & G.N.] will be appointed receiver. . . . The "true inwardness" of this movement appears to be this. The N.Y. crs. & stock & bond owners of this road are also largely interested in another road wh. has been running in opposition. The Texas crs. are interested only in this one road & are not disposed to join interests with the other one, it would therefore appear to be the aim of the Northern crs. when they get a receiver appointed to have the road sold out under a foreclosure & a new organization formed by wh. they can get control of the road & then operate in such a way that the two roads may run in harmony under the management of one interest. . . .

A number of New York capitalists are bondholders and stockholders in both the Texas Central and Texas International railroads, with a preponder-

64. The view that floating debts should take precedence over bonded debts was novel and the Taylor-Dodge group was criticized severely for this "dangerous" attitude. See, e.g., "Railroad Mortgages as Securities," *Commercial and Financial Chronicle*, XXIV (May 26, 1877), 479–480.

65. Phelps claimed the road owed: $1,465,110 to the N.Y. group for money loaned; $136,939 on supplies purchased in N.Y.; state taxes of $80,000; $300,000 in payrolls; paper on the company out and maturing within the year, $1,024,000; $550,000 "to certain parties and secured by pledge of bonds"; and U.S. taxes of $78,000. *Commercial and Financial Chronicle*, XXIV (April 14, 1877), 346, quoting Galveston *News*. For credit comment, see D. & B., Tex., vol. 15b, p. 287.

ating influence in favor of the International, which has never been a paying institution, while the Texas Central has. The latter . . . amassed a floating debt of $2,600,000 which amount was mainly advanced by capitalists in New York City; and they, in the hope of having a receiver appointed with the ultimate view of consolidating the two roads, have entered suit against the company for the amount due them.[66]

The Houston directors of the H. & T.C., who constituted a majority, took immediate steps to nullify the New Yorkers' bid for receivership and reorganization by putting themselves in the hands of Charles Morgan. He had been following the road's affairs closely and responded instantly. The depth of the Houstonians' concern and the trust they placed in Morgan are reflected in the directors' resolutions of March 23, 24, and 28, 1877:

Board met pursuant to adjournment. . . . On motion . . . the following resolutions were unanimously adopted viz. . . .

Whereas this board has been informed that a suit in chancery has been instituted in the Western District of Texas by Mesrs. Moses Taylor and others against this company to place the property of the company in the hands of a receiver, and this board has been further informed that Wm. E. Dodge President of this Company of his own motive and without the knowledge by this board of the existence of this suit has accepted Service and had an appearance for the Company. Now be it:

Resolved that the action of said President was without authority and does not bind this company and is not the appearance of this company to said suit, and that the attorneys of this company are hereby instructed to take all proper steps to deny and put in issue the jurisdiction of the court in the Western District of Texas over this company in said suit.

Whereas there are habilities of the company payable in the City of New York & other places now due and to become due which are secured by the mortgage bonds of the company held and pledged for the prompt payment of the same, & as this company is without present funds to meet said obligations & believing that Mr. Charles Morgan of the City of New York is willing to advance the amounts of money necessary to pay said debts.

Therefore be it Resolved that Mr. Charles Morgan of the City of New York is hereby requested and authorized to pay any and all such amounts of money as are now due and owing or which may hereafter become due by the Houston & Texas Central Railway Company in the City of New York or elsewhere and which amounts are or may be secured by first Mortgage bonds, Consolidated or second Mortgage bonds or other bonds or coupons executed by this company and upon payment of any portion of said debt, to receive said bonds,

66. D. & B., Tex., vol. 156, pp. 287, 331; *Commercial and Financial Chronicle*, XXIV (March 24, 1877) ; *Public*, X (March 15, 1877), 168.

coupons and other securities and hold the same pledged as security for the account of principal and interest so advanced and such further interest as may accrue while the said habilities are in his hands unpaid, and that he may hold the same with all the rights, liens, privileges and powers over the same held by the present or original holders of said indebtedness until paid by said Company.

Resolved that upon the payment by Mr. Charles Morgan of all or any of said accounts he shall thereby be entitled to the possession of said First Mortgage Bonds, Consolidated or Second Mortgage bonds or other Mortgage bonds or coupons and shall be subsigated [sic] to all the rights, privileges and powers over the same held by the present or original holders of the indebtedness of the Company. . . .

Whereas this Company owes a considerable amount of floating debt and is without available means for its prompt payment, and it is most important to the credit and business of the Company that the Company should be relieved from the immediate pressure of such indebtedness, therefore,

Resolved that the Executive Committee of this board or a majority thereof be and the same are hereby authorized to enter into any arrangement they may deem expedient with Mr. Charles Morgan by which he will guaranty [sic], assume, take up or become the owner of such indebtedness or any part or amount thereof: and to this end that the said Committee or the majority thereof may execute any and all obligations to Mr. Charles Morgan for the repayment thereof at such time and with such note of interest as they may deem proper, and to secure the payment of the same by any first or junior trustdeed, lien, mortgage or security on any lands, bonds, stock, property, assets and rights whatsoever of or belonging to this Company. . . .

Whereas this Co. is without funds in hand to pay the interest coupons on its Second Mortgage Consolidated Bonds maturing April 1st,

Resolved that Charles Morgan be & he hereby is authorized to purchase such coupons from the respective holders thereof for his own account to be held by him with all existing rights of lien.

Resolved that Charles Morgan be and he hereby is authorized to sell any of the first or second mortgage bonds of this Company which he may in pursuance of the resolutions of this board heretofore possess, reduce by the payment of the claims for which the same have been pledged by this Company, at such times, in such manner and upon such terms as he may deem best for the interest of this Company, and he is hereby further authorized to apply the proceeds of such sales to reimburse himself principal and interest for the moneys advanced by him for the redemption of said Bonds and for any moneys which he may expend in purchasing the coupons of this company's mortgage bonds.[67]

67. Minute Book No. 1, Board of Directors, H. & T.C., 328–331, H. & T.C. Records.

Given such broad discretion, Morgan acted swiftly to forestall receivership or foreclosure. His first actions were to meet April interest and tax payments of the road and to gain equity control of its affairs. Through the brokerage of William Brady in New York, Charles A. Whitney in New Orleans, Charles Fowler in Galveston, and William Marsh Rice in Houston and New York (the first being Morgan's personal broker; the second, his son-in-law and managing agent; the third, his Galveston agent; and the fourth, the H. & T.C.'s financial agent), he purchased 40,440½ shares of H. & T.C. at 15 and secured proxies from two Taylor-group defectors: 7,035 shares of John J. Cisco & Son and 6,675½ shares of William E. Dodge.[68]

At the regular annual meeting of the H. & T.C. stockholders, held May 7, 1877, Morgan purged the board of Taylor-Dodge men and elected a new slate of officers:

CHARLES MORGAN, Director

CHARLES A. WHITNEY, Director and President

ALEXANDER C. HUTCHINSON, Director

CHARLES FOWLER, Director and Executive Committee Member

GEORGE JORDAN, Director and Vice President

EBER W. CAVE, Director, Treasurer, and Executive Committee Member

ABRAM GROESBECK, Director

A. S. RICHARDSON, Director, Secretary, and Executive Committee Member

The first four need no introduction; Jordan was a professional engineer brought in from Tennessee; Cave, Groesbeck, and Richardson were long-time investors and officers in the H. & T.C. and eminently represented Houston's financial elite. Under this leadership the H. & T.C. became a key addition to the growing Morgan enterprises.

Morgan rescued the H. & T.C. with no illusions about speculative prof-

68. Morgan made the following block purchases and assignments of H. & T.C. stock: 40 to E. W. Cave (3/22/77; these were the 40 he bought 10/28/75); bought 35,000 (3/24/77); bought 5,000 (3/24/77); bought 440½ (3/24/77); 40 to C. A. Whitney (5/2/77); 40 to A. C. Hutchinson (5/2/77); 320½ to Charles Fowler (5/2/77); 40 to G. Jordan (5/2/77); and bought 320½ from Fowler (5/27/77). This gave Morgan 40,000 shares at the time of the annual meeting of May 7. Stock Ledger, G. & R.R.R.–H. & T.C., 3/22/77 to 5/27/77 and Minute Book No. 1, Board of Directors, H. & T.C., 333, H. & T.C. Records.

its or quick turnover. He was quoted that "The road in his estimation is valuable property, well able, with proper management, to meet its expenses. But its debts are . . . much heavier in fact than he supposed when he made his purchase and he says that it will require careful, earnest support from its managers and patience at the hands of its creditors."[69] And his activities indicated he had signed on for a long voyage. He persuaded the Taylor group to drop its motion for receivership and met numerous debts of the road with balance transfers from his other enterprises. In May 1877, the remaining floating debt was funded by payment of liabilities under $1,000 in cash or two-year notes and the flotation of a ten-year, $2,500,000, 7 per cent income and indemnity bond issue with Houston bankers Benjamin A. Sheppard and Thomas W. House (this to funded larger floating debts). Operating costs were reduced by a 10 per cent wage cut, effective April 1 and the discharge of "extramen."[70]

Most of the refinancing was complete by September, and the road recorded its revised indebtedness (see Table 9.4). By October, the H. & T.C.'s credit report noted "there seems to be consid. confidence felt that this road is in a shape for ultimate success."[71]

Although the "ultimate" history of the H. & T.C. under Morgan management belongs to the next chapter, why he committed himself to this debt-ridden railroad in 1877 should be made clear here. Looking ahead, he believed that he could help himself by helping the H. & T.C. He could gain control of an operating railroad which would give him through service over his own ships and tracks from New York, Havana, and New Orleans to the innermost hinterland of Texas. This was the goal he had set for himself, and he would achieve it before any competing transportation entrepreneur.

Morgan had seen his goal slip away at Indianola, but in the H. & T.C. he acquired a reality rather than a dream; a going concern which blended with his new focus on Houston and which could be connected to his Louisiana road, first by steamship via Brashear, ultimately, by track. His

69. *Commercial and Financial Chronicle*, XXIV (April 21, 1877), 370. See also, *ibid.*, XXX (March 13, 1880), 273.

70. Minute Book No. 1, Board of Directors, H. & T.C., 335–348, H. & T.C. Records; Income and Indemnity Mortgage of H. & T.C., Benjamin A. Sheppard and Thomas W. House, Trustees, May 7, 1877, H. & T.C., File (Corporation Records Division, Baker Library); Morgan to Whitney, May 17, 1877, M.L. & T.R. & S. Records; *Daily Picayune*, May 25, 1877.

71. D. & B., Tex., vol. 15b, p. 331 (October 27, 1877).

acquisition of the H. & T.C. also increased his competitive advantage over the railroads invading Texas from the North as well as over the Mallory steamships running between Galveston and New York. None of these enterprises could offer one-management, through service for northeast-southwest commerce, and none had as extensive a Cuban service as did Morgan.

All in all, then, the H. & T.C. was a calculated risk which brought Morgan closer to his goal of a network of railroads and steamships linking the Southwest with Mexico, Cuba, and the East. He knew full well that times were changing and that some of his traditional services would decline or be destroyed in the process of creating his larger rail-water system. Indeed, something of the ultimate pattern was already evident by 1877: his Galveston agency, for example, which had a gross volume of business averaging $60,000 per month in 1874, declined to $53,000 per month during 1875 and 1876, and to $28,000 during 1877; Indianola, which had averaged a gross volume of $24,000 per month during both 1874 and 1875, declined to $17,000 per month in 1876 and $16,000 per month in 1877.

On the brighter side, however, the Havana agency, which had averaged a gross volume of $31,000 per month in 1874, peaked at $75,000 per month in 1875, and held steady at $53,000 per month during 1876 and 1877. The New York agency, which opened in July 1875, averaged a gross volume of $61,000 per month over the next twenty-eight months, while Houston, which had no Morgan agency before October 1876, averaged a gross volume of $43,000 per month over the next eighteen months. At the smaller ports, where rail competition was not a factor, Morgan steamship service held the field: at Rockport the average gross volume was $7,000 per month by 1877; at Brazos St. Iago the average was $18,000 per month in 1874, $13,000 in 1875, $16,000 in 1876, and $17,000 during 1877.[72]

Thus Morgan's traffic patterns were gradually shifting toward new goals during the late 1860s and early 1870s. With the clearing of the political air in Louisiana, the achievement of his aims soon followed.

72. Compiled from Ledger No. 3, Charles A. Whitney & Co., 1874–1877, M.L. & T.R. & S. Records.

10

MORGAN'S LOUISIANA
AND TEXAS
RAILROAD AND STEAMSHIP
COMPANY, 1877–1885

MORGAN'S overriding goal, in the post–Civil War years, was the creation of a unified network of steamship and rail lines which would interlock the Gulf Southwest with the Mississippi Valley, northern Latin America, and the Atlantic and Pacific coasts. Between 1877 and 1885 much of this dream became reality through his own efforts and those of his key managers. A large, integrated transportation system flying the Morgan star crowned the effort begun decades before on the tiny deck of *Columbia*.

Yet at its peak of accomplishment, death and the railroad consolidation movement of the 1880s stripped the Morgan Line of its original identity. It lived on in name as an important segment of a transcontinental system, but 1885 marked the end of its founder's influence.

The initial steps in the ultimate integration of the Morgan Line began with the restoration of Bourbon control in Louisiana. Morgan had remained steadfastly Democratic throughout the uncertain days of Reconstruction, and his reward came in the form of corporate privilege. One of the first actions of the newly elected Democratic legislature in 1877 asked Morgan to "bring his great resources to assist" in the completion of a railroad to Texas. The result was the charter of Morgan's Louisiana and Texas Railroad and Steamship Company—"no more than was to be expected of a conservative Legislature . . . after . . . the legislative corruption and jobbery of Louisiana Radicalism."[1]

The new corporation created by the legislature and Morgan on March 8, 1877, was chartered indefinitely to purchase, maintain, and run his railroad from New Orleans to Morgan City, to own and operate his ships, and to extend his rail lines from Morgan City to the Sabine (and beyond) and to Opelousas (and beyond). The charter allowed the widest latitude in connecting with any or all Texas or Louisiana railways, but especially the New Orleans Pacific then projected westward from New Orleans to Opelousas and Shreveport. Morgan's company was capitalized at $5,000,000, its domicile set at New Orleans, and a five-man directorate established. Extension of his roads west of Morgan City was to begin within a year, and elaborate machinery was provided for judicial expropriation of lands for right-of-way. Morgan's tasks of extension were lessened by complementary state legislation approving general procedures for reorganizing foreclosed railroads and consolidating connecting or interesecting lines.[2]

Organization of a corporation took time, but commencement of construction was certified to the state on March 4, 1878, and formal incorporation soon achieved. Hutchinson (holding Morgan's power of attorney), Whitney, Pandely (superintendent of the M.L. & T.), and John B. Richardson (secretary of Whitney & Co.), met on March 25, in twenty minutes subscribed the entire 50,000 shares, named themselves and Morgan the required five directors, and elected Whitney president of the firm. Morgan took 49,940 shares in the company, the other four directors subscribed ten each, while Morgan's Louisiana attorney Henry J. Leovy and his grandson Charles Morgan Whitney purchased the remaining twenty shares. The corporation was authorized to purchase Morgan's railroad from New Orleans, the Atchafalaya Bay Co., any or all of Morgan's steamers, and any other property deemed necessary to achieve its goals.[3]

1. New Orleans *Times*, February 28–March 8, 1877; New Orleans *Daily Picayune*, February 28, March 8, 1877.
2. *Louisiana Acts* (1877), pp. 37–51; Acceptance of Act No. 27 by Morgan, March 2, 1877. Act before George W. Christy, N.A. (Orleans).
3. Service of Notice on Governor and Secretary of State of La. by M.L. & T.R. & S., March 6, 1878. Act before George W. Christy, N.A. (Orleans); Minute Book No. 1, Board of Directors, M.L. & T.R. & S., 1–5, M.L. & T.R. & S. Records.

The necessary transfers were completed by April 16. On April 1, Morgan had contracted to exchange property valued at $9,994,000 for stock and bonds in the new corporation. He relinquished his entire railroad between New Orleans and Morgan City, his claims against the N.O.M. & T. for properties beyond the Atchafalaya River, the levee portion of the Pontchartrain Railroad, the Houma Branch of his railroad, all his properties or claims to property in New Orleans, Algiers, Morgan City, or along the way of his line, sixteen steamships, two tugs, and three ferries, the assets of Whitney & Co., and his holdings in all related companies: 2,500 shares of the Atchafalaya Bay Company, 40,000 shares of the H. & T.C., 5,054 shares and 190 bonds of the Buffalo Bayou Ship Channel Company, 4,965 shares of the G.W.T. & P., two bonds of the Selma, Rome, and Dalton Railroad Co., and 263 shares and a $300,000 construction-claim against the Texas Transportation Company.[4] In exchange, Morgan received his 49,940 shares in the M.L. & T.R. & S. and $5,000,000 in first-mortgage bonds (due in 1918 and carrying 7 per cent interest) secured by the corporation's property.[5]

The formation of the M.L. & T.R. & S. was the closest Morgan's enterprises ever came to integration under a single proprietary, organizational, and operational unit. Before 1877 Morgan had owned his various businesses either as sole proprietor or as majority stockholder. Below him had been a variety of organizations for operation—some proprietary; some corporate; all pragmatically structured through time but all answering to his equity control. His exercise of this entrepreneurial control had been in person or through his lawful agents—first his captains or representatives; then through Harris & Morgan; finally through Whitney & Co. The M.L. & T.R. & S. changed this pattern. Henceforth, Morgan's equity and management were institutionalized in a closely held pyramid of interlocking corporations.

His motives for these consolidations are clear. Eighty-three years of age and weakened by Bright's disease, Morgan wished to guarantee completion of his plans. His purpose in incorporation (at the suggestion of Hutchinson) was to convert his assets into easily transferable property

4. Sale, Whitney to M.L & T.R. & S., March 2, 1878. Act before George W. Christy, N.A. (Orleans); Contract between Morgan and M.L. & T.R. & S., April 1, 1878. Deposited with Andrew Hero, Jr., April 12, 1878, *ibid.*

5. Sale, Morgan to M.L. & T.R. & S., April 9, 1878, Receipt, M.L. & T.R. & S. to Morgan, April 13, 1878, Mortgage, M.L. & T.R. & S. to Morgan, April 16, 1878. Acts before Andrew Hero, Jr., N.A. (Orleans).

and to centralize equity control in a perpetual decision-making body. Aware of his infirmity and desiring smooth continuation of his enterprises by the concentration of power in trusted hands, Morgan donated most of his new securities to selected heirs (with Whitney as trustee). Between April 13 and 15, 1878, 32,000 shares in the M.L. & T.R. & S. were distributed to his wife Mary Jane Sexton Morgan, his daughters Maria Louise Morgan Whitney and Frances Eliza Morgan Quintard, his grandson (Charles W.'s son) Richard Jessup Morgan (7,500 each); and his sons-in-law, Charles A. Whitney and George W. Quintard (1,000 each). Absent were gifts to grandson Montaigu Morgan (Henry R.'s son) or his family, whom Morgan disliked. Those closest to him testified in later years that Morgan's purposes for the gifts were, "perpetuating, as nearly as practicable, his own methods of management" and "dislike of a contest over the distribution of his property. . . . [based upon] horror at the conduct of some of Commodore Vanderbilt's children after the latter's death."[6]

Morgan's action proved wise. On May 9, 1878, seventeen days after his eighty-third birthday, he died in his residence at 7 West 26th Street, New York. Bedridden since early April, Morgan had allowed Hutchinson and Whitney to organize his final company, but thousands mourned him as the creator of the Morgan Line. His memorial services held at Rutgers Presbyterian Church and Green-Wood Cemetery, New York, on May 11 were attended by scores of business leaders, many serving as actual or honorary pallbearers, and messages of sympathy poured in from individuals and corporations with which he had been associated.[7]

Morgan's death did not affect the M.L. & T.R. & S., however—indeed, no resolution of sympathy was adopted by its directorate for fifty days following his death. The management, because of Morgan's bequests, remained securely in the hands of his family and his estate as administered through proxies by Whitney and Hutchinson. Morgan's wish to press on was honored.

President Whitney and Vice-President Hutchinson had actually as-

6. Surrogate's Court, County of New York, In the Matter of the Last Will of Charles Morgan, Allegations to Revoke Probate, May 31, 1879, and Points in Reply [n.d.], M.L. & T.R. & S. Records; *In the Matter of the Final Accounting of Morgan,* 104 New York Reports 74 (1887).

7. New York *Times,* May 9, 12, 1878; *Daily Picayune,* May 9, 1878; New Orleans *Democrat,* May 9, 1878; New Orleans *Price Current,* May 11, 1878; Galveston *Daily News,* May 9. 1878: *In Memoriam: Charles Morgan.*

sumed *de facto* control before Morgan's death and were busily pursuing a plan for extending their railroad in Louisiana and expanding their enterprises in Texas and at sea. Since their success so nearly approximated Morgan's oft-expressed desires, the Morgan Line drew on its founder long after his death.

The operation of the Morgan companies actually underwent two phases between 1877 and 1885. During the first period, 1877–1882, the actions of their managers most approximated Morgan's original plans for expansion and consolidation of his system. After 1882, however, the intrusion of Collis P. Huntington and Jay Gould into Southwestern railroading, basically modified the strategy and tactics of the Morgan enterprises. The companies became less and less "Morgan" operations and by 1885 had been subsumed by the Huntington and Gould systems. The last years of the original Morgan Line thus blended into the initial years of a mature southwestern railroad network (see Map 10.1).

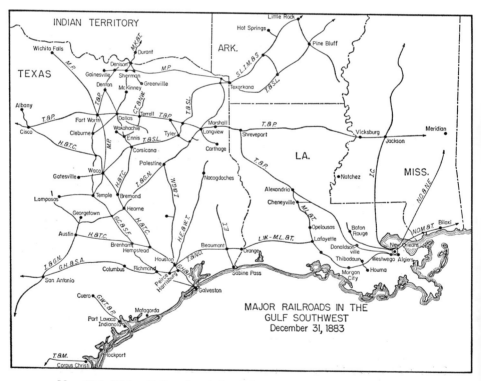

Map 10.1. Major Railroads of the Gulf Southwest, December 31, 1883.

In the period from 1877 to 1882 the parent M.L. & T.R. & S. company acted as planner, financier, and policy co-ordinator for all of the Morgan enterprises. In this sense it assumed the role previously held by Harris & Morgan and Whitney & Co. Single incorporation of the whole system was impossible as Texas law prohibited the consolidation of the G.W.T. & P., the H. & T.C., and the T.T. with "foreign corporations." Majority ownership in the Texas roads by the Louisiana corporation and careful interlocking of directorates, however, insured a community of interest in decision-making. The parent company also owned and operated all Morgan vessels and fulfilled its co-ordinate function as manager and consolidator of its Louisiana railroads.

Morgan policies in Texas before 1882 favored maintenance of the status quo on the G.W.T. & P., extension of the H. & T.C., and use of the Houston Ship Channel–Texas Transportation Company bypass of Galveston until an all-rail connection could be completed between New Orleans and Houston.

In Louisiana, plans called for regaining those franchises west of Morgan City to Vermillionville (now Lafayette) which had been lost to the N.O.M. & T. in 1871 and the extension of the M.L. & T. in two directions: one, a branch via Lafayette to connect near Opelousas with the New Orleans Pacific road (then building from New Orleans to Shreveport and a connection with the T. & P.); the other, a road between Lafayette and the Sabine River as the first segment in an all-rail line from New Orleans to Houston.

A conscious byproduct of these policies was redeployment of the Morgan steamers. Some continued to serve ports not yet connected to the railroad system (such as Rockport and Brazos St. Iago). Other steamers were diverted to the longer-haul trades to New York and Latin America as their traditional short-haul, intra-Gulf routes were antiquated by the completion of parallel railroads. The success of each of these plans will be considered in turn.

In his reorganization of the G.W.T. & P. in 1875–1876, Morgan had changed the road's financial structure and purpose. Its mortgage debt had been cancelled in favor of a new stock issue of $1,200,000, and its plans for interior extension had been dropped. With the transfer of Morgan's personal properties to the M.L. & T.R. & S. company in 1878, the G.W.T. & P. became a wholly owned subsidiary of the latter. Under these circumstances, the G.W.T. & P. was worked only for what it would produce in income for its parent. Since the road was never extended beyond Cuero, its expenses became only those of routine operation and its earnings only those of local traffic.[8]

Nevertheless, as can be seen from Table 10.1, the G.W.T. & P. remained a profitable, if small and isolated, Morgan subsidiary. Its ratio of gross earnings to operating expenses remained rather constant and high from 1879 to 1885. The parent company reinvested its earnings prior to March 31, 1882, but on that date the parent declared a four-year dividend of $24 per $250 share and transferred $120,000 from the G.W.T. & P. accounts to those of the M.L. & T.R. & S.

The net earning power of the H. & T.C. proved more of a disappointment, however (see Table 10.2). In keeping with its over-all plans, the Morgan parent actively managed the H. & T.C. between 1877 and 1882. The Morgan strategy called for the H. & T.C. to blanket the area north of the Colorado and west of the Trinity rivers, channeling imports and exports of this region via Houston and the Morgan steamers and commanding a substantial pro rata share of traffic between Texas points and Kansas City and St. Louis via its connection with the M.K. & T. Since it also crossed the east-west T. & P. at a number of junction points, the H. & T.C. also was to seek right-angle (north-south) extensions of that road's traffic. Its major competitor remained the I. & G.N.–S.L.I.M. & S. entente, which was pursuing similar goals east of the Trinity River.

To achieve the company's purposes, the Morgan managers streamlined the organization and operation of the H. & T.C. and centralized decision-making through an interlocking directorate. The physical condition of the road was improved, its entire gauge was standardized to 4′ 8½″, and significant new mileage was added to its main line.

The last was accomplished through the incorporation on May 28, 1879, of the Texas Central Railway—a joint venture of the H. & T.C. and the M.L. & T.R. & S.—which built 177 miles of track by 1882 from a junction with the H. & T.C. at Ross, through Cisco, to Albany and fifty-two additional miles from Garrett (on the H. & T.C. mainline) to Roberts. Supple-

8. There was talk of pushing on to San Antonio as late as 1881, but nothing came of the discussions. Minute Book No. 1, Board of Directors, M.L. & T.R. & S., 224–225, M.L & T.R. & S. Records; Stockholders Minute Book, Gulf Western Texas and Pacific Railway Co. (1878–1905), *passim*, G.W.T. & P. Records. Only routine matters are recorded here; important G.W.T. & P. matters were recorded on the M.L. & T.R. & S. books.

mental trackage was added through the H. & T.C. purchase of the Waxa-hachie Tap Railroad, which was reorganized into the Central Texas and Northwestern Railroad in 1881, and completion of its twelve-mile stem from Garrett to Waxahachie.[9]

M.L. & T.R. & S. management of the H. & T.C. included legal and debt services as well as construction. The parent company assumed the direction and costs of all litigation involving the subsidiary and regularly met the latter's bonded and floating debt payments.[10]

The H. & T.C. and its two associated companies were operating 761 miles of main line by 1882, and their physical condition rivaled any railroad in the South. Their profits, however, were disappointing. The difficulty still lay in their large bonded indebtedness and, increasingly, in the penetration of their hinterland by extensions of the I. & G.N. and the T. & P. As Table 10.2 indicates, gross earnings of the three roads peaked in 1880 and 1881, and operating expenses were kept relatively stable. The heavy expenditures for construction and improvement and for interest payments, however, steadily pushed total expenditures above gross earnings. A consolidation mortgage was floated in March 1881 through the Farmers Loan & Trust Company of New York, but physical and organizational improvements and debt refinancing were not enough. The net earning capacity and borrowing power of the parent M.L. & T.R. & S. and those of the G.W.T. & P. were used to keep the H. & T.C. solvent with periodic transfusions of cash or credit.[11]

The Morgan companies between Galveston and Houston were also profitably operated by the M.L. & T.R. & S. during the period between 1877 and 1882, but they were admittedly stopgap measures pending completion of a railroad between New Orleans and Houston. A. C. Hutch-

9. Minute Book No. 1, Board of Directors, M.L. & T.R. & S., 85–87, 112, 207–208, 224, 255–256, M.L. & T.R. & S. Records; Minute Book No. 1, Board of Directors, H. & T.C., *passim*, H. & T.C. Records; Stock Record Book, Central Texas and Northwestern Railway Co. (1881–1901), H. & T.C. Records.

10. E.g., Minute Book No. 1, Board of Directors, M.L. & T.R. & S., 69, 181, 185–186, M.L. & T.R. & S. Records. In June, 1878, the parent loaned the H. & T.C. $335,276.53 to meet July 1878 interest on the latter's bonds. The M.L. & T.R. & S. raised the money by drawing four 12-month notes @ 6 per cent on Central Trust Co. of N.Y. ($100,000), Second National Bank of N.Y. ($100,000), Amos H. Trowbridge of N.Y. ($50,000), and National Bank of State of New York ($100,000). *Ibid.*, 85–87, 108, 110–111.

11. General Mortgage, H. & T.C. to F.L. & T., April 1, 1881, H. & T.C. File (Corporation Records Division, Baker Library).

inson, in particular among Morgan men, was never keen on the Buffalo Bayou projects and, after Morgan's death, won his point.

Common sense could predict "the gradual withdrawal of business from Buffalo Bayou which must inevitably follow the opening of the road [from New Orleans to Houston]."[12] In the meantime, however, the Buffalo Bayou Ship Channel Company and the Texas Transportation Company continued to shunt Morgan cargoes around Galveston. The Houston Direct Navigation Company joined them as Morgan enterprises.

Morgan Line steamers continued to use the ship channel to bypass Galveston throughout the late 1870s except to lighter mail and passengers ashore. The contract with the Ship Channel Company granted them free passage while competing steamers and barge lines were charged a toll. Maintenance of advantage was guaranteed by the fact that the M.L. & T.R. & S. owned the majority share of the B.B.S.C. and the Clinton wharves and the T.T. The M.L. & T.R. & S. purchase of a majority in the H.D.N. between 1877 and 1878 further neutralized competition between Houston and Galveston. This move gave the Morgan companies the privileged use of small steamers and barges for lighterage and shallow-water work and tightened their control over the ship channel as well.

Only the Mallory Line of steamers to New York and its connections with the Texas interior via Galveston's two railroads—the G.H. & H. and the G.C. & S.F.—challenged the Buffalo Bayou enterprises of the Morgan parent company. It is quite clear, however, that the Morgan system saw no great threat in the Mallory connections after 1878. In that year a secret traffic agreement apportioned New York freights and rates between the Mallory and Morgan lines to the exclusion of outsiders. Their mutual philosophy soon became co-operative rather than competitive.[13] Anyway,

12. G. Jordan to Whitney, May 22, 1879, M.L. & T.R. & S. Records. For the B.B.S.C., the T.T.C., and the H.D.N. after 1877, see: *Daily Picayune*, September 14, 1877; *Daily News*, May 10, 1878; Q. A. Gillmore, *Galveston*, pp. 15–16; Minute Book No. 1, Board of Directors, H.D.N., 99 ff., H.D.N. Records. The M.L. & T.R. & S. held the following number of shares in the H.D.N.: 287 (1877); 292 2/3 (1879); 293 (1880); 297 2/3 (1881); 298 2/3 (1882); 269 2/3 (1883); 296 2/3 (1884); 294 (1885).

13. Charles H. Mallory Diary, July 31, August 28, September 14, 16, December 7, 1875, August 2, 1877, March 26, March 30, April 3–5, 9, 12, 27, May 1, 4, 8, 14, June 10, 1878, Mallory Papers; Minute Book No. 1, Board of Directors, M.L. & T.R. & S., 87, M.L. & T.R. & S. Records. The terms of the agreement have not survived. Whitney considered it "satisfactory"; Mallory hoped it "will prove in the end to have been the right thing to do."

the Morgan Ship Channel operations were scheduled for liquidation once the long-range plans of their parent company were achieved.[14]

These basic plans were nearing fruition in Louisiana. The new corporation flexed its muscles on the construction of branches and on improvement of its mainline. Construction of a four-mile spur from Terrebonne to Thibodaux was typical of the private-public effort involved. Morgan laid track, sidings, and turnouts in exchange for: a fifty-foot right-of-way donated by Edward J. Gay of Acadia Plantation; a station site in Thibodaux donated by Laurence Keefe; wharfage rights in Thibodaux donated by the town; the town's 270 shares in the Thibodaux Bridge Company; and a $5,000 bonus upon completion, payable by Lafourche Parish in five installments at 8 per cent interest.[15] Soon the company took on more ambitious tasks.

In June 1878, the Morgan road was able to repurchase the sixty-three miles of incomplete railroad between Morgan City and Lafayette from Frank Ames, trustee of the N.O.M. & T. Ames was persuaded to exclude this property from one of the periodic reorganizational sales of his road, and it was returned to the Morgan interests for the first time since its loss on December 12, 1871. Ames was paid $6,000 cash and accepted return and cancellation of 695 N.O.M. & T. first-mortgage bonds which Morgan had held since his sale of the franchises in 1871. Plans for completing the road to Lafayette were underway by November 1, 1878, as the M.L. & T.R. & S. authorized 6-per-cent construction bonds totaling $10,000 per mile.[16]

Whitney and Hutchinson were also pursuing with renewed vigor Morgan's plans for a railroad between New Orleans and Houston. In March 1878, they helped charter the Louisiana Western Railroad Company to construct a line from Lafayette to the Sabine River in Calcasieu Parish. The L.W., planned as an extension of the M.L. & T. (if and when the latter reached Lafayette), lagged until the franchises beyond Morgan

14. A stock majority of G.H. & H. was offered to the M.L. & T.R. & S. in 1879 for $125,000 but was refused on the grounds that the New Orleans–Houston and the Santa Fe roads would render it obsolete. G. Jordan to Whitney, May 22, 1879, M.L. & T.R. & S. Records.

15. Agreement between Thibodaux and M.L. & T.R. & S., June 1, 1878, Donation, Edward J. Gay to same, June 5, 1878. Acts before Hero, Jr., N.A. (Orleans); Minute Book No. 1, M.L. & T.R. & S., 34–35, 88–90, M.L. & T.R. & S. Records.

16. Sale, Ames to M.L. & T.R. & S., June 19, 1878. Deposited with Hero, Jr., June 25, 1878, N.A. (Orleans); Board Minute Book No. 1, M.L. & T.R. & S., 36, 62, 85–87, M.L. & T.R. & S. Records; *Daily Picayune*, April 11–June 26, 1878.

City were regained from Ames. By late 1878, however, a new scheme was in operation.[17]

On November 21, the interests of the L.W., the M.L. & T.R. & S., and the Texas and New Orleans Railroad Company of 1874 were combined. The last, chartered by Texas in 1856, had overcome the Civil War and two receiverships before opening its road from Houston to Orange in November 1876.[18] It now joined the two Louisiana lines in linking New Orleans and Houston.

The T. & N.O. agreed to extend its tracks from Orange to the Sabine River and share half the cost of a bridge with the L.W., which was to complete its road from Lafayette to the river within eighteen months. The M.L. & T. promised to build from Morgan City to Lafayette but reserved the right to connect with other roads if they be west of Lafayette, Louisiana, and south of Palestine, Texas. The signatories agreed to allocate 40 per cent of all traffic between Houston and New Orleans to Morgan's rail-water route (via Morgan City and Buffalo Bayou) and reserved the remaining 60 per cent to the New Orleans–Morgan City–Lafayette–Orange–Houston all-rail combination. Over the latter route, revenues would be pro rated by mileage of the carriers including a twenty-mile bonus for the M.L. & T. because of its terminal facilities in New Orleans. Revenues from New York–New Orleans–Texas through traffic were also pooled, with a 450 railroad-mile allowance for the Morgan Line's sea segment.[19]

Ratified in December, the pool allowed a gradual phasing out of Morgan's rail-water service while construction of its rail segments was co-ordinated by a tripartisan board. A Texas subsidiary of the T. & N.O. was chartered as the Louisiana Western Extension Railroad Company on March 31, 1879, and completed its 6.42 miles from Orange to the Sabine in March 1880.[20] The Louisiana Western segment from Lafayette to the Sabine opened August 28, 1880, thereby extending the M.L. & T. line which had reached Lafayette in April after construction expenditures

17. *Louisiana Acts* (1878), pp. 358–368; *Daily Picayune*, May 5, 1878.

18. "Record Book Containing the Records of the Proceedings of Oakes Ames, Edwin D. Morgan, Messrs. Morton, Bliss & Co., John T. Terry, John A. Griswold, Henry J. Gardiner, and George F. Tyler as Associates in a Certain Purchase of Bonds Issued by the Texas and New Orleans Rail Road Company" (1870–1888), pp. 3–76, T. & N.O. Records (S.P. Co.).

19. Agreement among M.L. & T.R. & S., L.W., and T. & N.O., November 21, 1878, M.L. & T.R. & S. Records.

20. "Record Book . . . Texas and New Orleans Rail Road Company," pp. 76 ff., T. & N.O. Records.

totaling $742,000. The pooled all-rail line from New Orleans to Houston opened on September 28, 1880, but as late as May 1881, Whitney still reported it not "as satisfactory as hoped for" because of the unfinished condition of the L.W. and the T. & N.O. and lack of a bridge between Morgan City and the opposite bank of the Atchafalaya River.[21]

Participation in the New Orleans–Houston pool was typical of Whitney and Hutchinson's active management of the M.L. & T.R. & S. between 1878 and 1882. Organizational machinery for control of the company's rail and steamship enterprises was improved and operations constantly diversified or expanded.

Under bylaws adopted July 13, 1878, and a charter amendment of January 30, 1879, responsibilities were allocated among officers of the corporation. A board of directors, elected every five years, in turn elected a president, vice president, managers, superintendent of railroads, auditor, treasurer, secretary, and attorney. The president, selected by and from the directorate every five years, was the only official not annually elected. The managers, however, were the key officials, supervising the monthly accounts of the secretary, treasurer, and superintendent and implementing the policy of the board. The auditor was the only nonresident officer, remaining in New York and supervising both the floating and bonded debts. Since Whitney and Hutchinson served as president and vice president and as managers, however, and since the other officers were all former members of the firm of Whitney & Co., their new titles were somewhat academic.[22]

The managers concentrated on improving rail service in Louisiana. In Morgan City almost unlimited trackage and ferry rights were secured; in 1880, a $220,000 contract was let for a bridge across the Atchafalaya which opened in 1882.[23] In New Orleans the St. Ann ferry rights were extended for thirty years in 1879, an adjoining square leased from the city for fifty years at $35,000, and trackage and batture rights between Marigny and Barracks streets reapproved. Property totaling $25,500 in

21. Minute Book No. 1, Board of Directors, M.L. & T.R. & S., 78–79, 88–90, 110–11, 138, 152, 221, M.L. & T.R. & S. Records; *Commercial and Financial Chronicle*, XXXI (September 4, 1880), 259.

22. Morgan's Louisiana and Texas Railroad and Steamship Co., *By-Laws* (New Orleans, 1878), pp. 3–8; *Louisiana Acts* (1879), pp. 20–22; Minute Book No. 1, Board of Directors, M.L. & T.R. & S., 4, 50–57, 72–75, 80, 145, 213, M.L. & T.R. & S. Records.

23. Minute Book No. 1, Board of Directors, M.L. & T.R. & S., 60, 152, 221, 227, M.L. & T.R. & S. Records.

value was added to the Algiers and New Orleans terminals through purchase from private individuals and $60,000 expended for the new ferry *Enterprise* to connect the two.[24]

A potential competitor on the New Orleans–Texas route was also absorbed. In July 1879, the M.L. & T.R. & S. purchased the railroad operated by the N.O.M. & T. between the Crescent City and Donaldsonville. For $300,000 in debentures, Whitney and Hutchinson acquired the only operative line running west from New Orleans besides their own and soon turned it into a neat profit.[25]

Plans for joining this Donaldsonville road with the Lafayette terminus of the L.W. were briefly considered, but were dropped upon completion of the pool among the M.L. & T.R. & S., the L.W., and the T. & N.O. The Morgan road's managers reshaped the Donaldsonville road to fit their second objective: a Louisiana connection with northeastern Texas. By early 1880 they began to extend their Morgan City–Lafayette road northward hoping to reach and "rest at Alexandria and await the building by other companies of a connecting Road thence to the Texas line." Six-per-cent construction-bonds totaling $12,000 per mile were authorized for the 160-mile extension from Morgan City to Opelousas and Alexandria, but as part of the same scheme the recently purchased Donaldsonville road was sold to a combination of interests representing Jay Gould and the New Orleans Pacific Railway Company.[26]

The N.O.P., chartered in 1875 and a veteran of five years of financial difficulties, was by 1880 co-operating to join New Orleans with the T. & P. railhead at Shreveport. Co-promoters of the scheme were Thomas A. Scott and Jay Gould of the T. & P. who were interested in access to New Orleans as part of their transcontinental rail plans.[27]

24. Acceptance of Ordinances 6015 A.S. and 6021 A.S. by M.L. & T.R. & S., June 30, 1879. Act before Hero, Jr., N.A. (Orleans); Lease, City of New Orleans to M.L. & T.R. & S., November 7, 1879. Act before Gustave Le Gardeur, *ibid.*; Sales, Albert N. Robelot, Widow Horatio V. Hills, Dominique Durroux, *et. als.*, and Bertrand Saloy to M.L. & T.R. & S., December 22, 31, 1879, April 22, 1880, July 8, 1881. Acts before Hero, Jr., N.A. (Orleans).

25. The debentures carried 6 per cent per annum interest and were to be issued in installments over a five-year term. Indenture, Frank M. Ames, *et. als.* to M.L. & T.R. & S., July 15, 1879. C.O. (Orleans), Book 110, pp. 964–967 (October 8, 1879); Minute Book No. 1, Board of Directors, M.L. & T.R. & S., 118–120, 129, 149–151, 154, M.L. & T.R. & S. Records.

26. Minute Book No. 1, Board of Directors, M.L. & T.R. & S., 149–152, 187–190, 192–193, 202–203, M.L. & T.R. & S. Records.

27. Charter, N.O.P.R., June 29, 1875. Act before John G. Eustis, N.A. (Or-

As early as May 1880 Gould had approached Whitney of the Morgan companies to sell the Donaldsonville road to Gould's American Railway Improvement Company (a T. & P.–N.O.P. construction company) as the first segment of a line from New Orleans to Alexandria and Shreveport.[28] Completion of the M.L. & T.R. & S.–L.W.–T. & N.O. pool eliminated the Morgan's need for the Donaldsonville line; thus Whitney complied with Gould's request on February 15, 1881.

Whitney sold sixty-eight miles of railroad (Westwego–Donaldsonville– White Castle) to the N.O.P. for $494,402.09 cash. In addition, all Morgan notes issued to the N.O.M. & T. since its sale of the road to the M.L. & T.R. & S. in 1879 and their interest due were to be purchased and canceled by N.O.P. The N.O.P. also agreed to build on to Shreveport and to connect their line near Alexandria with the Morgan extension already building from Lafayette via Opelousas. This transaction finally wiped the slate clean regarding the property so long disputed between Morgan and the Ameses and closed another chapter in the history of the Morgan Line.[29]

Gould's appearance as purchaser of the Donaldsonville road was part of the final episode. He was then locked in his manueverings against Collis P. Huntington for control of Southwestern railways. Since this struggle swirled the Morgan Line into its midst, its major contours bear review.

Jay Gould had entered the Southwest in October 1873 when he placed his man William Bond on the directorate of the M.K. & T. Shortly after Bond became president of the road, on June 1, 1877, Gould bought the Missouri Pacific Railroad and began to use it as the nucleus for his southwestern railroad plans.[30] By the end of 1880 he was active in both north-south and east-west lines.

Gould formed the Pacific Railway Improvement Company in December 1879 to extend the western end of the T. & P. from Forth Worth to El

leans); *Louisiana Acts* (1876), pp. 28–34; Odom, "Louisiana Railroads," pp. 242–250.

28. *From Ox-Teams to Eagles: A History of the Texas and Pacific Railway*, pp. 24, 31; Julius Grodinsky, *Jay Gould: His Business Career, 1867–1892*, pp. 252–253, 256–258; New Orleans *Times*, January 10, 1881.

29. Sale, M.L. & T.R. & S. to N.O.P., February 15, 1881. Act before Hero, Jr., N.A. (Orleans), C.O. (Orleans), Book 115, pp. 212–213 (February 24, 1881).

30. The best secondary sources on Gould's southwestern ventures are Grodinsky, *Gould*; Caudle, *Missouri Pacific*; and Masterson, *Katy*. See also the more general: Grodinsky, *Transcontinental Railway Strategy: A Study of Businessmen*; Ira G. Clark, *Then Came the Railroads: The Century from Steam to Diesel in the Southwest*; and Reed, *Texas Railroads*.

Paso. He organized the American Railway Improvement Company in February 1880 to extend the eastern end of the T. & P. from Shreveport to New Orleans. On December 1, 1880, he leased the M.K. & T. to the M.P., bought the St. Louis, Iron Mountain, and Southern, and organized the International Railway Improvement Company to extend the M.K. & T. to the Gulf and to Mexico City.

Most of Gould's moves had implications for the Morgan railroads. In Louisiana, the Morgan companies co-operated fully with Gould's plans as they did not conflict with Morgan plans: they sold him the Donaldsonville road on February 15, 1881; in April he purchased control of the T. & P. from Scott; on June 20 he bought the N.O.P.; and on September 5, 1880, he intersected the M.L. & T.R. & S. at Cheneyville (between Opelousas and Alexandria). This gave Gould his first access to New Orleans—via T. & P. tracks from Shreveport to Cheneyville and on Morgan tracks from Cheneyville via Opelousas and Morgan City to New Orleans. In return for their co-operation, the Morgan roads and steamships south of Cheneyville received a pro rata share in through freights to and from northern Louisiana and Texas via the Gould-Morgan pool. Gould achieved his second and more direct access to the Crescent City on September 12, 1882, when his Donaldsonville road was completed to Alexandria. This gave him his own tracks into New Orleans.[31]

It might appear that the Morgan road got the worst of its bargain with Gould after his own tracks were completed into New Orleans. To the Morgan managers, however, who were more interested in the road to Houston, Gould appeared a chicken well plucked. They had sold him the Donaldsonville road for a nice profit in ready cash and had secured an extension of the M.L. & T. into northern Louisiana and Texas without the expense of building it themselves. On balance, the Morgan-Gould deals in Louisiana were satisfactory to both parties.

Gould had less success with the Morgan managers in pursuing his Texas plans. There were many rumors that Gould wanted to purchase the H. & T.C. as the easiest way to extend the M.K. & T. to the Gulf. Its owners, however, wished to keep it as a feeder to Houston and New Orleans rather than a sea route for Kansas City and St. Louis (as Gould

31. Indenture, N.O.P. to T. & P., June 20, 1881. C.O. (Orleans), Book 116, pp. 612–614 (November 20, 1882); R. S. Hayes to Whitney & Co., June 17, July 16, 1881, Whitney to Hayes, July 19, 1881, Agreement between M.L. & T.R. & S. and T. & P., September 5, 1881, M.L. & T.R. & S. Records. See also works cited above.

envisaged it) and would not sell. Gould was therefore forced elsewhere in his north-south Texas plans: on June 1, 1881, the M.K. & T. leased the I. & G.N. to use it as a Gulf and Mexican extension; in February, M.K. & T. construction began anew, south of Denison, reaching Waco on January 23, 1882, Temple on March 23, and Taylor on June 9; on March 6, 1883, the I. & G.N. leased the G.H. & H., finally giving Gould his Gulf port at Galveston.

The opening of the M.L. & T.–L.W.–T. & N.O. pooled line between New Orleans and Houston on September 28, 1880, and the Morgan-Gould co-operation which gave the latter access to New Orleans were far from unnoticed by Gould's competitor for a southern transcontinental system—Collis P. Huntington. Huntington had been active in California and Atlantic Coast railroads since the late 1860s. By 1877–1878 he was planning to link them up via Texas and Louisiana: in the East, his Chesapeake and Ohio Railway Company was extending its Richmond–Huntington line northward toward Cincinnati and southward toward Lexington, Kentucky, and New Orleans; in the West, his Southern Pacific Railroad had reached Yuma in May 1877 and in October had received Presidential permission to build eastward across Federal territory to El Paso.[32]

The S.P. reached El Paso on May 19, 1881, and the C. & O. reached Lexington, Kentucky, on December 12, 1881. Both roads were aimed at New Orleans and both naturally became major elements of change in the existing Texas and Louisiana rail picture. And again, the Morgan roads were forced to adapt.

Huntington's first move in Texas was to secure construction franchises east of El Paso. This he accomplished through a community of interest agreement with Peirce's G.H. & S.A. The latter had reached San Antonio on February 6, 1877, and welcomed the chance to become part of a transcontinental line. On July 5, 1881, less than two months after the S.P. reached El Paso, the G.H. & S.A. board voted to contract with Huntington's Southern Development Company of California to build west of San Antonio to El Paso and a connection with the S.P.[33]

32. The best works on Huntington in the southwest are Cerinda W. Evans, *Collis Potter Huntington*; Neill C. Wilson and Frank J. Taylor, *Southern Pacific: The Roaring Story of a Fighting Railroad*; Grodinsky, *Transcontinental Railway Strategy*; and Reed, *Texas Railroads*.

33. Minute Book, Boston Board of Directors, G.H. & S.A. (1870–1881), July 5, 1881, November 7, 1881; Minute Book, Board of Directors, G.H. & S.A.

To balance his negotiations regarding the El Paso–San Antonio route, Huntington also sought a Houston–New Orleans connection. If both were achieved, his southern-transcontinental road would be complete from the Golden Gate to the mouth of the Mississippi. On June 16, 1881, he began buying into the T. & N.O. and by July 28, 1881, he held 20,379 common and 2,235 preferred shares. This gave him control of the T. & N.O. from Houston to Orange, of its subsidiary the L.W.E. from Orange to the Sabine, and made him a party to the M.L. & T.–L.W.–T. & N.O. pool between Houston and New Orleans.[34] This move guaranteed him access to New Orleans once the G.H. & S.A. reached El Paso—over G.H. & S.A. tracks from El Paso to Houston; over T. & N.O. tracks from Houston to the Sabine River; and over Morgan tracks from the Sabine to New Orleans. All that remained was to join San Antonio and El Paso.

Pouring funds into construction east of El Paso, Huntington completed ninety miles to Sierra Blanca on November 25, 1881, and forced his rival Gould into the famous compromise of November 26. This compromise was extremely important in the subsequent pattern of railway development in the Southwest and was especially relevant to the final episode of the Morgan enterprises.[35]

Gould's T. & P., which had built westward from Forth Worth to within ten miles of Sierra Blanca, was allowed to complete to that point and then use S.P. track into El Paso. "Unconsigned business" (i.e., freights on which the route was undesignated in advance) originating on the T. & P. but destined for points west of Sierra Blanca or El Paso were to be relinquished at those junctions to the S.P. Gould's T. & P. also turned over its land grants, franchises, and claims west of El Paso.

The agreement thus gave Huntington the upper hand west of Sierra Blanca–El Paso. East of those points Gould bargained more closely and must have thought he protected his interests—but events proved him woefully wrong. At the time the agreement was signed, Gould already had

(1877–1906), pp. 68–69, 71–72, 85, 91–92, 104–108, G.H. & S.A. Records (S.P. Co.); Agreement between S.D.C. and G.H. & S.A., July 15, 1881, Auditor's Central File #13–13 (S.P. Co.).

34. Stock Transfer Book, T. & N.O. (1881–1897), 6–16–81 ff., T. & N.O. Records.

35. The most accurate account of these agreements in secondary literature is in Reed, *Texas Railroads*, pp. 544–551. Because of Reed's factual lapses, the present account has been drawn from the original documents.

a Sierra Blanca–New Orleans line and Huntington did not, yet Gould agreed to equal division of gross earnings on business between those points. Gould had secured his New Orleans connection when the T. & P. joined the M.L. & T. at Cheneyville on September 5; Huntington had still to reach San Antonio before his S.P.–G.H. & S.A. line could reach New Orleans via the T. & N.O.–L.W.–M.L. & T. pool.

Similarly, Gould already had a Galveston connection through the M.K. & T. lease of the I. & G.N. on June 1, 1881, and the latter's traffic agreements with the T. & P. and the G.H. & H. Huntington would have access to Galveston (via G.H. & S.A.) only after the Sierra Blanca–San Antonio line was completed. Yet despite his advantage, Gould agreed to divide business between Galveston, El Paso, and Sierra Blanca two thirds to Huntington and one third to himself.

From this analysis, the Gould-Huntington "agreement" is revealed as Huntington's victory. Gould recognized his rival's superior geographic position regarding New Orleans and Galveston connections and capitulated. Huntington included a weak promise not to parallel Gould's roads east of the Sabine. This, however, was totally deceitful, as Huntington was already deep in negotiations to do just that.[36]

Despite his pledge of November 1881 not to parallel Gould into New Orleans, Huntington forged ahead toward access to the Crescent City over his own tracks. And like Gould before him, the Morgan system figured in his plans. He had opened negotiations with Hutchinson and Whitney in September 1881 *two months before the Gould agreement*—and on March 14, 1882, pooled their interests with his.[37]

In the new agreement, the old New Orleans–Houston traffic pool of December 1878 was reaffirmed and extended west to San Antonio. Through rates were to be fixed by Huntington but were divided according to mileage operated. The Morgan road was allowed a bonus of seventy-six miles over their actual New Orleans–Vermillionville mileage of 145 miles, and their New Orleans–New York steamship service again counted as 450 railroad miles in extending the pool to include eastern freights.

36. The Huntington–Gould agreement appears in the following original sources with related contracts and operations orders: Minute Book, Boston Board of Directors, G.H. & S.A., December 24, 1881, G.H. & S.A. Records; "Record Book . . . Texas and New Orleans Rail Road Company," pp. 87–88, T. & N.O. Records.
37. Hutchinson to Whitney, September 28, 1881, M.L. & T.R. & S. Records.

The arrangement was to be extended west of San Antonio upon completion of Huntington's trackage there and was binding until December 20, 1898.[38]

By March 1882 the Morgan system had thus provided Gould and Huntington with the means to enter New Orleans. In return it had turned a good profit on sales to Gould and had secured traffic pools to El Paso via Alexandria, Shreveport, and Fort Worth on Gould's T. & P. and to San Antonio and ultimately to the Pacific on Huntington's S.P. The Morgan corporation also continued to operate the H. & T.C., the G.W.T. & P., its Louisiana roads, and a variety of steamship lines.

Completion of the Morgan company's railroad network had dictated constant redeployment of its vessels. While service was continued from Morgan City to Brazos St. Iago, Rockport–Corpus Christi, and Indianola, the opening of the railroad pool to Houston ended Morgan sailings to Galveston and Houston from Louisiana in October 1880.[39] More emphasis was placed on the expansion of service to New York and Latin America: weekly schedules were maintained between New Orleans and New York; the Texas–Havana steamers were continued (one ran weekly, direct with cattle only until 1884; another ran weekly from New Orleans via Key West with passengers and freight commencing in 1880); twice-monthly sailings between New Orleans and Vera Cruz were begun in 1881.[40]

With new services came new vessels. The company refurbished its older vessels and between 1877 and 1882 added six new steamships: *Aransas* (1877; 1,157 tons), a shallow-draught ship designed for the shallow approaches to Rockport and Corpus Christi; *Mary Morgan* (1878; 370 tons), intended as a yacht for Morgan but used for charter work until she could be turned in for credit on more practical vessels; *Louisiana* (1880; 2,840 tons), *Chalmette* (1880; 2,983 tons), *Willamette* (1881; 2,264 tons), and *Excelsior* (1882; 3,264 tons), large coastal steamers used in the New York trade. *Chalmette* was the largest

38. Contract between M.L & T.R. & S. and Huntington, March 14, 1882, M.L. & T.R. & S. Records.

39. "Contracts for Carrying the Mails, 1879," *House Exec. Docs.*, 46 Cong., 2 Sess., No. 47 (Serial 1924), 1479, 1505; *ibid.*, 1880, *House Exec. Docs.*, 46 Cong., 3 Sess., No. 55 (Serial 1977), 1483, 1505; *ibid.*, 1881, *House Exec. Docs.*, 47 Cong., 1 Sess., No. 40 (Serial 1987), 1981.

40. Minute Book No. 1, Board of Directors. M.L. & T.R. & S., 85–87, 100, 175–177, 222–223, 232–333, 276–277, 282–283, M.L. & T.R. & S. Records; *Times-Democrat Almanac for the Year 1883* (New Orleans, 1882), 57; *ibid.*, 1884 (New Orleans, 1883), 31.

American-built coastal steamship at the time of her launch. *Excelsior* would set a New York to New Orleans record run of 1,695 miles in five days and fifty-four minutes, dock to dock (June 17–22, 1885). Her round voyage record was thirteen days, ten hours, including discharging and loading of full cargoes in New Orleans.[41]

By 1883, then, the "Morgan" system had reached its zenith and had achieved its founder's dream: a network of railroads and steamships interlocking the Gulf Southwest with the eastern United States and northern Latin America. Reference to Table 10.3 provides an appreciation of the extent of the system. Note that during calendar 1883, the five Morgan railroads in Texas operated 13 per cent of the rail mileage, owned 16 per cent of the state's locomotives, 13 per cent of the passenger cars, and 14 per cent of the freight cars in that state. This rolling stock accounted for 17 per cent of Texas' reported passenger mileage and 12 per cent of its reported ton-mileage. In Louisiana, the two Morgan roads operated 25 per cent of the rail mileage of the state with 31 per cent of the state's locomotives, 30 per cent of its passenger cars, and 45 per cent of its freight cars. This rolling stock traveled at least 57 per cent of Louisiana's reported passenger mileage and at least 50 per cent of its reported ton-mileage.

Table 10.4 summarizes the financial structure, earning power, and profitability of the Morgan system and puts it in its state and national contexts. First, it should be noted that the equity shares per mile of Morgan railroads were well below state and national averages. In Texas, the equity per mile of the five Morgan railroads averaged 79 per cent of the state average; in Louisiana, equity per mile in the two Morgan roads ran 86 per cent of the state average; nationally, the average ran 206 per cent of the Morgan average.

The absence of dividends on the Morgan roads can be explained in several ways. First, shipowning tradition made Morgan less sensitive to what Arthur S. Dewing refers to as the firm's obligation to superimpose "a regularity in dividend payments . . . on an irregularity of earnings," since return on investment in ships was calculated at voyage's end, not at arbitrary intervals on the calendar. Also, since Morgan's corporations

41. Hutchinson to Whitney, September 28, 1881, Minute Book No. 1, Board of Directors, M.L. & T.R. & S., 45, 76, 85–90, 11, 148–149, 222, 252, 276–277, M.L. & T.R. & S. Records; *Scientific American*, XLI (November 29, 1879), 345; Fairburn, *Merchant Sail*, V, 1399–1400.

were closely held by himself and his managers, there was less demand for return on equity. Stock was primarily a means of control, not of income.

The totals also suggest that Morgan did not engage in excessive stock-watering. In the cases of the G.W.T. & P., the H. & T.C., and the C.T. & N.W., whose equity per mile was high by Texas standards if not by national standards, some watering had taken place at the time of Morgan's entry into the corporation—usually to permit his entry. On the whole, however, no Vanderbilt-, Fisk-, or Drew-style dilution of equity occurred in any of the Morgan roads. For Morgan himself, the sole proprietorship and the closely held corporation were related mechanisms of control, not to be subverted by the squabblings of contending shareholders.

Lack of dividends was a characteristic of many young transportation ventures after the Civil War. As Dewing has shown, it is the nature of such businesses that their indivisibilities or "blocs of needs" may require capital expenditures unrelated to the amount of net earnings available for reinvestment. Under such circumstances, the best business policy may be to retain all earnings "in order to bring to fruition a carefully planned long-term program of expansion under conditions of increasing profits." Writing in the twentieth century, Dewing found these situations rare.[42] In the nineteenth century they were commonplace, especially in the South, and Morgan's railroads reflect their existence and acceptance.

As a shipowner, Morgan's preference for equity-financing proved difficult to sustain in the Reconstruction South. Thus for his railroads he turned increasingly to debt-financing in eastern capital markets through mortgage bonds and debentures. His bankers were primarily John J. Cisco & Son and the Farmers Loan and Trust Co., both of New York, and both specialists in southern railroads.

By 1883 the bonded debt of the five Morgan roads in Texas ran 162 per cent of the state average; in Louisiana, the average of the two Morgan roads was 115 per cent of that for all roads in the state. Morgan and his managers thus used bonds more than most of their contemporaries in Texas and Louisiana—but they used them far less than was common nationally. The average bonded debt per mile for the seven Morgan roads ran only 76 per cent of the national average for all roads. Morgan took

42. *Financial Policy of Corporations*, II, 795–848.

his own profits out of his roads through the medium of bonds (after 1877) and his heirs and managers followed suit. Other investors were also respected: the Morgan roads paid 22 per cent of all interest payments on bonded indebtedness paid by Texas railroads in 1883; in Louisiana, the Morgan share was 24 per cent of the state total.

One would expect the low gross and net earnings for Morgan's five Texas roads shown in Table 10.4. Except for the G.W.T. & P., all of these roads were in highly competitive growth situations, spending large sums on construction and improvement in expectation of future return on investment. Thus the high value of expenditures as a percentage of gross earnings (74 per cent) found among Morgan's five Texas roads is not surprising. In Louisiana, however, the high gross and net earnings of the two Morgan roads connote mature, well-managed, high-volume earning power. The fact that the measure of expenditures as a percentage of gross earnings for Morgan's two Louisiana roads is 59 per cent of the state average and 76 per cent of the national average is the clue to Morgan's use of his highly profitable steamships and Louisiana roads to subsidize the expansion of his roads in Texas. His ability to do this is suggested when the expenditures–gross earnings ratio for all seven of his roads is calculated: it is a very respectable 66 per cent, only 3 per cent above the national average for 1883.

Table 10.5 provides a closer look at the changing sources of revenue of the Morgan system and its changing traffic pattern by spotlighting key income and expense items of the parent company. Aggregate data for the parent are presented in Table 10.6. First, note the gradual decline in the receipts for freight and passage to and from Louisiana points and Texas ports via the combined rail-water route. Canceling this decline, however, was the tremendous increase in receipts from "through" freight and passengers which followed the opening of the all-rail, New Orleans–Houston pool on September 1, 1880. The table reflects a polarization of "Texas freight and passage" between Texas ports not yet part of the railroad network (such as Indianola, Rockport, and Brazos St. Iago) which sent their goods by steamer, and Texas points able and willing to use all-rail service to and from New Orleans.

Thus in the New Orleans–Texas trade, which had always been Morgan's specialty, there was a redistribution of traffic between steamships and railroads after 1880. Initially, the redistribution was gradual and something of its nature can be gained from the following statement of selected items of "Inward Freight" from Texas received at New Orleans between September 1, 1880, and March 31, 1881:[43]

Item	All Rail	All Water
Cotton for N.O.	54,465 bales	36,187 bales
Cotton for re-export to N.Y.	7,373 bales	22,320 bales
Cattle	9,970 head	7,712 head
Sheep	6,888 head	700 head
Horses and Mules	1,272 head	553 head
Cottonseed	115 carlds.	63,348 sacks
Grain	209 carlds.	20,029 sacks

The pattern of redistribution was much clearer by March 31, 1882, when even some through freights from California were to be found in the annual totals:[44]

Item	All Rail	All Water
Cotton	67,517 bales	51,495 bales
Cottonseed	98 carlds.	21,164 sacks
Cottonseed oil	14,630 bbls.	5,093 bbls.
Cottonseed meal & cakes	11,204 sacks	6,178 sacks
Sugar	246 hhds.; 18 bbls.	22 hhds.
Molasses	8 bbls.	441 bbls.
Cereal grains	696 carlds.	286 bbls.; 8,454 sacks
Livestock	44,205 head	12,925 head
Wool	16,522 bags	28,761 bags
Peltries	248 bales	2,705 bales
Dry hides	583 bales/1,774 bales; 38,207 loose	
Green hides	0	53 bndls.
Tallow	11 bbls.	223 bbls.
Bone	92 carlds.	3,235 sacks
Flour from Tex.	248 bbls.	305 bbls.
Flour from Calif.	760 qtr. sacks	0
Wine from Calif.	710 bbls.	0
Lead from Calif.	1,588,250 lbs.	2,468,605 lbs.
Brass & Copper	28,186 lbs.	14,142 lbs.
Scrap Iron	201,200 lbs.	12,720 lbs.
Machinery	114,719 lbs.	74,939 lbs.
Rags & Junk	210,755 lbs.	194,007 lbs.
Mdse. & Hshld. goods	7,672 pkgs.	5,952 pkgs.
Pecans	1,454 bbls.	0
Eggs	0	11,190 doz.
Silver ore	0	35,242 lbs.
Specie	0	$1,310,252

43. M.L. & T.R. & S., *Annual Report, 1881*, p. 49.
44. *Ibid.* (1882), bet. 42 and 43.

These data should make it clear that the Morgan railroads and the Morgan steamships were complementary, not competitive. Each carried the products unique to those regions which they served, and in those few regions where shippers had an option, they sent about as much by one form of Morgan service as by the other.

From Table 10.5 one should also note the earning and traffic patterns of Morgan's all-water services to and from New York, Cuba, and Mexico. The New York–Gulf trade increased steadily, suggesting that competition with the Mallorys was not destructive to Morgan. The cattle trade from Rockport and Indianola to Havana bloomed between 1879 and 1882 but had disappeared (as previously described) by 1885. Service between New Orleans, Key West, and Havana was begun in late 1879 and early 1880 and soon reached a plateau of profitability. The major items in this trade are suggested by selected items of "Inward Freight" received at New Orleans during the year ending March 31, 1882. This statement also includes items carried in the New Orleans–Vera Cruz service which the Morgan Line opened in 1881:[45]

Item	Amount
Sugar from Cuba & Fla.	5,912 hhds.; 46 bbls.
Leaf tobacco from Cuba	1,421 bales
Mixed fruit from Cuba	731 pkgs.
Oranges from Cuba	1,849 bbls.
Oranges from Fla.	2,079 bbls.
Vegetables from Fla.	5,179 crates
Potatoes from Fla.	24 bbls.
Coffee from Mex.	29,739 sacks
Rubber from Mex.	54 bales
Jalap from Mex.	133 bales
Ixtle from Mex.	3,165 bales

In terms of income, the very large increase in "Local" passengers and freight should be noticed. These items represent freight and passage receipts for service between New Orleans and Louisiana points. The nature of this trade is suggested by a statement of "Inward Freight" received at New Orleans for the year ending March 31, 1882:[46]

45. *Ibid.*
46. *Ibid.*

Item	Amount
Cotton	44,409 bales
Cottonseed	51,007 sacks
Cottonseed oil	936 bbls.
Sugar	24,468 hhds.; 23,120 bbls.
Molasses	52,022 bbls.
Rice	5,282 bbls.; 78,669 sacks
Livestock	14,349 head
Wool	923 bags
Peltries	192 bales
Dry hides	255 bales; 11,115 loose
Green hides	133 hhds.; 448 bbls.; 3,528 bndls.
Tallow	72 bbls.
Bone	11 carlds.
Flour	163 bbls.
Salt	4,603 sacks
Pecans	576 bbls.
Oranges	366 bbls.
Potatoes	15,919 sacks; 748 bbls.
Vegetables	214 pkgs.
Poultry	633 coops
Eggs	367,105 doz.
Lumber	194,161 feet
Machinery	266,845 lbs.
Scrap iron	1,476,637 lbs.
Lead	825 lbs.
Brass & copper	2,056 lbs.
Junk	15,851 lbs.
Moss	5,849 bales
Mdse. & Hshld. goods	16,407 pkgs.

Table 10.5 also presents selected expense items of the parent Morgan company. Note that, despite increased traffic and earnings, voyage and agency expenses were kept relatively stable—again a sign of good management. The major expense items which continued to increase throughout the period were those of railroad management, especially payrolls, and fuel.

Thus the flourishing Morgan system demonstrated its character and profitability, and it was admirable testimony to the man whose name it bore. But even as its founder's dreams were realized, his legacy dimmed, and by 1885, the company remained "Morgan's" in name and tradition alone.

The death of President Charles A. Whitney on October 29, 1882, triggered changes in the nature and management of the corporation. Having left management of the firm to Hutchinson, Whitney had summered at Newport, Rhode Island, and was preparing to leave New York on a European tour when death came. Although it was not immediately apparent, the end of the M.L. & T.R. & S. as a family enterprise would soon follow the death of Morgan's son-in-law.[47]

The ambitious Hutchinson assumed the presidencies of the M.L. & T.R. & S. and its subsidiaries on November 21 and was confirmed by election on December 23. Hutchinson, long the junior partner of Whitney & Co. and the highest-ranking nonrelative in the Morgan management was now on his own. More testy and pedantic than Whitney, Hutchinson was bound to assert himself, once in control. His first action was to tighten the managerial organization of the corporation.[48]

By March 1883, with Hutchinson voting 48,950 of 50,000 shares (through proxies from the Morgan estate, Mary Jane Morgan, Richard J. Morgan, and Frances Morgan Quintard, *and his own ten shares*), the charter and bylaws of the company were amended to allow annual election of the board and all officers, abolition of separate "managers," and expansion of the duties of the vice president. As his new vice-president–manager, Hutchinson elected J. George Schriever. Promoted from the ranks, Schriever purchased the ten shares necessary to hold office from Henry J. Leovy, thus removing that old friend and attorney of Morgan from the board. Another "Morgan-man," George Pandely, was replaced by the elevation of Julius Kruttschnitt from the engineering department to superintendency of railroads. These changes in key personnel placed men loyal to Hutchinson, but not necessarily to the Morgan-Whitney tradition, at the managerial helm of the M.L. & T.R. & S.[49]

Hutchinson's greatest and most lasting departure from precedent was the sale of a majority share in the M.L. & T.R. & S. (and thereby in its associated enterprises) to a three-man syndicate headed by Huntington.

47. New York *Times*, October 30, 1882; *Daily Picayune*, October 30, 1882.
48. Minute Book No. 1, Board of Directors. M.L. & T.R. & S., 296–307, M.L. & T.R. & S. Records. For recollections of Hutchinson's personality see the testimony of his "right-hand man" Julius Kruttschnitt, in U.S. District Court, District of Utah, *Record in Equity No. 420: United States v. Southern Pacific Company, Central Pacific Railway Company, et. al.*, I, 705 ff., esp., 709–710.
49. Minute Book No. 1, Board of Directors, M.L. & T.R. & S., 311–319, M.L. & T.R. & S. Records.

The stock was transferred by Hutchinson as proxy for the Morgan heirs in return for $7,500,000 payable in three equal installments. Never before had stockholders outside the family owned over ten shares. Huntington received his first block of 100 shares on April 27, 1883, replaced Richard J. Morgan on the M.L. & T.R. & S. board on May 1, and by April 1884 owned 13,985 shares in the company. Hutchinson, as trustee for various heirs, delivered the remaining 36,015 votes on demand, and managerial policy was securely formulated between him and Huntington.[50]

Control of the M.L. & T.R. & S. gave Huntington control of the H. & T.C., the G.W.T. & P., the T.T., the B.B.S., and the H.D.N.—as majority shares in all those corporations were owned by their Morgan parent. He secured control of the L.W. by purchase of 33,600 of its 43,600 outstanding shares on November 16, 1883. This gave him what he had sought, his own system from San Francisco to New Orleans.[51]

Huntington's intrusion into the Morgan system was inevitable. His line between Sierra Blanca and San Antonio was completed on January 12, 1883, the New Orleans–San Francisco pool was activated, and through trains departed simultaneously from both ends of the line on February 5. Between 1882 and 1885, with the help of Hutchinson, Huntington consolidated his position. Systematically enlarging his equity in the former Morgan companies as well as the G.H. & S.A. and the T. & N.O., Huntington merged them with his new Southern Pacific Company of Kentucky—a holding company created to integrate management of his southern transcontinental line—on December 31, 1884.[52]

Hutchinson's reward came early in 1885. On February 10, 1885, Huntington's rail holdings east of El Paso, including the M.L. & T.R. & S., the H. & T.C., and the G.W.T. & P., were leased to a new Atlantic Division of Southern Pacific (now known as Texas and Louisiana Lines Division), and A. C. Hutchinson was named general manager. His ap-

50. *Ibid.*, 342, 345.
51. Capital Stock Ledger, L.W. (1883–1913), pp. 1–91, L.W. Records (S.P. Co.).
52. For first-hand accounts of the Sierra Blanca–El Paso completion, see testimony of Timothy Hopkins and Julius Kruttschnitt, *Record in Equity No. 420, op. cit.*, pp. 656–661, 705–713. Huntington's "Omnibus Lease" of the Texas and Louisiana lines and his formation of the S.P. Co. of Ky. are well covered in Evans, *Huntington*; Clark, *Then Came the Railroads*; Wilson and Taylor, *Southern Pacific*; Grodinsky, *Transcontinental Railway Strategy*; and 36 ICC Val. Rep., pp. 345–714.

pointment was opposed by many of Huntington's older associates, but, as the latter informed Hutchinson, "I have great faith in your manner of working railroad property . . . [and my associates] have all finally come to my way of thinking."[53]

Transfer of the M.L. & T.R. & S. to the Huntington interests between 1882 and 1885 ended the Morgan Line's corporate existence. S.P. retained the name for bookkeeping and advertising purposes as late as 1939, but it was mostly applied to the Southern Pacific Steamship Company—the descendant of Morgan's vessels. The true Morgan Line, however, had passed into history between the deaths of Morgan in 1878 and Whitney in 1882.

Although not so apparent then, the end of the "Morgan" enterprises truly marked an era in the economic history of the Gulf South. The responsible purposefulness and "can-do" image of such men as Morgan, which had made them prime decision makers in the process of resource allocation and economic development, were gradually replaced by the no less purposeful but far more impersonal activities of national corporations. The public increasingly took the existence of transportation and financial intermediaries as "given" and turned its attention to their regulation—forgetting, as new generations always do, the time when transportation, communication, and capital accumulation were not so easy or so sure. And, as national and state governments matured and broadened their financial base, they took on many of the projects which had, in earlier, less-affluent days, been left to private initiative. In short, the evolution of the modern "mixed" economy shifted into a higher gear —but a gear anchored in the achievements of such men as Charles Morgan.

53. Minute Book No. 1, Board of Directors, M.L. & T.R. & S., 377–438, Huntington to Hutchinson, March 30, 1885, M.L. & T.R. & S. Records.

APPENDIXES
BIBLIOGRAPHY
INDEX

APPENDIX 1

STEAMSHIPS OWNED BY CHARLES MORGAN
OR HIS CORPORATE ENTERPRISES, 1833–1885

Vessel	Tonnage	Acquisition[a]	Disposition[b]
ATLANTIC AND GULF COAST			
David Brown	190	P-1833	Sk-1836
William Gibbons	294	P-1833	Sk-1836
Columbia	423	B-1835	S-1839
New York	365	B-1837	Sk-1846
Home	550	B-1837	Sk-1837
Neptune	745	B-1837	S-1838
Savannah	305	P-1839	Sk-1841
Republic	262	B-1844	?
Galveston	548	B-1845	Sk-1851
New Orleans	869	B-1847	S-1847
Palmetto	533	P-1847	Sk-1851
Yacht	249	P-1847	Sk-1853
Portland	445	P-1847	D-1854
Globe	481	P-1847	Sk-1851
Jerry Smith	159	P-1849	D-1850
Louisiana	1,056	B-1850	Sk-1857
Mexico	1,043	B-1850	Sz-1861
Meteor	542	B-1851	Sk-1852
Perseverance	827	B-1852	Sk-1856
Cincinnati	276	P-1852	Sk-1853
Texas	1,151	B-1852	Sz-1861
Charles Morgan	1,215	B-1854	Sz-1861
Nautilus	898	B-1854	Sz-1856
Tennessee	1,149	P-1856	Sz-1862
Atlantic	623	P-1856	Sz-1861
Calhoun	508	P-1856	Sz-1861
Gen. Rusk	417	B-1857	Sz-1861
Galveston	945	P-1858	Sz-1861
Orizaba II	595	P-1858	Sz-1861
Suwanee	494	P-1858	Sz-1861
Magnolia	843	P-1858	Sz-1861

STEAMSHIPS OWNED BY CHARLES MORGAN
OR HIS CORPORATE ENTERPRISES, 1833–1885 *(Cont.)*

Vessel	Tonnage	Acquisition[a]	Disposition[b]
ATLANTIC AND GULF COAST *(Cont.)*			
Matagorda	616	P-1858	Sz-1861
Arizona	578	B-1858	Sz-1861
Austin	603	B-1860	Sz-1861
W. G. Hewes	747	B-1860	Sz-1861
St. Mary	678	B-1862	S-1885
Crescent	678	B-1862	Sk-1868
Clinton	721	B-1863	S-1885
Frances I	679	B-1863	Sk-1865
Louise	1,351	B-1864	S-1874
Frances II	988	B-1865	S-1871
Morgan	994	B-1865	S-1885
Lady of the Lake	716	B-1865	?
I. C. Harris	994	B-1865	S-1885
Harlan	1,163	B-1865	S-1885
Mary	1,096	B-1865	Sk-1876
Manhattan	1,339	B-1865	S-1875
Vera Cruz	1,339	B-1865	Sk-1866
City of Norfolk	1,040	B-1866	S-1884
Laura	1,098	B-1866	S-1871
Agnes	583	P-1866	?
Alabama	510	P-1866	D-1875
Josephine	1,282	B-1867	S-1885
Tartar	692	P-1867	S-1868
Charleston	1,517	P-1867	S-1872
Champion	1,452	P-1867	Sk-1879
A. C. Hutchinson	1,435	B-1870	S-1885
Whitney	1,338	B-1871	S-1885
Thomas Kelso	1,430	P-1871	S-1873
Gussie	998	B-1872	?
Lone Star	2,255	B-1875	S-1885
New York	2,255	B-1875	S-1885
Brashear	1,735	B-1875	R-1876
Morgan City	2,271	B-1876	S-1885
Algiers	2,270	B-1876	S-1885
Aransas	1,157	B-1877	S-1885
Mary Morgan	370	B-1878	S-1879
Louisiana	2,840	B-1880	S-1885
Chalmette	2,983	B-1880	S-1885
Willamette	2,264	B-1881	S-1885
Excelsior	3,264	B-1882	S-1885

STEAMSHIPS OWNED BY CHARLES MORGAN
OR HIS CORPORATE ENTERPRISES, 1833–1885 (*Cont.*)

Vessel	Tonnage	Acquisition[a]	Disposition[b]
PANAMA AND NICARAGUA ROUTES			
Crescent City	1,291	P-1848	S-1850
Empire City	1,751	B-1849	S-1850
Northerner	1,012	B-1850	S-1850
Prometheus	1,207	P-1853	S-1857
Pacific	1,207	P-1853	S-1857
Daniel Webster	1,035	P-1853	S-1857
Brother Jonathan	1,359	P-1853	S-1857
Northern Light	1,767	P-1853	S-1857
Star of the West	1,172	P-1853	S-1857
S. S. Lewis	1,103	P-1853	Sk-1853
Independence	613	P-1853	Sk-1853
Sierra Nevada	1,246	P-1853	S-1857
Uncle Sam	1,433	P-1853	S-1856
Yankee Blade	1,767	P-1853	Sk-1854
J. M. Clayton	150	P-1853	S-1857
H. Bulwer	150	P-1853	S-1857
Director	87	P-1853	D-1856
La Virgen	?	B-1853	S-1857
Central America	?	B-1853	S-1857
Ometepe	?	B-1853	Sk-1854
Orizaba I	1,335	B-1854	S-1860
J. Ogden	150	B-1854	S-1857
I. C. Lea	158	B-1854	Sk-1854
San Carlos	421	B-1854	S-1857
C. Morgan	?	B-1855	S-1857
J. L. White	?	B-1855	S-1857
Col. Wheeler	?	B-1856	S-1857
E. L. Hunt	?	B-1856	S-1857
H. L. Routh	?	B-1856	S-1857
FERRIES AND TUGS			
Porter	288	P-1866	?
Sarah	405	P-1866	?
Lucretia	428	P-1866	?
Louise	134	P-1866	?
Endeavor	634	B-1871	?
Restless	54	B-1875	S-1885
Fidget	54	B-1875	Sk-1884
Juno	80	B-1879	?
Enterprise	1,041	B-1880	S-1885

a. P: Purchased; B: Built.
b. S: Sold; Sk: Sunk; Sz: Seized; D: Dismantled; R: Renovated.

MARINE ENGINES BUILT BY MORGAN IRON WORKS AND PREDECESSOR T. F. SECOR & CO., 1838–1867

Vessel	Builder	Tonnage	Eng. Type	Cyl. Dia. (in.)	Stroke Length (ft.)	Wheel Dia. (ft.)
1838						
Savannah		305	V.B.			
1840						
Troy	Capes—N.Y.C.	724	H.B. (2)	44	10	29
1843						
Empire	Brown—N.Y.C.	936	H.B. (2)	48	12	32
1846						
Atlantic	Simonson—N.Y.C.	1,112	V.B.	72	11	36
John Stevens	Stevens—Hbkn.	686	V.B.	75	8	
Perry	Burtis—N.Y.C.	255	V.B.	36	9	22
Thomas Powell	Sneeden—N.Y.C.	585	V.B.	48	11	30
T. F. Secor		210	V.B.			
1847						
Antelope	Simonson—N.Y.C.	425	V.B.			28
New Orleans	Brown—N.Y.C.	869	V.B.	55	11	32
1848						
Crescent City	Brown—N.Y.C.	1,289	S.L.	80	9	34
New World		1,312	V.B.	76	15	45
Ontario	Merrick—N.Y.	832	V.B.	50	11	28
Queen City		906				
United States	Webb—N.Y.C.	1,875	S.L.	72	10	
Connecticut	Sneeden—N.Y.C.	1,129	V.B.	72	12	35
1849						
Empire City	Brown—N.Y.C.	1,751	S.L.	75	9	
Georgia	Dimon—N.Y.C.	2,727	S.L. (2)	90	8	36
Goliah	Webb—N.Y.C.	333	V.B.	50	8	
Ocean	Sanford—N.Y.C.	658	V.B.	48	11	
Ohio	Simonson—N.Y.C.	2,432	S.L. (2)	90	8	36
Gold Hunter	Westervelt—N.Y.C.	436	S.L. (2)			26
1850						
Boston	Brown—N.Y.C.	630	V.B.	44	11	
Louisiana	Westervelt—N.Y.C.	1,056	V.B.	56	10	
Prometheus	Simonson—N.Y.C.	1,207	V.B. (2)	42	10	
Reindeer	Collyer—N.Y.C.	790	V.B.	56	12	34
St. Lawrence	Collyer—N.Y.C.	588	V.B.	44	11	

MARINE ENGINES BUILT BY MORGAN IRON WORKS AND PREDECESSOR T. F. SECOR & CO., 1838–1867 (*Cont.*)

Vessel	Builder	Tonnage	Eng. Type	Cyl. Dia. (in.)	Stroke Length (ft.)	Wheel Dia. (ft.)
1851						
Brother Jonathan	Patterson—N.Y.C.	1,359	V.B.	72	11	33
Mexico	Collyer—N.Y.C.	1,043	V.B.	56	10	
North America	Sneeden—N.Y.C.	1,440	V.B.	60	12	
Roanoke	Westervelt—N.Y.C.	1,071	V.B. (2)	42	10	
Winfield Scott	Westervelt—N.Y.C.	1,291	S.L. (2)	66	8	
1852						
City of Hartford	Sneeden—N.Y.C.	814	V.B.	60	12	35
Cortes	Westervelt—N.Y.C.	1,117	V.B. (2)	42	10	32
Northern Indiana	Bidwell—N.Y.	1,475	V.B.	72	12	38
Perseverance	Westervelt—N.Y.C.	827	V.B.	56	12	
Sierra Nevada	Collyer—N.Y.C.	1,246				
Southern Michigan	Bidwell—N.Y.	1,470	V.B.	72	12	38
1853						
Crescent City	Bidwell—N.Y.	1,746	V.B.	80	12	40
George Law	Webb—N.Y.C.	2,141	O. (2)	65	10	
Golden Age	Brown—N.Y.C.	2,281	V.B.	83	12	35
Granite State	Sneeden—N.Y.C.	887	V.B.	52	12	35
Jamestown	Westervelt—N.Y.C.	1,300	V.B. (2)	40	10	
Josephine		552	V.B. (2)	40	14	
San Francisco	Webb—N.Y.C.	2,272	O. (2)	65	8	28
1854						
Charles Morgan	Westervelt—N.Y.C.	1,215	V.B.	60	11	31
Nautilus		898	V.B.	44	11	
Orizaba I	Westervelt—N.Y.C.	1,335	V.B.	65	11	30
Sonora	Westervelt—N.Y.C.	1,616	V.B. (2)	50	10	30
St. Louis	Westervelt—N.Y.C.	1,621	V.B. (2)	50	10	30
1855						
Commonwealth.	Lawrence—N.Y.C.	1,732	V.B.	76	12	38
Island Home	Sneeden—N.Y.C.	481	V.B. (2)	40	11	28
1856						
Christoval Colon	Sneeden—N.Y.C.	450	V.B.	48	10	28
Everglade	Sneeden—N.Y.C.	406	O.	32	8	28
Fulton	Dimon—N.Y.C.	2,307	O. (2)	65	10	36
1857						
Eastern Queen	Englis—N.Y.C.	695	V.B.	48	11	30
Independence	Sneeden—N.Y.C.	354	V.B. (2)	32	8	28
Yangtsze	Collyer—N.Y.C.	1,003	O. (2)	38	8	
City of Buffalo	Bidwell—N.Y.	2,026	V.B.	76	12	38
1858						
Huntsville	Westervelt—N.Y.C.	817	G.S.	56	4	14
Montgomery	Westervelt—N.Y.C.	787	G.S.	56	4	14
Ocean Queen	Westervelt—N.Y.C.	2,801	V.B.	90	12	38
1859						
Alabama	Sneeden—N.Y.C.	510	V.B.	50	10	30

MARINE ENGINES BUILT BY MORGAN IRON WORKS AND PREDECESSOR T. F. SECOR & CO., 1838–1867 (*Cont.*)

Vessel	Builder	Tonnage	Eng. Type	Cyl. Dia. (in.)	Stroke Length (ft.)	Wheel Dia. (ft.)
De Soto	Lawrence—N.Y.C.	1,600	V.B. 65		11	30
John Brooks	Sneeden—N.Y.C.	780	V.B.	56	12	
Peiho	Collyer—N.Y.C.	1,113	O.	52	8	28
White Cloud	Collyer—N.Y.C.	520	V.B.	44	10	26
Yorktown	Webb—N.Y.C.	1,403	V.B.	50	10	30
U.S.S. Seminole	U.S.N.—Fla.	801	G.S. (2)	50	3	10
1860						
Bienville	Lawrence—N.Y.C.	1,558	V.B.	68	11	
Flushing	Sneeden—N.Y.C.	333	V.B.	36	10	26
Charleston	Westervelt—N.Y.C.	1,517	V.B.	71	12	
Peruano	Westervelt—N.Y.C.	570	V.B.	44	11	28
Wm. G. Hewes	Harlan—Wlmtng.	747	V.B.	50	11	30
Zouave	Englis—N.Y.C.	750	V.B.	50	11	31
1861						
Continental	Sneeden—N.Y.C.	686	V.B.	70	11	34
Cosmopolitan	Englis—N.Y.C.	774	V.B.	50	11	31
Hankow	Collyer—N.Y.C.	725	V.B.	48	12	29
Mary Benton	Goodspeed—Conn.	365	V.B.	44	10	26
New Brunswick	Englis—N.Y.C.	804	V.B.	48	11	31
South America	Webb—N.Y.C.	2,150	V.B.	80	11	34
Westfield	Simonson—N.Y.C.	891	V.B.	50	10	
U.S.S. Chippewa	Webb—N.Y.C.	507	G.S.			
U.S.S. Katahdin	Larrabee—Bath	507	G.S.			
U.S.S. Kineo	Dyer—Ptlnd.	507	G.S.			
U.S.S. Mahaska	U.S.N.—Me.	832	V.B.			
U.S.S. Wachusett	U.S.N.—Mass.	1,032	G.S.	50	3	
1862						
Chekiang	Steers—N.Y.C.	1,264	V.B.	70	11	30
Fohkien	Steers—N.Y.C.	1,947	V.B.	81	12	
New England	Englis—N.Y.C.	852	V.B.	52	11	27
U.S.S. Ticonderoga	U.S.N.—N.Y.C.	1,533	G.S.	42	3	
U.S.S. Tioga	U.S.N.—Mass.	819				
1863						
Morning Star	Roosevelt—N.Y.	2,022	V.B.	80	12	
Western Metropolis	Tucker—N.Y.C.	2,269	V.B.	74	12	
U.S.S. Ascutney	Jackman—Nbrypt.	974				
U.S.S. Chenango	Simonson—N.Y.C.	974				
U.S.S. Onondaga	Morgan—N.Y.C.	1,250	G.S. (4)	30	18	
Re Don Luige De Portugallo	Webb—N.Y.C.			84	4	
1864						
Gen. J. K. Barnes	Lawrence—N.Y.C.	1,365	V.B.	60	10	
Golden Rule	Steers—N.Y.C.	2,767	V.B.	81	12	30
Herman Livingston	Lawrence—N.Y.C.	1,314	V.B.	60	10	
Oriflamme	Lawrence—N.Y.C.	1,204	V.B.	60	10	
U.S.S. Ammonoosuc	U.S.N.—Mass.	2,190	G.S. (2)	100	4	
U.S.S. Muscoota	U.S.N.	(No other information found.)				

MARINE ENGINES BUILT BY MORGAN IRON WORKS AND PREDECESSOR T. F. SECOR & CO., 1838–1867 (Cont.)

Vessel	Builder	Tonnage	Eng. Type	Cyl. Dia. (in.)	Stroke Length (ft.)	Wheel Dia. (ft.)
1865						
Albemarle	Lawrence—N.Y.C.	871	V.B.	44	11	20
Hatteras	Lawrence—N.Y.C.	868	V.B.	44	11	20
Manhattan	Lawrence—N.Y.C.	1,337	V.B.	66	11	26
Nevada	Simonson—N.Y.C.	1,691	V.B.	85	12	35
New York	Simonson—N.Y.C.	2,217	V.B.	78	12	35
Raleigh	Lawrence—N.Y.C.	868	V.B.	44	11	20
Rapidan	Lawrence—N.Y.C.	868	V.B.	44	11	20
Vera Cruz	Lawrence—N.Y.C.	1,340	V.B.	66	11	26
U.S.S. Idaho	Forbes—N.Y.C.	2,638	G.S. (4)	30	8	
1866						
Villa Clara		1,095	V.B.	52	4	
1867						
Cambridge		1,337	V.B.	60	11	

Notes: Dates are date of launch. Engine types are those described at date of launch and are as follows: V.B. = vertical-beam; H.B. = horizontal beam; O. = oscillating; G.S. = geared screw; S.L. = side-lever.

245

APPENDIX 3

SLAVES BOUGHT OR SOLD BY CHARLES MORGAN OR HIS AGENTS,
1846–1862

Name, Age	Purchase price, date		Sale price, date	
Joe, 31;				
Jacob, 29	$1,000	6– 2–46		
Reuben, 27	505	6– 2–46		
William, 29	350	7– 5–46		
John, 21	750	1– 3–48		
Daniel, 35	200	1– 2–50	$ 135	2–24–51
Sealey Benton, 40	345	2–28–50		
Jane, 18	700	3–15–50	650	2–24–53
Ann, 29;				
Arthur, 2			700	3–15–50
Archy, 50;				
Hester, 40	450	3–22–50		
Jane, 40;				
Cornelius, 5;				
George, 3	300	11–21–50	300	6–30–51
John, 27	381.20	12–24–50	460	4– 7–53
Angeline, 28;				
Robert, 8	1,225	1–22–51	1,300	2–24–53
Nancy, 26;				
George, 9	1,000	3–29–51		
Ben, 35	300	4– 1–51	200	10–30–51
Eliza, 16			650	2–24–53
Betsy, 33; and				
4 children			1,000	4–28–53
Dick, 27	700	7–21–54		
Martin, 26;				
Lewis, 24;				
John Lewis, 28	3,150	7–27–54		
Bill, 28	1,000	7–28–54		

246

SLAVES BOUGHT OR SOLD BY CHARLES MORGAN OR HIS AGENTS, 1846–1862 (*Cont.*)

Name, Age	Purchase price, date		Sale price, date	
Frank Anderson, 19;				
Jefferson, 21	2,150	7–29–54		
Frederick, 24	1,000	8– 3–54		
Edward, 35	725	8–11–54	700	5–29–55
Jules, 12	100	8–21–54		
Hiram, 22	1,500	12–20–54		
Sarah, 45;				
William, 21;				
Rosalie, 15	1,500	7–30–55		
Louisa, 13	746.13	11–21–55	746	6–12–56
Eliza, 23			900	1–24–56
Mary Jane, 25			575	6–19–56
Horace, 31	1,150	4–29–58		
Louis, 23	1,050	9–18–58		
Cyrus, 23;				
Doze, 16;				
Jacob, 21;				
Joe, 27;				
Charles, 22;				
William, 24	7,500	11–12–58		
Jordan, 24;				
Isaac, 25;				
Dave, 19	3,800	12– 4–58		
Andrew, 22;				
Dick, 25;				
Walker, 22	3,750	12– 4–58		
Albert, 13	1,250	9–13–59		
Lina, 36;				
Louisa, 9	2,400	9–29–59	2,400	3– 2–60
Harry, 36	1,000	10– 4–59		
Gus, 20;				
Alfred, 28	3,000	3– 2–60		
Sidney, 27	1,250	3– 8–60		
Joe, 24	1,600	4–25–60		

Compiled from original bills of sale deposited in Notarial Archives of Orleans Parish, Louisiana. Note that some purchases and sales were individual and that other slaves changed hands in lots.

TABLE 1.1—CHARLES MORGAN'S EQUITY IN SAILING VESSELS, 1819–1846

Type, Name, and Tonnage	Morgan's[a] Share		Period of His Equity	Trade[b] Route	Line or[c] Tramp
PACKETS					
Sp. *Franklin* (213)	1 of 4	b, h	11–1–19/4–28–25	N.Y.–C.	"Ship"
Sp. *Washington* (318)	1 of 3–4	b, h	5–4–22/	N.Y.–C.	"Ship"
Sp. *Calhoun* (285)	1 of 6–7	x	10–2–23/10–1–27	N.Y.–C	"Ship"
Sp. *Commodore Perry* (263)	1 of 5	h	10–30–23/?–?–27	N.Y.–C.	"Ship"
Sp. *President* (244)	1 of 7	h	12–20–23/	N.Y.–C.	"Ship"
Sp. *Niagra* (319)	1 of 5–6	h	12–31–23/9–19–28	N.Y.–C.	"Ship"
				N.Y.–N.O.	"New"
Sp. *Charleston* (167)	1 of 7	h	2–20–24/2–21–25	N.Y.–C.	"Ship"
Sp. *Lafayette* (342)	1 of 6–7		5–22–24/4–3–37	N.Y.–C.	"Ship"
				N.L.–L.	"Black Ball"
				N.Y.–C.	"Established"
				N.Y.–N.O.	"New"
Sp. *Othello* (264)	1 of 5–6	h	9–21–24/1–4–31	N.Y.–C.	"Ship"
Sp. *Saluda* (289)	1 of 8–10		9–23–25/9–29–37	N.Y.–C.	"Ship"
Bg. *Lawrence* (170) *	1 of 1–5	b, h	9–29–30/8–7–32	N.Y.–W.I.	"Jamaica"
				N.Y.–N.O.	"Brig"
Sp. *John W. Cater* (217)	1 of 1–4	b, h	10–4–31/	N.Y.–W.I.	"Jamaica"
Sp. *Amelia* (244)	1 of 4		1–20–32/	N.Y.–C.	"Ship"
Sp. *Orbit* (283)	1 of 4		11–3–32/	N.Y.–W.I.	"Jamaica"
				N.Y.–S.	"Old"
				N.Y.–S.	"Established"
Sp. *Sutton* (346)	1 of 9		12–1–32/12–16–36	N.Y.–C.	"Ship"
Sp. *H. Alen* (323)	1 of 5	x	12–22–32/1–9–34	N.Y.–C.	"Ship"
Bg. *Neptune* (154)	1 of 3	h	1–18–33/	N.Y.–W.I.	"Jamaica"
Sp. *Emily* (298) **	1 of 2–6	b, h	11–18–35/	N.Y.–W.I.	"Jamaica"
				N.Y.–N.O.	"Merchant's"
				N.Y.–S.	"Georgia"
				N.Y.–N.O.	"Union"
NON-PACKETS					
Sch. *Empire* (93)	1 of 1–5	h	4–2–25/	N.Y.–W.I.	tramp
Sch. *Syren* (82)	1 of 2	h	4–9–25/	N.Y.–W.I.	tramp
Bg. *Spartan* (129)	1 of 1–3	h	11–16–25/	N.Y.–W.I.	tramp
Sch. *Exchange* (314)	1 of 2–4	h	10–19–27/	N.Y.–W.I.	tramp
Bg. *Matteawan* (163)	1 of 1–2	h	11–5–27/	N.Y.–W.I.	tramp
Sch. *Angerona* (106)	1 of 1–2	h	12–11–28/10–9–30	N.Y.–W.I.	tramp
Bg. *Lawrence* (170) *	1 of 1–5	b, h	9–29–30/8–7–32	N.Y.–W.I.	tramp
Slp. *Franklin* (31)	1 of 2	h	5–6–31/7–11–31	N.Y.–W.I.	tramp
Sch. *Northampton* (68)	1 of 2–3		2–23–32/12–21–34	N.Y.–W.I.	tramp
				N.Y.–VA.	coaster

TABLE 1.1—CHARLES MORGAN'S EQUITY IN SAILING VESSELS, 1819–1846 *(Cont.)*

Type, Name, and Tonnage	Morgan's[a] Share		Period of His Equity	Trade[b] Route	Line or[c] Tramp
Sch. *Richard & Douglass* (48)	1 of 3		4–4–32/	N.Y.–W.I.	tramp
				N.Y.–VA.	coaster
Bg. *Russian* (222)	1 of 4		4–30–32/	N.Y.–E.	tramp
Slp. *Nancy Finly* (50)	1 of 7	x	10–31–32/6–1–33	N.Y.–CT.	coaster
Sp. *Ganges* (396)	1 of 4	h	7–2–33/10–23–33	N.Y.–E.	tramp
Slp. *Ludlow* (65)	1 of 6–7	x	4–18–34/10–8–36	N.Y.–CT.	coaster
Sp. *Emily* (298) **	1 of 2–6	b, h	11–18–35/	N.Y.–E.	tramp
Slp. *Susan* (67)	1 of 6	x	11–9–36/7–12–38	N.Y.–CT.	coaster
Slp. *Emily* (59)	1 of 4–6	x	9–12–38/1–8–46	N.Y.–CT.	coaster

Sources: Ship Registers and Enrollments, New York City, RG 36, National Archives; *ibid.*, Middletown and Hartford District, Conn. (WPA transcripts), Marine Historical Assn., Mystic, Conn.; Carl C. Cutler, *Queens of the Western Ocean.*

a. Ship registers and enrollments before 1850 rarely show fractional shares. Other symbols: b = Morgan was builder; x = was one of original builders; h = was ship's husband sometime during his equity.

b. N.Y. = New York; C. = Charleston; N.O. = New Orleans; L. = Liverpool; S. = Savannah; W.I. = West Indies; VA. = Chesapeake Bay area; E. = Europe; CT. = Connecticut shore of Long Island Sound.

c. Names of packet lines are given in quotation marks.

* ** Same vessels.

TABLE 1.2—WEST INDIAN IMPORTS TO "CHARLES MORGAN & CO.," 1825–1826

Sugar	4 hhds., 3 tcs., 10 bbls.
Molasses	225 hhds., 11 bbls., 1 punch
Rum	4 hhds.
Salt	3,750 bus.
Hides	1,179 pcs. and "quantities"
Cocoanuts	1,200 pcs.
Palm Oil	2 bbls.
Lignum vitae	1,200 lbs.
Fustic	17,000 lbs.
Indigo	65 ceroons
Limes	2 bbls. and "quantities"
Tamarinds	9½ bbls., 51 kegs
Oranges	2,500 pcs. and "quantities"
Old lead[a]	7,000 lbs. and "quantities"
Old copper, pewter, and brass	7,700 lbs. and "quantities"
Old iron	57,000 lbs. and "quantities"
Specie	$5,822 and "quantities"

Source: New York *Shipping & Commercial List,* December 24, 1825, February 22, March 18, June 14, July 26, December 6, 13, 30, 1826.

a. "Old" metals were used metal artifacts as differentiated from the "scrap" metals produced by trimming processes at time of manufacture. Both were in demand by New York's ironmasters. *Ibid.,* November 26, 1831.

TABLE 1.3—OWNERSHIP AND AGENCY OF NEW YORK–CHARLESTON STEAM-PACKET LINES, 1832–1838

Vessel	Date of Document and Owners Listed		New York Agent
David Brown	E 9–26–32	James P. Allaire	Master
	E 9–13–33	James P. Allaire Thomas Andrews Benjamin Aymar John Q. Aymar John Haggerty Charles Morgan	Morgan
	E 9–29–34	James P. Allaire John Haggerty Charles Morgan	Morgan
	R 12– 8–35	Same	Morgan
William Gibbons	E 2– 1–34	James P. Allaire	Master
	E 2– 4–34	James P. Allaire Thomas Andrews Benjamin Aymar John Q. Aymar John Haggerty Charles Morgan	Morgan
	E 9–29–34	James P. Allaire John Haggerty Charles Morgan	Morgan
	E 9–19–36	Same	Same
	E 5– 4–36	John Haggerty Charles Morgan	Same
Columbia	E 3–14–35	John Haggerty Charles Morgan	Morgan
	E 4–30–36	Same	Same
	R 10–25–37	Same	Same
New York	E 6–14–37	John Haggerty Charles Morgan	Morgan
	E 10– 3–38	John Haggerty Charles Morgan John T. Wright (master)	Same
	R 1– 2–39	Same	Same
Home	E 1–19–37	James P. Allaire	Morgan
	E 9– 6–37	Same	Same
Neptune	R 1–27–38	James Pennoyer Various South Carolinians	Pennoyer
	E 2– 1–38	Same	Same

Sources: Ship Registers and Enrollments, New York City, RG 36, National Archives; Hal Allaire Papers; New York Herald, 1832–1838; Alexander Crosby Brown, "An Early American Neptune," American Neptune, XII (April 1952), 148–150.

TABLE 2.1—STEAMSHIPS RUNNING BETWEEN NEW ORLEANS AND GALVESTON, 1837–1845

Vessel	Dates on Run	Round Voyages	Passengers East	Passengers West
September 1, 1837–August 31, 1838				
Columbia*	11/25/37–8/27/38	18	954(17)	90(1)
Cuba	6/ 8/38–7/ 1/38	2	92(2)	(0)
Constitution	1/11/38–1/29/38	1	39(1)	(0)
September 1, 1838–August 31, 1839				
Columbia*	9/ 3/38–8/25/39	21	903(18)	799(14)
Cuba	11/ 8/38–6/12/39	14½	729(14)	722(9)
New York*	2/ 1/39–6/11/39	9	527(9)	606(9)
Charleston	3/14/39– ?	1	(0)	100(1)
Constitution	5/21/39– ?	1	(0)	18(1)
September 1, 1839–August 31, 1840				
Columbia*	9/ 3/39–8/31/40	19	916(18)	264(6)
New York*	11/ 8/39–6/ 8/40	14	721(13)	45(2)
Neptune	11/20/39–6/10/40	11	402(10)	102(2)
September 1, 1840–August 31, 1841				
Savannah*	10/17/40–8/22/41	20	651(18)	(0)
New York*	11/ 8/40–6/15/41	16	524(15)	(0)
Neptune	11/ ?/40–6/ 3/41	13	546(11)	(0)
Kingston	6/25/41–8/30/41	5½	90(5)	(0)
Maryland	1/ 3/41–3/18/41	1	10(1)	(0)
September 1, 1841–August 31, 1842				
New York*	11/ 6/41–7/19/42	16	524(12)	492(11)
Neptune	11/13/41–6/13/42	12	289(7)	(0)
Merchant	7/ 9/42–8/31/42	2	80(2)	(0)
Kingston	9/ 1/41–9/24/41	1½	41(2)	(0)
Belle of Attakapas	1/28/42–2/ 9/42	1	(0)	(0)
Monmouth	2/19/42–3/ 2/42	1	(0)	(0)
September 1, 1842–August 31, 1843				
Neptune	10/26/42–6/12/43	13	165(10)	(0)
New York*	11/ 7/42–6/ 4/43	12	354(11)	137(5)
Sarah Barnes	7/? /43–8/31/43	4	90(4)	(0)
Merchant	9/ 8/42– ?	2	16(1)	(0)
September 1, 1843–August 31, 1844				
New York*	11/ 4/43–7/11/44	14	479(14)	(0)
Neptune	11/15/43–6/13/44	12	426(12)	(0)
Sarah Barnes	9/ 1/43–9/ ?/43	1	10(1)	(0)
Republic*	8/ 4/44–8/28/44	1	37(1)	(0)
September 1, 1844–August 31, 1845				
New York*	11/ 7/44–6/17/45	15	438(13)	(0)
John S. McKim	12/19/44–8/29/45	12	364(12)	(0)
Republic*	9/12/44–2/15/45	5	73(4)	(0)
Marmora	3/22/45–4/28/45	2	48(2)	(0)
September 1, 1845–December 31, 1845				
New York*	10/18/45–12/31/45	7	170(6)	(0)
John S. McKim	9/ 1/45–12/31/45	4½	14(3)	(0)
Galveston*	11/26/45–12/31/45	3	133(3)	(0)
Cincinnati	10/11/45–12/31/45	1½	31(1)	(0)

Source: Numbers of voyages and passenger statistics compiled from newspapers, custom-house records, and passenger lists as cited in text.

 * Vessels owned and operated by Charles Morgan.

 Figures in parentheses following passenger statistics represent number of voyages for which statistics are available.

TABLE 4.1—FINANCIAL STATEMENT, ACCESSORY TRANSIT COMPANY OF NICARAGUA, DECEMBER 31, 1853

Assets:

8 Ocean steamers, cost	$1,575,000.00
Repairs, alterations, and increased accommodations on ocean steamers	100,000.00
10 Lake and river steamboats, cost	162,175.00
Add ⅔ for expense of getting them in position, materials and labor in fitting up, and increased value in use	108,116.00
Construction of road from Virgin Bay to Pacific	126,000.00
Depots, landings, ways, stations, shops, stores and supplies on hand, and balances unexpended with agents on Isthmus	100,000.00
Coal on hand on the Pacific, after paying the account of $183,000 for coal and coal hulks, besides 1,500 tons on the way from New York	150,000.00
2,400 shares of Company's stock, cost	63,193.00
Cash on hand	33,000.00
Total assets	$2,417,484.00

Liabilities:

S.S. Lewis, lost, uninsured	$ 125,000.00
10% depreciation on river and lake steamboats	27,029.00
Current engagements: notes for insurance on ships, due next year	45,000.00
Drafts of agents, accepted & advised	20,000.00
Due for supplies sent to the Isthmus	5,500.00
Provision for account of Nicaraguan gov't.	20,000.00
Bonds for half purchase money of *Cortes* due on 3/21 and 6/21/54	113,000.00
Total liabilities	$ 355,529.00
Surplus	$2,061,955.00

Unvalued Assets:
Nicaraguan franchise
Unvalued Liabilities:
Capital stock
Account with Cornelius Vanderbilt

Source: Adapted from "To the Stockholders of the Accessory Transit Company of Nicaragua, Statement of the Affairs of the Company . . . 31st December 1853 " New York *Tribune*, January 6, 1854.

TABLE 6.1—FEDERAL CHARTERS HELD BY MORGAN VESSELS, 1861–1866

Vessel	Type of Charter[a]	Period	Fee[b]
General Rusk	A @ $ 12,000	3/3/61 ff.	$ 12,000.00 G
St. Mary	B @ 700/day	8/28/62–2/4/63	
Crescent	A @ 12,000	1/26/63 ff.	12,000.00 G
Crescent	B @ 700/day	2/13/63–9/14/63	
St. Mary	A @ 15,000	2/15/63 ff.	15,000.00 G
St. Mary	B @ 700/day	3/5/63–8/17/63	
Crescent, St. Mary, Clinton	B @ 500/day	9/1/63–7/31/65	612,185.00 N
Frances I	B @ 150/day	3/17/64–6/30/64	15,750.00 G
Louise	B @ 600/day	12/07/64–5/18/65	145,482.64 G
Louise	B @ 600/day	5/20/65–9/19/65	24,300.00 G (to 6–30–65)
Frances I	B @ 150/day	6/25/65–3/17/66	787.50 G (to 6–30–65)
Crescent, St. Mary, Clinton	D @ 251,533	8/1/65	251,533.00 N
Crescent, St. Mary, Clinton	C @ 10,800/mo.	8/1/65–8/1/66	237,600.00 G

Source: Vessel Charter Files, Quartermaster General, U.S. Army, RG 92, National Archives.

a. A-type charters were for one voyage only with shipowner assuming all expenses in return for a flat fee. B-type charters were time charters. These became the most common. The shipowner "manned, victualled, tackled, apparelled, and ballasted, and furnished in every respect fit for merchant service" and assumed marine risk; the government paid a per diem rate with allowances for lay days, "all pilotage and port charges," "all fuel," and assumed war risk. Vessels were appraised upon charter and when 60 to 70% of the total net earnings of the shipowner (i.e., after "actual cost of running and keeping in repair") equaled the appraisal price, the vessel became the property of the government at no extra cost. A C-type contract was for "victualling and manning" of vessels owned by the government. A D-type purchase was one in which the government paid the difference up to the appraised value in a B-type charter in order to take title to the vessel. (These categories A, B, C, and D are my own, formulated in the absence of official nomenclature).

b. G = gross amount paid Morgan; N = net amount realized as profit by Morgan. Gaps in the appropriate records preclude any totalization of either G or N amounts.

TABLE 6.2—NAVAL CONTRACTS COMPLETED BY
MORGAN IRON WORKS, 1858–1867

Vessel & Flag	Contract For	Contract Date	Contract Price	Delivered Price
Seminole (U.S.)	Machinery	10–28–58	$120,000	$ 120,000.00
Wachusett (U.S.)	Machinery	6–29–61	104,000	104,000.00
Chippewa (U.S.)	Machinery	7– 8–61	46,000	46,218.50
Katahdin (U.S.)	Machinery	7– 8–61	45,500	44,880.15
Kineo (U.S.)	Machinery	7– 8–61	46,500	45,989.70
Mahaska (U.S.)	Machinery	8–21–61	50,000	50,000.00
Ticonderoga (U.S.)	Machinery	10–14–61	110,000	110,000.00
Tioga (U.S.)	Machinery	11–25–61	50,000	50,000.00
Chenango (U.S.) ⎫ *Ascutney* (U.S.) ⎭	Machinery	8–15–62	164,000	215,652.67
Onondaga (U.S.)	Complete	5–26–62	625,000	759,673.08
Idaho (U.S.)	Machinery	9–22–63	?	?
Ammonoosuc (U.S.)	Machinery	?– ?–63	700,000	729,565.00
General J. K. Barnes (U.S.)	Machinery	?– ?–64	?	?
Re Don Luige de Portugallo (IT.)	Machinery	?– ?–62	?	?
Partial Total				$2,275,991.10

Sources: Record of Payments on Contracts for Ships ("Bill Book"), 1861–1864, Records of the Bureau o Ships, U.S. Navy, RG 19, National Archives; "Contracts for Vessels for War," *Senate Exec. Docs.*, 39 Cong. 1 Sess., No. 18 (Serial 1237); "Naval Vessels," *House Exec. Docs.*, 40 Cong., 2 Sess., No. 280 (Serial 1343); Frank M. Bennett, *The Steam Navy of the United States.*

TABLE 9.1—INVESTMENT IN ROAD AND EQUIPMENT, MORGAN'S
LOUISIANA AND TEXAS RAILROAD, 1870–1878

Road and equipment purchased under foreclosures on properties of the N.O.O. & G.W.:		
Completed road		
Recorded money outlay	$ 701,825.00	
Funded debt assumed (agreed amount)	1,348,175.00	
		$2,050,000.00
Partially built road, recorded money outlay		250,000.00
(This amount when applied in partial settlement of judgments against the N.O.O. & G.W. was distributed, to Charles Morgan $197,025.03 and, to various parties $52,974.97)		
Road purchased from PRR, recorded money outlay		250,000.00
Construction, additions, and betterments, construction of Schriever to Houma branch, and improvements on whole property, recorded money outlay		1,284,053.55
Total		3,834,053.55
Less road and equipment retired:		
Retirement of road, sale to the N.O.M. & T. for the consideration of $283,205.47, of the partially built road acquired from the N.O.O. & G.W., resulting in a retirement from investment account of the amount for which this property had been purchased	250,000.00	
Retirement of equipment at sale price of	31,000.00	
		281,000.00
Total recorded at March 31, 1878		3,553,053.55
Construction of 125 freight cars, recorded money outlay charged to operating expenses		70,621.43
Alteration of gauge, equipment, and turntable charged to Morgan		95,177.23
Grand total		$3,718,852.21

Source: This statement covers the period November 1, 1870, through March 31, 1878, and was compiled by valuation reporters of the Interstate Commerce Commission. (36 Val. Rep. 693–694). It has been verified by the present writer from the original journals and ledgers in possession of the Southern Pacific Company in Houston.

TABLE 9.2—RESULTS OF CORPORATE OPERATIONS, MORGAN'S LOUISIANA AND TEXAS RAILROAD, 1870–1878

Operating income:		
Railway operating revenues	$7,872,033.30	
Railway operating expenses	4,537,452.69	
Net revenue from railway operations	3,334,580.61	
Railway tax accruals	134,273.99	
Total operating income	3,200,306.62	
Nonoperating income:		
Hire of equipment	60.00	
Miscellaneous rent income	545.00	
Income from funded securities	4,980.36	
Miscellaneous income	227.80	
Total nonoperating income	5,813.16	
GROSS INCOME		$3,206,119.78
Deductions from gross income:		
Interest on funded debt	163,390.98	
Interest on unfunded debt	49,219.97	
Total deductions	212,610.95	
NET INCOME (transferred to Morgan's personal account)		$2,993,508.83

(Note that there was no profit and loss account on the books to which this income credit balance would under normal accounting procedures of the day have been transferred. Rather, all transactions affecting income and its disposition were passed to Charles Morgan's open account. This open account was a clearing account for transactions affecting both investment and operations.)

Source: This statement covers the period November 1, 1870, through March 31, 1878, and was compiled by valuation reporters of the Interstate Commerce Commission (36 Val. Rep. 692–693). It has been verified by the present writer from the original journals and ledgers in possession of the Southern Pacific Company in Houston.

TABLE 9.3—EARNINGS AND EXPENDITURES, HOUSTON & TEXAS CENTRAL RAILWAY, 1870–1876

Fiscal Year Ending	Gross Earnings	Operating Expenses Including Taxes[a]	Interest on Floating Debt	Fixed Interest Charges	Total Expenditures
1870	$1,463,132.80	$ 750,917.33	$269,502.72	$ 176,903.00	$1,197,323.05
1871	1,708,170.32	883,820.81	323,844.16	376,123.93	1,583,788.90
1872	2,239,456.26	1,462,101.79	292,040.52	562,422.94	2,316,565.25
1873	3,013,465.68	1,891,505.78	206,698.95	704,433.06	2,802,637.79
1874	3,165,179.88	1,975,562.57	313,272.57	959,304.43	3,248,139.57
1875	2,980,218.56	1,857,296.56	290,268.79	1,077,189.60	3,224,754.95
1876	3,161,011.76	1,891,118.44	335,352.61	1,168,863.94	3,395,334.99

Source: Copy of MS report by Frederick W. Foote, partner in John J. Cisco & Son, "Houston and Texas Central Railway and Texas Central Railway Matters, New York, February 25th, 1885." In possession of author.

a. "During these years the road was in progress of construction to its termini and ["construction and improvement," i.e., capital] expenditures were derived mainly from proceeds of Bonds sold. Whatever net earnings there may have been were also expended in construction of road, etc." Capital expenditures are not included in this column.

TABLE 10.1—EARNINGS AND EXPENDITURES, GULF, WESTERN TEXAS & PACIFIC RAILWAY, 1872–1885

Year Ending:	Gross Earnings	Balance from Previous Year after Interest and Dividends	Operating Expenses	Net Earnings before Interest and Dividends
5–1–72 (8 mos.)	$131,999.76	$?	$ 70,393.69	$ 61,606.05
3–30–73	232,979.30	?	104,817.77	128,161.53
3–31–74	242,300.54	54,486.35	149,788.36	139,979.35
3–31–75	164,454.33	14,397.56	114,291.71	64,560.18
3–31–76	?	56,139.29	?	?
No reports issued from 3–31–75 to 3–31–79				
3–31–79	112,357.94	?	82,652.36	29,705.58
12–31–80	134,278.12	?	89,523.64	44,754.48
12–31–81	129,249.31	?	98,236.35	31,012.96
3–31–83	128,616.64	?	96,126.51	32,490.13
3–31–84	114,556.05	?	93,072.03	21,484.02
3–31–85	97,108.98	?	89,108.98	8,416.96

Source: Manual of the Railroads of the United States.

TABLE 10.2—EARNINGS AND EXPENDITURES, HOUSTON & TEXAS CENTRAL RAILWAY AND SUBSIDIARIES, 1877–1884

Fiscal Year Ending	Gross Earnings	Operating Expenses including Taxes	Construction & Improvement	Interest on Floating Debt	Fixed Interest Charges	Total Expenditures
			Houston & Texas Central Railway			
1877	$2,628,053.77	$1,570,808.33	$ 119,241.67	$113,484.39	$ 992,839.02	$2,796,373.41
1878	2,920,996.64	1,752,038.94	36,933.04	239,384.87	1,044,322.50	3,072,689.35
1879	3,205,684.88	1,773,771.27	43,507.13	207,670.80	1,059,260.00	3,084,209.20
1880	3,741,000.37	2,007,323.35	181,797.83	112,283.72	1,099,475.00	3,400,879.70
1881	3,748,655.10	2,141,872.22	1,063,113.91	74,305.48	1,139,965.56	4,419,257.17
1882	3,156,517.51	1,748,954.36	549,207.90	95,382.41	1,193,255.00	3,586,749.67
1883	3,251,875.89	1,743,771.28	782,791.12	103,092.74	1,193,200.00	3,822,855.14
1884	2,547,847.41	1,578,190.15	641,920.38	126,018.31	1,193,200.00	3,539,328.84
			Texas Central Railway			
1881	$ 282,724.27	$119,030.07			$ 154,875.00	$ 273,905.07
1882	$ 205,887.32	157,896.73			207,235.00	365,131.73
1883	290,262.45	261,751.05			237,930.00	499,681.05
1884	283,637.74	253,199.51			237,930.00	491,129.51
			Central Texas & Northwestern Railway			
1881	$ 38,414.40	$ 19,700.40			$ 2,100.00	$ 21,800.40
1882	45,792.00	26,792.00			3,600.00	30,392.00
1883	50,158.53	53,760.55			3,600.00	57,360.55
1884	36,523.71	31,318.44			3,600.00	34,918.44

Source: Copy of MS report by Frederick W. Foote, partner in John J. Cisco & Son, "Houston and Texas Central Railway and Texas Central Railway Matters, New York, February 25th, 1885." In possession of author.

TABLE 10.3—THE MORGAN RAILROAD SYSTEM AT ITS PEAK, 1883

Railroad	Mileage	Locos.	Pass Cars.	Frt. Cars	Pass. miles (millions)	Ton-miles (millions)
In Texas:						
H. & T.C.	521.75	69	31	1,807	26.5	80.0
T.C.	228.60	8	6	203	?	?
G.W.T. & P.	66.00	6	3	71	0.5	2.0
C.T. & N.W.	12.00	1	1	2	.5	.1
T.T.	8.00	2	0	50	?	?
In Louisiana:						
M.L. & T.R. & S.	245.00	44	36	849	26.5	50.0
L.W.	112.00	9	5	327	?	?

Sources: Manual of the Railroads of the United States for 1884; Minute Book No. 1, M.L. & T.R. & S., *passim.*

TABLE 10.4—THE MORGAN RAILROAD SYSTEM IN STATE AND NATIONAL CONTEXTS, AS OF DECEMBER 31, 1883

Item	Texas	Louisiana	National
Morgan av. stock/mi.	$11,389 (5)	$25,331 (2)	$14,846
State/National av.	$13,760 (25)	$29,417 (14)	$30,759
Morgan av. bonds/mi.	$20,819 (5)	$23,418 (2)	$21,561
State/National av.	$12,551 (29)	$20,357 (14)	$28,650
Morgan av. gross/mi.	$ 3,343 (4)	$ 5,376 (1)	—
State/National av.	$ 4,500 (12)	$ 4,500 (6)	$ 7,461
Morgan av. net/mi.	$ 994 (4)	$ 2,331 (1)	—
State/National av.	$ 1,366 (12)	$ 1,333 (4)	$ 2,702
Morgan expenditures as % gross earnings	73.88 (4)	48.74 (2)	65.50
State/National av.	61.25 (12)	82.33 (6)	63.78
Int. on bonds paid by Morgan rrs.	$1,535.1M (3)	$625.2M (2)	$2,160.3M
Morgan % of state	21.63 (13)	23.81 (5)	—
Div. on stock paid by Morgan rrs.	0 (5)	0 (2)	—
No. of rrs. paying as per Poor's	0 (29)	1 (14)	—

Source: Compiled from *Manual of the Railroads of the United States for 1884.* Numbers in parentheses are number of roads reporting. Total for Texas was 29 and for Louisiana, 14.

TABLE 10.5—SELECTED ITEMS OF GROSS EARNINGS AND EXPENDITURES, MORGAN'S LOUISIANA & TEXAS RAILROAD AND STEAMSHIP COMPANY, 1879–1885

(to nearest $1,000)

Items	Fiscal Years Ending March 31:					
	1879	1880	1881	1882	1884	1885
Gross Earnings:						
NY freight	965	1,094	1,110	1,146	1,497	1,558
Tex. freight by ss. & rr.	674	740	745	727	472	420
Tex. passengers by ss. & rr.	147	151	118	125	64	35
Local freight by rr.	384	392	448	601	920	685
Local passengers by rr.	91	147	247	313	363	233
Through freight by rr.	(9–1–80 ff.)	0	169	287	592	456
Through passengers by rr.	(9–1–80 ff.)	0	41	69	177	182
Texas–Havana cattle ss.	195	191	148	139	29	0
Cattle on own account	18	22	25	17	0	0
N.O.–Key West–Havana ss.	0	3	42	32	40	49
N.O.–Vera Cruz ss.	0	0	19	58	51	13
Mail Service	47	65	64	32	30	27
Express freight by rr.	0	0	0	24	42	30
Expenditures:						
NY ss. on voyage account	474	532	539	491	n.a.	758
Tex.–Hav.–Mex. ss. account	428	474	473	529	n.a.	358
Gen. agency expenses	200	211	229	245	n.a.	199
Gen. rr. expenses	215	366	323	528	n.a.	472
Rr. Payrolls	251	269	438	558	n.a.	579
Fuel	41	48	72	96	n.a.	104
Taxes	30	1	48	55	n.a.	79

Sources: M.L. & T.R. & S. Co., *Annual Reports* (New York, 1879, 1880, 1881, 1882, and 1885).

TABLE 10.6—EARNINGS AND EXPENDITURES, MORGAN'S LOUISIANA & TEXAS RAILROAD & STEAMSHIP COMPANY, 1879–1885

Fiscal Year Ending 3–31	Gross Earnings	Total Expenditures	Net Earnings
1879	$2,549,418.94	$1,660,126.49	$ 889,292.45
1880	2,915,362.04	2,315,347.46	600,014.58
1881	3,224,401.48	2,501,950.75	722,450.73
1882	4,188,622.14[a]	2,937,846.02	1,250,776.12
1883	3,953,145.03	2,846,817.69	1,106,327.34
1884	4,372,951.09	3,091,386.70	1,281,564.39
1885	3,764,723.14[b]	3,177,131.25[b]	587,591.89

Source: Minute Book No. 1, Board of Directors, M.L. & T.R. & S.

a. Includes $439,746.59 profit on sale of Donaldsonville railroad and $120,000.00 of G.W.T. & P. net earnings transferred to M.L. & T.R. & S.

b. Losses in earnings and increased expenditures resulted primarily from heavy flooding on line.

BIBLIOGRAPHY

Acts Passed by the General Assembly of the State of Louisiana. Baton Rouge and New Orleans, 1835–1885.

Adams, Ephraim D. (editor). *British Diplomatic Correspondence Concerning the Republic of Texas, 1838–1846.* Austin: Texas State Historical Association [1917].

Albion, Robert G. "Early Nineteenth-Century Shipowning: A Chapter in Business Enterprise," *Journal of Economic History,* I (May 1941), 1–11.

———. *The Rise of New York Port [1815–1860].* New York: C. Scribner's Sons, 1939.

———. *Square-Riggers on Schedule: The New York Sailing Packets to England, France, and the Cotton Ports.* Princeton: Princeton University Press, 1938.

Allaire (Hal) Papers. In possession of Mrs. M. Taylor, Brielle, New Jersey.

Allaire v. American Insurance Co. N. Y. Super. Ct., March 15, 1841 (reported in New York *Shipping & Commercial List,* March 20, 1841).

Allhands, J. L. *Uriah Lott.* San Antonio: Naylor, 1949.

The American Coast Pilot. 11th and 14th eds. New York: E. and G. W. Blunt, 1827 and 1842.

American Lloyd's Register of American and Foreign Shipping. New York: J. W. Pratt, 1864, 1865, 1867, 1877.

American Railroad Journal. New York, 1849–1850.

American Railroad Manual. New York: Edward Vernon, 1874.

Ames, John W. "Leaving Texas," *Overland Monthly,* XII (February 1874), 130–137.

Annual List of Merchant Vessels of the United States. Washington: Government Printing Office, 1868–1885.

Annual Report of the Chief of Engineers to the Secretary of War. Washington: Government Printing Office, 1866–1886.

"Annual Report of the Postmaster General."

> *Note:* During the nineteenth century this report was published annually in the Executive Document series of the U.S. Congress. In the preparation of this study all reports between 1820 and 1886 were consulted. Those cited in the text of this study are:

1846. *S.E.D.,* 29 Cong., 2 Sess., No. 1 (Serial 493).

1847. *S.E.D.,* 30 Cong., 1 Sess., No. 1 (Serial 503).

1848. *H.E.D.*, 30 Cong., 2 Sess., No. 1 (Serial 537).

1849. *H.E.D.*, 31 Cong., 1 Sess., No. 1 (Serial 569).

1850. *S.E.D.*, 31 Cong., 2 Sess., No. 1 (Serial 587).

1853. *S.E.D.*, 33 Cong., 1 Sess., No. 1 (Serial 692).

1854. *S.E.D.*, 33 Cong., 2 Sess., No. 1 (Serial 757).

1855. *S.E.D.*, 34 Cong., 1 Sess., No. 1 (Serial 812).

1856. *S.E.D.*, 34 Cong., 3 Sess., No. 5 (Serial 876).

1857. *S.E.D.*, 35 Cong., 1 Sess., No. 1 (Serial 921).

1858. *S.E.D.*, 35 Cong., 2 Sess., No. 1 (Serial 977).

1859. *S.E.D.*, 36 Cong., 1 Sess., No. 2 (Serial 1025).

1860. *S.E.D.*, 36 Cong., 2 Sess., No. 1 (Serial 1080).

1861. *S.E.D.*, 37 Cong., 2 Sess., No. 1 (Serial 1119).

Annual Report of the Superintendent of the Coast Survey. Washington: Government Printing Office, 1845–1865.

Annual Report on Commerce, Navigation, and Tonnage. Washington: Government Printing Office, 1830–1883.

Annual Report on the Internal Commerce of the United States. Washington: Government Printing Office, 1879–1889.

Appleton's Annual Cyclopaedia. New York: Appleton, 1861–1887.

Armstrong, A. B. "Origins of the Texas and Pacific Railway," *Southwestern Historical Quarterly*, LVI (April 1953), 489–497.

Armstrong, Leroy and J. O. Denny. *Financial California: An Historical Review of the Beginnings and Progress of Banking in the State.* San Francisco: Coast Banker Publishing Company, 1916.

Army and Navy Chronicle. Washington, 1835–1842.

"Attack on Steamboat *Columbia*," *House Exec. Docs.*, 25 Cong., 2 Sess., No. 360 (Serial 330).

Bankers' Magazine. Baltimore, 1847–1885.

Barksdale, E. C. *The Meat Packers Come to Texas.* Austin: University of Texas Press, 1959.

Barrett, Walter [pseud. of J. A. Scoville]. *The Old Merchants of New York City.* New ed. 5 vols. New York: Carleton, 1889.

Barringer, Graham A. (editor), "The Mexican War Journal of Henry S. Lane," *Indiana Magazine of History*, LIII (December 1957), 383–434.

Bayley, G. W. R. "History of the Railroads of Louisiana," New Orleans *Daily Picayune*, March 10–December 17, 1873.

Bennett, Frank M. *The Steam Navy of the United States.* Pittsburgh: W. T. Nicholson, 1896.

Benns, F. Lee. *The American Struggle for the British West India Carrying-Trade, 1815–1830.* Bloomington: Indiana University Press, 1923.

"Berwick Bay, Louisiana," *House Exec. Docs.*, 43 Cong., 1 Sess., No. 82 (Serial 1607).

Best, Gerald M. and David L. Joslyn. *Locomotives of the Southern Pacific Company.* Boston: Railway and Locomotive Historical Society, 1956.

Bieber, Ralph P. "California Gold Mania," *Mississippi Valley Historical Review,* XXXV (June 1948), 3–28.

———. *Southern Trails to California in 1849.* Glendale: Arthur H. Clark Company, 1937.

Biesele, Rudolph L. *The History of the German Settlements in Texas, 1837–1861.* Austin: Von Boeckmann–Jones Co., 1930.

Bigelow, John. *Jamaica in 1850.* New York: G. P. Putnam, 1851.

Bishop, J. Leander. *A History of American Manufactures from 1608 to 1860.* 3rd ed. 3 vols. Philadelphia: E. Young & Co., 1868.

Blackwood, Emma J. (editor). *To Mexico with Scott: Letters of Captain E. Kirby Smith to His Wife.* Cambridge: Harvard University Press, 1917.

Blanchard, A. G. *Report of the Preliminary Survey of the Algiers and Opelousas Railroad.* New Orleans: The Company, 1852.

Bonsteel v. Vanderbilt. 21 Barbour (N.Y.) 26 (1855).

[Bonzano (M.)] Diary, 1845–1846. Archives, Howard-Tilton Library, Tulane University.

Boulding, Kenneth E. *The Image.* Ann Arbor: University of Michigan Press, 1956.

Boyer, Frederic Q. and Herbert A. Poole (compilers). "The Quintard Family in America," *New England Historical and Genealogical Register,* CIX (July 1955), 184–193; CIX (October 1955), 257–266.

Braman, D. E. E. *Braman's Information about Texas, Carefully Prepared.* Philadelphia: J. B. Lippincott & Co., 1857.

Braynard, Frank O. *Famous American Ships.* New York: Hastings House, 1956.

Briggs v. Vanderbilt, 19 Barbour (N.Y.) 222 (1855).

"British Correspondence in Relation to the Attack on the American Steamer *Prometheus* by the British Brig-of-War *Express,*" *Senate Exec. Docs.,* 32 Cong., 1 Sess., No. 30 (Serial 618).

Brown, Alexander C. "An Early American *Neptune,*" *American Neptune,* XII (April 1952), 148–153.

Brown, James S. *Allaire's Lost Empire: A Story of the Forges and Furnaces of the Manasquan.* Freehold, N. J.: Transcript Printing House, 1958.

"The Building of the Ship," *Harper's Monthly Magazine,* XXIV (April 1862), 608–620.

Bureau of the Census. *Heads of Families at the First Census of the United States Taken in the Year 1790: Connecticut.* Washington: Government Printing Office, 1908.

———. *Historical Statistics of the United States, 1789–1945.* Washington: Government Printing Office, 1949.

Bureau of Customs. *Passenger Lists of Vessels Arriving at New Orleans, 1820–1902.* 93 rolls. National Archives Microfilm Publication M-259.

———. *Quarterly Abstracts of Passenger Lists of Vessels Arriving at New Orleans, 1820–1875.* 17 rolls. National Archives Microfilm Publication M-272.

Calvert, Alfred. *Shipping Office Organisation, Management, and Accounts.* London: Sir I. Pitman & Sons, 1929.

Campbell, E. G. "Indebted Railroads: A Problem of Reconstruction," *Journal of Southern History*, VI (May 1940), 167–188.

Cannon v. New Orleans. 20 Wallace (U.S.) 577 (1874).

Carman, Harry J. and Reinhard H. Luthin. *Lincoln and the Patronage.* New York: Columbia University Press, 1943.

Carr, Albert H. Z. *The World and William Walker.* New York: Harper & Row, 1963.

Carrollton *Louisiana State Register.* 1869–1874.

"Case of Carmick and Ramsey," *House Exec. Docs.*, 35 Cong., 2 Sess., No. 30 (Serial 1004).

Caudle, Robert E. *History of the Missouri Pacific Lines, Gulf Coast Lines and Subsidiaries. International–Great Northern.* Mimeographed. Houston: The Author, 1949.

Cauley, T. J. "Early Meat Packing Plants in Texas," *Southwestern Political and Social Science Quarterly*, IX (March 1929), 464–478.

"Causes of the Reduction of American Tonnage," *House Reports*, 41 Cong., 2 Sess., No. 28 (Serial 1436).

"Century of Progress in Louisiana, 1852–1952," *Southern Pacific (Texas and Louisiana Lines) Bulletin*, XXV (October 1952), 1–55.

Chandler, Alfred D., Jr. and Fritz Redlich. "Recent Developments in American Business Administration and Their Conceptualization," *Business History Review*, XXXV (Spring 1961), 1–27.

"Charles Morgan: His Courage Helped Build an Empire," *Southern Pacific (Texas and Louisiana Lines) Bulletin*, VIII (May 1936), 4–5, 13.

Charter and Act of Incorporation of the American Atlantic and Pacific Ship Canal Company and Treaty of Protection Negotiated between the United States and Great Britain. New York: The Company, 1850.

Charter and Act of Incorporation of the American Atlantic & Pacific Ship Canal Company, As Amended; Also, Treaty of Protection Negotiated between the United States and Great Britain; and Charter Granted by the State of Nicaragua to the Accessory Transit Company. New York: The Company, 1852.

Childs, Orville W. *Engineer's Report of the Cost of Constructing the Ship Canal of Nicaragua As Estimated at New York Prices.* New York: W. C. Bryant & Co., 1852.

————— and John D. Fay. *Map and Profile of the Route for the Construction of a Ship Canal from the Atlantic to the Pacific Oceans across the Isthmus in the State of Nicaragua, Central America; Surveyed for the American Atlantic and Pacific Ship Canal Company.* New York: W. C. Bryant & Co., 1852.

—————. *Report of the Survey and Estimate of the Cost of Constructing the Inter-Oceanic Ship Canal from the Harbor of San Juan del Norte on the Atlantic to the Harbor of Brito on the Pacific in the State of Nicaragua, Central America; Made for the American Atlantic and Pacific Ship Canal Co. in the Years 1850–51.* New York: W. C. Bryant & Co., 1852.

Christian, Asa K. "The Tariff History of the Republic of Texas," *Southwestern Historical Quarterly*, XX (April 1917), 315–340; XXI (July 1917), 1–35.

Church, William C. *The Life of John Ericsson*. 2 vols. New York: C. Scribner's Sons, 1906.

City of Galveston Island, in Texas, with a History of the Title of the Proprietor and a Brief Account of All its Advantages; Accompanied with a Plan of the City and Harbor, and a Map of Texas, Showing the Commercial Channels with the Interior through Which the City is to Derive Its Extensive Trade. New Orleans: Hotchkiss & Co., 1837.

Claims against Costa Rica under the Convention of 1860. Record Group 76, National Archives.

Clark, Ira G. *Then Came the Railroads: The Century from Steam to Diesel in the Southwest*. Norman: University of Oklahoma Press, 1958.

"Clayton-Bulwer Treaty and the Monroe Doctrine," *Senate Exec. Docs.*, 47 Cong., 1 Sess., No. 194 (Serial 1991).

Clews, Henry. *Twenty-eight Years in Wall Street*. New York: Irving Publishing Co., 1888.

Clinton: Its Old Houses and Legends. Clinton, Conn.: First Church of Christ (Congregational), 1951.

"Clopper Correspondence, 1834–1838," *Quarterly of the Texas State Historical Association*, XIII (October 1909), 128–144.

Cochran, Thomas C. *The Inner Revolution: Essays on the Social Sciences in History*. New York: Harper & Row, 1964.

———. *Railroad Leaders, 1845–1890: The Business Mind in Action*. Cambridge: Harvard University Press, 1953.

Cohen's New Orleans Directory. Annually. New Orleans: H. and A. Cohen, 1849–1856.

Cole, Arthur H. "An Approach to the Study of Entrepreneurship: A Tribute to Edwin F. Gay," *Journal of Economic History*, VI (Supplement, 1946), 1–15.

———. *Business Enterprise in Its Social Setting*. Cambridge: Harvard University Press, 1959.

———. "What Is Business History?" *Business History Review*, XXXVI (Spring 1962), 98–106.

Coleman-Fulton Pasture Company Records, 1876–1885. University of Texas Archives.

"Commerce of Galveston," *De Bow's Review*, XXV (December 1858), 710–711.

"Commerce of Galveston, Texas, 1860," *De Bow's Review*, XXIX (October 1860), 529.

"Commerce of the Port of Brazos de St. Iago," *Senate Exec. Docs.*, 31 Cong., 1 Sess., No. 69 (Serial 562).

Commercial and Financial Chronicle. New York, 1865–1885.

"Condition of Texas," *House Exec. Docs.*, 24 Cong., 2 Sess., No. 35 (Serial 302).

Congressional Globe. Washington, 1834–1872.

Congressional Record. Washington, 1873–1885.

"Connecting with Texas by Railroad," *De Bow's Review*, XXIX (October 1860), 530–533.

Connor, Seymour V. and Virginia H. Taylor (editors). *Texas Treasury Papers:*

Letters Received in the Treasury Department of the Republic of Texas, 1836–1846. 4 vols. Austin: Texas State Library, 1955–1956.

"Contracts for Carrying the Mails."

Note: During the nineteenth century this report was published annually in the Executive Document series of the U. S. Congress. In the preparation of this study all reports between 1819 and 1886 were consulted. Those cited in the text of this study are:

1838. *S.E.D.*, 25 Cong., 3 Sess., No. 254 (Serial 341).
1853. *H.E.D.*, 33 Cong., 1 Sess., No. 125 (Serial 735).
1854. *H.E.D.*, 33 Cong., 2 Sess., No. 86 (Serial 789).
1858. *H.E.D.*, 35 Cong., 2 Sess., No. 109 (Serial 1013).
1859. *H.E.D.*, 36 Cong., 1 Sess., No. 86 (Serial 1057).
1871. *H.E.D.*, 42 Cong., 2 Sess., No. 191 (Serial 1513).
1875. *H.E.D.*, 44 Cong., 1 Sess., No. 191 (Serial 1693).
1879. *H.E.D.*, 46 Cong., 2 Sess., No. 47 (Serial 1924).
1880. *H.E.D.*, 46 Cong., 3 Sess., No. 55 (Serial 1977).
1881. *H.E.D.*, 47 Cong., 1 Sess., No. 40 (Serial 1987).

"Contracts for Vessels of War," *Senate Exec. Docs.*, 39 Cong., 1 Sess., No. 18 (Serial 1237).

"Contracts, Quartermaster Department."

Note: During the nineteenth century this report was published annually in the Executive Document series of the U. S. Congress. In the preparation of this study all reports between 1863 and 1870 were consulted. Those cited in the text of this study are:

1866. *H.E.D.*, 39 Cong., 2 Sess., No. 28 (Serial 1289).
1867. *S.E.D.*, 40 Cong., 2 Sess., No. 59 (Serial 1316).
1867. *H.E.D.*, 40 Cong., 2 Sess., No. 35 (Serial 1330).

"Contracts, War Department."

Note: During the nineteenth century this report was published annually in the Executive Document series of the U. S. Congress. In the preparation of this study all reports between 1817 and 1887 were consulted. Those cited in the text of this study are:

1836. *H.E.D.*, 24 Cong., 2 Sess., No. 99 (Serial 303).
1837. *H.E.D.*, 25 Cong., 2 Sess., No. 174 (Serial 327).
1839. *H.E.D.*, 26 Cong., 1 Sess., No. 89 (Serial 365).
1845. *H.E.D.*, 29 Cong., 1 Sess., No. 51 (Serial 482).
1846. *H.E.D.*, 29 Cong., 2 Sess., No. 46 (Serial 499).
1847. *H.E.D.*, 30 Cong., 1 Sess., No. 29 (Serial 516).
1848. *H.E.D.*, 30 Cong., 2 Sess., No. 44 (Serial 541).
1849. *H.E.D.*, 31 Cong., 1 Sess., No. 38 (Serial 576).
1853. *H.E.D.*, 33 Cong., 1 Sess., No. 63 (Serial 721).
1854. *H.E.D.*, 33 Cong., 2 Sess., No. 68 (Serial 788).
1855. *H.E.D.*, 34 Cong., 1 Sess., No. 17 (Serial 851).
1857. *H.E.D.*, 35 Cong., 1 Sess., No. 58 (Serial 955).
1858. *H.E.D.*, 35 Cong., 2 Sess., No. 50 (Serial 1006).

1859. *H.E.D.*, 36 Cong., 1 Sess., No. 22 (Serial 1047).

1860. *H.E.D.*, 36 Cong., 2 Sess., No. 47 (Serial 1099).

1861. *H.E.D.*, 37 Cong., 2 Sess., No. 101 (Serial 1136).

Corporate History of the Direct Navigation Company as of June 30, 1918. Southern Pacific Company (Texas and Louisiana Lines), Houston, Texas, Auditor's Central File No. 110–3.

Corporate History of the Galveston, Harrisburg, and San Antonio Railway Company and Predecessor Companies as of June 30, 1918. Southern Pacific Company (Texas and Louisiana Lines), Houston, Texas, Auditor's Central File No. 110–3.

Corporate History of Houston & Texas Central Railroad Company and Predecessor Companies as of June 30, 1918. Southern Pacific Company (Texas and Louisiana Lines), Houston, Texas, Auditor's Central File No. 110–3.

Corporate History of Texas and New Orleans Railroad Company and Predecessor Companies as of June 30, 1918. Southern Pacific Company (Texas and Louisiana Lines), Houston, Texas, Auditor's Central File No. 110–3.

"Correspondence with the United States Board of Navy Commissioners: Being Replies to Their Circular Asking Information Relative to Steam Navigation," *Journal of the Franklin Institute*, XI (April–June 1846), 216–236, 288–310, 361–380; XII (July–August 1846), 1–18, 89–91.

Coulter, E. Merton. *The Confederate States of America, 1861–1865.* Baton Rouge: Louisiana State University Press, 1950.

Crandall v. Nevada. 6 Wallace (U.S.) 35 (1867).

Crane, Robert E. L., Jr. "The History of the Revenue Service and the Commerce of the Republic of Texas" (Ph.D. dissertation, University of Texas, 1950).

Cushman (William A.) Letterbook, 1868–1869. In possession of author.

Cutler, Carl C. *Queens of the Western Ocean: The Story of America's Mail and Passenger Sailing Lines.* Annapolis: U.S. Naval Institute, 1961.

Daly, R. R. *Shipping Accounts.* London: Gee & Co., 1905.

Daubeny, Charles G. B. *Journal of a Tour through the United States and in Canada, Made during the Years 1837–38.* Oxford: T. Combe, 1843.

Davenport, Herbert. "Notes on Early Steamboating on the Rio Grande," *Southwestern Historical Quarterly*, XLIX (October 1945), 288–289.

Davis, Ralph. *The Rise of the English Shipping Industry in the Seventeenth and Eighteenth Centuries.* London: Macmillan, 1962.

Dayton, Fred E. *Steamboat Days.* New York: Frederick A. Stokes Company, 1925.

DeBow's Review. New Orleans, 1846–1880.

DeLoosey (Charles F.) Papers, 1860–1869. New York Historical Society.

Dewing, Arthur S. *The Financial Policy of Corporations.* 4th ed. 2 vols. New York: Ronald Press Company, 1941.

"Documents and Correspondence Relating to the Government of Nicaragua," *Senate Exec. Docs.*, 34 Cong., 1 Sess., No. 68 (Serial 822).

Dodd, Dorothy. "The Wrecking Business on the Florida Reef, 1822–1860," *Florida Historical Quarterly*, XXII (April 1944), 171–199.

Doggett's New York City Directory. Annually. New York: John Doggett, Jr., 1842–1851.

Doster, James F. *Railroads in Alabama Politics, 1875–1914.* University, Ala.: University of Alabama Press, 1957.

Doyle, Elisabeth J. "Greenbacks, Car Tickets, and the Pot of Gold: The Effects of Wartime Occupation of the Business Life of New Orleans, 1861–1865," *Civil War History,* V (December 1959), 347–362.

Dun & Bradstreet Credit Ledgers. Baker Library, Harvard Graduate School of Business Administration.

Eclipse Towboat Co. v. Pontchartrain Railroad Co. 24 Louisiana Ann. 1 (1872).

Edwards, Emory. *Modern American Marine Engines, Boilers, and Screw Propellors.* Philadelphia: H. C. Baird & Co., 1886.

Eldrege Collection of Beam Engine Plans. The Mariners Museum, Newport News, Virginia.

Elliott, Claude. "The Building of the Southern Pacific Railroad through Texas" (M.A. thesis, University of Texas, 1928).

Ellis, David M. "Railroad Land Grant Rates, 1850–1945," *Journal of Land and Public Utility Economics,* XXI (August 1945), 207–222.

Emmerson, John C., Jr. (compiler). *Steam Navigation in Virginia and Northeastern North Carolina Waters, 1826–1836.* Portsmouth, Va.: The Author, 1949.

Evans, Cerinda. *Collis Potter Huntington.* 2 vols. Newport News, Va.: Mariners' Museum, 1954.

Evans, George H., Jr. *Business Incorporation in the United States, 1800–1943.* New York: National Bureau of Economic Research, 1948.

Ewbank, Thomas. "Account of the Explosion of the Boiler of the Steamboat *Wm. Gibbons*," *Journal of the Franklin Institute,* N.S., XVII (May 1836), 298–302.

Fairburn, William M. *Merchant Sail.* 6 vols. Center Lovell, Me.: Fairburn Marine Educational Foundation, 1945–1955.

Fayssoux (Callendar I.) Collection of William Walker Papers, 1855–1860. Middle American Research Institute Library, Tulane University.

Fazende v. Morgan. 31 Louisiana Ann. 549 (1879).

Fetter, Theodore A. *Southwestern Freight Rates.* Boston: Christopher Publishing House, 1934.

Field, David D. *A Statistical Account of the County of Middlesex in Connecticut.* Middletown: Connecticut Academy of Arts & Sciences, 1819.

Financier. New York, 1872–1875. (Became *Public.*)

"Fines and Deduction, Mail Contractors."
   Note: During the nineteenth century this report was published annually in the Executive Document series of the U.S. Congress. In the preparation of this study all reports between 1837 and 1886 were consulted. Those cited in the text of this study are:
   1851. *H.E.D.,* 32 Cong., 1 Sess., No. 56 (Serial 643).
   1853. *H.E.D.,* 33 Cong., 1 Sess., No. 22 (Serial 717).
   1854. *H.E.D.,* 33 Cong., 2 Sess., No. 92 (Serial 790).
   1855. *H.E.D.,* 34 Cong., 1 Sess., No. 112 (Serial 859).

1857. *H.E.D.*, 35 Cong., 1 Sess., No. 81 (Serial 956).

1868. *H.E.D.*, 40 Cong., 3 Sess., No. 88 (Serial 1381).

1869. *H.E.D.*, 41 Cong., 2 Sess., No. 289 (Serial 1426).

Fleming, Howard. *Narrow Gauge Railways in America.* 2nd ed. Philadelphia: Inquirer Printing & Publishing Co., 1876.

Flint, Henry M. *The Railroads of the United States.* Philadelphia: J. G. Potter & Co., 1868.

Fluth, Alice F. "Indianola, Early Gateway to Texas" (M.A. thesis, St. Mary's University, 1939).

Foner, Philip S. *Business & Slavery: The New York Merchants & the Irrepressible Conflict.* Chapel Hill: University of North Carolina Press, 1941.

Foote, Frederick W. "Houston and Texas Central Railway and Texas Central Railway Matters, February 25, 1885." Copy of MS report by partner in John J. Cisco & Company, New York. In possession of author.

"Foreign Commerce and Decadence of American Shipping," *House Exec. Docs.*, 41 Cong., 2 Sess., No. 111 (Serial 1417).

"Foreign Commerce and the Practical Workings of Maritime Reciprocity," *House Exec. Docs.*, 41 Cong., 3 Sess., No. 76 (Serial 1454).

Fornell, Earl W. *The Galveston Era: The Texas Crescent on the Eve of Secession.* Austin: University of Texas Press, 1961.

Forney, John W. *What I Saw in Texas.* Philadelphia: Ringwalt & Brown [1872].

Frazer, Robert W. "Maximilian's Propaganda Activities in the United States, 1865–1866," *Hispanic-American Historical Review*, XXIV (February 1944), 4–29.

Galveston City Directory. Annually. Galveston: John H. Heller, 1870–1880.

Galveston *Civilian and Galveston City Gazette.* 1838–1845.

Galveston *Commercial and Weekly Prices Current*, September 1, 1856.

Galveston Custom House Records, 1835–1845. Rosenberg Library, Galveston, Texas.

Galveston *Daily Galvestonian.* 1840–1841.

Galveston *Daily News.* 1870–1885.

Galveston Directory. Galveston: W. and D. Richardson, 1859, 1866.

Galveston Directory for 1856–7. Galveston: A. De Lono, 1856.

Galveston, Harrisburg, and San Antonio Railway Co., et al. 36 ICC Val. Rep. 377–438.

Galveston, Harrisburg, and San Antonio Railway Company Records. Southern Pacific Company (Texas and Louisiana Lines), Houston, Texas.

Galveston, Houston and Henderson Railroad Company File. Corporation Records Division, Baker Library, Harvard Graduate School of Business Administration.

Galveston *Tri-Weekly News.* 1855–1861.

Galveston Wharf Company. *A Brief History of the Galveston Wharf Company.* Galveston: The Company, 1927.

Galveston Wharf Company. *Report of H. de St. Cyr.* Galveston: News Steam Book and Job Establishment, 1874.

Galveston Wharf Company Records, 1854–1926. The Galveston Wharves Office, Galveston, Texas.

Gammel, H. P. N. (editor). *The Laws of Texas*. 10 vols. Austin: Gammel Book Co., 1898.

Gardner's New Orleans Directory. Annually. New Orleans: Charles Gardner, 1857–1861.

Garrison, George P. (editor). *The Diplomatic Correspondence of the Republic of Texas*. 3 vols. Washington: Government Printing Office, 1908–1911.

Giddings, Luther. *Sketches of the Campaign in Northern Mexico*. New York: G. P. Putnam, 1853.

Gillmore, Q. A. *Galveston*. New York: C. Scribner's Sons, 1879.

[Gilman, S. H.]. *The Tributary and Economical Relations of the Railway Systems of the United States to the Commerce of Galveston*. Galveston: News Steam Book and Job Office, 1871.

Goldberg, Joseph P. *The Maritime Story: A Study in Labor-Management Relations*. Cambridge: Harvard University Press, 1958.

Goodrich, Carter. *Government Promotion of American Canals and Railroads, 1800–1890*. New York: Columbia University Press, 1960.

———. "Public Aid to Railroads in the Reconstruction South," *Political Science Quarterly*, LXXI (September 1956), 407–442.

———. "The Revulsion against Internal Improvements," *Journal of Economic History*, X (November 1950), 145–169.

Goodwin, J. H. *Goodwin's Improved Book-Keeping and Business Manual*. 28th ed. New York: J. H. Goodwin, 1913.

Gordon, Clarence. *Report on Cattle, Sheep, and Swine Supplementary to Enumeration of Live Stock on Farms in 1880 (Tenth Census of the United States, III)*. Washington: Government Printing Office, 1883.

Gouge, William M. *The Fiscal History of Texas*. Philadelphia: Lippincott, Grambo and Co., 1852.

Graebner, Norman A. "United States Gulf Commerce with Mexico, 1822–1848," *Inter-American Economic Affairs*, V (Summer 1951), 36–51.

Graf, LeRoy P. "The Economic History of the Lower Rio Grande Valley, 1820–1875" (Ph.D. dissertation, Harvard University, 1942).

Gras, N. S. B. *Business and Capitalism: An Introduction to Business History*. New York: F. S. Crofts and Co., 1939.

———. "Stages in Business History," *Studi in Onore di Armando Sapori* (2 vols., Milan, 1957), I, 5–27.

———. "Stages in Economic History," *Journal of Economic and Business History*, II (May 1930), 395–418.

"Great Commercial Advantages of the Gulf of Mexico," *DeBow's Review*, VII (December 1849), 510–523.

Greer, James K. (editor). "Journal of Ammon Underwood, 1834–1838," *Southwestern Historical Quarterly*, XXXII (October 1928), 124–151.

Grodinsky, Julius. *Jay Gould: His Business Career, 1867–1892*. Philadelphia: University of Pennsylvania Press, 1957.

————. *Transcontinental Railway Strategy: A Study of Businessmen.* Philadelphia: University of Pennsylvania Press, 1962.

"Growth of Galveston, Texas," *DeBow's Review*, XXIII (November 1857), 554–555.

Gulf, Western Texas, and Pacific Railway Company Records. Southern Pacific Company (Texas and Louisiana Lines), Houston, Texas.

Gulick, Charles A., Jr. and Willie Allen (editors). *The Papers of Mirabeau Buonaparte Lamar.* 6 vols. Austin: A. C. Baldwin & Sons, 1914–1927.

Haggerty v. Allaire Works. 5 Sanford (N.Y. Super. Ct.) 230 (1851).

Hall, Henry (editor). *America's Successful Men of Affairs: An Encyclopedia of Contemporaneous Biography.* 2 vols. New York: New York Tribune, 1895.

Hall, Henry. *Report on the Ship-Building Industry of the United States (Tenth Census of the United States, VIII).* Washington: Government Printing Office, 1884.

Hamilton, Holman. "Texas Bonds and Northern Profits: A Study in Compromise, Investment, and Lobby Influence," *Mississippi Valley Historical Review*, XLIII (March 1957), 579–594.

Hamilton v. Accessory Transit Co. 26 Barbour (N.Y.) 45 (1857).

"The Harlan & Hollingsworth Company," *Nautical Gazette*, October 27, 1875.

Harlan and Hollingsworth Company. *Semi-Centennial Memoir of the Harlan & Hollingsworth Company, Wilmington, Delaware, U.S.A., 1836–1886.* Wilmington: The Company, 1886.

Harlan and Hollingsworth Corporation, Wilmington, Delaware, Plans of Vessels of Various Kinds, 1849–1896. The Mariners Museum, Newport News, Virginia.

Hartmann, Heinz. "Managers and Entrepreneurs: A Useful Distinction?" *Administrative Science Quarterly*, III (March 1959), 429–451.

Haswell, Charles H. *Reminiscences of an Octogenarian.* New York: Harper & Bros., 1896.

Haviland, Edward K. "American Steam Navigation in China, 1845–1878," *American Neptune*, XVI (July 1956), 157–179 (October, 1956), 243–269; XVII (January 1957), 38–73 (April 1957), 134–151 (July 1957), 212–230 (October 1957), 298–314; XVIII (January 1958), 59–85.

Hazard, John L. *Crisis in Coastal Shipping: The Atlantic-Gulf Case.* Austin: Bureau of Business Research, University of Texas, 1955.

Heyl, Erik. *Early American Steamers.* 5 vols. Buffalo: The Author, 1953–1967.

Hill, Ralph N. *Sidewheeler Saga: A Chronicle of Steamboating.* New York: Rinehart, 1953.

Hirschman, Albert O. *The Strategy of Economic Development.* New Haven: Yale University Press, 1958.

Hodder, Frank H. (editor). *Audubon's Western Journal, 1849–1850.* Cleveland: A. H. Clark Co., 1906.

Hodge, P. R. *The Steam Engine: Its Origin and Gradual Improvements from the Time of Hero to the Present Day.* 2 vols. New York: D. Appleton & Co., 1840.

Hogan, William R. "A Social and Economic History of the Republic of Texas" (Ph.D. dissertation, University of Texas, 1942).

————. *The Texas Republic: A Social and Economic History.* Norman: University of Oklahoma Press, 1946.

Holdcamper, Forrest R. (editor). *Merchant Steam Vessels of the United States, 1807–1868: The "Lytle List."* Mystic, Conn.: Marine Historical Assn., 1952.

House Misc. Docs., 47 Cong., 1 Sess., No. 53 (Serial 2036).

Houston and Texas Central Railway Company. *The First Mortgage Land Grant Sinking Fund Bonds of the Houston and Texas Central Railway Co. . . . together with Copies of Its Charter, Forms of Bond, and Trust Deeds, May 1, 1871.* New York: The Company, 1871.

————. *Meeting of First Mortgage Bondholders (and First Report of Bondholder's Committee) . . . Held at No. 50 Wall Street, New York City, on the 27th Day of January, 1885.* New York: The Company, 1885.

————. *Statement by B. G. Clarke and Charles Dillingham, Receivers, New York, March 31st, 1886.* New York: The Company, 1886.

————. *The State of Texas.* Chicago: Rand, McNally & Co., 1879.

Houston and Texas Central Railway Company File. Corporations Records Division, Baker Library, Harvard Graduate School of Business Administration.

Houston and Texas Central Railway Company Records. Southern Pacific Company (Texas and Louisiana Lines), Houston, Texas.

Houston Direct Navigation Company Records. Southern Pacific Company (Texas and Louisiana Lines), Houston, Texas.

Houstoun, Matilda C. F. *Hesperos: or, Travels in the West.* 2 vols. London: John W. Parker, 1850.

————. *Texas and the Gulf of Mexico: or, Yachting in the New World.* 2 vols. London: J. Murray, 1844.

Howland, S. A. *Steamboat Disasters and Railroad Accidents in the United States.* Worcester, Mass.: W. Lazell, 1840; Rev. ed., Worcester, Mass.: W. Lazell, 1846.

Huber, Leonard V. and Clarence A. Wagner. *The Great Mail: A Postal History of New Orleans.* State College, Pa.: American Philatelic Society, 1949.

Huebner, Solomon S. *Marine Insurance.* New York: D. Appleton & Co., 1920.

Hunter, Louis C. *Steamboats on the Western Rivers.* Cambridge: Harvard University Press, 1949.

Hunt's Merchant's Magazine and Commercial Review. New York, 1839–1870.

Hutchins, John G. B. *The American Maritime Industries and Public Policy, 1789–1914.* Cambridge: Harvard University Press, 1941.

Indianola Scrap Book: Fiftieth Anniversary of the Storm of August 20, 1886. Victoria, Tex.: Advocate Office, 1936.

Indianola (Tex.) *Bulletin.* 1853–1860.

Indianola (Tex.) *Courier.* 1859–1861.

Indianola (Tex.) *Indianolian.* 1857.

Indianola (Tex.) *Times.* 1866.

Indianola (Tex.) *Weekly Bulletin.* 1871–1872.

"Inducements to Settle or to Invest Capital in Texas," *DeBow's Review,* XI (November 1851), 533–537.

"Information in Relation to Contracts for the Transportation of the Mails by Steamships between New York and California," *Senate Exec. Docs.*, 32 Cong., 1 Sess., No. 50 (Serial 619).

"Information in Relation to the Firing into and Seizure of the American Steamship *Prometheus* by a British Vessel of War," *Senate Exec. Docs.*, 32 Cong., 1 Sess., No. 6 (Serial 614).

In Memoriam: Charles A. Whitney. New Orleans: n.p. [1882].

In Memoriam: Charles Morgan. [New York: n.p., 1878].

In the Matter of the Final Accounting of Morgan. 104 N.Y. Reports 74 (1887).

"Investigation by the Committee on Naval Affairs," *House Misc. Docs.*, 44 Cong., 1 Sess., No. 170 (9 pts. Serials 1703–1705).

Jewell's Digest of the City Ordinances . . . of the City of New Orleans. New Orleans: Edwin L. Jewell, 1882.

Johnson, Allen and Dumas Malone (editors). *Dictionary of American Biography.* 20 vols. and index. New York: C. Scribner's Sons, 1928–1937.

Johnson, Arthur M. and Barry E. Supple. *Boston Capitalists and Western Railroads: A Study in the Nineteenth-Century Railroad Investment Process.* Cambridge: Harvard University Press, 1967.

Jones, Fred M. *Middlemen in the Domestic Trade of the United States, 1800–1860.* Urbana: University of Illinois, 1937.

Journal of the Congress of the Confederate States of America, 1861–1865. 7 vols. Washington: Government Printing Office, 1904–1905.

Journal of the Franklin Institute. Philadelphia, 1830–1885.

Kaiser, Leo M. (editor). "The Civil War Diary of Florison D. Pitts," *Mid-America*, XL (January 1958), 22–63.

Kemble, John H. "The Gold Rush by Panama, 1848–1851," *Pacific Historical Review*, XVIII (February 1949), 45–56.

———. *The Panama Route, 1848–1869.* Berkeley: University of California Press, 1943.

Kendall, George W. *Narrative of the Texas Santa Fe Expedition.* 2 vols. New York: Harper and Brothers, 1844.

Kennedy, William. *Texas: The Rise, Progress, and Prospects of the Republic of Texas.* 2 vols. London: R. Hastings, 1841.

Kenny, Norris. "The Transportation of Government Property and Troops over Land-Grant Railroads," *Journal of Land and Public Utility Economics*, IX (November 1933), 368–381.

Kerr's General Advertiser and Directory. New Orleans: R. C. Kerr, 1856.

Killingworth Land Records. Town Clerk's Office, Killingworth, Connecticut.

Kirkland, Edward C. *Dream and Thought in the Business Community, 1860–1900.* Ithaca: Cornell University Press, 1956.

———. *Industry Comes of Age: Business, Labor, and Public Policy, 1860–1897.* New York: Holt, Rinehart and Winston, 1961.

———. *Men, Cities, and Transportation: A Study in New England History, 1820–1900.* 2 vols. Cambridge: Harvard University Press, 1948.

Lane, Carl D. *American Paddle Steamboats.* New York: Coward-McCann, 1943.

Lane, Wheaton J. *Commodore Vanderbilt: An Epic of the Steam Age.* New York: A. A. Knopf, 1942.

Larson, Henrietta M. (editor). *Guide to Business History.* Cambridge: Harvard University Press, 1948.

The Laws and Revised Ordinances of the Town of Brashear. Brashear, La.: W. Bartholomew Merchant, 1872.

Leovy, Henry J. and C. H. Luzenberg. *The Laws and General Ordinances of the City of New Orleans.* New Orleans: L. R. Simmons & Co., 1870.

Lewis, Oscar. *Sea Routes to the Gold Fields: The Migration by Water to California in 1849–1852.* New York: A. A. Knopf, 1949.

Linn, John J. *Reminiscences of Fifty Years in Texas.* New York: D. & J. Sadlier & Co., 1883.

Lively, Robert A. "The American System: A Review Article," *Business History Review,* XXIX (March, 1955), 81–95.

London *Times.* 1850.

Longworth's American Almanac, New-York Register, and City Directory. Annually. New York: David and Thomas Longworth, 1797–1842.

Louisiana Western Railroad Company Records. Southern Pacific Company (Texas and Louisiana Lines), Houston, Texas.

Lowitt, Richard. *A Merchant Prince of the Nineteenth Century: William E. Dodge.* New York: Columbia University Press, 1954.

Lowrey, Walter Mc. "Navigational Problems at the Mouth of the Mississippi River, 1698–1880" (Ph.D. dissertation, Vanderbilt University, 1956).

Luke, Myron H. "The Port of New York, 1800–1810: The Foreign Trade and Business Community" (Ph.D. dissertation, New York University, 1950).

Lynch and Aymar Papers. New York Historical Society and Columbia University.

Lytle, William M. "Iron Construction in the United States," *Annual Report of the Commissioner of Navigation for 1899* (Washington: Government Printing Office, 1899), I, 217–222.

McCampbell, Coleman. *Saga of a Frontier Seaport.* Dallas: Southwest Press, 1934.

McCoy, Joseph G. *Historic Sketches of the Cattle Trade of the West and Southwest.* Kansas City, Mo.: Ramsey, Millett and Hudson, 1874.

Macdonald v. Garrison and Morgan. 2 Hilton (N.Y. Common Pleas) 510 (1859).

"Mail Steamers," *House Exec. Docs.,* 32 Cong., 1 Sess., No. 91 (Serial 644).

"Mails to Texas: Arrangement Respecting Postage," *House Exec. Docs.,* 27 Cong., 3 Sess., No. 146 (Serial 421).

Mallory Papers, 1865–1885. Marine Historical Association, Mystic, Connecticut.

Manning, William R. (editor). *Diplomatic Correspondence of the United States: Inter-American Affairs, 1831–1860.* 12 vols. Washington: Carnegie Endowment for International Peace, 1932–1939.

Manual of the Railroads of the United States. Annually. New York: H. V. & H. W. Poor, 1868–1885.

Manufactures of the United States in 1860 (Eighth Census of the United States, III). Washington: Government Printing Office, 1865.

Martin, Margaret E. *Merchants and Trade of the Connecticut River Valley, 1750–1820*. Northampton, Mass.: Smith College, 1939.

Master and Wardens of Port of New Orleans v. CHARLES MORGAN. 14 Louisiana Ann. 595 (1859).

Masterson, V. V. *The Katy Railroad and the Last Frontier*. Norman: University of Oklahoma Press, 1952.

The Merchant's and Shipmaster's Guide. 3rd ed. Boston: Frederic W. Sawyer, 1843.

"Message on Attack on Steamboat *Columbia*," *House Exec. Docs.*, 25 Cong., 2 Sess., No. 360 (Serial 330).

Mexican Ocean Mail and Inland Company. *Annual Report*. New York: The Company, 1853.

Michel's New Orleans Annual and Commercial Register. New Orleans: Edward A. Michel & Co., 1833–1849.

Miller, Edmund T. *A Financial History of Texas*. Austin: University of Texas, 1916.

Miller, William (editor). *Men in Business: Essays on the Historical Role of the Entrepreneur*. Harper Torchbook ed. New York: Harper & Row, 1962.

Mills, C. Wright. "The American Business Elite: A Collective Portrait," *Journal of Economic History*, V (December 1945), 20–44.

Missouri, Kansas, and Texas Railway Company. *Annual Report*. New York: The Company, 1872–1879.

Missouri, Kansas, and Texas Railway Co., et al. 34 ICC Val. Rep. 293–673.

Missouri, Kansas, and Texas Railway Company File. Corporation Records Division, Baker Library, Harvard Graduate School of Business Administration.

Missouri Pacific Railroad Co., et al. 40 ICC Val. Rep. 249–721.

Monthly Nautical Magazine and Quarterly Review. New York, 1854–1858. (After 1855, called *U.S. Nautical Magazine and Naval Journal Monthly*).

Moore, A. B. "Railroad Building in Alabama during the Reconstruction Period," *Journal of Southern History*, I (November 1935), 421–441.

Moran v. New Orleans. 112 U.S. 69 (1884).

"The Morgan Line and Its Founders: A Sketch of Mr. Charles Morgan," *Nautical Gazette*, November 3, 1875.

Morgan, Nathaniel H. *Morgan Genealogy: A History of James Morgan of New London, Conn., and His Descendants, from 1607 to 1867*. Hartford: Case Lockwood & Brainard, 1869.

Morgan v. Dibble and Seeligson. 29 Texas Reports 108 (1867).

Morgan v. Graham. 17 Federal Cases 749 (1871).

Morgan v. Louisiana. 3 Otto (U.S.) 217 (1876).

Morgan v. New Orleans, Mobile, and Texas Railroad Co., et al. 17 Federal Cases 754 (1876).

Morgan v. Parham. 16 Wallace (U.S.) 471 (1873).

Morgan v. PHILIP DE PEYSTER. 17 Federal Cases 758 (1848).

Morgan v. Skiddy, et al. 62 N.Y. Reports 319 (1875).

Morgan's Louisiana and Texas Railroad. *New and Reduced Freight and Passen-*

ger Tariff of Morgan's Louisiana and Texas Railroad from New Orleans to Brashear City. New Orleans: The Company, 1869.

———. New and Reduced Freight and Passenger Tariff of Morgan's Louisiana and Texas Railroad from New Orleans to Brashear City, Bayou Teche, and Houma Branch. New Orleans: The Company, 1872.

"Morgan's Louisiana and Texas Railroad," Senate Reports, 45 Cong., 3 Sess., No. 732 (Serial 1838).

Morgan's Louisiana and Texas Railroad and Steamship Company. Annual Report. New Orleans: The Company, 1879–1882, 1885.

———. By-Laws. New Orleans: The Company, 1878.

———. Charter. New Orleans: The Company, 1878.

———. Charter of Morgan's Louisiana and Texas Railroad and Steamship Company, Together with Statutes, Ordinances, By-Laws, etc., Relating to the Company. New Orleans: The Company, 1884.

Morgan's Louisiana and Texas Railroad and Steamship Company Records. Southern Pacific Company (Texas and Louisiana Lines), Houston, Texas.

Morgan's Steamship Co. v. La. Board of Health. 118 U.S. 455 (1886).

Morrison and Fourmy's General Directory of the City of Galveston. Annually. Galveston: Morrison & Fourmy, 1880–1883.

Morrison, John H. History of American Steam Navigation. New York: W. F. Sametz & Co., 1903.

———. History of New York Ship Yards. New York: W. F. Sametz & Co., 1909.

———. "Iron and Steel Hull Steam Vessels of the United States," Scientific American Supplement, LX (October 21–November 25, 1905), 24918–24920, 24928–24930, 24943–24945, 24964–24966, 24980–24982, 24996–24998.

Muir, Andrew F. "The Destiny of Buffalo Bayou," Southwestern Historical Quarterly, XLVIII (October 1943), 91–106.

——— (editor). "Diary of a Young Man in Houston, 1838," Southwestern Historical Quarterly, LIII (January 1950), 276–307.

———. "Railroads Come to Houston, 1857–1861," Southwestern Historical Quarterly, LXIV (July, 1960), 42–63.

———. Texas in 1837: An Anonymous Contemporary Narrative. Austin: University of Texas Press, 1958.

———. "The Thirty-Second Parallel Pacific Railroad in Texas to 1872" (Ph.D. dissertation, University of Texas, 1949).

Murray, Amelia M. Letters from the United States, Cuba, and Canada. New York: G. P. Putnam & Co., 1856.

Mustang Island Pilot Station, Aransas Bar, Texas, Log Books, 1866–1881. In possession of Mrs. Robert A. Mercer, Aransas Pass, Texas.

Myers, William S. (editor). The Mexican War Diary of George B. McClellan. Princeton: Princeton University Press, 1917.

Mygatt and Co.'s Directory. New Orleans: Mygatt & Co., 1857.

Nautical Gazette. New York, 1871–1887.

"Naval Vessels," House Exec. Docs., 40 Cong., 2 Sess., No. 280 (Serial 1343).

Naylor, Robert A. "The British Role in Central America Prior to the Clayton-

Bulwer Treaty of 1850," *Hispanic American Historical Review,* XL (August 1960), 361–382.

Neu, Irene D. *Erastus Corning: Merchant and Financier, 1794–1872.* Ithaca: Cornell University Press, 1960.

Nevins, Allan (editor). *The Diary of Philip Hone, 1828–1851.* 2 vols. New York: Columbia University Press, 1927.

———— and Milton H. Thomas (editors). *The Diary of George Templeton Strong, 1835–1875.* 4 vols. New York: Columbia University Press, 1952.

New Iberia *Louisiana Sugar Bowl.* 1871–1877.

New Orleans *Bee.* 1835–1885.

New Orleans *Commercial Bulletin.* 1835–1871.

New Orleans *Daily Crescent.* 1848–1869.

New Orleans *Daily Delta.* 1845–1862.

New Orleans *Daily Picayune.* 1837–1885.

New Orleans *Democrat.* 1875–1881.

New Orleans, Mobile, and Chattanooga Railroad Company. *Charter of the New Orleans, Mobile, and Chattanooga Railroad Company and Laws Relating Thereto.* New York: The Company, 1869.

New Orleans, Mobile, and Chattanooga Railroad Co. v. City of New Orleans, et al. 26 Louisiana Ann. 478 (1874).

New Orleans, Mobile, and Chattanooga Railroad Co. v. City of New Orleans, et al. 26 Louisiana Ann. 517 (1874).

New Orleans, Opelousas, and Great Western Railroad Company. *Annual Report of the President and Directors.* New Orleans: The Company, 1853–1857, 1859–1863, 1867–1969.

————. *By-Laws and Charter.* New Orleans: The Company, 1866.

————. *Legal Documents and By-Laws.* New Orleans: The Company, 1866.

————. *List of Stockholders.* New Orleans: The Company, 1852.

New Orleans, Opelousas, and Great Western Railroad Co. v. Morgan. 10 Wallace (U.S.) 256 (1870).

New Orleans, Opelousas, and Great Western Railroad Company Records. Southern Pacific Company (Texas and Louisiana Lines), Houston, Texas.

New Orleans *Price Current.* 1834–1885.

New Orleans Real Estate Assessment Rolls, 1857–1875. New Orleans Public Library.

New Orleans *Republican.* 1867–1878.

New Orleans *Times.* 1863–1881.

New Orleans *Times-Democrat.* 1881–1914.

New Orleans *True Delta.* 1851–1861.

New-York As It Is. Annually. New York: Edwin Williams and J. Disturnell, 1833–1837.

New York *Evening Post.* 1838.

New York *Herald.* 1848–1865.

New-York Marine Register: A Standard of Classification of American Vessels. New York: J. W. Pratt, 1857.

New York *Shipping & Commercial List*. 1825–1860.

New York *Sun*. 1835–1886.

New York *Times*. 1851–1885.

New York *Tribune*. 1841–1885.

Nichols, Thomas L. *Forty Years of American Life*. 2nd ed. London: J. Maxwell and Co., 1874.

Niles' Weekly Register. Baltimore, 1811–1849.

Nims, Dorothy L. "History of the Village of Rockport" (M.A. thesis, Southwest Texas State Teachers College, 1939).

Norfolk (Va.) *American Beacon*. 1832–1836.

Norfolk and Portsmouth (Va.) *Herald*. 1833–1836.

North, Thomas. *Five Years in Texas: or, What You Did Not Hear During the War*. Cincinnati: Elm Street Printing Co., 1871.

Oaksmith (Appleton) Papers, 1855–1857. Manuscript Division, Duke University Library.

Obregon-Loria, Rafael. *La Campaña del Transito, 1856–1857*. San José, C.R.: A. Lehmann, 1956.

Odom, E. Dale. "Louisiana Railroads, 1830–1880: A Study of State and Local Aid" (Ph.D. dissertation, Tulane University, 1961).

Official Records of the Union and Confederate Navies in the War of the Rebellion. 30 vols. and index. Washington: Government Printing Office, 1894–1927.

Office of Naval War Records. *Office Memoranda No. 3: Chronological Tables, December 26, 1860–November 6, 1865*. Washington: Government Printing Office, 1895.

Olson, Albert L. *Agricultural Economy and the Population in Eighteenth-Century Connecticut*. New Haven: Yale University Press, 1935.

Ouachita Packet Co. v. Aiken. 121 U.S. 444 (1887).

Opelousas (La.) *Journal*. 1871–1877.

Orleans Parish Conveyance Office Records, XX–CXXII, 1835–1885. Recorder of Conveyances, Orleans Parish Courthouse, New Orleans.

Orleans Parish Mortgage Office Society Books, I–VII, 1825–1869. Recorder of Mortgages, Orleans Parish Courthouse, New Orleans.

Orleans Parish Notarial Acts, 1835–1885. Custodian of Notarial Records, Orleans Parish Courthouse, New Orleans.

Osbon, B. S. "The New Morgan Steamers," *Nautical Gazette*, April 21, 1875.

"Particulars of the Steamer *Wm. G. Hewes*," *Journal of the Franklin Institute*, XLI (April 1861), 270.

Passenger Cases. 7 Howard (U.S.) 282 (1849).

Patten v. Accessory Transit Co. (Reported in New York *Tribune*, October 1856–March 1857).

Paul, Robert B. *Shipping Finance and Accounts*. London: I. Pitman & Sons, 1923.

Payne, Buckner H. *Report on the Algiers and Opelousas Railroad*. New Orleans: Picayune Office, 1851.

Peete v. Morgan. 19 Wallace (U.S.) 581 (1874).

Perkins, Dexter. *The Monroe Doctrine, 1826–1867*. Baltimore: Johns Hopkins Press, 1933.

Pierce, Henry. *Colonial Killingworth: A History of Clinton and Killingworth*. Clinton, Conn.: Clinton Historical Society, 1961.

Potts, Charles S. *Railroad Transportation in Texas*. Austin: University of Texas, 1909,

Price, Marcus W. "Ships that Tested the Blockade of the Gulf Ports, 1861–1865," *American Neptune*, XI (October 1951), 262–290; XII (January–July 1952), 52–59, 154–161, 229–256.

Prichard, Walter (editor). "A Forgotten Louisiana Engineer: G. W. R. Bayley and His 'History of the Railroads of Louisiana,'" *Louisiana Historical Quarterly*, XXX (October 1947), 1065–1325.

"Prize Vessels," *House Exec. Docs.*, 40 Cong., 2 Sess., No. 279 (Serial 1343).

Public. New York, 1876–1883. (Formerly *Financier*.)

Puckett, Erastus P. "The Attempt of New Orleans to Meet the Crisis in Her Trade with the West," *Mississippi Valley Historical Association*, Proceedings for the Year 1920–1921 (Cedar Rapids, 1921), 481–495.

Purdy, T. C. *Report on Steam Navigation in the United States (Tenth Census of the United States, IV)*. Washington: Government Printing Office, 1883.

Quimby v. Vanderbilt. 3 Smith (N.Y.) 306 (1858).

Quintard, et al. v. Secor et al. 3 E. D. Smith (N.Y. Common Pleas) 614 (1855).

"Railroad Mortgages as Securities," *Commercial and Financial Chronicle*, XXIV (May 26, 1877), 479–480.

"Ramsey and Carmick Contract," *House Exec. Docs.*, 33 Cong., 2 Sess., No. 47 (Serial 783).

Rawley, James A. *Edwin D. Morgan, 1811–1883: Merchant in Politics*. New York: Columbia University Press, 1955.

Record of American and Foreign Shipping. New York: American Ship Masters' Association, 1871.

Record of Payments on Contracts for Ships ("Bill Book"), 1861–1864. Record Group 19. National Archives.

Redlich, Fritz. "Approaches to Business History," *Business History Review*, XXXVI (Spring 1962), 61–70.

Reed, Merl E. "Boom or Bust—Louisiana's Economy during the 1830's," *Louisiana History*, IV (Winter 1963), 35–54.

———. *New Orleans and the Railroads: The Struggle for Commercial Empire, 1830–1860*. Baton Rouge: Louisiana State University Press, 1966.

Reed, S. G. *A History of the Texas Railroads and of Transportation Conditions under Spain and Mexico and the Republic and the State*. Houston: St. Clair Publishing Co., 1941.

"Refusal of the [Morgan's] Louisiana and Texas Railroad to Transport Troops," *House Exec. Docs.*, 43 Cong., 2 Sess., No. 94 (Serial 1646).

Register of Texas Debt Warrants, 1856–1861. Record Group 39. National Archives.

Report of the Commissioner of Corporations on Transportation by Water in the United States. 4 pts. Washington: Government Printing Office, 1909.

Report of the New York Ladies' Southern Relief Association. New York: The Association, 1868.

"Report of the Select Committee on Naval Contracts and Expenditures," *House Reports*, 35 Cong., 2 Sess., No. 184 (Serial 1019).

"Report of the Select Committee on Transportation Routes to the Seaboard with Appendix and Evidence," *Senate Reports*. 43 Cong., 1 Sess., No. 307 (Serial 1589).

"Report on Case of Harris & Morgan," *House Reports*. 35 Cong., 1 Sess., No. 99 (Serial 964).

"Report on the Steam Marine of the United States," *Senate Exec. Docs.*, 32 Cong., 1 Sess., No. 42 (Serial 640).

Rightor, Henry. *Standard History of New Orleans.* Chicago: Lewis Publishing Co., 1900.

Robinson, William M., Jr. *The Confederate Privateers.* New Haven: Yale University Press, 1928.

Rockport Book of Ordinances, 1870–1890. City Hall, Rockport, Texas.

Rockport City Council Minute Book, Volume I. City Hall, Rockport, Texas.

Rockport (Tex.) *Transcript.* 1870, 1874.

Rode's New York City Directory. New York: Charles R. Rode, 1850.

Rodriguez, Mario. *A Palmerstonian Diplomat in Central America: Frederick Chatfield, Esq.* Tucson: University of Arizona Press, 1964.

Roeder, Robert E. "Merchants of Ante-Bellum New Orleans," *Explorations in Entrepreneurial History*, First Series, X (April 1958), 113–122.

Rogers, Augustus C. (editor). *Sketches of Representative Men, North and South.* New York: Atlantic Publishing Co., 1872.

Rostow, W. W. *The Process of Economic Growth.* 2nd ed. New York: W. W. Norton & Co., 1962.

Runge (Henry J.) Papers, 1868–1898. Rosenberg Library, Galveston, Texas.

Russel, Robert R. *Improvement of Communication with the Pacific Coast as an Issue in American Politics, 1783–1864.* Cedar Rapids: Torch Press, 1948.

Rydell, Ramond A. "The Cape Horn Route to California, 1849," *Pacific Historical Review*, XVII (May 1948), 149–163.

"Sale of Public Vessels," *House Exec. Docs.*, 40 Cong., 2 Sess., No. 282 (Serial 1343).

Saturday Review. Galveston, 1897.

Sawyer, John E. "Entrepreneurial Error and Economic Growth," *Explorations in Entrepreneurial History*, First Series, IV (May 1952), 199–204.

———. "Entrepreneurship in Periods of Rapid Economic Growth: The United States in the 19th Century," *Papers Presented at a Conference Sponsored Jointly by the Committee on Economic Growth of the Social Science Research Council and the Harvard University Research Center in Entrepreneurial History, Cambridge, Massachusetts, November 12 and 13, 1954.* Mimeographed copy in Baker Library, Harvard Graduate School of Business Administration.

Saybrook Land Records. Town Clerk's Office, Old Saybrook, Connecticut.

Schmidt, Charles F. (editor and translator). *Texas in 1848 by Viktor Bracht.* San Antonio: Naylor, 1931.

Schumpeter, Joseph A. "The Creative Response in Economic History," *Journal of Economic History,* VII (November 1947), 149–159.

Scientific American. New York, 1851–1885.

Scientific American Supplement. New York, 1876–1885.

Scroggs, William O. *Filibusters and Financiers: The Story of William Walker and His Associates.* New York: Macmillan Co., 1916.

Selznick, Philip. *Leadership in Administration: A Sociological Interpretation.* Evanston: Row, Peterson, 1957.

Seymour, William H. *The Story of Algiers, Now Fifth District of New Orleans.* New Orleans: Democrat Publishing Co., 1896.

Sharp, Henry S. *The Physical History of the Connecticut Shoreline.* Hartford: State Geological and Natural History Survey, 1929.

Sherman (Sidney) Papers, 1837–1870. Rosenberg Library, Galveston, Texas.

Sheldon, George W. "Old Shipping Merchants of New York," *Harper's Monthly Magazine,* LXXXIV (February 1892), 457–471.

———. "The Old Packet and Clipper Service," *Harper's Monthly Magazine,* LXVIII (January 1884), 217–237.

———. "The Old Ship-Builders of New York," *Harper's Monthly Magazine,* LXV (July 1882), 223–241.

Ship Registers and Enrollments, Middletown and Hartford District, 1815–1885. (WPA transcripts). Marine Historical Association, Mystic, Connecticut.

Ship Registers and Enrollments, New York City, 1815–1885. Record Group 41. National Archives.

Shuman, Armin E. *Statistical Report of the Railroads in the United States (Tenth Census of the United States,* IV). Washington: Government Printing Office, 1883.

Shuck, O. T. *Representative and Leading Men of the Pacific Coast.* San Francisco: Bacon and Co., 1870.

Sinclair, Harold. *The Port of New Orleans.* Garden City: Doubleday, Doran & Co., 1942.

Smith and Armistead v. Croom. 7 Florida 81 (1857).

Smith (James Norman) Memoirs, 1789–1875. Typescript by Thomas D. Smith, 4 vols. Waco, 1936. In possession of William R. Hogan, New Orleans.

Somers, Robert. *The Southern States since the War, 1870–1.* London: Macmillan & Co., 1871.

Soule, Frank, John H. Gihon, and James Nisbet. *The Annals of San Francisco.* New York: D. Appleton & Co., 1854.

"Southern Pacific—Morgan's Louisiana & Texas—Houston & Texas Central," *Commercial and Financial Chronicle,* XXXVI (February 24, 1883), 212.

Southern Pacific (Texas and Louisiana Lines) Bulletin. Houston, 1927 to present.

Southern Pacific Company. *Historical Sketch of the Origin and Development of the Transportation Properties Operated As A Part of the Southern Pacific System*. San Francisco: The Company, 1933.

Southern Steamship Co. v. Master and Wardens of Port of New Orleans. 6 Wallace (U.S.) 31 (1867).

The Souvenir Power's Pocket Companion and Guide Prepared Expressly for the Use of Planters, Merchants, and Travelers. New Orleans: Steve Power, 1873.

Stansifer, Charles L. "The Central American Career of E. George Squier" (Ph.D. dissertation, Tulane University, 1959).

Stanton (Adam) General Store Records. Clinton, Connecticut.

Stanton, Lewis E. *An Account of the Dedication of Morgan School Building, Clinton, Conn., Thursday, December 7th, 1871*. New York: F. Hart and Co., 1873.

Stanton, Samuel W. *American Steam Vessels*. New York: Smith & Stanton, 1895.

State Freight Tax Cases. 15 Wallace (U.S.) 284 (1872).

State of Louisiana, Eighth District Court, Parish of Orleans. *Record of Suit No. 19: New Orleans, Mobile, and Chattanooga Railroad Co. v. City of New Orleans, et al.* New Orleans: L. R. Simmons & Co., 1871.

———. *Record of Suit No. 21: New Orleans, Mobile, and Chattanooga Railroad Co. v. Pontchartrain Railroad Co., et al.* New Orleans: L. R. Simmons & Co., 1871.

State of Louisiana, Supreme Court. *Eclipse Towboat Co. v. Pontchartrain Railroad Co.: Answer of Defendants, April 29, 1871*. New Orleans: L. R. Simmons & Co., 1871.

———. *Eclipse Towboat Co. v. Pontchartrain Railroad Co.: Appeal by Plaintiffs, April 17, 1871*. New Orleans: L. R. Simmons & Co., 1871.

State of New York, Supreme Court. *David Colden Murray, Receiver of the Accessory Transit Company v. Cornelius Vanderbilt: Complaint*. New York: W. C. Bryant & Co., 1859.

———. *David Colden Murray, Receiver of the Accessry [sic] Transit Company v. Cornelius Vanderbilt: Deposition of Joseph N. Scott*. New York: W. C. Bryant & Co., 1861.

State of New York, Surrogate's Court, County of New York. *In the Matter of the Last Will of Charles Morgan: Allegations to Revoke Probate, May 31, 1879 and Points in Reply*. New York: n.p., n.d. In possession of author.

State Tax on Railway Gross Receipts. 15 Wallace (U.S.) 284 (1872).

State Tonnage Tax Cases. 12 Wallace (U.S.) 204 (1870).

State v. Morgan. 28 Louisiana Ann. 482 (1876).

State v. Southern Steamship Co. 13 Louisiana Ann. 497 (1858).

"Statement of Vessels Chartered or Employed by the Quartermaster's Department during the Fiscal Year Ending June 30 . . ." (title varies).

Note: Contained in the *Annual Report of the Secretary of War*, as follows:
1864. (Washington: Government Printing Office, 1865), 185–223.
1865. (2 vols., Washington: Government Printing Office, 1866), I, 304–407.
1866. (Washington: Government Printing Office, 1867), 123–137.

The Statistics and the Wealth and Industry of the United States (*Ninth Census of the United States*, III). Washington: Government Printing Office, 1872.

"Steamboats and Other Vessels Owned in the Loyal States," *House Reports*, 41 Cong., 2 Sess., No. 23 (Serial 1436).

"Steam-Engines," *House Exec. Docs.*, 25 Cong., 3 Sess., No. 21 (Serial 345).

Stephens, A. Ray. *The Taft Ranch: A Texas Principality*. Austin: University of Texas Press, 1964.

Stillman (James) Letterbook, 1867–1871. Baker Library, Harvard Graduate School of Business Administration.

Stover, John F. "Colonel Henry S. McComb, Mississippi Railroad Adventurer," *Journal of Mississippi History*, XVII (July 1955), 177–190.

———. "Northern Financial Interests in Southern Railroads, 1865–1900," *Georgia Historical Quarterly*, XXXIX (September 1955), 205–220.

———. *The Railroads of the South, 1865–1900: A Study in Finance and Control*. Chapel Hill: University of North Carolina Press, 1955.

———. "Southern Ambitions of the Illinois Central Railroad," *Journal of Southern History*, XX (November 1954), 499–510.

Sturmey, S. G. "Some Aspects of Ocean Liner Economics," *Paper before the Manchester Statistical Society*. Manchester, March 11, 1964.

———. *On the Pricing of Tramp Ship Freight Service*. Bergen: Institute for Shipping Research, 1965.

A Summary Historical, Geographical, and Statistical View of the City of New York. New York: J. H. Colton & Co., 1836.

Superintendent of Immigration of the State of Texas. *Annual Report*. Austin: J. Cardwell, 1872–1874.

Sutherland, Mary A. *The Story of Corpus Christi*. Houston: Rein & Sons, 1916.

Survey of Federal Archives (Louisiana). *Excerpts from Letter Books of United States Custom House, New Orleans, Louisiana, 1834–1912*. Baton Rouge: W.P.A. (Louisiana), 1937–1938.

———. *Navigation Casualties, 1866–1910: Casualties of Steamboats and Vessels and Loss of Life to Passengers and Crews as Reported to the 10th District*. Baton Rouge: W.P.A. (Louisiana), 1937–1938.

———. *Passenger Lists Taken from Manifests of the Customs Service, 1813–1867*. 6 vols. Baton Rouge: W.P.A. (Louisiana), 1940–1941.

———. *Registers and Enrollments of New Orleans, Louisiana, 1804–1870*. 6 vols. Baton Rouge: W.P.A. (Louisiana), 1942.

———. *Wreck Reports: A Record of Casualties to Persons and Vessels on the Mississippi River, Its Tributaries, on Lakes and Other Waterways of the U.S. Customs District, Port of New Orleans, 1873–1924*. Baton Rouge: W.P.A. (Louisiana), 1938.

Swann, Leonard A., Jr. "John Roach: Maritime Entrepreneur" (Ph.D. dissertation, Harvard University, 1963).

———. *John Roach, Maritime Entrepreneur: The Years as Naval Contractor, 1862–1886*. Annapolis: U. S. Naval Institute, 1965.

Taussig, F. W. and C. S. Joslyn. *American Business Leaders: A Study in Social Origins and Social Stratification*. New York: Macmillan Co., 1932.

Taylor, George R. *The Transportation Revolution, 1815–1860*. New York: Rinehart, 1951.

Taylor (Moses) Collection. New York Public Library.

TePaske, John J. "Appleton Oaksmith, Filibuster Agent," *North Carolina Historical Review*, XXXV (October 1958), 427–447.

Texas and New Orleans Railroad Company Records. Southern Pacific Company (Texas and Louisiana Lines), Houston, Texas.

Texas and Pacific Railway Company. *From Ox-Teams to Eagles: A History of the Texas and Pacific Railway.* Dallas: The Company [1946].

The Texas Almanac. Galveston: W. and D. Richardson, 1857–1864, 1866–1873.

Texas Rural Almanac. Houston: J. Burke, Jr., 1875, 1876, 1885.

Texas State Register. Annually. Galveston: Albert Hanford, 1858–1879.

Thompson, Robert T. *Colonel James Neilson: A Business Man of the Early Machine Age in New Jersey, 1784–1862.* New Brunswick: Rutgers University Press, 1940.

Thornburgh, Conway deC. "The History of the New Orleans, Opelousas, and Great Western Railroad, 1851–1861" (M.A. thesis, Tulane University, 1950).

Thorburn, Thomas. *Supply and Demand of Water Transport.* Stockholm: Business Research Institute at the Stockholm School of Economics, 1960.

"Thoughts on a Rail-Road System for New-Orleans," *De Bow's Review*, X (February 1851), 175–188.

Thrall, Homer S. *A Pictorial History of Texas.* 2nd ed. St. Louis: N. D. Thompson & Co., 1879.

"Tigre Island and Central America," *House Exec. Docs.*, 31 Cong., 1 Sess., No 75 (Serial 579).

Tilton, Cecil G. *William Chapman Ralston: Courageous Builder.* Boston: Christopher Publishing House, 1935.

The Times-Democrat Almanac. New Orleans: *Times-Democrat*, 1882–1885.

Travis, Ira D. *The History of the Clayton-Bulwer Treaty.* Ann Arbor: American Historical Association, 1900.

Trow's New-York City Directory. Annually. New York: John F. Trow, 1853–1879.

Trumbull, James H., Charles J. Hoadly, Leonard W. Labaree, and Albert E. Van Dusen (editors). *The Public Records of the State of Connecticut.* 9 vols. Hartford: Connecticut State Library, 1894–1953.

Tuel, J. E. *The Steam Marine of the Port of New-York Examined in Its Connection with the Southern Ports of the United States and the West Indies and in Its Communication with the Atlantic and Pacific Oceans.* Albany: C. Van Benthuysen, 1853.

Tyler, David B. *The American Clyde: A History of Iron and Steel Shipbuilding on the Delaware from 1840 to World War I.* Newark: University of Delaware Press, 1958.

U. S. Circuit Court, District of Louisiana. *Record in Suit No. 5788: Charles Morgan v. New Orleans, Opelousas, and Great Western Railroad Co.* New Orleans: L. R. Simmons & Co., 1871.

———. *Record in Suit No. 6178: Morgan v. New Orleans, Mobile, and Chattanooga Railroad Co.* New Orleans: L. R. Simmons & Co., 1871.

———. *Record of Suit No. 116: Pontchartrain Railroad Co. v. New Orleans,*

Mobile, and Chattanooga Railroad Co. New Orleans: L. R. Simmons & Co., 1871.

U. S. District Court, District of Utah. *Record in Equity No. 420: United States v. Southern Pacific Company, Central Pacific Railway Company, et al.* 3 vols. Washington: Government Printing Office, 1915.

U. S. Express Guide and Shipping Directory for 1867–8; Revised January 1st, 1867. Baltimore: G. W. Hawes, 1867.

U. S. House of Representatives. *Journal.* Washington: Government Printing Office, 1830–1885.

U. S. Senate. *Journal.* Washington: Government Printing Office, 1830–1885.

U. S. Supreme Court. *N. A. Cowdrey et al. v. Galveston, Houston, and Henderson Railroad Company, Thomas W. Pierce, et al.: Brief of Complainants.* New York: Evening Post Steam Presses, 1871.

Untitled Workbook Pertaining to the Texas Debt of 1850. Record Group 56. National Archives.

Van Alstyne, Richard W. "The Central American Policy of Lord Palmerston, 1846–1848," *Hispanic American Historical Review,* XVI (August 1936), 339–359.

Vanderbilt v. Garrison. 5 Duer (N.Y. Superior) 689 (1856).

Vessel Charter Files, Quartermaster General, U.S. Army. Record Group 92. National Archives.

"Vessels Bought, Sold, and Chartered by the United States, April, 1861–July, 1868," *House Exec. Docs.,* 40 Cong., 2 Sess., No. 337 (Serial 1346).

Victoria (Tex.) *Advocate.* 1874.

Vielé, Teresa. *"Following the Drum:" A Glimpse of Frontier Life.* New York: Rudd & Carleton, 1858.

Vose, Reuben. *The Rich Men of New York, Series 4.* New York: The Author, 1862.

———. *Wealth of the World Displayed.* New York: The Author, 1859.

Walker, William. *The War in Nicaragua.* Mobile: S. H. Goetzel & Co., 1860.

The War of the Rebellion: A Compilation of the Official Records of the Union and Confederate Armies. 69 vols., index, and atlas. Washington: Government Printing Office, 1902.

Waters, L. L. *Steel Trails to Santa Fe.* Lawrence: University of Kansas Press, 1950.

Watson, J. W. "Along the Wharves," *Harper's Monthly Magazine,* XXV (August 1862), 307–325.

Webb, Walter P. *The Great Plains.* New York: Ginn & Co., 1931.

———. *The Texas Rangers: A Century of Frontier Defense.* Boston: Houghton Mifflin Co., 1935.

——— and H. Bailey Carroll (editors). *The Handbook of Texas.* 2 vols. Austin: University of Texas Press, 1952.

Weinberger, Abe L. "The History and Development of the Houston Ship Channel and the Port of Houston" (M.A. thesis, University of Texas, 1940).

Wells, William V. *Walker's Expedition to Nicaragua: A History of the Central American War.* New York: Stringer & Townsend, 1856.

[White, Carleton]. *Narrative of the Loss of the Steam-Packet Home, Carleton White, Master, on a Voyage from New York to Charleston, with Affidavits Disproving the Charges of Misconduct against the Master.* New York: J. Ormond, 1837.

Williams, Harry, Jr. "The Development of a Market Economy in Texas: The Establishment of the Railway Network, 1836–1890" (Ph.D. dissertation, University of Texas, 1957).

Williams, Mary W. *Anglo-American Isthmian Diplomacy, 1815–1915.* Washington: American Historical Association, 1916.

———— (editor). "Letters of Ephraim George Squier to John M. Clayton, 1849–1850," Hispanic American Historical Review, I (November 1918), 429–431.

Williams (Samuel May) Papers, 1819–1864. Rosenberg Library, Galveston, Texas.

Williams v. Vanderbilt. 1 Tiffany (N.Y.) 217 (1863).

Williamson, Harold F. "The Uses of Business History: A Comment," *Business History,* VII (January 1965), 57–59.

Wilson, George W. *Essays on Some Unsettled Questions in the Economics of Transportation.* Bloomington: Indiana University, 1962.

Wilson, Neill C. and Frank J. Taylor. *Southern Pacific: The Roaring Story of a Fighting Railroad.* New York: McGraw-Hill, 1951.

Wilson, Robert A. *Mexico and Its Religion, with Incidents of Travel in That Country During Parts of the Years 1851–52–53–54.* New York: Harper & Bros., 1855.

Wiltsee, Ernest A. *Gold Rush Steamers of the Pacific.* San Francisco: The Grabhorn Press, 1938.

Winkler, William (editor). *Journal of the Secession Convention of Texas, 1861.* Austin: Texas State Historical Association, 1912.

Winston, James E. "New Orleans and the Texas Revolution," *Louisiana Historical Quarterly,* X (July 1927), 317–354.

————. "New York and the Independence of Texas," *Southwestern Historical Quarterly,* XVIII (April 1915), 368–385.

————. "Notes on Commercial Relations between New Orleans and Texas Ports, 1838–1839," *Southwestern Historical Quarterly,* XXXIV (October 1930), 91–105.

————. "Notes on the Economic History of New Orleans, 1803–1836," *Mississippi Valley Historical Review,* XI (September 1924), 200–226.

Wyllie Irvin G. *The Self-Made Man in America: The Myth of Rags to Riches.* New Brunswick, N.J.: Rutgers University Press, 1954.

Youngson, A. J. *Possibilities of Economic Progress.* Cambridge: Cambridge University Press, 1959.

Zeichner, Oscar. *Connecticut's Years of Controversy, 1750–1776.* Chapel Hill: University of North Carolina Press, 1949.

Ziegler, Jesse A. *Wave of the Gulf.* San Antonio: Naylor, 1938.